W9-BUV-780

HTML, XHTML & CSS

FOR

DUMMIES®

7TH EDITION

by Ed Tittel and Jeff Noble

Foreword by Eric A. Meyer

WILEY

Wiley Publishing, Inc.

HTML, XHTML & CSS For Dummies®, 7th Edition

Published by
Wiley Publishing, Inc.
111 River Street
Hoboken, NJ 07030-5774

www.wiley.com

Copyright © 2011 by Wiley Publishing, Inc., Indianapolis, Indiana

Published by Wiley Publishing, Inc., Indianapolis, Indiana

Published simultaneously in Canada

No part of this publication may be reproduced, stored in a retrieval system or transmitted in any form or by any means, electronic, mechanical, photocopying, recording, scanning or otherwise, except as permitted under Sections 107 or 108 of the 1976 United States Copyright Act, without either the prior written permission of the Publisher, or authorization through payment of the appropriate per-copy fee to the Copyright Clearance Center, 222 Rosewood Drive, Danvers, MA 01923, (978) 750-8400, fax (978) 646-8600. Requests to the Publisher for permission should be addressed to the Permissions Department, John Wiley & Sons, Inc., 111 River Street, Hoboken, NJ 07030, (201) 748-6011, fax (201) 748-6008, or online at http://www.wiley.com/go/permissions.

Trademarks: Wiley, the Wiley Publishing logo, For Dummies, the Dummies Man logo, A Reference for the Rest of Us!, The Dummies Way, Dummies Daily, The Fun and Easy Way, Dummies.com, Making Everything Easier, and related trade dress are trademarks or registered trademarks of John Wiley & Sons, Inc. and/or its affiliates in the United States and other countries, and may not be used without written permission. All other trademarks are the property of their respective owners. Wiley Publishing, Inc., is not associated with any product or vendor mentioned in this book.

LIMIT OF LIABILITY/DISCLAIMER OF WARRANTY: THE PUBLISHER AND THE AUTHOR MAKE NO REPRESENTATIONS OR WARRANTIES WITH RESPECT TO THE ACCURACY OR COMPLETENESS OF THE CONTENTS OF THIS WORK AND SPECIFICALLY DISCLAIM ALL WARRANTIES, INCLUDING WITHOUT LIMITATION WARRANTIES OF FITNESS FOR A PARTICULAR PURPOSE. NO WARRANTY MAY BE CREATED OR EXTENDED BY SALES OR PROMOTIONAL MATERIALS. THE ADVICE AND STRATEGIES CONTAINED HEREIN MAY NOT BE SUITABLE FOR EVERY SITUATION. THIS WORK IS SOLD WITH THE UNDERSTANDING THAT THE PUBLISHER IS NOT ENGAGED IN RENDERING LEGAL, ACCOUNTING, OR OTHER PROFESSIONAL SERVICES. IF PROFESSIONAL ASSISTANCE IS REQUIRED, THE SERVICES OF A COMPETENT PROFESSIONAL PERSON SHOULD BE SOUGHT. NEITHER THE PUBLISHER NOR THE AUTHOR SHALL BE LIABLE FOR DAMAGES ARISING HEREFROM. THE FACT THAT AN ORGANIZATION OR WEBSITE IS REFERRED TO IN THIS WORK AS A CITATION AND/OR A POTENTIAL SOURCE OF FURTHER INFORMATION DOES NOT MEAN THAT THE AUTHOR OR THE PUBLISHER ENDORSES THE INFORMATION THE ORGANIZATION OR WEBSITE MAY PROVIDE OR RECOMMENDATIONS IT MAY MAKE. FURTHER, READERS SHOULD BE AWARE THAT INTERNET WEBSITES LISTED IN THIS WORK MAY HAVE CHANGED OR DISAPPEARED BETWEEN WHEN THIS WORK WAS WRITTEN AND WHEN IT IS READ. FULFILLMENT OF EACH COUPON OFFER IS THE SOLE RESPONSIBILITY OF THE OFFEROR.

For general information on our other products and services, please contact our Customer Care Department within the U.S. at 877-762-2974, outside the U.S. at 317-572-3993, or fax 317-572-4002.

For technical support, please visit www.wiley.com/techsupport.

Wiley also publishes its books in a variety of electronic formats. Some content that appears in print may not be available in electronic books.

Library of Congress Control Number: 2010941511

ISBN: 978-0-470-91659-9

Manufactured in the United States of America

10 9 8 7 6 5 4 3 2

WILEY

About the Authors

Ed Tittel is a freelance writer, consultant, and occasional expert legal witness on Web technologies who works at home near beautiful Austin, Texas. Ed has written for the trade press since 1986 and has worked on more than 140 books. Ed has worked on many other titles for Wiley, too, including *Windows Server 2008 For Dummies, XML For Dummies,* and *Networking with NetWare For Dummies*. Lately, he's worked on various *For Dummies* custom titles, including booklets on clustered computing, mobile backhaul, XBRL Markup, and carrier Ethernet.

Ed blogs, provides expert Q&A, and writes for several TechTarget.com Web sites, such as SearchNetworking.com and SearchWindows.com. He also writes for ITExpertVoice, Tom's Hardware, Tom's Guide, and more. When he's not busy working, Ed likes to travel, shoot pool, and spend time with his family. He also loves to spend time in the kitchen cooking like mad, or sous-cheffin' for his cuisine-crazy wife, Dina. Contact Ed by e-mail at `etittel@ yahoo.com`.

Jeff Noble leads a team of designers as a product design manager at a global software company, CA Technologies, is the associate editor of UItrends.com (a blog about the good, the bad, and the ugly of user interface design), and owner of Conquest Media (`www.conquestmedia.com`), a small Web and application design company in Austin, Texas. Jeff has more than twelve years of design experience and specializes in all aspects of Web sites and enterprise software applications (designing, building, optimizing, explaining, and so on). In addition to this title, he's handled technical editing on six other *For Dummies* Web design and programming titles for Wiley. In what little spare time he has away from the computer, Jeff enjoys childish activities like eating unhealthy amounts of candy and breaking things, as well as relaxing hobbies like hiking, traveling, and gardening. Jeff is available for Web site and enterprise application consulting. You can contact him by e-mail at `jeff@conquestmedia.com`.

Authors' Acknowledgments

Wow! It's hard to believe we've hit the "lucky 13th edition" for *HTML For Dummies*. Of all the books I've worked on, this one's covered more time and versions than the rest. So thanks again readers, for keeping this book going strong. We'd also like to thank our readers and the Wiley editors for providing welcome feedback to drive continuing improvement of this book. Don't stop now — keep telling us what you want. Especially, tell us what you liked and didn't like about this second full-color edition.

Let me also thank some people from previous editions, including J. Michael Stewart, Natanya Anderson, Dori Smith, Tom Negrino, Mary Burmeister, Brock Kyle, Chelsea Valentine, Dawn Davidson, and Kim Lindros. And, for the second time, I'm indebted to my co-author and friend, Jeff Noble, for infusing insight and enthusiasm. I am grateful for your ideas, your hard work, and your experience in reaching budding Web experts. Thanks, too, to Mary Kyle Inks, who expertly project-managed this effort.

At Wiley, I must thank Bob Woerner and Jean Nelson for their outstanding efforts, and Brian Walls, Teresa Artman, and Christopher McGee for their efforts on design, layout, content, and coverage. A special shout-out to the friendly folks in Composition Services for artful page layouts, and for keeping all the color-coded elements straight.

Thanks to my lovely wife, Dina Kutueva-Tittel, and inquisitive son, Gregory, for putting up with my sometimes whacky and intense schedule. I'm not always as easy to live with as I could be, but hopefully, I'll improve with time and effort. Also, thanks to my Dad, Al Tittel, for all he's done for my family and me, and for dropping in more frequently. I hope you're around to see our 14th edition come to print! Finally, profound thanks and remembrances to Cecilia Katherine Kociolek Tittel (4/3/1919–9/11/2009). Thanks, Mom, for encouraging my love of words and writing: I still miss you every day.

Ed Tittel

Special thanks to Ida F. Orengo, M.D. and the rest of the staff from the Baylor College of Medicine in Houston, Texas. Without all of you, there is a decent chance I wouldn't even be alive now.

Thanks to Ed Tittel for allowing me to sit in again and handle even more responsibility with this latest edition. This title has been one of the biggest accomplishments in my life and has opened up incredible opportunities to me and I thank you sincerely. To Slade Deliberto, it seems like only yesterday you taught me how to design my first Web site. Technology and software changes over time, but a lot of what I've accomplished so far professionally goes all the way back to your initial design and Photoshop lessons more than twelve years ago.

Big thanks to my boss and mentor Russell Wilson, you've always supported and believed in me and without a doubt have made me a better designer and a better person. I don't say it as much as I should, I owe you big time and I appreciate everything you have done for me — there, you have it in writing.

To CSS master Eric Meyer, thanks for agreeing to write the Foreword to this book. I've learned a lot from your volume of work over the years and having my name noted on a book with yours is a huge honor. I'd also like to dedicate this book in memory of my friend Zach Beatty who was tragically killed by a drunk driver in 1997. Please don't drink and drive, you might kill someone a lot cooler than you.

Jeff Noble

Publisher's Acknowledgments

We're proud of this book; please send us your comments at http://dummies.custhelp.com. For other comments, please contact our Customer Care Department within the U.S. at 877-762-2974, outside the U.S. at 317-572-3993, or fax 317-572-4002.

Some of the people who helped bring this book to market include the following:

Acquisitions, Editorial, and Media Development

Project Editor: Jean Nelson

Executive Editor: Bob Woerner

Copy Editor: Brian Walls

Technical Editor: Christopher McGee

Editorial Manager: Kevin Kirschner

Media Development Project Manager: Laura Moss-Hollister

Media Development Assistant Project Manager: Jenny Swisher

Media Development Associate Producers: Josh Frank, Marilyn Hummel, Douglas Kuhn, and Shawn Patrick

Editorial Assistant: Amanda Graham

Sr. Editorial Assistant: Cherie Case

Cartoons: Rich Tennant (www.the5thwave.com)

Composition Services

Project Coordinator: Kristie Rees

Layout and Graphics: Samantha K. Cherolis, Joyce Haughey, Lavonne Roberts

Proofreaders: Laura Bowman, Lindsay Littrell

Indexer: BIM Indexing & Proofreading Services

Special Help: Teresa Artman

Publishing and Editorial for Technology Dummies

Richard Swadley, Vice President and Executive Group Publisher

Andy Cummings, Vice President and Publisher

Mary Bednarek, Executive Acquisitions Director

Mary C. Corder, Editorial Director

Publishing for Consumer Dummies

Diane Graves Steele, Vice President and Publisher

Composition Services

Debbie Stailey, Director of Composition Services

Contents at a Glance

Foreword ....*xix*

Introduction 1

Part 1: Getting to Know (X)HTML and CSS 7
Chapter 1: The Least You Need to Know about HTML, CSS, and the Web.............. 9
Chapter 2: Creating and Viewing a Web Page 31
Chapter 3: Proper Planning Prevents Poor Page Performance...................... 43

Part 11: Formatting Web Pages with (X)HTML 61
Chapter 4: Creating (X)HTML Document Structure 63
Chapter 5: Text and Lists 73
Chapter 6: Linking to Online Resources 91
Chapter 7: Finding and Using Images 105

Part 111: Taking Precise Control over Web Pages and Styles 119
Chapter 8: Deprecated (X)HTML Markup... 121
Chapter 9: Introducing Cascading Style Sheets 129
Chapter 10: Using Cascading Style Sheets..................................... 147
Chapter 11: Getting Creative with Colors and Fonts........................... 169

Part 1V: Scripting and (X)HTML 189
Chapter 12: Top 20 CSS Properties.. 191
Chapter 13: Scripting Web Pages 211
Chapter 14: Working with Forms 221
Chapter 15: Bring the Best of the Web to Your Web Site 251
Chapter 16: Fun with Client-Side Scripts..................................... 265
Chapter 17: Content Management Systems....................................... 279

Part V: The Future of (X)HTML 291
Chapter 18: Mobile Web Design.. 293
Chapter 19: Party On with HTML5 305
Chapter 20: CSS3... 325

Part VI: The Part of Tens 343

Chapter 21: Ten HTML Do's and Don'ts 345
Chapter 22: Ten Ways to Exterminate Web Bugs 353
Chapter 23: Ten Cool HTML Tools and Technologies 361

Appendix A: Twitter Supporters 373

Index 377

Table of Contents

Foreword...*xix*

Introduction 1
    About This Book 1
    How to Use This Book...2
    Three Presumptuous Assumptions.............................3
    How This Book Is Organized 3
        Part I: Getting to Know (X)HTML and CSS..............4
        Part II: Formatting Web Pages with (X)HTML 4
        Part III: Taking Precise Control over Web Pages and Styles 4
        Part IV: Scripting and (X)HTML 5
        Part V: The Future of (X)HTML 5
        Part VI: The Part of Tens 6
    Icons Used in This Book 6
    Where to Go from Here...6

Part 1: Getting to Know (X)HTML and CSS 7

Chapter 1: The Least You Need to Know about HTML, CSS, and the Web 9
    Web Pages in Their Natural Habitat...........................10
        Hypertext 10
        Browsers 13
        Web servers 14
    Anatomy of a URL..15
    (X)HTML's Component Parts....................................16
        HTML and XHTML: What's the difference? 16
        Syntax and rules...17
        Markup color-coding 18
        Elements...18
        Attributes 21
        Entities 22
    Parts Is Parts: What Web Pages Are Made Of 25
        Organizing HTML text 26
        Images in HTML Documents...................................27
        Links and navigation tools.....................................27
    Listing 1-1: Meet an Author!.....................................28

Chapter 2: Creating and Viewing a Web Page **31**

Before You Get Started 31
Creating a Page from Scratch.. 32
    Step 1: Planning a simple design.................................... 33
    Step 2: Writing some HTML 34
    Step 3: Saving your page 37
    Step 4: Viewing your page 38
Editing an Existing Web Page 40
Posting Your Page Online 41

Chapter 3: Proper Planning Prevents Poor Page Performance **43**

Planning Your Site 44
    Design matters 45
    Mapping your site 46
    Building solid navigation 49
    Planning outside links 53
Hosting Your Web Site 54
    Hosting your own Web site.. 55
    Using a hosting provider 56
    Obtaining your own domain 57
    Moving files to your Web server 57

Part II: Formatting Web Pages with (X)HTML *61*

Chapter 4: Creating (X)HTML Document Structure **63**

Establishing a Document Structure.. 63
Labeling Your (X)HTML Document.. 64
    Adding an HTML DOCTYPE declaration 64
    Adding an XHTML DOCTYPE declaration...................... 65
    The <html> element.. 65
    Adding the XHTML namespace 65
Adding a Document Header 66
    Giving your page a title 66
    Defining metadata 67
    Redirecting users to another page 69
Creating the (X)HTML Document Body.................................. 71

Chapter 5: Text and Lists **73**

Formatting Text 73
    Paragraphs... 74
    Headings... 75
Controlling Text Blocks 77
    Block quotes.. 77
    Preformatted text.. 78
    Horizontal rules.. 80

Organizing Information 82
 Numbered lists 82
 Bulleted lists 85
 Definition lists 87
 Nesting lists 89

Chapter 6: Linking to Online Resources 91

Basic Links 91
 Link options 92
 Common mistakes 95
Customizing Links 97
 New windows 97
 Locations in Web pages 99
 Non-HTML resources 102

Chapter 7: Finding and Using Images 105

The Role of Images in a Web Page 105
Creating Web-Friendly Images 106
Adding an Image to a Web Page 108
 Image location 108
 Using the <img /> element 108
 Adding alternative and title text 110
 Specifying image size 112
 Image borders and alignment 114
Images That Link 115
 Triggering links 115
 Building image maps 116

**Part III: Taking Precise Control over
Web Pages and Styles 119**

Chapter 8: Deprecated (X)HTML Markup 121

And Now, A Word from Our Sponsor 122
Deprecated Elements 123
Deprecated Attributes 124
How to Handle Deprecated Markup 127

Chapter 9: Introducing Cascading Style Sheets 129

Advantages of Style Sheets 130
 What CSS can do for a Web page 131
 What you can do with CSS 132
 Property measurement values 133

CSS Structure and Syntax 134
    Selectors and declarations 136
    Working with style classes 138
    Working with style IDs 140
    Inheriting styles 141
Using Different Kinds of Style Sheets 142
    Internal style sheets 143
    External style sheets 144
Understanding the Cascade 145

Chapter 10: Using Cascading Style Sheets 147

Managing Layout and Positioning 148
    Visual layouts 149
    Positioning 151
Changing Fonts for Visual Interest and Better Readability 153
    Body text 154
    Headings 155
    Hyperlinks 155
Externalizing Style Sheets 157
Using CSS with Multimedia 158
    Visual media styles 159
    Paged media styles 165

Chapter 11: Getting Creative with Colors and Fonts 169

Color Values 170
    Color names 170
    Color numbers 171
Color Definitions 172
    Text 173
    Links 173
    Backgrounds 175
Fonts 176
    Font family 176
    Sizing 178
Positioning Blocks of Text 182
    Aligning text 182
    Indenting text 183
Text Treatments 184
    Embolden with bold 184
    Emphasizing with italic 184
    Changing capitalization 185
    Getting fancy with the text-decoration property 187
The Catchall Font Property 187

Part IV: Scripting and (X)HTML *189*

Chapter 12: Top 20 CSS Properties 191
  Background Properties.. 191
    background-color.. 192
    background-image... 192
  Border and Outline Properties 193
    border 195
  Dimension... 195
    height and width... 196
  Fonts and Font Properties 197
    font-family.. 197
    font-weight... 198
    font-size.. 198
  Spacing Properties: Margin and Padding 199
    margin 200
    padding 200
  Positioning.. 201
    float... 202
    z-index.. 202
    clear.. 203
    cursor.. 204
  Text... 204
    color.. 206
    line-height.. 206
  Pseudo Classes 207
    :hover, :link, and :visited.. 207
  Best CSS Resources 208
    W3Schools.com.. 208
    Firebug 209
    Eric Meyer's Reset 209
    Spoon Browser Sandbox.. 209
    W3C CSS Validation Service....................................... 209
    Web-Developer's Handbook 210
    YSlow... 210

Chapter 13: Scripting Web Pages 211
  Finding Out What JavaScript Can Do for Your Pages 212
  Using JavaScript to Arrange Content Dynamically 214
  Working with Browser Windows 216
  Soliciting and Verifying User Input..................................... 217
  But Wait . . . There's More!.. 219

Chapter 14: Working with Forms..............................**221**

    Uses for Forms 221
        Search forms... 222
        Data collection forms 223
    Creating Forms.. 224
        Structure 225
        Input tags 226
        Input fields 227
        Form validation 241
    Processing Data 241
        Processing forms on your pages.............................. 242
        Sending form data by e-mail 243
    Designing User-Friendly Forms... 244
    Other Noteworthy Forms-Related Markup.............................. 246
    Form Frameworks.. 248
    CAPTCHA This! 249

Chapter 15: Bring the Best of the Web to Your Web Site **251**

    What's Up with Content Embedding? 252
        Using a Twitter widget 252
        Working with Flickr.. 255
        Creating a map 256
        Other embeddings to check out 258
    Mashups: Two or More Sites... 258
        Creating a Yelp/Google Maps mashup 259
        Crafting a Twitter/Google Maps mashup 262

Chapter 16: Fun with Client-Side Scripts......................**265**

    Adding Rollovers to Your Pages 265
        Text rollovers with CSS 266
        Image rollovers with CSS 268
        Custom button rollovers with CSS........................... 271
    Working with Cookies 272
    Working with jQuery and FancyBox Lightbox 274

Chapter 17: Content Management Systems.....................**279**

    Comparing CMS Sites to HTML Sites....................................... 279
    Popular CMS Sites and Programs 280
        WordPress 281
        Drupal.. 281
        Joomla! 282
    Customizing CSS on a CMS 283
        WordPress and CSS 283
        Drupal and CSS.. 285
        Joomla and CSS 287
    Pssst! Hey Buddy! Wanna See Some CMS? 289

Part V: The Future of (X)HTML 291

Chapter 18: Mobile Web Design 293
Understanding Different Mobile Devices...................................... 293
Optimizing Mobile Web Site Design 296
Designing for small screens..297
Optimizing for low bandwidth 297
Navigating on mobile devices 298
Designing for distracted surfers 299
Surfing the Web on many mobile devices....................................299
Best Practices for Mobile Web Sites 299
Set up mobile Web addresses 300
Create a virtual demo or showcase...300
Location, location, location 300
Don't make users type or click too much 301
Mobile Frameworks.. 301
Sencha Touch 302
jQTouch...302
Additional Resources 303

Chapter 19: Party On with HTML5 305
HTML5 Highlights: Why It's Important 306
HTML5 and Flash 307
Simplified and Enhanced HTML5 Markup 308
Simplified doctype 309
Simplified character encoding 309
What's New and Improved in HTML5 310
Elements new in HTML5...311
Attributes new in HTML5..312
Deprecated elements gone from HTML5 315
Absent and removed HTML5 attributes 316
New Input Types in HTML5.. 318
HTML5 Web APIs 320
Limits to HTML5 Access and Use 320
Additional HTML5 Resources 322
Introducing HTML5 323

Chapter 20: CSS3 325
About the CSS3 "Standard" 325
CSS3 Highlights Hint at Riches Available.................................... 330
Fonts...331
Borders..332
Backgrounds...334
Shadows 334

CSS3 Transitions and Animations 337
    Transitions..337
    Animations...338
Transform Your Content 339
CSS3 Limitations 340
Finding More on CSS3 341

Part VI: The Part of Tens................................. 343

Chapter 21: Ten HTML Do's and Don'ts 345

Don't Lose Sight of Your Content..345
Do Structure Your Documents and Your Site......................................346
Do Make the Most from the Least 346
Do Build Attractive Pages...347
Don't Lose Track of Those Tags 347
Do Avoid Browser Dependencies 349
Don't Make It Hard to Navigate Your Wild and Woolly Web 349
Don't Think Revolution, Think Evolution 350
Don't Get Stuck in the Two-Dimensional-Text Trap............................351
Don't Let Inertia Overcome You 351

Chapter 22: Ten Ways to Exterminate Web Bugs. 353

Make a List and Check It — Twice..353
Master Text Mechanics..354
Lack of Live Links — A Loathsome Legacy 355
When Old Links Must Linger 356
Make Your Content Mirror Your World..356
Look for Trouble in all the Right Places 357
Cover all the Bases with Peer Reviews 358
Use the Best Tools of the Testing Trade 358
Schedule Site Reviews...358
Foster User Feedback...359
If You Give to Them, They'll Give to You! 360

Chapter 23: Ten Cool HTML Tools and Technologies 361

WYSIWYG HTML Editors 362
    Dreamweaver...362
    Other WYSIWYG editors 363
Helper HTML Editors 363
    Aptana Studio..364
    Other helper editors 364
Inexpensive Graphics Editors 365
Professional Graphics Editors 366
    Adobe Photoshop..366
    Adobe Fireworks...367

W3C Link Checker..367
Other Link Checkers..368
HTML Validators..368
FTP Clients..370
Miscellaneous Helpful Web Tools 370

Appendix A: Twitter Supporters.................................... 373

Index.. 377

Foreword

*W*hat you hold in your hands is the first step into a larger world.

How so? It's an introduction to the fundamental underpinnings of the web. With the knowledge gained from this book, you can start building your own web pages — and what's more, look at web pages that already exist and understand how they were assembled. It's like having a second sight, a magic crystal ball, X-ray vision. What's more, it's all a lot easier than you think.

That may sound crazy, but it really isn't. The entire list of HTML elements can be written on a piece of paper, and the 80% of elements you need to work with on a daily basis are easy to understand. You can pick them up in well under an hour. CSS is a bit more complicated than that — writing all its properties on one piece of paper might require legal-disclaimer-sized type — but the basics are very straightforward and the rest of it comes with experience.

Why, you may wonder, do you need to learn all this stuff when there are programs like Dreamweaver that will do it for you? For the same reason a sculptor needs to know how to chisel rock or an auto mechanic needs to understand how engines and transmissions work. When something goes wrong, you need to have the skills to get in there and fix it. And eventually, with practice, you'll get to the point where you can build pages from scratch much more efficiently and elegantly than any point-and-click tool can manage.

And that's why, even if you're not usually comfortable with code listings and other monospaced-font text, you should relax. (Come on, deep breath. Hold it — and release. Good.) Think of the things you learn about in this book as Lego® pieces. Each piece on its own is very simple, but you can put them together in all kinds of interesting and sometimes astonishing ways. That's the fun of it!

Every epic journey starts with a single step. Your first steps await in the pages that follow. Savor them. You'll never look at the web in the same way again.

Eric A. Meyer
Cleveland Heights, OH
8 September 2010

Introduction

Welcome to the wild, wacky, and wonderful possibilities of the World Wide Web, or more simply, *the Web*. In this book, we reveal the ins and outs of the markup languages that are the Web's lifeblood — the Hypertext Markup Language (HTML) and its cousin, XHTML, along with the Cascading Style Sheet (CSS) language used to make other stuff look good. Because HTML and XHTML (we use *(X)HTML* in this book to refer to both) and CSS are used to build Web pages, learning to use them brings you into the fold of Web authors and content developers.

If you've tried to build your own Web pages but found it too forbidding, now you can relax. If you can dial a telephone or find your keys in the morning, you too can become an (X)HTML author. No kidding!

This book keeps the technobabble to a minimum and sticks with plain English whenever possible. Besides plain talk about hypertext, (X)HTML, and the Web, we include lots of examples, plus tag-by-tag instructions to help you build Web pages with minimum of fuss. We also provide examples about what to do with your Web pages after they're created so you can publish them. We explain the differences between HTML4, HTML5, and XHTML as well, so you can decide whether you want to stick with the best-known and longest-lived Web markup language (HTML) or its later and greater successor (XHTML).

This book has a companion Web site that contains (X)HTML and CSS examples from its chapters in usable form — plus pointers to cool widgets you can use to embellish your own documents and amaze your friends. Visit www.dummieshtml.com and start browsing from there.

About This Book

Think of this book as a friendly, approachable guide to taking up (X)HTML and CSS and building readable, attractive Web pages. These things aren't hard to learn, but they pack lots of details that you must handle as you build your own Web pages. Topics in this book include:

- ↳ Designing and building Web pages
- ↳ Uploading and publishing Web pages for the world to see
- ↳ Testing and debugging your Web pages
- ↳ Introducing HTML5 and Cascading Style Sheets 3

You can build Web pages without years of arduous training, advanced aesthetic talents, or ritual ablutions in ice-cold streams. If you can tell someone how to drive to your house, you can build a useful Web document. The purpose of this book isn't to turn you into a rocket scientist (or, for that matter, rocket science into (X)HTML). The purpose is to show you the design and technical elements needed for a good-looking, readable Web page and to give you the confidence to build one!

How to Use This Book

This book tells you how to use (X)HTML and CSS to get your Web pages up and running on the World Wide Web. We tell you what's involved in designing and building effective Web documents that can bring your ideas and information to the online world — if that's what you want to do — and maybe have some high-tech fun communicating them.

To make this book easier to read, we use some conventions with the text. For example, all (X)HTML and CSS code appears in monospaced type like this:

```
<head><title>What's in a Title?</title></head>...
```

When you type (X)HTML code, CSS, or other related stuff, be sure to copy the information exactly as you see it, including the angle brackets (< and >), because that's part of the magic that makes (X)HTML and CSS work. Otherwise, you learn how to marshal and manage the content that makes your pages special, and we tell you exactly what to do to mix elements of (X)HTML and CSS with your own work.

The margins on a book page don't have the same room as the vast reaches of cyberspace. Therefore, long lines of (X)HTML and CSS markup, or designations for Web sites (called *URLs,* for *Uniform Resource Locators*), may wrap across two or more lines. Remember, your computer shows such lines as a *single line of (X)HTML or CSS,* or as a single URL — so if you type that hunk of code, do it on one line. Don't insert any hard returns if you see the line wrap. We clue you in that the markup is supposed to be *all one line* by breaking the line at a punctuation character and by indenting the overage, like this:

```
http://www.infocadabra.transylvania.com/nexus/plexus/lexus/praxis/okay/this/
   is/a/make-believe/URL/but/some/real/ones/are/SERIOUSLY/long-too.html
```

HTML4 doesn't care if you type tag text in uppercase, lowercase, or both (except for character entities, also known as character codes). HTML5, XHTML, and CSS, however, want tag text in lowercase only. Thus, to make your work look like ours as much as possible, enter all (X)HTML and CSS tag text, and all other code, *in lowercase only.*

If you have an older edition of this book, this reverses earlier instructions. The keepers of the eternal and ever-awesome HTML standard, the World Wide Web Consortium (W3C), have changed the rules, so we follow their lead. We don't make the rules, but we *do* know how to play the game!

Our code listings are color-coded where specific colors signify different types of markup. We explain this in Chapter 1 in the section about color-coding markup. (Notice all the illustrations use pretty colors, too!)

Three Presumptuous Assumptions

They say that making assumptions makes a fool out of the person who makes them and the person who is subject to those assumptions. (And just who are *they,* anyway? We *assume* we know, but . . . never mind.)

You don't need to be a wizard in the arcane arts of programming, nor do you need a PhD in computer science. You don't even need a detailed sense of what's going on in the innards of your computer to deal with the material in this book.

Even so, practicality demands us to make a few assumptions about you, gentle reader: You can turn your computer on and off; you do know how to use a mouse and a keyboard; and you want to build your own Web pages for fun, profit, or some esoteric reason entirely of your own. We also assume you have a working Internet connection and a Web browser.

If you can write a sentence and know the difference between a heading and a paragraph, you can build and publish your own documents on the Web. The rest consists of details — and we help you with those!

How This Book Is Organized

This book contains six major parts, arranged like Russian *Matrioshki* (nesting dolls). Parts contain at least three chapters, and each chapter contains several modular sections. This way, you can use this book to jump around, find topics or keywords in the index or table of contents, or read the whole book from cover to cover.

Part 1: Getting to Know (X)HTML and CSS

This part sets the stage for, overviews, and introduces the Web and the software that people use to mine its treasures. It also explains how the Web works, including the (X)HTML and CSS that this book covers, and the server-side software and services that deliver these goods to end users (when we aren't preoccupied with the innards of our systems).

(X)HTML documents, also called *Web pages,* are the fundamental units of information, organization, and delivery on the Web. Here, you also discover what HTML is about, how hypertext can enrich ordinary text, and what CSS does to modify and manage how that text looks on display. Next you take a walk on the Web side and build your very first (X)HTML document.

Part 11: Formatting Web Pages with (X)HTML

HTML mixes ordinary text with special characters called *markup,* used to instruct browsers how to display (X)HTML documents. In this part, you find out about markup in general and (X)HTML in particular. We start with a fascinating discussion of (X)HTML document organization and structure. (Well . . . *we* think it's fascinating, and we hope you do, too.) Next we explain how text can be organized into blocks and lists. Then we tackle how the hyperlinks that put the *H* into (X)HTML work. After that, we discuss how you can find and use graphical images in your Web pages and make some fancy formatting maneuvers to spruce up those pages.

Throughout this part, we include discussion of (X)HTML markup elements *(tags)* and how they work. By the time you finish Part II, expect to have a good overall idea of what HTML is and how to use it. Heck, we even include a chapter at the end of Part II that steers you clear of obsolete or no-longer-recommended markup so you'll know it when you see it (and avoid using that stale dross yourself).

Part 111: Taking Precise Control over Web Pages and Styles

Part III starts with a discussion of Cascading Style Sheets (CSS) — another form of markup language that lets (X)HTML deal purely with content while it deals with how Web pages look when they're displayed in a Web browser or as rendered on other devices (PDAs, mobile phones, and special assistive devices for visually impaired users). After exploring CSS syntax and structures and discovering how to use them, you find out how to manipulate color and typefaces for text, backgrounds, and more on your Web pages. We give you lots of examples to help you design and build commercial-grade (X)HTML documents. You can get started working with related (X)HTML tag syntax and structures that you need to know so you can build complex Web pages.

Part IV: Scripting and (X)HTML

(X)HTML isn't good at snazzing up text and graphics when they're on display (that's where CSS excels). And (X)HTML really can't *do* much by itself. Web designers often build interactive, dynamic Web pages using scripting tools to add interactivity to an (X)HTML framework.

In this part, you find out about scripting languages that enable Web pages to interact with users and that also provide ways to respond to user input or actions and to grab and massage data along the way. You're introduced to general scripting languages, and we jump directly into the most popular such language — JavaScript. You discover the basic elements of this scripting language and how to add interactivity to Web pages. You also explore typical uses for scripting that you can extend and add to your own Web site. We go on to explore how you can embed content from third parties into your Web pages, leverage other people's dynamic content, spruce up your site with very little effort, and get lots of nice returns from services like Flickr, Twitter, YouTube, and Google Maps.

Throughout this part, examples, advice, and details show you how scripting and embedded components can enhance your Web site's capabilities — and your users' experiences when visiting your pages.

Part V: The Future of (X)HTML

Big things are happening in the (X)HTML world, with lots of changes on the way. In this part, we lay the new stuff on you, show you how it looks and what it can do (when browsers cooperate, that is), and tell you what to soon expect.

You find a chapter on (X)HTML for mobile devices, such as smartphones, iPads, and other portable electronic doo-dads with Web access. You also find a chapter on a new and improved version of HTML — namely, HTML5 — coming soon to a browser near you and maybe to your Web site. Plus, there's another chapter on an upcoming version of CSS — namely, CSS3. We provide cool examples, all of which you can view on our companion Web site at www. dummieshtml.com (or not, as your Web browser permits).

Part VI: The Part of Tens

In this part, we sum up and distill the very essence of the mystic secrets of (X)HTML. Here you can read further about cool Web tools, review top do's and don'ts for HTML markup, and review how to catch and kill potential bugs and errors in your pages before anybody else sees them.

Icons Used in This Book

This icon signals technical details that are informative and interesting but aren't absolutely critical to writing HTML.

This icon flags useful information that makes HTML markup or other important stuff even less complicated than you feared it might be.

This icon calls out stuff you shouldn't pass by — don't overlook these gentle reminders (the life, sanity, or page you save could be your own).

Watch out when you see this icon. It warns you of things you shouldn't do; consequences can be severe if you ignore accompanying bits of wisdom.

Information highlighted with this icon gives best practices — advice we wish we'd had when we first started out! These techniques can save you time and money on migraine medication.

Where to Go from Here

This is where you pick a direction and hit the road! Where you start out doesn't matter. Don't worry. You can handle it. We know you're getting ready to have the time of your life. Enjoy!

Part I
Getting to Know (X)HTML and CSS

The 5th Wave — By Rich Tennant

RURAL WEB DESIGN

"What you want to do, is balance the image of the pick-up truck sittin' behind your home page, with a busted washing machine in the foreground."

In this part . . .

Here, we explore and explain basic HTML document links and structures. We also explain the role that Web browsers play in delivering all this stuff to people's desktops. We even explain where the *(X)* comes from — namely, a reworking of the original description of HTML markup using XML syntax to create (X)HTML — and go on to help you understand what makes (X)HTML different (and possibly better, according to some) than plain old HTML. We also look at general Web page anatomy, the various pieces and parts that make a Web page, and how CSS helps manage their presentation, placement, and even color when they appear on somebody's display.

Next, we take you through the exercise of creating and viewing a simple Web page so you can understand what's involved. We also explain making changes to an existing Web page and how to post your changes (or a new page) online.

This part concludes with a rousing exhortation to figure out what you're doing before making too much markup happen. A well built house starts with a set of blueprints and architectural drawings, and a Web page (and site) should start with a plan or a map, too, with some idea of where your pages will reside in cyberspace and how hordes of users can find their way to them.

Chapter 1

The Least You Need to Know about HTML, CSS, and the Web

In This Chapter

▶ Creating HTML in text files

▶ Serving and browsing Web pages

▶ Understanding links and URLs

▶ Understanding basic HTML syntax

▶ Understanding basic CSS

*W*elcome to the wonderful world of the Web, (X)HTML, and CSS. With just a little knowledge, some practice, and something to say, you can build your own little piece of cyberspace or improve on existing work.

You'll notice we use (X)HTML throughout this book. This is an acronym we made up to stand for "either HTML or XHTML," where HTML is Hypertext Markup Language, and XHTML is Extensible Hypertext Markup Language. Although HTML and XHTML aren't exactly identical, they're enough like each other for this reference to make sense.

This book is your down-and-dirty guide to understanding Web documents, sprucing up an existing page, or creating complex and exciting pages that integrate intricate designs, multimedia, and scripting.

The best way to start working with HTML is to jump right in, so that's what this chapter does: It brings you up to speed on the basics of how (X)HTML and CSS work behind the scenes inside Web pages, introducing you to their underlying building blocks. When you're done with this chapter, you'll know how (X)HTML and CSS work so you can start creating or editing Web pages right away.

Web Pages in Their Natural Habitat

Web pages can accommodate many kinds of content, such as *text, graphics, forms, audio and video files,* and even *interactive games.*

Browse the Web for only a moment, and you see a buffet of information and content displayed in many ways. Every Web site is different, but most have one thing in common: the Hypertext Markup Language (also known as HTML). You'll also run into Extensible Hypertext Markup Language (XHTML) and Cascading Style Sheets (CSS) pretty regularly, too.

Whatever information a Web page contains, every Web page is created using HTML (or some reasonable facsimile). HTML is the mortar that holds Web pages together; graphics, content, and other information are the bricks; CSS tells Web pages how they should look when on display.

HTML files that produce Web pages are just text documents, as are XHTML and CSS files. This use of text documents is why the Web works as well as it does. Text is a universal language for computers. Any text file you create on a Windows computer — including any HTML, XHTML, or CSS file — works equally well on a Mac or any other operating system.

But Web pages aren't *merely* text documents. Web pages are made with special, attention-deprived, sugar-loaded text called HTML, XHTML, or CSS. Each uses its own specific set of instructions that you include (along with your content) inside text files to specify how a page should look and behave.

Stick with us to discover everything you need to know about (X)HTML and CSS!

Hypertext

Special instructions in HTML permit lines of text to point (that is, *link*) to something else in cyberspace. Such pointers are called *hyperlinks.* Hyperlinks are the glue that holds the World Wide Web together. In your Web browser, hyperlinks usually appear in blue and are underlined. When you click a hyperlink, it takes you somewhere else.

Hypertext or not, a Web page is a text file, which means you can create and edit a Web page in any application that creates plain text (such as Notepad or TextEdit). Some software tools offer fancy options and applications (covered in Chapter 23) to help you create Web pages, but they generate the same text files that you create with plain-text editors. We're of the opinion, though, that those just getting started with HTML are best served by a simple text editor. Just break out Notepad on the PC (or TextEdit on the Mac), and you're ready to go.

Steer clear of word processors like WordPad or Microsoft Word when creating HTML. They introduce all kinds of extra code to Web pages that you may neither want nor need.

The World Wide Web comes by its name honestly. It's quite literally a web of online pages hosted on Web servers around the world, connected in trillions of ways by hyperlinks that tie pages together. Without such links, the Web would be just a bunch of standalone pages.

Much of the Web's value comes from its ability to link to pages and other resources (such as images, downloadable files, and media presentations) on either the same Web site or at another site. For example, USA.gov (www.usa.gov) is a *gateway* Web site — its sole function is to provide access to other Web sites. If you aren't sure which government agency handles first-time loans for homebuyers, or you want to arrange a tour of the Capitol, visit the site shown in Figure 1-1 to find out.

Figure 1-1: USA.gov uses hyperlinks to help visitors find government information.

Web browsers were created specifically for the purpose of reading HTML instructions (known as *markup*) and displaying the resulting Web page.

Markup lives in a text file (with your content) to give orders to a browser. For example, look at the page shown in Figure 1-2. You can see how the page is made up and how it is formatted by examining its underlying HTML.

Figure 1-2: To achieve its present good looks, this Web page incorporates multiple parts and numerous bits of HTML and CSS markup.

This page includes an image, a heading that describes the page, several paragraphs of text about one of your authors, and an address block with links to a résumé and a list of publications.

However, different components of the page use different formatting:

- The heading at the top of the page is larger than text in the paragraphs.
- Blocks of text are separated by more blank space than between contiguous lines of text within blocks.
- Some text is in white, some orange, and some light blue.

The browser knows to display these components of the page in specific ways thanks to the *HTML markup,* shown in Listing 1-1. (You'll see Listing 1-1 in all its glory at the end of the chapter.)

Any text enclosed between angle brackets (less-than and greater-than signs: < >) is an HTML *tag* (often called the *markup*). For example, a p within brackets (`<p>`...`</p>` tags) identifies text inside paragraphs. The markup between `<style>` and `</style>` tags at the head of the file uses CSS to define the look and feel for various HTML elements used on this page. That's really all there is to it. You embed the markup in a text file, along with text for readers to view, to tell the browser how to display your Web page.

Tags and the content between (and within) the tags are collectively called *elements.* Angle brackets < > enclose HTML and XHTML markup, curly braces { } enclose CSS markup.

Browsers

The user's piece in the Web puzzle is a Web browser. Web browsers read instructions written in HTML, XHTML, and CSS, and use those instructions to display Web page content on your screen.

You should always write your HTML with the idea that people will view the content using a Web browser. Just remember that there's more than one kind of browser out there, and each one comes in several versions.

Usually, Web browsers request and display Web pages available via the Internet from a Web server. You can also display HTML pages you've saved on your own computer before making them available on a Web server on the Internet. When you're developing your own HTML pages, you view these pages (called *local* pages) in your browser. You can use local pages to get a good idea of what people see after the page goes live on the Internet.

Each Web browser interprets HTML in its own way. The same HTML may not look exactly alike from one browser to the next. When you work with basic HTML, variations will be minor, but as you add other elements (such as scripting and multimedia), rendering markup gets hairy.

Chapter 2 shows how to use a Web browser to view a local copy of your first Web page.

Some people use text-only Web browsers, such as Lynx, because either

- They're visually impaired and can't use a graphical display.
- They like a lean, fast Web browser that displays only text.

A bevy of browsers

The Web world is full of browsers of many shapes and sizes — or rather versions and feature sets. Some popular browsers are Microsoft Internet Explorer, Mozilla Firefox, Apple Safari, and Google Chrome. Other browsers, such as Opera and Lynx, are also widely used. As an HTML developer, you must think beyond your own browser experience and preferences. Every user has his or her personal browser preferences and settings.

Each browser renders HTML a bit differently. Every browser handles JavaScript, multimedia, style sheets, and other HTML add-ins differently too. Throw different operating systems into the mix, and things get really fun.

Usually differences between browsers are minor. But sometimes a combination of HTML, text, and media brings a specific browser to its knees. When you work with HTML, test your pages on as many different browsers as you can. Install at least three different browsers on your own system for testing. We recommend the latest versions of Internet Explorer, Firefox, and Chrome.

Yahoo! has a fairly complete list of browsers at

```
http://dir.yahoo.com/Computers_and_Internet/Software/Internet/World_Wide_Web/
       Browsers
```

Web servers

Your HTML pages aren't much good if you can't share them with the world. Web servers make that possible. A *Web server* is a computer that

- Connects to the Internet
- Runs Web-server software
- Responds to requests from Web browsers for Web pages

Almost any computer can be a Web server, including your home computer. But Web servers generally are computers dedicated to the task. You don't need to be an Internet or computer guru to publish your Web pages, but you must find a Web server to serve your pages:

- If you're building pages for a company Web site, your IT department may have a Web server. (Ask your IT guru for the information.)
- If you're starting a new site, you need a host for your Web pages.

 Finding an inexpensive host is easy — all it takes is a simple Google search. One inexpensive host is GoDaddy (www.godaddy.com), with current monthly fees as low as $1.99 a month. You can even find free hosts for your Web site with a little effort. Free Web Hosts maintains a list of free host providers. Check them out at `www.free-webhosts.com`. Chapter 3 shows how to determine your hosting needs and find the perfect provider.

Anatomy of a URL

The Web is made up of billions of resources, each of them linkable. A resource's exact location is the key to linking to it. Without an exact address (a *Uniform Resource Locator,* or *URL*), you can't use the Address bar in a Web browser to visit a Web page directly.

URLs are the standard addressing system for Web resources. Each resource (Web page, site, or individual file) has a unique URL. URLs work a lot like your postal address. Figure 1-3 identifies the components of a URL.

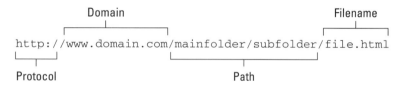

Figure 1-3: The components of a URL help it define an exact location for a file on the Web.

Introducing Internet protocols

Interactions between browsers and servers are made possible by a set of computer-communication instructions: Hypertext Transfer Protocol (HTTP). This protocol defines how browsers should request Web pages and how Web servers should respond to those requests.

HTTP isn't the only protocol at work on the Internet. The Simple Mail Transfer Protocol (SMTP) and Post Office Protocol (POP) make e-mail exchange possible, and the File Transfer Protocol (FTP) allows you to upload, download, move, copy, and delete files and folders across the Internet. The good news is that Web browsers and servers do all the HTTP work for you, so you only have to put your pages on a server or type a Web address into a browser.

To see how HTTP works, check out David Gourley and Brian Totty's chapter on HTTP Messages, available through Google book search with "understanding http transactions" as the search string. Start your search at `http://books.google.com`, then scroll down until you see the link to "HTTP: the definitive guide" and check out Page 80.

Each URL component helps define the location of a Web page or resource:

- **Protocol:** Specifies the protocol the browser follows to request the file.

  The Web page protocol is `http://` (the usual start to most URLs).

- **Domain:** Points to the general Web site (such as `www.oracle.com/US/SUN/index.html`) where the file resides. A domain may host a few files (like a personal Web site) or millions of files (like a large corporate site, such as `www.sun.com`).

- **Path:** Names the sequence of folders through which you must navigate to get to a specific file.

  For example, to get to a file in the `evangcentral` folder that resides in the `developers` folder, you use the `/developers/evangcentral/` path.

- **Filename:** Specifies which file in a directory path the browser accesses.

Although the URL shown in Figure 1-3 is not publicly accessible, it points to the domain and offers a path that leads to a specific file named `file.html`:

```
http://www.domain.com/mainfolder/subfolder/file.html
```

 Chapter 6 provides the complete details on how you use HTML and URLs to add hyperlinks to your Web pages, and Chapter 3 shows how to obtain a URL for your own Web site after you're ready to move it to a Web server.

(X)HTML's Component Parts

The following section removes the mystery from the *X*. This section shows

- The differences between HTML and XHTML
- How HTML is written (its *syntax*)
- Rules that govern use of HTML (and XHTML)
- Names for important pieces and parts of HTML (and XHTML) markup
- How to make the best, most correct use of (X)HTML capabilities

HTML and XHTML: What's the difference?

HTML is *Hypertext Markup Language,* markup developed in the late 1980s and early 1990s to describe Web pages. HTML is now enshrined in numerous standard descriptions *(specifications)* from the World Wide Web Consortium (W3C). The last HTML specification was done in 1999.

When you put an *X* in front of HTML to get XHTML, you get a new, improved version of HTML based on the *eXtensible Markup Language (XML)*. XML is designed to work and behave well with computers, software, and the Internet.

The original formulation of HTML has some irregularities that can cause heartburn for software that reads HTML documents. XHTML, on the other hand, uses an extremely regular and predictable syntax that's easier for software to handle. XHTML will replace HTML someday, but HTML keeps on ticking. This book covers both varieties and shows you the steps to put the X in front of your own HTML documents and turn them into XHTML.

- ✔ Most HTML and XHTML markup is identical.
- ✔ In a few cases, HTML and XHTML markup looks a little different.
- ✔ In a few cases, HTML and XHTML markup must be used differently.

This book shows how to create code that works in both HTML and XHTML.

Syntax and rules

HTML is a straightforward language for describing Web page contents. XHTML is even less demanding. Their components are easy to use — when you know how to use a little bit of (X)HTML. Both HTML and XHTML markup have three types of components:

- ✔ **Elements:** Identify different parts of an HTML page by using tags.
- ✔ **Attributes:** Information about an instance of an element.
- ✔ **Entities:** Non-ASCII text characters, such as copyright symbols (©) and accented letters (É). Entities originate from the Standard Generic Markup Language, or SGML.

Every bit of HTML and/or XHTML markup that describes a Web page's content includes some combination of elements, attributes, and entities.

This chapter covers basic form and syntax for elements, attributes, and entities. Parts II and III of the book show how elements and attributes:

- ✔ Describe kinds of text (such as paragraphs or tables)
- ✔ Create an effect on the page (such as changing a font style)
- ✔ Add images and links to a page

Markup color-coding

As we present HTML, XHTML, and CSS information in our code samples, we use color-coding to help you distinguish what's what by way of markup. Here is a color key that you should keep in mind as you read all of our code listings:

- **Purple** Indicates the DOCTYPE declaration used in (X)HTML documents. This is actually a totally different markup language known as the Standard Generalized Markup Language, or SGML. SGML is used to identify what specific set of rules that (X)HTML documents follow in their construction and content. It also applies to codes for character entities, such as the following:

  ```
  &pos;
  &123;
  ```

- Light green Indicates ordinary garden variety XHTML and HTML markup

- Dark green Indicates XML markup

- Orange Indicates Cascading Style Sheet, or CSS, markup

- Blue Indicates JavaScript

We only colorize markup in code listings and code blocks because it affects readability too much when code appears in body copy. In that case, we simply use a different, monospaced font — as you'll see in the discussions of the <html>, <head>, and <title> elements in our first paragraph that discusses HTML markup here.

One more thing: If you use an HTML editor, such as HTML Kit, Dreamweaver, Kompozer, or whatever, you find these tools also use text color to help you identify different kinds of markup. The thing is that none of these tools do this the same way, and none of them match the way we do it here — we picked out colors that would be easy to see (and distinguish) when viewed on a four-color printed page; whereas others picked their colors to look good on LCD displays.

Elements

Elements are the building blocks of (X)HTML. You use them to describe every piece of text on your page. Elements are made up of tags and the content within those tags. There are two main types of elements:

- Elements with content made up of a tag pair and whatever content sits between the opening and closing tags in the pair

- Elements that insert something into the page, using a single tag

Tag pairs

Elements that describe content use a *tag pair* to mark the beginning and the end of the element. Start and end tag pairs look like this:

```
<tag>...</tag>
```

Content — such as *paragraphs, headings, tables,* and *lists* — always uses a tag pair:

- ✔ The start tag (`<tag>`) tells the browser, "The element begins here."
- ✔ The end tag (`</tag>`) tells the browser, "The element ends here."

Actual content is what occurs between a start tag and an end tag. For example, the Ed Tittel page in Listing 1-1 uses a paragraph element (`<p>`) to surround text for a paragraph (we omit CSS inline markup for clarity):

```
<p>Ed started writing about computing subjects in 1986 for a
Macintosh oriented monthly magazine. By 1989 he had contributed to such
publications as LAN Times, Network World, Mac World, and LAN Magazine. He worked
on his first book in 1991, and by 1994 had contributed to over a dozen different
titles.</p>
```

Single tags

Elements that insert something into the page are called *empty elements* (because they enclose no content) and use just a single tag, like this:

```
<tag />
```

Images and line breaks insert something into the HTML file, so they use one tag.

One key difference between XHTML and HTML is that, in XHTML, all empty elements must end with a slash before the closing greater-than symbol. This is because XHTML is based on XML, and the XML rule is that you close empty elements with a slash, like this:

```
<tag/>
```

However, to make this kind of markup readable inside older browsers, you should insert a space before the closing slash, like this:

```
<tag />
```

This space allows older browsers to ignore the closing slash (because they don't know about XHTML). Newer browsers that understand XHTML ignore the space and interpret the tag exactly, which is `<tag/>` (as per the XML rules).

HTML doesn't require a slash with empty elements, but this markup is *deprecated* (that is, identified as obsolete even though it still occurs in some markup). An HTML empty element looks like this:

```
<tag />
```

You can use the image element (`<img />`) to include an image on a web page, using this kind of markup:

```
<img src="images/header.gif" alt="header graphic" width="794" height="160" />
```

The `<img />` element references an image. When the browser displays the page, it replaces the `<img />` element with the file that it points to (an attribute does the pointing, as shown in the next section). Following the XHTML rule introduced earlier, what appears in HTML as `<img>` appears in XHTML as `<img />` (and this applies to all single tag elements).

You can't make up HTML or XHTML elements. Legal elements for (X)HTML belong to a very specific set — if you use elements that aren't part of that set, every browser ignores them. The elements you can use are defined in the HTML 4.01 or XHTML 1.0 specifications. (The specs for HTML 4.01 can be found at `www.w3.org/TR/html4`, while the specs for XHTML 1.0 can be found at `www.w3.org/TR/xhtml1`.)

Nesting

Many page structures combine nested elements. Think of your nested elements as *suitcases* that fit neatly inside one another.

For example, a bulleted list uses two kinds of elements:

- The `<ul>` element specifies that the list is unordered (bulleted).
- The `<li>` elements mark each item in the list.

When you combine elements by using this method, be sure you close the inside element completely before you close the outside element:

```
<ul>
  <li>Item 1</li>
  <li>Item 2</li>
</ul>
```

Attributes

Attributes allow variety in how an element describes content or works. Attributes let you use elements differently depending on circumstances. For example, the <img /> element uses the src attribute to specify the location of the image you want to include on your page:

```
<img src="images/header.gif" alt="header graphic" width="794" height="160" />
```

In this bit of HTML, the <img /> element itself is a general flag to the browser that you want to include an image; the src attribute provides the specifics on the image you want to include — header.gif in this instance. Other attributes (such as width and height) provide information about how to display that image, while the alt attribute provides a text alternative to the image that a text-only browser can display (or a text-to-speech reader can read aloud, for the visually impaired).

Chapter 7 describes the <img /> element and its attributes in detail.

You include attributes within the start tag of the element you want them with — after the element name but before the ending sign, like this:

```
<tag attribute="value" attribute="value">
```

XML syntax rules decree that attribute values must always appear in quotation marks, but you can include the attributes and their values in any order within the start tag or within a single tag.

Every (X)HTML element has a collection of attributes that can be used with it, but you can't mix and match attributes and elements however you please. Some attributes can take any text as a value because the value could be anything, like the location of an image or a page you want to link to. Others have a specific list of values the attribute can take, such as your options for aligning text in a table cell.

The HTML 4.01 and XHTML 1.0 specifications define exactly which attributes you can use with any given element and which values (if explicitly defined) each attribute can take.

Each chapter in Parts II and III covers which attributes you can use with each (X)HTML element. Also, see our online content for complete lists of deprecated (X)HTML tags and attributes.

Entities

Text makes the Web possible, but it has limitations. *Entities* are special characters that you can display on your Web page.

Non-ASCII characters

Basic American Standard Code for Information Interchange (ASCII) text defines a fairly small number of characters. It doesn't include some special characters, such as *trademark symbols, fractions,* and *accented characters.*

For example, if we translate a paragraph of text from the page in Figure 1-2 into German, the result includes three *u* characters with umlauts *(ü),* as shown in Figure 1-4.

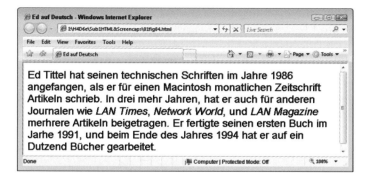

Figure 1-4: ASCII text can't represent all text characters, so HTML entities do the job instead.

ASCII text doesn't include an umlauted *u,* so HTML uses *entities* to represent such characters. The browser replaces the entity with the character it references. Each entity begins with an ampersand (&) and ends with a semicolon (;); entities come originally from SGML, so we color-code them in purple to reflect their origins. The following markup shows entities in bold:

```
<html>
<head>
<style type="text/css">
  body {
    font-family: sans-serif;
    font-size: large;
    }
  cite {
    font-family: serif;
    font-style: italic;
    }
```

```
</style>
<title>Ed auf Deutsch</title>
</head>
<body>
<p>Ed Tittel hat seinen technischen Schriften im Jahre 1986 angefangen, als er
f&uuml;r einen Macintosh monatlichen Zeitschrift Artikeln schrieb. In drei mehr
Jahren, hat er auch f&uuml;r anderen Journalen wie <cite>LAN Times</cite>,
<cite>Network World</cite>, und <cite>LAN Magazine</cite> mehrere Artikeln
beigetragen. Er fertigte seinen ersten Buch im Jarhe 1991, und beim Ende des
Jahres 1994 hat er auf ein Dutzend B&uuml;cher gearbeitet.</p>
</body>
</html>
```

The entity that represents the umlauted *u* is `&uuml;`.

(X)HTML character codes

The encodings for the ISO-Latin-1 character set are supplied by default, and related entities (a pointer to a complete table appears in Chapter 24) can be invoked and used without special contortions. But using other encodings mentioned earlier requires inclusion of special markup to tell the browser it must interpret Unicode character codes. (Unicode is an international standard — ISO standard 10646, in fact — that embraces enough character codes to handle most unique alphabets, plus plenty of other symbols and nonalphabetic characters as well.) This special markup takes the form `<meta http-equiv="Content-Type" content="text/html; charset=UTF 8">`; because the value for `charset` reads `UTF-8`, you can reference common Unicode values that appear in our Web Exclusive —Ten Tip-Top Online HTML References (`http://www.dummieshtml.com/wp-content/downloads/bonus.pdf`).

Although today's browsers support UTF-8 across the board, you can expect to see support for UTF-16 character codes showing up in the next year or two. This will let browsers deal more effectively with non-Roman alphabets like Arabic, kata kana (Japanese), or Hangul (Korean), which some browsers struggle to render correctly today.

Tag characters

HTML-savvy software assumes that some HTML characters, such as the greater-than and less-than signs, are meant to be hidden and not displayed on your finished Web page. If you actually want to show a greater-than or less-than sign on your page, you're going to have to make your wishes clear to the browser. The following entities let you display characters that normally are part of the hidden HTML markup:

- **less-than sign (<):** `&lt;`
- **greater-than sign (>):** `&gt;`
- **ampersand (&):** `&amp;`

The < and > signs are used in markup, but these symbols are *instructions to the browser* and won't show up on the page. If you need these symbols on the Web page, include the entities for them in your markup, like this:

```
<p>The paragraph element identifies some text as a paragraph:</p>
<p>&lt;p&gt;This is a paragraph.&lt;/p&gt;</p>
```

In the preceding markup, the first line uses *tags* to describe a paragraph, and the second line shows how *entities* describe the < and > symbols.

Figure 1-5 shows these entities as characters in a browser window.

Figure 1-5: Entities let <, >, and & symbols appear in a browser window.

Parts Is Parts: What Web Pages Are Made Of

Comments include text in (X)HTML files that isn't displayed in the final page. Each comment is identified with two special sequences of markup characters:

- Begin each comment with the string `<!--`
- End each comment with the string `-->`

In the following code, comments explain how each markup element functions and where it fits into the HTML markup hierarchy.

Elements are organized into a structure:

- Some elements can occur only inside other elements.
- Some elements are required for a well-structured (X)HTML document.

```
<html>  <!-- This tag should always occur at or near the beginning of any
            well-formed HTML document -->
<head>  <!-- The head element supplies information to label the whole HTML
            document -->
```

```
<title>Welcome to Ed Tittel.com</title> <!-- The text in the title element
           appears in the title bar of the browser window when the page
           is viewed -->
</head> <!-- closes the head element -->

<body>  <!-- The content that appears on any Web page appears or is
           invoked from inside the body element -->
       <!-- Skip a bunch of copy here . . . -->
<!-- Subtitle text -->
  <h1>Contact:</h1>
  <!-- List -->
    <ul>
      <li><b>Email:</b> etittel at yahoo dot com</li>
      <li><b>Address:</b> 2443 Arbor Drive, Round Rock, TX 78681-2160</li>
      <li><b>Phone:</b> 512-252-7497 (No solicitors, please)</li>
      <li>List of publications available in: <a href="docs/v_et.doc"
          target="_blank">MS Word</a></li>
      <li>Resume available in: <a href="docs/Resu-et13.doc" target="_
          blank">
          MS Word</a></li>
    </ul></body>  <!-- End of the body section -->
</html>  <!-- End of the HTML document -->
```

The preceding document is broken into a head and a body. Within each section, certain kinds of elements appear. Many combinations are possible —
and that's what you see throughout this book!

To see complete, valid HTML files for any and all screen captures of pages
we build in this book, visit the Web site at www.dummieshtml.com and
check the area for each chapter. The preceding markup appears therein as
01Listing01.html, for example.

Organizing HTML text

Beyond the division into head and body sections, text can be organized in
plenty of ways in HTML documents.

Document heads

Inside the head section, you can define all kinds of labels and information
besides a title, primarily to describe the document that follows, such as the
character sets used, meta data about the current document, scripts to be
invoked, and style information. The body section is where real content lives
and most (X)HTML elements appear.

Document headings

Headings (denoted using elements h1 through h6) are different from the HTML document head. Individual headings structure the text that follows them, whereas the head identifies or describes the whole document.

In the Ed Tittel page example, the h1 element sets off the Contact block at the bottom of the page.

Paragraphs and more

When you want running text on a Web page, the paragraph element, p (which includes the <p> and </p> tags), breaks text into paragraphs. You can also create horizontal rules (lines) by using the <hr /> element.

HTML also includes all kinds of ways to emphasize or identify text inside paragraphs; Parts II and III of this book show a few of them.

Lists

HTML permits easy definition of unordered or bulleted lists. Various mechanisms to create other kinds of lists, including numbered lists, are also available. Lists can be nested within lists to create as many levels of hierarchy as your list might need (perhaps when outlining a complex subject or modeling a table of contents with several heading levels you want to represent). Chapter 5 covers creating lists in more detail.

Tables

In addition to providing a variety of listing mechanisms, HTML also includes markup for defining tables. (Tables were really popular at one time in HTML design, and they were used for all kinds of page layouts; today, they're used for tables, as they should be.) Structure is part of how markup works, so within the definition of a table, you can

- Distinguish between column heads and table data
- Manage how rows and columns are laid out

Cascading Style Sheet markup

CSS markup can occur in separate style-sheet documents, in a block of text in the head of an HTML document, or appended in the style attribute within individual HTML elements — and even in some combination of all three such forms! What CSS does is provide much more detailed control over font selection, use of color for text and backgrounds, positioning of text and other elements on the page, and (as the old Ronco ad intones) "much, much more."

You delve into CSS in detail in Part III of this book, but we cover bits and pieces of CSS throughout the book as appropriate for the subject matter at hand. You can build a Web site without using CSS (using CSS makes more work), but it's the right tool for precise control over look and layout!

Images in HTML Documents

Adding an image to any HTML document is easy. Careful and well-planned use of images adds greatly to Web pages. Chapter 7 shows how to grab images from files. Chapter 9 shows how to use complex markup to position and flow text around graphics. Along the way, you also discover how to select and use interesting and compelling images to add both allure and information to your Web pages.

Links and navigation tools

Web page structure should help visitors find their way around collections of pages, look for (and hopefully, find) items of interest, and get where they most want to go quickly and easily. Links provide the mechanism to bring people into your Web pages, so Chapter 6 shows how to

- Reference external items or resources
- Jump from one page to the next
- Jump around inside a page
- Add structure and organization to your pages

    The importance of structure and organization increases in relation to the amount of information that you want to present to your visitors.

Navigation tools (which establish standard mechanisms and tools for moving around inside a Web site) provide ways to create and present your Web page (and site) structure to visitors as well as mechanisms for users to grab and use organized menus of choices

When you add everything up, your result should be a well-organized set of information and images that are easy to understand, use, and navigate.

Listing 1-1: Meet an Author!

Listing 1-1 is reproduced in its entirety here, color-coded to distinguish the various types of markup it uses. Lest you think this is mere vanity on Ed's part, we also hasten to point out that this is the basis for the "About me" page described in Chapter 16 of this book, which we hope only makes it more interesting, rather than the reverse!

Listing 1-1: Ed Tittel's "About Me" Web Page

```
<!DOCTYPE html PUBLIC "-//W3C//DTD XHTML 1.0 Transitional//EN" "http://www.
          w3.org/TR/xhtml1/DTD/xhtml1-transitional.dtd">
<html xmlns="http://www.w3.org/1999/xhtml">
<head>
<meta http-equiv="Content-Type" content="text/html; charset=UTF-8" />
<title>Ed Tittel - Edtittel.com</title>
<style type="text/css">

body {
   background-image: url(images/background_page.gif);
   font-family: Verdana, Arial, Helvetica, sans-serif;
   font-size: .9em;
   line-height: 1.3;
   color: #FFF;
   margin: 0px;
   padding: 0px; }
#container{
   width: 794px;
   margin: 0px auto; }
#headerGraphic{
   background-image: url(images/header.gif);
;
   width: 794px;
   height: 160px; }
b {
   font-weight: bold;
   }
h2 {
   font-weight: bold;
   font-size: 1.5em;
   color:#96CDFF;
   border-bottom: 1px solid white; }

h1 {
   font-weight: bold;
   font-size: 1.2em;
   color:#96CDFF; }
ul{
   list-style-type: none;
   margin: 0px;
   padding: 0px; }
```

```
a:link {
  font-weight : bold;
  text-decoration : none;
  color: #FF7A00;
  background: transparent; }
a:visited {
  font-weight : bold;
  text-decoration : none;
  color: #91a3b4;
  background: transparent; }
a:hover {
  color: #FA0000;
  background: transparent;
  text-decoration : underline; }
a:active {
  color: #494949;
  background: transparent;
  font-weight : bold;
  text-decoration : underline; }
</style>
</head>

<body>
<div id="container">
<!-- Top graphic of Ed and title -->
<div id="headerGraphic"></div>
<!-- Header text -->
  <h2>About me</h2>
  <!-- Paragraphs -->
    <p>Ed Tittel has been working in and around the computer industry since the
    early 1980s, at which point he left academia to work as a programmer. After
    seven years of writing code and managing development projects, he switched
    to the softer side of the industry in pre-sales technical and marketing
    roles. In the period from 1981 to 1994 he worked for 6 companies that
    included Information Research Associates, Burroughs, Schlumberger, and
    Novell.</p>
    <p>Ed started writing about computing subjects in 1986 for a Macintosh
    oriented monthly magazine. By 1989 he had contributed to such publications
    as LAN Times, Network World, Mac World, and LAN Magazine. He worked on his
    first book in 1991, and by 1994 had contributed to over a dozen different
    titles.</p>
    <p>Ed has been freelancing full-time since 1994, with two
    brief stints of other employment interspersed therein (1987-8 at Tivoli,
    and 2006 at NetQoS, Inc.). He has contributed to over 140 computer
    books, including numerous ...For Dummies titles, college textbooks,
    certification preparation materials, and more. These days, Ed revises an
    occasional book, writes for Tom's Hardware, TechTarget, and ITExpertVoice,
    and teaches online courses for large corporations such as HP.</p>
    <p>To learn more about Ed's professional history, please
    read his <a href="bio.htm">professional bio</a>.</p>
```

(continued)

Listing 1-1 *(continued)*

```
  <!-- Subtitle text -->
  <h1>Contact:</h1>
  <!-- List -->
  <ul>
    <li><b>Email:</b> etittel at yahoo dot com</li>
    <li><b>Address:</b> 2443 Arbor Drive, Round Rock, TX 78681-2160</li>
    <li><b>Phone:</b> 512-252-7497 (No solicitors, please)</li>
    <li>List of publications available in: <a href="docs/v_et.doc"
        target="_blank">MS Word</a></li>
    <li>Resume available in: <a href="docs/Resu-et13.doc" target="_blank">
        MS Word</a></li>
  </ul>

</div>
</body>
</html>
```

That's a huge amount of HTML to pore over at the very beginning of this book. Please take our word for it, though: If you read enough of this book's contents, all of it makes perfect sense!

If you check out our Web site for this book (www.dummieshtml.com), you find it's broken down chapter by chapter. If you grab the downloads for Chapter 1, you find the source code for the page shown in Listing 1-1, named aboutme.html. You also want to grab two image files — background_ page.gif and header.gif. The HTML files for various other screen shots in this chapter depicting Web pages we've built are also part of the Chapter 1 downloads (there's no file named 01fig01.html in this collection — that's Uncle Sam's page! — but you will find pages named 01fig04.html and 01fig05.html).

Chapter 2

Creating and Viewing a Web Page

· ·

In This Chapter

▶ Planning your Web page

▶ Writing some HTML

▶ Saving your page

▶ Viewing your page offline and online

· ·

*C*reating your very own Web page may seem daunting, but it's definitely fun, and experience tells us that the best way to get started is to jump right in with both feet. You might splash around a bit at first, but you can keep your head above water without too much thrashing.

This chapter walks you through the basic steps to create a Web page. We don't stop and explain every bit of markup you use — we save that for other chapters. Instead, we want to make you comfortable working with markup and content to create and view a suitably simple Web page.

Before You Get Started

Creating HTML documents differs from creating word processor documents using an application like Microsoft Word because you end up having to use two applications:

✔ You create the Web pages in your text or HTML editor.

✔ You view the results in your Web browser.

Even though many HTML editors, such as Dreamweaver and HTML-Kit, provide a browser preview, it's still important to preview your Web pages inside actual Web browsers (such as Internet Explorer, Firefox, or Safari) so you can see them as your end users do. Editing inside one application and then switching to another to look at your work might feel odd, but you'll be switching from text or HTML editor to browser and back like a pro in (almost) no time.

Because not all Web browsers are created equal (or identical), your Web pages may look different depending on which Web browser you use. Get in the habit and regular practice of previewing Web pages in multiple browsers so that you see what your end users see when they open the same page.

To get started on your first Web page, you need two types of software:

▸ **A text editor, such as Notepad, TextPad, or SimpleText**

We discuss these tools in more detail in Chapter 23, but here's the thumbnail sketch. Notepad is a native text editor in Windows. TextPad is a shareware text editor available from `www.textpad.com`. SimpleText is part of the Macintosh operating system.

▸ **A Web browser**

We're going to recommend that you use a plain text editor for your first Web page and here's why:

▸ An advanced HTML editor, such as Expression Web or Dreamweaver, often *hides* your HTML from you. For your first page, you want to see your HTML in all of its (limited) glory.

You can easily view your HTML if you are using Dreamweaver CS5 or later. Simply click the Code tab and your hidden HTML appears. You can also set Dreamweaver to permanently view HTML by specifying the default to Code View in the Preferences file.

You can make a smooth transition to a more advanced editor after you become familiar with HTML, XHTML, and CSS markup, syntax, and document structure.

▸ Word processors decked out with bells and whistles (such as Microsoft Word, in other words) often insert extra file information behind the scenes (for example, formatting instructions to display or print files). You can't see or change that extra information while you're editing, but what's worse, it interferes with your HTML or XHTML.

Creating a Page from Scratch

Using HTML to create a Web page from scratch takes four basic steps:

1. **Plan your page design.**

2. **Combine HTML and text in a text editor to make that design a reality.**

3. **Save your page.**

4. **View your page in a Web browser.**

Break out your text editor and Web browser — and roll up your sleeves.

Step 1: Planning a simple design

We've discovered that a few minutes spent planning a general approach to the page at the outset of work makes the creation process faster and easier.

You don't have to create a complicated diagram or elaborate graphical display in this step. Just jot down some ideas for what you want on the page and how you want it arranged.

You don't even have to be at your desk to plan a simple design. Take a notepad and pencil outside and design in the sun, or scribble on a napkin while you're having lunch. Remember, this is supposed to be fun!

The example in this chapter is our take on the traditional "Hello World" exercise used in just about every existing programming language: The first thing you learn when tackling a new programming language is how to display Hello World onscreen. In our example, we create a short letter to the world instead, so the page is more substantial with more text to work with. Figure 2-1 shows our basic design for this page.

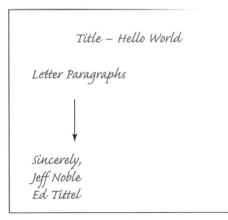

Figure 2-1: Taking a few minutes to sketch your page design makes writing HTML easier.

The design for the page includes four components:

- ✒ A serviceable title: Hello World
- ✒ A few paragraphs explaining how HTML can help you communicate with the whole world
- ✒ A closing: Sincerely
- ✒ A signature

Jot down some notes about the color scheme you want to use on the page. For our example page, we use a teal background and white text with the title HTML Makes the Web Go Round.

When you know what kind of information you want on the page, you can move on to Step 2 — writing the markup.

Step 2: Writing some HTML

You have a couple of different options when you're ready to create your HTML. In the end, you'll probably use some combination of these options:

- ✒ If you already have some text that you just want to describe with HTML, save that text as a plain text file and add HTML markup around it.
- ✒ Start creating markup and add the content while you go.

Our example in this chapter starts with some text in Word 2007 document format. We saved the content as a text file, opened the text file in our text editor, and added markup around the text.

To save a Word 2007 file as a text document, choose File➪Save As. In the dialog box that appears, choose Text Only (*.txt) from the Save As Type drop-down list. (In older versions of Word, the file type name may be slightly different. For example, in Word 2003, you'll choose Plain Text (*.txt) from the Save As Type drop-down list. Just make certain you choose the text or *.txt option in older versions of Word.)

Figure 2-2 shows how our draft letter appears in Microsoft Word before we convert it to text for our page.

Listing 2-1 shows you what you must add to the prose from Microsoft Word to turn it into a fully functional HTML file.

Figure 2-2: The letter that is the text for our page, in word processing form.

Listing 2-1:   The Complete HTML Page for the "Hello World!" Letter

```
<!DOCTYPE html PUBLIC "-//W3C//DTD XHTML 1.0 Transitional//EN"
         "http://www.w3.org/TR/xhtml1/DTD/xhtml1-transitional.dtd">
<html xmlns="http://www.w3.org/1999/xhtml">

  <head>
    <title>HTML Makes the Web Go Round</title>
    <meta http-equiv="Content-Type" content="text/html;charset=utf-8" />
  </head>

  <body style="color: white;
               background-color: teal;
               font-size: 12pt;
               font-family: sans-serif;">

  <h1>Hello World!</h1>

  <p>We sincerely believe that basic HTML knowledge is essential to
     designing, building, and maintaining readable and workable Web
     pages. Our goal in this book is to explain what HTML, XHTML, and
     CSS are and how they work, and then to show you exactly how to
     use them to best advantage.
  </p>
```

(continued)

Listing 2-1 *(continued)*

```
<p>Along the way, we will examine the principles and best practices
   that govern Web page design and construction, and help you
   understand how to make your content accessible to the broadest
   possible audience.
</p>

<p>By the time you work your way through this book's contents, you
   should feel comfortable with creating and managing your own Web
   site. You should also understand what it takes to identify your
   audience, communicate with that audience, and keep your content
   fresh and interesting to keep them coming back for more.
</p>

<p>Sincerely,</p>
   <p>Jeff Noble and Ed Tittel, your humble authors</p>

</body>
</html>
```

The HTML markup includes a collection of markup elements and attributes that describe the letter's contents:

- ✔ The `<html>` element defines the document as an HTML document.
- ✔ The `<head>` element creates a header section for the document.
- ✔ The `<title>` element defines a document title that is displayed in the browser's title bar.

  The `<title>` element is *inside* the `<head>` element.

- ✔ The `<body>` element holds the text that appears in the browser window.

  The markup that follows the `style=" "` attribute inside the `<body>` element is CSS, otherwise known as the Cascading Style Sheet markup language. CSS says we want white text on a teal background, where the text is larger than usual, and in a sans-serif font. (You find out all about styles and attributes in Chapters 9 and 10.)

- ✔ The `<h1>` element marks the Hello World text as a first-level heading.
- ✔ The `<p>` elements identify each paragraph of the document.

Don't worry about the ins and outs of how the HTML elements work. They are covered in detail in Chapters 4 and 5. Also, a Web page includes graphics, scripts, and other elements that we deliberately avoid in this contrived and simple example to keep things, well, simple! We cover all these things in profuse detail later in the book, though.

After you create an HTML page (or the first chunk of it that you want to review), you must save it before you can see your work in a browser.

Step 3: Saving your page

You use a text editor to create HTML documents and a Web browser to view them. Before you can let your browser loose on your HTML page, you must save that page. When you're just building a page, you should save a copy of it to your local hard drive and view it locally with your browser.

Choosing a location and name for your file

When you save your file to your hard drive, keep the following in mind:

✔ You need to be able to find it again.

✔ The name should make sense to you so you can identify file contents without actually opening the file.

✔ The name should work well in a Web browser.

Create a folder on your hard drive especially for your Web pages. Call it Web Pages or HTML (or any other name that makes sense to you), and be sure to put it somewhere easy to find.

Don't use spaces in page names. Some operating systems — most notably Unix and Linux (the most popular Web-hosting operating systems around) — don't tolerate spaces in filenames; use an underscore (_) or hyphen (-) instead. Avoiding other punctuation characters in filenames and generally keeping them as short as you can is also a good idea.

In our example, we saved our file in a folder called Web-Pages and named it (drum roll, please) `html-letter.html`, as shown in Figure 2-3.

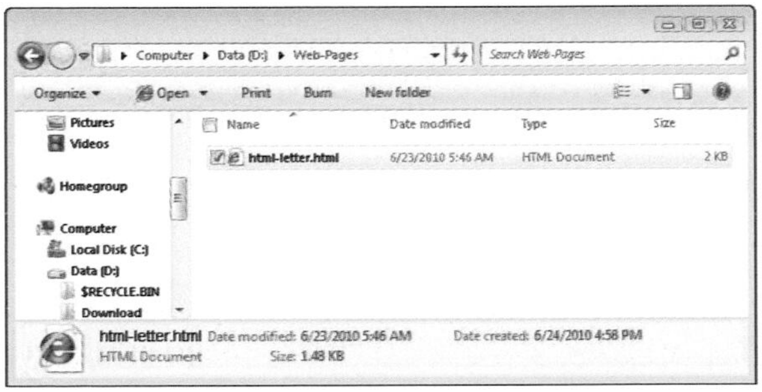

Figure 2-3: Use a handy location and a logical filename for HTML pages.

.htm or .html

You can actually choose from one of two suffixes for your pages: .html or
.htm. (Our example filename, html-letter.html, uses the .html suffix.)

The shorter .htm is a relic from the "8.3" DOS days when filenames could
only include eight characters plus a three-character suffix that described the
file's type. Today, operating systems can support long filenames and suffixes
that are longer than three letters, so we suggest you stick with .html.

Web servers and Web browsers handle both .htm and .html equally well.

Stick with one filename option. .html and .htm files are treated the same by
browsers and servers, but they're actually different suffixes, so they create
different filenames. (The name html-letter.html is different from html-
letter.htm.) This difference matters a lot when you create *hyperlinks* (covered in Chapter 6).

Step 4: Viewing your page

After you save a copy of your Web page, you're ready to view it in a Web
browser. Follow these steps to view your Web page in Internet Explorer.
(Steps may be different if you're using a different browser.)

1. **If you haven't opened your browser, do that now.**

2. **Choose File⇨Open.**

3. **In the Open dialog box that appears, click the Browse button.**

4. **In the new dialog that appears, navigate your file system until you find
   your HTML file, and then select it so it appears in the File Name area.**

   Figure 2-4 shows a highlighted HTML file ready to be opened.

5. **Click the Open button.**

   You are brought to the Open dialog box. (***Note:*** If you're already connected to the Internet, some versions of Internet Explorer warn you that
   for security reasons they must open a new browser window for your
   local file; this is perfectly okay.)

6. **Click OK.**

   The page appears in your Web browser in all its glory, as shown in
   Figure 2-5.

You aren't actually viewing this file on the Web just yet; you're just viewing
a *copy* of it saved on your local hard drive. So don't give anyone the URL for
this file — but do feel free to edit the HTML source file and view any changes
you make.

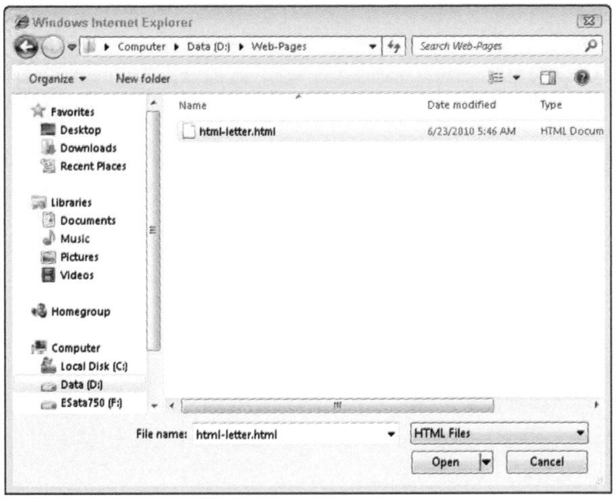

Figure 2-4: Use Internet Explorer to navigate to your Web pages.

An even faster way to view a Web page locally in a browser is to drag and drop the HTML file into an open browser window. You can do this from Windows Explorer or any program that gives you file-level access.

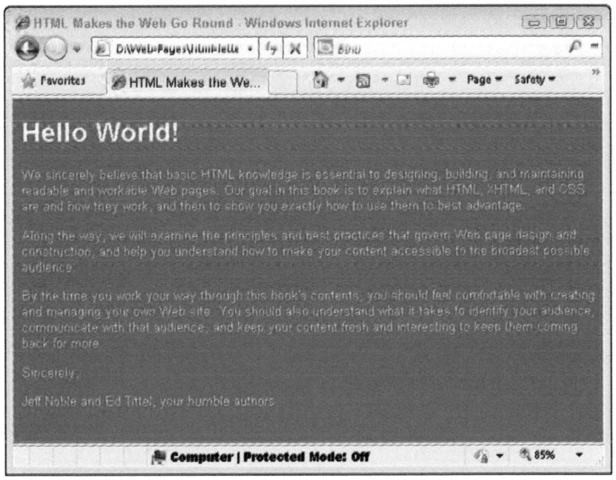

Figure 2-5: Viewing a local file in your Web browser.

Editing an Existing Web Page

Chances are you'll want to change one thing (at least) about your page after you view it in a Web browser for the first time. After all, you can't really see how the page looks when you're creating the markup. You might decide that a first-level heading is too big or that you really *want* purple text on a green background (horrible idea, actually).

To make changes to the Web page you've created in a text editor and are viewing in a browser, repeat these steps until you're happy with its final appearance:

1. **Leave the browser window with the HTML page display open, and go back to the text editor.**

2. **If the HTML page isn't open in the text editor, open it.**

   You should have the same file open in both the browser and the text editor, as shown in Figure 2-6.

3. **Make your changes to the HTML and its content in the text editor.**

4. **Save the changes.**

   This is an important step. If you don't save your changes, you won't see them in the Web browser.

5. **Move back to the Web browser and click the Refresh button.**

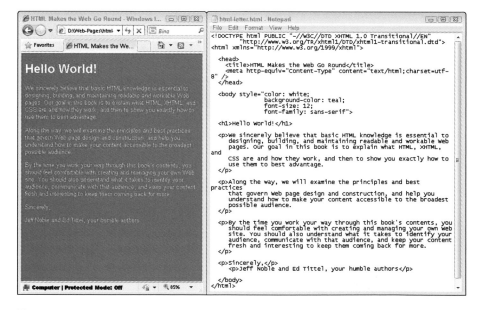

Figure 2-6: Viewing an HTML file in your text editor and Web browser at the same time.

If you keep an HTML file open in both a text editor and a browser while you work, checking changes is a breeze. You can quickly save a change in the editor, flip to the browser and refresh, flip back to the editor to make more changes, save, then flip back to the browser and refresh again, and so on.

In our example letter, we decided — after our initial draft of the HTML page — that we should add a date to the letter. Figure 2-7 shows the change we made to the HTML to add the date, and the resulting display in the Web browser.

This approach to editing an HTML page applies only to pages saved *on your local hard drive.* If you want to edit a page that you've stored on a Web server, you have to save a copy of the page to your hard drive, edit it, verify your changes, and then upload the file again to the server, as discussed in the following section.

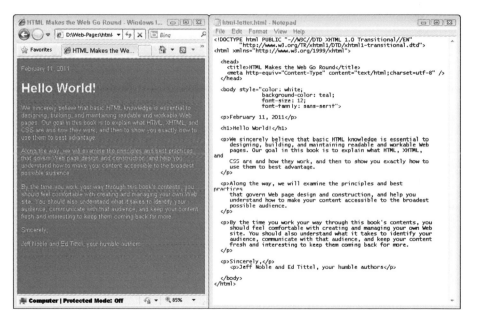

Figure 2-7: A change in the HTML displays in a browser after a quick save and refresh.

Posting Your Page Online

After you're happy with your Web page, it's time to put it online. Chapter 3 includes a detailed discussion of what you need to do to put your page online, but to sum it up in a few quick steps:

1. **Find a Web hosting provider to proffer your Web pages.**

   Your Web host might be a company Web server or a server that you pay an Internet service provider (ISP) to use. If you don't have a host yet, double-check with your Internet ISP to find out whether you get Web-server access along with your service package. Regardless of where you find space, get details from the provider on where to move your site's files and what URL to use.

2. **Use an FTP client or a Web browser to make a connection to your Web server.**

   Use the username and password, as specified in the information from your hosting provider, to transfer files to your Web server.

3. **Copy the HTML file from your hard drive to the Web server.**

4. **Use your Web browser to view the file via the Internet.**

For example, to host our letter online at `www.dummieshtml.com/examples/ch02`, we used Internet Explorer to access the site and provided the appropriate name and password, which we got from our ISP. A collection of folders and files appeared.

We copied the file to the server with a simple drag-and-drop operation from Windows Explorer to Internet Explorer.

The URL for this page is `http://www.dummieshtml.com/examples/ch02/html-letter.html`, and the page is now served from the Web browser instead of from a local file system, as shown in Figure 2-8.

Chapter 3 has details on how to serve your Web pages to the world.

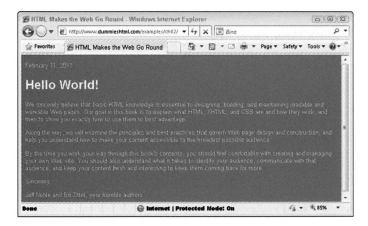

Figure 2-8: A file on a Web server is available to anyone with an Internet connection.

Chapter 3

Proper Planning Prevents Poor Page Performance

In This Chapter

▶ Planning your Web page

▶ Defining your Web site hierarchy

▶ Creating user-friendly navigation

▶ Hosting your site

▶ Uploading and editing your Web site

*T*he overall design of a site defines its *user interface* (UI). When you design a good UI, you provide tools to move through your site with minimum fuss. This chapter outlines standard Web site design principles for (X)HTML and CSS. These principles ensure a usable and effective UI.

The UI is the mechanism that gives users access to information on your site. Each UI is unique but made from the same elements (text, graphics, and media files) and held together with (X)HTML.

Visitors probably won't return to your site if

✓ It's hard to navigate.

✓ It's cluttered with flashing text and clashing colors.

✓ It doesn't help people find what they're looking for.

You've created a solid UI if

✓ Your site's navigation is intuitive.

✓ Images and media accent your design without overpowering it.

✓ You do all you can to help people find the information they want.

This chapter walks you through simple steps to design a Web site and your basic Web page. (Other chapters explain every nuance of the markup.)

Planning Your Site

One important first step in creating an effective site UI has nothing to do with markup, but everything to do with planning. Before your site grows too large (or before you build your site if you haven't yet started), scope out your site's exact purpose and goals. When you know your site's scope and goals, you can create a better interface to embody them.

Before designing your site, ask yourself these questions:

- Why are you creating this site?
- What do you want to convey to users?
- Who is your target audience? For example:
  - What's the average age of your users?
  - How well does your audience work with the Internet?
- How many pages do you need in your site?
- What kind of hierarchy will you use to organize your pages? For example:
  - Will users go through your site linearly?
  - Will users jump from topic to topic?

After you answer these questions, you can better understand your site's goals and needs. For example, an online store might have these goals:

- Let visitors browse an online catalog and put items in a shopping cart.
- Provide visitors a way to purchase the items in their cart.
- Help users make smart purchasing decisions.
- Ease merchandise returns and exchanges.
- Solicit feedback from users about products they want to see in the catalog or ways to make the site better.
- Enable users to comment on and rate products.

Stating clear goals helps you get a better sense of what you must do on your Web site to fulfill these goals. To do the things an online store does, for example, your site is going to need the following:

- An online catalog, complete with shopping cart
- Buying guides or other information that can help users make better purchasing decisions

✔ Help and feedback sections, perhaps with message forums to let users and experts interact

✔ A set of tools to expedite returns and exchanges

When you establish goals for your site, you can identify those elements best suited for inclusion, such as

✔ A navigation system, such as a site map, navigation menu, or bread-crumbs to identify major areas of the site, to help users

- Quickly identify what part of the site they're in

- Move from one part of the site to others without getting lost

✔ A set of standard design elements, such as buttons, page-title styles, and color specifications, to keep users oriented while they move from page to page on the same site

✔ A standard display for catalog items, including product-related infor-mation, such as product images and descriptions, prices, and availabil-ity data

✔ Well-designed forms to help users find products in the catalog, put items in their shopping carts and purchase them, request a refund or return an item, and submit comments to the site

✔ Pages that explain purchasing options, product returns, and other help-ful information but are still easy to read and to navigate

Your site's goals should dictate your site's

✔ **UI elements**

When you add to an existing site, identify UI elements that

- Meet the goals of the new section of the site

- Complement the overall site UI design

✔ **Design**

✔ **Organization**

Design matters

This chapter recommends good design principles, but it's up to you to choose color schemes and the overall look and feel for your site. What looks great to one person may be ugly to someone else.

A site built for a business, which provides a first impression for potential customers or clients, should reflect your business style. If you run an architecture firm, for example, strong lines and a clean look may be the best way to present the company image. If you run a flower shop, your site may be a bit more organic (okay, *flowery*) and decorated to remind visitors what to expect when they walk into your store.

If you're new to Web design or graphics and you need a site that stamps your business presence on the Web, consider getting help from a Web design professional. Use the images, layouts, and navigational aids he creates to build and manage the site yourself. Once established, a distinctive and consistent look and feel for a site is easy to maintain.

Regardless of who designs your site, take the time to get critiques from peers, friends, family members, and anyone else who is willing to be honest about how good (and even how bad) it looks. A negative-but-constructive critique from someone who knows and respects you beats a "Gee, that's ugly" from someone whose business you are trying to acquire. Plus, it's always less stressful to get beat up in private than to take a licking in public!

Mapping your site

It's easier to get where you're going if you know how to get there. Mapping your Web site can be a vital step in planning — and later running — that site. This process involves two creative phases:

- ✔ **Creating a visual guide on paper or electronically that you can use to guide the development of your site**
- ✔ **Creating a visual guide on your Web site to help visitors find their way around after it's up and running**

Both have a place in good UI design, so each gets its own section.

Using a map for site development

A *site map* is a supplemental navigational tool to give users a different way to find what they seek. A site map lays out all contents of your site so visitors can see all their options at once.

When you create and use a site map during the development of a Web site — even a Web site that includes only a few pages — you can identify

✔ Pages that you need to build

  ✔ How pages relate to each other

  ✔ Navigation elements that you need

As a bonus, a site map provides you with a *checklist* of pages.

For example, Figure 3-1 shows part of the site map for the Internal Revenue Service (IRS) Web site (www.irs.gov/sitemap).

Figure 3-1: The site map for the Internal Revenue Service Web site.

This map shows that the IRS site includes numerous main sections. Each main sections displays anywhere from 2 to 26 subsections. Each subsection links to a page or a document pertinent to that subsection's topics and coverage.

If you build your site one piece at a time . . .

If you plan to build your Web site a page or section at a time, you can create a map of the final site and then decide which pages make the most sense to build first. When you have a good working idea of how your site will grow, you can plan for further expansion during each stage. For example, suppose you create a site map for your company's Web site and the site needs an FAQ section. If the FAQ section isn't quite finished when the site launches, disaster need not ensue — provided someone planned ahead to accommodate new sections and built that capability into the site. Just leave out links to (and mentions of) the FAQ section when you launch the site.

When the FAQ section is ready:

✔ Add the section to the site

✔ Add a link to the main navigation elements

If you know resources are coming, you can create a navigation scheme that accommodates the FAQ section when it's ready to go. Without a site map and a complete plan for the site, however, integrating new sections can require lots of time and effort.

Don't create *under construction* sections that don't include anything except a hint that something might appear someday. Users are disappointed if your site hints at information it doesn't really offer. Instead, consider using a small section of your home page to highlight "coming soon" items so visitors know new information will be available later, but don't integrate anything that's inaccessible into your navigation bar or buttons.

Use a map as a visual user guide

Give visitors as many options as you (realistically) can to help them navigate around your site because people use many approaches to find stuff:

✔ Some people like to be led.

✔ Some people like to rummage around.

✔ Some people like to see every possible option and choose one.

Site maps grow as your site grows. If your site is large and complex, your map may take several screens to display. When you surf the Web, massive sites, such as www.microsoft.com, www.hp.com, and www.amazon.com, don't offer site maps because maps of their sites would be huge and unwieldy. But smaller Web sites (such as www.symantec.com) use site maps effectively.

You need to decide whether a site map is a good navigation tool for your site. Here are some points to ponder as you make this decision:

✔ A site map may be *unnecessary* if you have only a few pages.

✔ A site map may be the *best* choice if

- Your site has several sections.

- You can't think of other easy ways to access your content.

Many experts believe that site maps are always good. They're especially good for visitors who surf the Web using assistive devices (screen readers, Braille printers, and so forth). Site maps are also handy for navigating a site that lacks footer links or that uses graphics instead of HTML markup as a navigation technique. Site maps also help users who've turned their browser's JavaScript functions off (sites that use rollover images for navigation become unusable in that case). As an added bonus, site maps also help search engines map all the pages on a site, too.

Building solid navigation

The navigation you use on a site can make it or break it. If visitors can't find what they're looking for on your site, they'll probably leave and never come back. The type of navigation you use on your site depends on:

✔ **How many pages your site has:** If there are only a few pages, navigation might use a simple list of links on the home page to help users jump to each of the other pages.

✔ **How you organize your pages:** If your site has many pages organized into different sections, your home page might link only to section heads (not to each individual page).

The www.dummies.com site houses a large collection of pages organized as a variety of sections; therefore, it is impractical to link to all the pages in any navigation scheme. Also, the site includes articles, cheat sheets, and videos on a wide variety of topics, as well as book information. This site could be organized into books, articles, cheat sheets, and videos, but visitors are more likely to look for information on specific subjects, so the organization is topical. The home page (see Figure 3-2) displays these topic areas proudly.

If you click a topic area, you can still access all topic areas by clicking the See All Topics button at the top left (shown in Figure 3-3). You needn't return to the home page just to choose a new topic; you can open the pop-up menu shown any time you like.

Topics link to information (books, videos, articles, and cheatsheets)

Figure 3-2: The Dummies.com site is organized by topic.

Figure 3-3: The main topic areas for this site remain accessible via a See All Topics button.

Figure 3-4 shows the Games Topics navigation area (at left, echoing the home page layout) for its subtopics. The links differ, but the general navigation scheme is consistent throughout the site. A Cheat Sheets area appears below the local Topics, and Most Popular articles appear in the center column based on user access. That shows visitors what to expect as they move around the site.

Figure 3-4: The Games area includes subtopics, cheat sheets, and popular articles.

The topmost navigation area on each page includes a regular collection of links that appear on every page of the site to help visitors quickly access important areas from anywhere: a search box plus Store (shopping) and Help buttons. At the bottom of every page is a set of links to information on the Dummies.com Web site: Subscribe or Unsubscribe to E-Mail Newsletters, My Account, Store (shopping), Privacy Policy, Contact Us, and so forth (see Figure 3-5). Like a shopping cart and help links, links such as these (and a site copyright statement) must be on every page, but need not be displayed prominently. Including the links in a consistent site footer keeps them around without obscuring key content for given topics or subtopics.

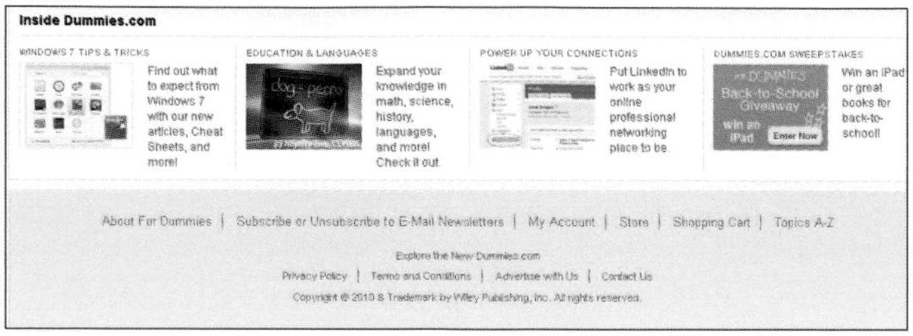

Figure 3-5: The bottom of the page provides further navigation aids to visitors.

If you build a map to aid site development, it can help you design your site navigation, too. Consider each page on the map in turn; list the links that each page must include. Normally, a pattern emerges to help you identify main navigation elements (such as links to main topic areas and copyright notice) and sub-navigation elements (links to subtopics on the topic pages) for your site.

After you know what you need, you can design a visual scheme for your UI. Do you want to use buttons across the top, buttons down the side, or both? Do you need a footer that links to copyright or privacy information? If you have sections within sections within sections, how can you best help people navigate through them? Answering questions like these is the route to a solid navigation system that helps users find their way around your site — letting them focus on what they came for, not on how to get there.

Whatever navigation scheme you devise, always give your visitors a way back to your home page from anywhere on the site. Your site's home page is the gateway to the rest of the site. If visitors get lost or want to start over, make sure they can get back to Square One without trouble.

After you design a site navigation scheme and put together a few pages, ask someone who isn't familiar with your site to use it. To help that person along, provide a list of three or four tasks you'd like to see completed — pages to visit or a form to fill out, perhaps. If your test visitor gets lost or has lots of questions about navigation, rework your scheme. A reviewer can also suggest ways to make navigation features clearer and easier to use. You might know your site and its content *too well* to see navigation issues that a first-time user will discover immediately. Ignorance may not always be bliss, but it sure can be informative!

Planning outside links

The Web wouldn't be the Web without hyperlinks. After all, hyperlinks connect your site to the rest of the Web and turn a collection of pages into a cohesive site. But overusing or misusing links detracts from a site — and may even cost you some business.

Choose off-site links wisely

Internal linking is a walk in the park compared to external linking; after all, when you link to pages on your own site, all such pages are under your control. You know what's on them today, whether they will exist tomorrow, and what will be on them. When you link to resources on someone else's site, however, all bets are off:

- ✔ You don't maintain the pages.
- ✔ You can't modify the page's content.
- ✔ You certainly don't know whether the pages will disappear.

  Neither will your visitors — until they slam into a 404 File or Directory Not Found message (the usual sign of a *broken link* that now goes nowhere). The text in 404 messages varies depending on the server that hosts the Web site with the broken link.

Links to other sites are more useful when they're stable and have less chance of breaking. We recommend these guidelines:

- ✔ **Link to a section of a site, not to a specific page.** Pages come and go, but general organization lasts longer.
- ✔ **Link to corporate Web sites.** Corporate sites have more staying power than sites maintained by an individual.
- ✔ **Don't link directly to media files, such as PDFs and images.** If you want to link to resources on another Web site, link to the page that links to those resources instead of the actual media files. Sites often update resources or give them new names. The page that links to the resource, however, is almost always certain to be updated to reflect new names. Therefore the resource page is a safer linking bet.

Linking to other sites implies your support or endorsement of those sites. When visitors follow links from your site to other sites, they assume you approve of that new site. That implied approval makes a couple of guidelines necessary:

✔ **If you don't want to be associated with content on another site, don't link to that site.** The only way to find out whether you approve of a seemingly relevant site is to visit it and check it out before you link.

✔ **Periodically review your links.** Be sure that

- The sites' owners are the same.

- The content remains appropriate.

When domain names expire, new owners may take them over and post new content that's

- Completely irrelevant

- Damaging to your image (by showing pornography, for example)

Craft useful link text

The text you associate with links is as important as the links you use. That text tells users about where a link takes them so they can decide to go along for the ride. Thus, *Visit Dummies.com to read more about this book* is more helpful than *Read more about this book*.

The first example tells visitors that they're going to leave the current site to visit Dummies.com and read more about a book there. The second example just tells visitors they're going to read more about the book — they may be surprised to find themselves flung from one site onto another.

Generally, when you create link text, let users know the following:

✔ **Whether they're leaving your site**

✔ **What kind of information the page they're linking to contains**

✔ **How the linked site relates to the current content or page**

The goal of your link text should be to inform users and build their trust. If your link text doesn't give them solid clues about what to expect from your links, they just won't trust your links or follow them.

Don't use *Click here* to label a link. If your link text is well-crafted, you don't need those extra words to prompt the user to click. Link text must speak for itself: Let it *invite* a click; it needn't *demand* one.

Hosting Your Web Site

The first (and most important) step in putting your pages online is finding someplace on the Web to display them — a host. Generally, you have two choices when it comes to hosting your pages:

- Host them yourself.
- Pay someone else to host them.

Host is used in the Web industry to mean a Web server set up to hold Web pages (and related files) that can be accessed by the rest of the world. This chapter (and the industry) uses *host* in the following ways:

- **Host as a noun:** The physical machine that holds the Web pages
- **Host as a verb:** The act of serving up the Web pages

You must decide whether to host your own pages or pay someone else to host them. This chapter describes both approaches and gives you the skinny on each one so you can decide which option is best for you.

You aren't stuck with a hosting decision for life. If you find hosting your own pages overwhelming, you can move your files to a service provider (or vice versa, if the provider's service is underwhelming). To decide which hosting option is best for you, consider your needs for the next year, but plan to review your needs in no more than six months.

Hosting your own Web site

This section illustrates an average-size site (up to about 100 pages) that doesn't include more than a couple of multimedia files and doesn't have any special security or electronic commerce (e-commerce) applications.

If you need to run a complex site, such as a large corporate site or an online store, you need more expertise, equipment, and software than this section outlines. The following resources can help:

- Books such as *E-Commerce For Dummies* and *Webmastering For Dummies,* 2nd Edition, can get you started setting up e-commerce and other complex sites.
- Consult a Web professional who has practical experience building and maintaining complex Web sites.

You can set up your own Web server and host your Web pages. To do this, you need:

- **A computer designated as your Web server:** Web servers are often *dedicated* to this task, leaving word processing and other activities to a different computer.
- **Web server software:** Common Web server software packages include Apache and Microsoft Internet Information Server (IIS), called Internet Information Services in modern Windows versions.

In the Web world, *Web server* refers to both

- A dedicated computer (the actual hardware)
- Web server software

You can't use one without the other.

✔ **A dedicated, high-speed Internet connection:** A Web server isn't useful or reliable if it connects to the Internet only when you fire up a dialup link. It can also be painful to use if the Internet link to which it's connected is slow (these days, slow is T-1 speeds of 1.544 Mbps or less).

If hosting a Web site yourself sounds complicated and expensive, you're right. Not only do you have to pay for the equipment and an Internet connection, but you also have to know how to set up and administer a Web server and keep all its pieces working 24/7. Defending against hackers and protecting either your data or your customers' information (credit card numbers, names, addresses, and so on) can also be problematic for the Web hosting novice. On top of these problems, you also have to worry about how to keep your Web hosting system running during power outages or when your Internet service provider goes down. All these Web hosting problems add up to a pile of frustration and headaches that most people would rather avoid. Whenever possible, consider a hosting provider first.

Using a hosting provider

A *hosting provider* manages all the technical aspects of Web hosting, from hardware to software to Internet connections. You just manage your Web pages. Back when the Web was young, hosting provider options were scarce, and what *was* available was expensive. Times have changed — and needs have grown — so reasonably priced hosting providers are abundant nowadays.

If someone else hosts your pages, two choices cover all costs:

✔ **Nothing:** Some services actually host your pages for free. That's it; you pay zip, zero, nada to put pages on the Web. What's the catch? You have to "pay" in other ways, usually by letting advertising onto your site.

✔ **Something:** Most Web hosting services, however, do charge a fee, from a few dollars to triple digits per month. The trick to making the most of your budget is to find the right service to meet your needs.

Read more about inexpensive Web hosting options at www. thehostingchart.com.

Obtaining your own domain

A *domain name* is a high-level address for a Web site. Examples of domain names are `microsoft.com`, `apple.com`, `w3c.org`, and `dummies.com`.

You might want your own domain name (and your own domain) to reflect your business name (or even your personality). If you don't get a domain name of your own, your pages will be part of someone else's domain name — usually your hosting provider's. For example, a hypothetical personal Web site hosted without a domain name at `io.com` could use this URL

```
http://www.io.com/~edtittel
```

With the domain name `edtittel.com`, the same Web site becomes

```
http://www.edtittel.com
```

One domain name is easier to remember than the other. Is that a good enough reason to have your own domain? Maybe . . . maybe not. Businesses or other entities that want to maintain a constant Web presence should probably invest in a domain name; hobbyists or enthusiasts don't need one.

Any good hosting provider can give detailed instructions on how to register a domain name in the provider's system or attach your domain name to a Web site on its computers. If you're changing from one hosting provider to another, the new provider should help you transfer your domain. Most providers either give you this information up front or offer online help to walk you through the process. If it isn't immediately clear how to set up a domain, ask for help. If you don't get it, change providers.

Moving files to your Web server

After you secure a Web host or decide to put up your own Web server, you need a way to move the Web pages you create on your local computer to that server. This isn't a one-time activity, either. While you maintain your Web site, you constantly move files you've built on your local computer to the Web server to refresh your site's contents.

How you move files to your Web server and manage the files when they're on the server depends entirely on how your Web server is set up. Normally, you have a couple of transfer options:

- ✔ **Using File Transfer Protocol (FTP)**
- ✔ **Using a Web interface provided by your hosting provider**

UI design resources

We recommend these Web sites and books on site and interface design if you want to create great UIs:

- For a crash course on design basics, read the "Basics" and "Design Process" articles at www.webdesignfromscratch.com.

- Jakob Nielsen is committed to creating accessible Web content, which means that all content is available to all visitors, including those with various handicaps that might prevent them from following visual or audible cues for navigation. His Web site, http://useit.com, is chock-full of resources and articles on creating accessible sites.

- One of this book's authors, Jeff Noble, is the Associate Editor for the UI Trends Web site (http://uitrends.com), which covers interesting user interface designs and trends as they relate to Web site and Web application designs.

- Hey, negative examples are useful too. Web Pages That Suck guides you to good design by evaluating bad design. Be sure your site doesn't look like any of those featured at www.webpagesthatsuck.com.

- *Web Design For Dummies,* 2nd Edition, by Lisa Lopuck, is another step in the direction of a sophisticated Web site with a knockout look.

- *Web Usability For Dummies,* by Richard Mander and Bud Smith, can help you fine-tune your site to make it amazingly easy to use, which is a great help in keeping your visitors coming back for more.

- *Web Designer Depot* (www.webdesignerdepot.com) is a community site dedicated to all things related to Web site design — typography, design techniques, coding (to name a few). This is a great place to come and find answers to all your design questions.

- *Smashing Magazine* (www.smashingmagazine.com) can help you find anything you need from inspiration (photos, examples, showcases) to design (Photoshop Documents, also commonly referred to as PSD, fonts) to coding (CSS, JavaScript, WordPress) to graphics (wallpapers, backgrounds, icons) and everything in between.

Using FTP to transfer files

Of these two options, FTP is nearly always a possibility. FTP is a standard way to transfer files on the Internet, and any hosting provider should offer FTP access to your Web server. When you set up your site with a provider, it usually gives you written documentation (either on paper or on the Web) to tell you how to transfer files to your Web server. Included in that information will be an FTP URL that usually takes the form ftp://ftp.*domain*.com.

You can use an FTP client, such as SmartFTP (`www.smartftp.com`), WS_FTP (`www.ipswitch.com/Products/WS_FTP`), and the free FileZilla (`filezilla-project.org`), to open a connection to the FTP URL. (Macintosh users will probably prefer Fetch at `www.fetchsoftworks.com` or Cyberduck at `cyberduck.ch`.) Your provider will give you a username and password to use to access your Web server directory via FTP. Then you can move files to your site using the client interface. It's really that easy. If you want to grab a copy of a file from your Web site and modify it, you can do so in three steps:

1. **Use the FTP client's interface to download a copy.**

2. **Make your modification.**

3. **Use the FTP client's interface to upload the changed file.**

Each FTP client's interface is different, but they're all pretty simple. Chapter 23 includes more information on finding a good FTP client; so when you do find one, spend a few minutes reading its documentation.

You might not need FTP software to move files to your Web server:

- ✔ Many browsers, such as current versions of Internet Explorer and Firefox, include basic, built-in FTP support. You can upload or download files, but you may be unable to create or delete directories.

- ✔ Many Web utilities, such as Dreamweaver, also include file-management capabilities.

Using your hosting provider's Web site to transfer files

To enhance usability and reduce technical support calls, many Web hosting providers offer Web pages to help you upload and manage your Web site files without using a separate FTP utility or even the FTP tools inside (X)HTML editors. Most of these tools let you manage your site in various ways, such as

- ✔ Uploading and downloading files
- ✔ Creating and deleting directories
- ✔ Moving files around
- ✔ Deleting files

If you work with a hosting provider, find out whether it has a set of Web-based tools for managing your site.

Keep these thoughts in mind while you decide on a provider:

- ✔ Read the provider's documentation before you start to transfer your files. Every provider's interface is different.

- ✔ Most providers who offer Web interfaces won't stop you from managing your site with FTP.

  Use FTP if a provider's interface is tricky, or if you prefer FTP.

Part II
Formatting Web Pages with (X)HTML

The 5th Wave   By Rich Tennant

FREELANCER NED WILLIS CONSULTS WITH A MEMBER OF HIS TECHNICAL STAFF

"...and that's pretty much all there is to converting a document to an HTML file."

In this part . . .

Here, we describe the markup and document structures that make Web pages workable and attractive.
We examine HTML document structure (including document headers and bodies) and show you how to put the
pieces together correctly. After that, we talk about organizing text in blocks and lists.

Next, we explain how linking in (X)HTML provides the
glue that ties the entire World Wide Web together. To
help you illustrate your words, we explain adding graphics to your pages, too. Thus, we cover the basic building
blocks for well-constructed, properly proportioned Web
pages — and not by coincidence, either.

The final chapter in Part II deals with *deprecated* markup —
namely, HTML elements and attributes that are no longer
safe or smart to use. Although these deprecated elements
and attributes work in HTML4, only some of them work in
XHTML, and none of them work in HTML5. That's why we
want you to know them when you see them, and why we
advise you to avoid them when creating your Web pages.

Chapter 4

Creating (X)HTML Document Structure

. . . .

In This Chapter

▶ Creating a basic (X)HTML document structure

▶ Defining the (X)HTML document header

▶ Creating a full-bodied (X)HTML document

. . . .

*T*he framework for a simple (X)HTML document consists of a head and body. The *head* provides information about the document to the browser, and the *body* contains content that appears in the browser window. The first step in creating any (X)HTML document is to define its framework.

This chapter covers all major elements needed to craft the basic structure of an (X)HTML document — including its head and body. We also show you how to tell a browser which version of HTML or XHTML you're using. Although version information isn't necessary for users, browsers use it to make sure they display document content correctly.

Establishing a Document Structure

Although no two (X)HTML pages are alike — each employs a unique combination of content and elements to define a page — every properly constructed (X)HTML page follows the same basic document structure:

✔ A statement that identifies the document as an (X)HTML document

✔ A document header

✔ A document body

Each time you create an (X)HTML document, you start with these elements. Then you fill in your content and markup to create an individual page.

TIP

Although a basic document structure is a requirement for every (X)HTML document, creating it over and over again can get monotonous. Most (X)HTML-editing tools set up basic document structure automatically whenever you create a new document.

Labeling Your (X)HTML Document

First up in any (X)HTML document sits a Document Type Declaration (DTD), or `DOCTYPE` declaration. This line of markup specifies which version of HTML or XHTML you're using and also lets browsers know how to interpret what follows. We use the XHTML 1.0 specification in this chapter because that's what most browsers and editing tools expect to see.

Adding an HTML DOCTYPE declaration

If you choose to create an HTML 4.01 document instead of an XHTML document, you can pick from three possible `DOCTYPE` declarations:

- **HTML 4.01 Transitional:** This is the most inclusive version of HTML 4.01, and it incorporates all HTML structural elements as well as all presentation elements:

    ```
    <!DOCTYPE HTML PUBLIC "-//W3C//DTD HTML 4.01 Transitional//EN"
            "http://www.w3.org/TR/html4/loose.dtd">
    ```

- **HTML 4.01 Strict:** This streamlined version of HTML excludes all presentation-related elements in favor of style sheets as the means to drive page display:

    ```
    <!DOCTYPE HTML PUBLIC "-//W3C//DTD HTML 4.01//EN"
            "http://www.w3.org/TR/html4/strict.dtd">
    ```

- **HTML 4.01 Frameset:** This version begins with HTML 4.01 Transitional and adds all the elements that make frames possible:

    ```
    <!DOCTYPE HTML PUBLIC "-//W3C//DTD HTML 4.01 Frameset//EN"
            "http://www.w3.org/TR/html4/frameset.dtd">
    ```

WARNING!

Although using HTML 4.01 Frameset is still a perfectly valid way to create your `DOCTYPE` declaration, framesets are no longer considered a best practice, and caution should be exercised before deciding to use framesets.

Adding an XHTML DOCTYPE declaration

To create an XHTML document, use one of the following `DOCTYPE` declarations:

✔ **XHTML 1.0 Transitional:**

```
<!DOCTYPE html PUBLIC "-//W3C//DTD XHTML 1.0 Transitional//EN"
        "http://www.w3.org/TR/xhtml1/DTD/xhtml1-transitional.dtd">
```

✔ **XHTML 1.0 Strict:**

```
<!DOCTYPE html PUBLIC "-//W3C//DTD XHTML 1.0 Strict//EN"
        "http://www.w3.org/TR/xhtml1/DTD/xhtml1-strict.dtd">
```

✔ **XHTML 1.0 Frameset:**

```
<!DOCTYPE html PUBLIC "-//W3C//DTD XHTML 1.0 Frameset//EN"
        "http://www.w3.org/TR/xhtml1/DTD/xhtml1-frameset.dtd">
```

Like with HTML framesets, using XHTML framesets is no longer considered a best practice.

The XHTML DTD descriptions are similar to the HTML DTD descriptions defined in Chapter 1. The HTML DTDs are documented in detail at www. w3.org/TR/html401/sgml/dtd.html; the XHTML DTDs are documented at www.w3.org/TR/xhtml1/dtds.html.

The <html> element

After you specify which version of (X)HTML the document follows, add an <html> element to contain all other (X)HTML elements in your page:

```
<!DOCTYPE html PUBLIC "-//W3C//DTD XHTML 1.0 Transitional//EN"
        "http://www.w3.org/TR/xhtml1/DTD/xhtml1-transitional.dtd">

<html>



</html>
```

Adding the XHTML namespace

A *namespace* is a collection of names used by the elements and attributes in an XML document. XHTML uses a special collection of names; therefore, it needs an XML namespace definition that looks like this:

```
<!DOCTYPE html PUBLIC "-//W3C//DTD XHTML 1.0 Transitional//EN"
        "http://www.w3.org/TR/xhtml1/DTD/xhtml1-transitional.dtd">

<html xmlns="http://www.w3.org/1999/xhtml">



</html>
```

Don't get bogged down by namespaces. If you work with other XML vocabularies, you need to know about namespaces. For simple XHTML documents, you just need to remember to include the XHTML namespace. The preceding code snippet shows you exactly how to do so! If you skip this step, though, your XHTML files will not validate at `validator.w3.org`.

Adding a Document Header

The *head* of an (X)HTML document is one of two main components in any such document; the *body* is the other main component. The head, or *header,* provides basic information about the document, including its title and *metadata* (information about information), such as keywords, character encoding, author information, and a description. If you wish to use a style sheet within a page, information about that style sheet also goes into the header.

Chapter 9 provides a complete overview of creating Cascading Style Sheets (CSS) and shows how to include them in (X)HTML documents.

The `<head>` element, which defines the page header, immediately follows the `<html>` opening tag:

```
<!DOCTYPE html PUBLIC "-//W3C//DTD XHTML 1.0 Transitional//EN"
        "http://www.w3.org/TR/xhtml1/DTD/xhtml1-transitional.dtd">

<html xmlns="http://www.w3.org/1999/xhtml">
  <head>
    <meta http-equiv="Content-Type" content="text/html; charset=UTF-8" />
  </head>
</html>
```

The metadata element for character encoding

```
<meta http-equiv="Content-Type" content="text/html; charset=UTF-8">
```

is also required for a Web page to validate at `validator.w3.org`. Don't leave it out!

Giving your page a title

Every (X)HTML page needs a descriptive title to tell visitors what the page is about. This text appears in the title bar at the very top of the browser window, as shown in Figure 4-1. A page title should be concise yet informative. (For example, *My home page* isn't as informative as *Jeff's Web Design Services.*)

Define a page title by using the `<title>` element inside the `<head>` element:

```
<!DOCTYPE html PUBLIC "-//W3C//DTD XHTML 1.0 Transitional//EN"
        "http://www.w3.org/TR/xhtml1/DTD/xhtml1-transitional.dtd">

<html xmlns="http://www.w3.org/1999/xhtml">
  <head>
    <meta http-equiv="Content-Type" content="text/html; charset=UTF-8" />
    <title>Jeff's Web Design Services</title>
  </head>

</html>
```

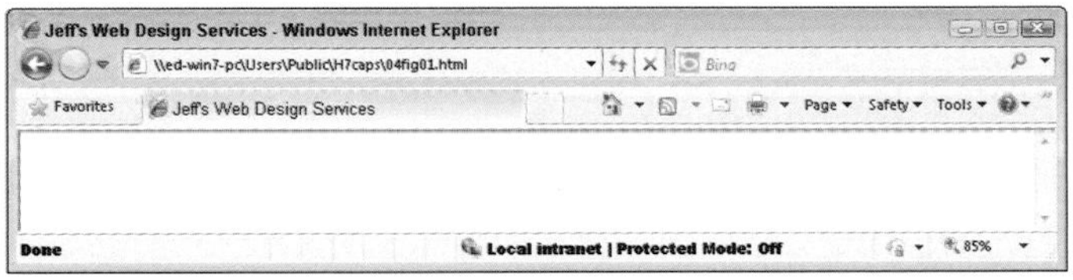

Figure 4-1: (X)HTML page titles appear in a Web browser's title bar.

Search engines use `<title>` content to list Web pages in response to a query. A page title may be the first thing a Web surfer reads about your page, especially if she finds it via a search engine. In fact, a search engine will probably list your page title among many others on a results page, which gives you only one chance to grab a surfer's attention and convince her to choose your page. A well-crafted title can do just that.

The title is also used for Bookmarks and in a browser's History, so keep your titles short and sweet.

Defining metadata

Metadata refers to data about data. In the context of the Web, that means data that describes your Web page. Metadata for a page may include

- Keywords
- A description of your page
- Information about the page author
- The software application you used to create the page

Elements and attributes

You define each piece of metadata for your (X)HTML page with

- The `<meta />` element
- The `name` and `content` attributes

For example, the following elements create a list of keywords and a description for a consulting-service page:

```
<!DOCTYPE html PUBLIC "-//W3C//DTD XHTML 1.0 Transitional//EN"
        "http://www.w3.org/TR/xhtml1/DTD/xhtml1-transitional.dtd">

<html xmlns="http://www.w3.org/1999/xhtml">
  <head>
  <title>Jeff's Web Design Services</title>
    <meta http-equiv="Content-Type" content="text/html; charset=UTF-8" />
    <meta name="keywords"
      content="Web consulting, page design, site construction" />
    <meta name="description"
      content="Synopsis of Jeff's skills and services" />
  </head>
</html>
```

Custom names

The (X)HTML specification doesn't

- Predefine what kinds of metadata you can include in your page
- Specify how to name different bits of metadata, such as keywords and descriptions

So, for example, instead of using `keywords` and `description` as names for keyword and description metadata, you can just as easily use `kwrd` and `desc`, as in the following markup:

```
<!DOCTYPE html PUBLIC "-//W3C//DTD XHTML 1.0 Transitional//EN"
        "http://www.w3.org/TR/xhtml1/DTD/xhtml1-transitional.dtd">

<html xmlns="http://www.w3.org/1999/xhtml">
  <head>
    <title>Jeff's Web Design Services</title>
    <meta http-equiv="Content-Type" content="text/html; charset=UTF-8" />
    <meta name="kwrd"
      content=" Web consulting, page design, site construction " />
    <meta name="desc" content="Synopsis of Jeff's skills and services" />
  </head>
</html>
```

If you can use just any old values for `<meta>` name and content attributes, how do systems know what to do with metadata? The answer is that they don't. Each search engine works differently. Although *keywords* and *description* are commonly used names, search engines may not recognize or use other metadata names that you include. Despite an occasional failure of search engines to recognize any metadata names you might include, their use remains an effective way to increase the chance that your Web site will be found in a search engine.

Many developers use metadata to either

✔ Leave messages for those who look at source code for the page

✔ Prepare for future browsers and search engines to use such metadata

Although keywords and page descriptions are optional, search engines use them to collect information about your Web site. In the past, some people would completely overload their Web site `<meta />` tags in an attempt to try to have their Web site show up as many times as possible. Modern search engines are "smart" enough to take this into account, though, and will either de-emphasize the `<meta />` tags or ignore them completely for rankings. Be sure to include detailed and concise information in your `<meta />` tag if you want your Web site discovered by search engine robots, or bots for short.

Redirecting users to another page

You can use metadata in your header to send messages to Web browsers about how they should display (or otherwise handle) your Web page. Web builders commonly use the `<meta />` element this way to redirect page visitors from one page to another automatically. For example, if you've ever come across a page that reads `This page has moved. Please wait 10 seconds to be automatically sent to the new location.` (or something similar), you've seen this trick at work.

To use the `<meta />` element to send messages to the browser, here are the general steps you need to follow:

1. **Use the `http-equiv` attribute in place of the `name` attribute.**

2. **Choose from a predefined list of values that represent instructions for the browser.**

   These values use instructions that you can send to a browser in the HTTP header, but changing the HTTP header for a document is harder than embedding the instructions into the Web page itself.

To instruct a browser to redirect users from one page to another, here's what you need to do in particular:

1. **Use the `<meta />` element with `http-equiv="refresh"`.**

2. **Adjust the value of `content` to specify how many seconds before the refresh happens and what URL you want to jump to.**

For example, the `<meta />` element line in the following markup creates a refresh that jumps to `www.w3.org` after 15 seconds:

```
<!DOCTYPE html PUBLIC "-//W3C//DTD XHTML 1.0 Transitional//EN"
        "http://www.w3.org/TR/xhtml1/DTD/xhtml1-transitional.dtd">

<html xmlns="http://www.w3.org/1999/xhtml">
  <head>
    <title>All About Markup</title>
    <meta http-equiv="Content-Type" content="text/html; charset=UTF-8" />
    <meta http-equiv="refresh" content="15; url= http://www.w3.org/" />
  </head>

  <body>
    <p>This page is still in development. Until we are done, please visit
       the <a href="http://www.w3.org">W3C Website</a> for the definitive
       collection of markup-related resources.
    </p>

    <p>Please wait 10 seconds to be automatically redirected to the W3C.</p>
  </body>
</html>
```

Use metadata with caution when redirecting a Web page. When some search engines see metadata redirects in use, they think the site is trying to spam. This could result in your Web site or page being *delisted,* or removed from the search engine's listings. When you become a pro at using metadata to redirect, you can step up to the next level and try redirecting using the HTTP code number 301 to force a server-based redirect from an `*.htaccess` file located in the root directory on your Web server. While server-based 301 redirects are outside the scope of this book, a simple Google search can lead you to a number of good resources such as the .htaccess file Redirect/Rewrite Tutorial on Master Site Manager located at `www.mastersitemanager.com/857/301-htaccess-redirect-tutorial`.

Older Web browsers may not know what to do with `<meta />` elements that use the `http-equiv` element to redirect a page. Be sure to include some text and a link on the page so a visitor can link manually to your new target page if your `<meta />` element fails to work. Linking, which uses the anchor (`<a>`) element, is discussed in Chapter 3.

If a user's browser doesn't know what to do with your redirect, the user simply clicks a link on the page to go to the new page, as in Figure 4-2.

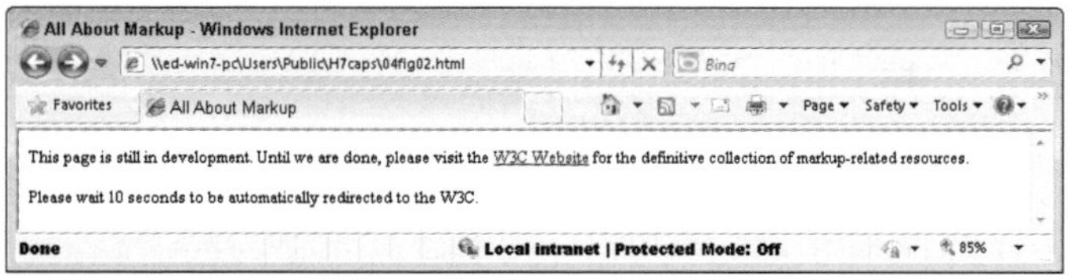

Figure 4-2: When you use a `<meta />` element to create a page redirector, include a link in case the redirector fails.

You can use the `http-equiv` attribute with the `<meta />` element for a variety of purposes, such as setting an expiration date for a page and specifying a character set (the language) for the page to use. To find out what your `http-equiv` options are (and how to use them), check out this Dictionary of HTML META Tags at the following URL:

```
http://vancouver-webpages.com/META/metatags.detail.html
```

Creating the (X)HTML Document Body

After you set up a page header, create a title, and define some metadata, you're ready to create (X)HTML markup and content that will show up in a browser window. The `<body>` element holds your document content.

If you want to see something in your browser window, put it in the `<body>` element, like this:

```
<!DOCTYPE html PUBLIC "-//W3C//DTD XHTML 1.0 Transitional//EN"
        "http://www.w3.org/TR/xhtml1/DTD/xhtml1-transitional.dtd">

<html xmlns="http://www.w3.org/1999/xhtml">
  <head>
    <meta http-equiv="Content-Type" content="text/html; charset=UTF-8" />
    <title>Jeff's Web Design Services</title>
    <meta name="kwrd"
          content=" Web consulting, page design, site construction " />
    <meta name="desc" content="Synopsis of Jeff's skills and services" />
  </head>


<body  style="color: white;
      background-color: teal;
```

```
      font-size: 1.2;
      font-family: sans-serif">
  <h1>Jeff's Web Design Services</h1>
  <p>Jeff has helped many Texas clients, large and small, to design and
     publish their company and professional Web sites. He specializes in
     cutting-edge Web designs, dynamic multimedia, and companion print-
     design solutions to suit all business needs.</p>

  <p>For more information, e-mail
     <a href="mailto:jeff@conquestmedia.com>Jeff Noble</a></p>
 </body>
</html>
```

Figure 4-3 shows how a browser displays this complete (X)HTML page:

- ✔ The content of the `<title>` element is in the window's title bar.

- ✔ The `<meta />` elements don't affect the page appearance at all.

- ✔ Only the paragraph text contained in the `<h1>` and `<p>` elements (in the `<body>` element) actually appears in the browser window.

Figure 4-3: Only content in the `<body>` element appears in the browser window.

Chapter 5

Text and Lists

In This Chapter

▶ Working with basic blocks of text

▶ Manipulating text blocks

▶ Creating bulleted, numbered, and definition lists

*H*TML documents include text, images, multimedia files, links, and other bits of content that you mold into a Web page by using markup elements and attributes. You use blocks of text to create such things as headings, paragraphs, and lists. The first step in creating a solid HTML document is laying a firm foundation to establish the document's structure.

Formatting Text

Here's an ultra-technical definition of a *block of text:* some chunk of content that fills one or more lines inside an HTML element.

In fact, any HTML page is a collection of blocks of text:

✓ Every bit of content on your page must be part of some block element.

✓ Every block element sits inside the <body> element on your page.

HTML recognizes several kinds of text blocks that you can use in your document, including (but not limited to)

✓ Paragraphs

✓ Headings

✓ Block quotes

✓ Lists

✓ Tables

✓ Forms

Inline elements versus text blocks

The difference between inline elements and a block of text is important. HTML elements in this chapter describe blocks of text. An *inline element* is a word or string of words *inside* a block element (for example, text-emphasis elements, such as `<em>` or `<strong>`). Inline elements must be nested within a block element; otherwise, your HTML document isn't syntactically correct.

Inline elements, such as linking and formatting elements, are designed to link from (or change the appearance of) a few words or lines of content found inside those blocks.

Paragraphs

Paragraphs appear more often than any other text block in Web pages.

HTML browsers don't recognize hard returns that you enter when you create your page inside an editor. You must use a `<p>` element to tell the browser to package all text up to the closing `</p>` tag as a paragraph.

Formatting

To create a paragraph, follow these steps:

1. **Add `<p>` in the body of the document.**

2. **Type the content of the paragraph.**

3. **Add `</p>` to close that paragraph.**

Here's what it looks like:

```
<!DOCTYPE html PUBLIC "-//W3C//DTD XHTML 1.0 Transitional//EN"
        "http://www.w3.org/TR/xhtml1/DTD/xhtml1-transitional.dtd">
<html xmlns="http://www.w3.org/1999/xhtml" xml:lang="en" lang="en">
  <head>
    <meta http-equiv="Content-Type" content="text/html; charset=ISO-8859-1" />
    <title>All About Blocks</title>
  </head>

  <body>
    <p>This is a paragraph. It's a very simple structure that you will use
       time and again in your Web pages.</p>
    <p>This is another paragraph. What could be simpler to create?</p>
  </body>
</html>
```

This HTML page includes two paragraphs, each marked with a separate `<p>` element. Most Web browsers add a line break and a full line of white space after every paragraph on your page, as shown in Figure 5-1.

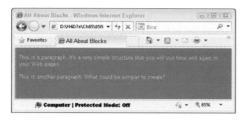

Figure 5-1: Web browsers delineate paragraphs with line breaks.

Sloppy HTML coders don't use the closing </p> tag when they create paragraphs. Although some browsers permit this dubious practice without yelling, omitting the closing tag isn't good practice because it:

- Isn't correct syntax
- Causes problems with style sheets
- Can cause a page to appear inconsistently from one browser to another

You can control paragraph formatting (color, style, size, and alignment) with Cascading Style Sheets (CSS), covered in Chapters 9–12.

Headings

Headings break a document into sections. This book uses headings and subheadings to divide each chapter into sections, and you can do the same with your Web page. Headings

- Create an organizational structure
- Break up the text flow on the page
- Provide visual cues as to how pieces of content are grouped

HTML includes six elements for different heading levels in documents:

- <h1> is the most prominent heading (Heading 1)
- <h6> is the least prominent heading (Heading 6)

Follow numerical order from lowest to highest as you use HTML heading levels. That is, don't use a second-level heading until you use a first-level heading, don't use a third-level heading until you use a second, and so on. If you want to change how headings look, Chapters 10 and 11 show you how to use style sheets for that purpose.

Formatting

To create a heading, follow these steps:

1. **Add `<hn>` in the body of your document.**
2. **Type the content for the heading.**
3. **Add `</hn>`.**

When used in this context, *n* means the number of the heading level you want to create. For example, to create a level 1 heading, you would substitute the number 1 for *n* and would add `<h1>` to your page, for a level 2 heading, add `<h2>`, and so forth.

Browser displays

Every browser has a different way of displaying heading levels, as you see in the next two sections.

Graphical browsers

Most graphical browsers use a distinctive size and typeface for headings:

- First-level headings (`<h1>`) are the largest (usually two or three font sizes larger than the default text size for paragraphs).
- All headings use boldface type by default, and paragraph text uses plain (nonbold) type by default.
- Sixth-level headings (`<h6>`) are the smallest and may be two or three font sizes *smaller* than the default paragraph text.

The following snippet of HTML markup shows all six headings at work:

```
<!DOCTYPE html PUBLIC "-//W3C//DTD XHTML 1.0 Transitional//EN"
        "http://www.w3.org/TR/xhtml1/DTD/xhtml1-transitional.dtd">
<html xmlns="http://www.w3.org/1999/xhtml" xml:lang="en" lang="en">
  <head>
    <meta http-equiv="Content-Type" content="text/html; charset=ISO-8859-1" />
    <title>All About Blocks</title>
  </head>

  <body>
    <h1>First-level heading</h1>
    <h2>Second-level heading</h2>
    <h3>Third-level heading</h3>
    <h4>Fourth-level heading</h4>
    <h5>Fifth-level heading</h5>
    <h6>Sixth-level heading</h6>
  </body>
</html>
```

Figure 5-2 shows the headings in the HTML page as rendered in a browser.

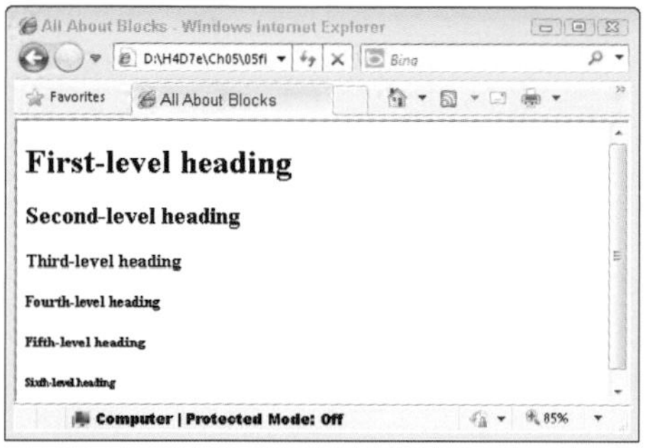

Figure 5-2: Web browsers display headings from level one to level six.

Use CSS to control how headings look, including color, size, spacing, and alignment.

By default, most browsers use Times Roman fonts for headings. The font size decreases as the heading level increases. (Default sizes for first- through sixth-level headings are, respectively, 24, 18, 14, 12, 10, and 8 point font.) You can override any of this formatting by using CSS.

Text browsers

Text-only browsers use heading conventions different from those of graphical browsers because text-only browsers use a single character size and font to display all content. Some good text-only browsers to consider include Lynx, ELinks, Cygwin, and MIRA.

Controlling Text Blocks

Blocks of text build the foundation of your page. You can break those blocks into smaller pieces to better guide readers through your content.

Block quotes

A *block quote* is a quotation, or an excerpt from a copyrighted source, that you set apart on a page. Use the <blockquote> element to enclose quotations:

```
<!DOCTYPE html PUBLIC "-//W3C//DTD XHTML 1.0 Transitional//EN"
        "http://www.w3.org/TR/xhtml1/DTD/xhtml1-transitional.dtd">
<html xmlns="http://www.w3.org/1999/xhtml" xml:lang="en" lang="en">
  <head>
    <meta http-equiv="Content-Type" content="text/html; charset=ISO-8859-1" />
    <title>Famous Quotations</title>
  </head>

  <body>
    <h1>An Inspiring Quote</h1>
    <p>When I need a little inspiration to remind me of why I spend my days
       in the classroom, I just remember what Lee Iococca said:</p>
    <blockquote>
      In a completely rational society, the best of us would be teachers
      and the rest of us would have to settle for something else.
    </blockquote>
  </body>
</html>
```

Most Web browsers display block quote content with a slight left indent, as shown in Figure 5-3.

Figure 5-3: Web browsers typically indent a block quote to separate it from paragraphs.

Preformatted text

Ordinarily, HTML ignores white space inside documents. A browser won't display a block element's

- ✔ Hard returns
- ✔ Line breaks
- ✔ Large white spaces

The following markup includes various hard returns, line breaks, and lots of spaces. Figure 5-4 shows that the Web browser ignores all of this.

```
<p>This is a paragraph

   with a lot of white space

       thrown in for fun (and as a test of course).</p>
```

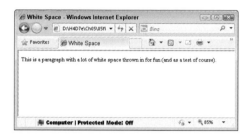

Figure 5-4: Web browsers routinely ignore white space.

The preformatted text element (`<pre>`) instructs browsers to keep all white space intact while it displays your content (see the following sample). Use the `<pre>` element in place of the `<p>` element to make the browser apply all your white space, as shown in Figure 5-5.

```
<!DOCTYPE html PUBLIC "-//W3C//DTD XHTML 1.0 Transitional//EN"
        "http://www.w3.org/TR/xhtml11/DTD/xhtml11-transitional.dtd">
<html xmlns="http://www.w3.org/1999/xhtml" xml:lang="en" lang="en">
  <head>
    <meta http-equiv="Content-Type" content="text/html; charset=ISO-8859-1" />
    <title>White Space</title>
  </head>

  <body>
    <pre>This is a paragraph

                      with a lot of white space

                              thrown in for fun (and as a test of course).

    </pre>
  </body>
</html>
```

You may want the browser to display white spaces in an HTML page where proper spacing is important, such as for

✔ Code samples

✔ Columnar data, numbers, or other format-sensitive text

✔ Text tables

Figure 5-5: Use preformatted text to force browsers to recognize white space.

You can nest `<pre>` elements inside `<blockquote>` elements to carefully control how lines of quoted text appear on the page. Or better still, forget about these tags and use CSS to position text blocks inside `<div>` elements.

Horizontal rules

Using a horizontal rule element (`<hr />`) helps you include solid straight lines *(rules)* on your page.

The browser creates the rule based on the `<hr />` element, so users don't wait for a graphic to download. A horizontal rule is a good option to

- Break a page into logical sections.
- Separate headers and footers from the rest of the page.

Formatting

When you include an `<hr />` element on your page, as in the following XHTML, the browser replaces it with a line, as shown in Figure 5-6.

```
<!DOCTYPE html PUBLIC "-//W3C//DTD XHTML 1.0 Transitional//EN"
        "http://www.w3.org/TR/xhtml1/DTD/xhtml1-transitional.dtd">
<html xmlns="http://www.w3.org/1999/xhtml" xml:lang="en" lang="en">
  <head>
    <meta http-equiv="Content-Type" content="text/html; charset=ISO-8859-1" />
    <title>Horizontal Rules</title>
  </head>

  <body>
    <p>This is a paragraph followed by a horizontal rule.</p>

    <hr />

    <p>This is a paragraph preceded by a horizontal rule.</p>
  </body>
</html>
```

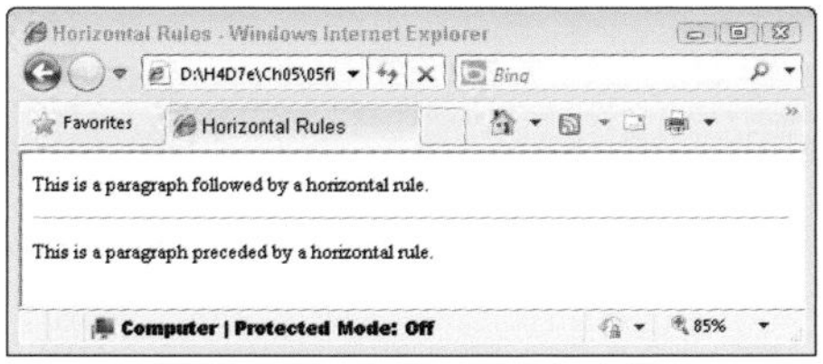

Figure 5-6: Use the `<hr />` element to add horizontal lines to your page.

A horizontal rule always sits on a line by itself; you can't add the `<hr />` element in the middle of a paragraph (or other block element) and expect the rule to appear in the middle of the block.

This bit of HTML creates a horizontal rule that takes up 45 percent of the page width, is 4 pixels (px) high, is aligned to the center, and has shading turned off:

```
<p>This is a paragraph followed by a horizontal rule.</p>

<hr width="45%" size="4" align="center" noshade="noshade" />

<p>This is a paragraph preceded by a horizontal rule.</p>
```

Figure 5-7 shows how adding these attributes alters how the rule is displayed. (***Note:*** These attributes are deprecated, and are better replaced with CSS equivalents as described in Chapters 9–12. Deprecated attributes are covered in Chapter 8.)

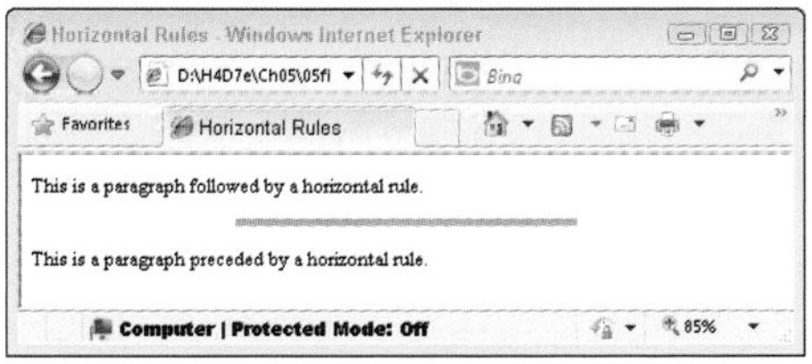

Figure 5-7: Horizontal rule markup enables a browser to display a rule sized to the current page display.

Figure 5-8 shows how you can use horizontal rules in the real world to highlight important content. The EdTittel.com home page uses a colored hard rule to separate the footer from the rest of the page.

Figure 5-8: The EdTittel.com home page uses a colored rule to separate page content from page-footer information.

As the `<style>` section in the file header clearly illustrates, CSS gives you great control over color, width, and page coverage for horizontal rules.

Organizing Information

Lists are powerful tools to group similar elements, and lists give visitors to your site an easy way to zoom in on groups of information. Just about anything fits in a list, from sets of instructions to collections of links.

Lists use a combination of elements — at least two components:

- A markup element that says, "Hey browser! The following items go in a list."
- Markup elements that say, "Hey browser! This is an item in the list."

HTML supports three types of lists:

- Numbered lists
- Bulleted lists
- Definition lists

Numbered lists

A *numbered list* consists of at least two items, each prefaced by a number. Use a numbered list when the order or priority of items is important.

You use two kinds of elements for a numbered list:

- The ordered list element (`<ol>`) specifies a numbered list.
- List item elements (`<li>`) mark each item in the list.

Formatting

A numbered list with three items requires elements and content in the following order:

1. `<ol>`

2. `<li>`

3. Content for the first list item

4. `</li>`

5. `<li>`

6. Content for the second list item

7. `</li>`

8. `<li>`

9. Content for the third list item

10. `</li>`

11. `</ol>`

The following markup defines a three-item numbered list:

```
<!DOCTYPE html PUBLIC "-//W3C//DTD XHTML 1.0 Transitional//EN"
        "http://www.w3.org/TR/xhtml1/DTD/xhtml1-transitional.dtd">
<html xmlns="http://www.w3.org/1999/xhtml" xml:lang="en" lang="en">
  <head>
    <meta http-equiv="Content-Type" content="text/html; charset=ISO-8859-1" />
    <title>Numbered Lists</title>
  </head>

  <body>
    <h1>Things to do today</h1>
    <ol>
      <li>Feed cat</li>
      <li>Wash car</li>
      <li>Grocery shopping</li>
    </ol>
  </body>
</html>
```

Figure 5-9 shows how a browser renders this markup. You don't actually have to specify a number for each item in the list; the browser identifies the list items from the markup and adds the numbers, including a period after each list number by default.

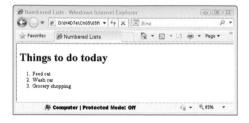

Figure 5-9: Use `<ol>` and `<li>` tags to create a numbered list.

If you swap the first two items in the list, they're still numbered in order when the page appears, as shown in Figure 5-10.

```
<ol>
  <li>Wash car</li>
  <li>Feed cat</li>
  <li>Grocery shopping</li>
</ol>
```

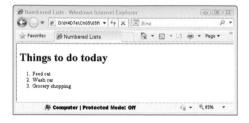

Figure 5-10: Web browsers set numbers for your list according to order of appearance.

Numbering

Two different `<ol>` attributes control the appearance of a numbered list:

✔ `start`: Specifies the first number in the list.

   • The default starting number is 1, although you can specify any number as the start number for the new list.

   Specify a start number when you resume a list after an unnumbered paragraph or some other block element.

✔ type: Specifies the numbering style from the list. You can choose from five predefined numbering styles:

- 1: Decimal numbers
- a: Lowercase Romans letters
- A: Uppercase Roman letters
- i: Lowercase Roman numerals
- I: Uppercase Roman numerals

The following markup uses ordered elements and attributes to build a list that uses uppercase Roman numerals starting at 5 (V in Roman numerals):

```
<ol start="5" type="I">
  <li>Wash car</li>
  <li>Feed cat</li>
  <li>Grocery shopping</li>
</ol>
```

Figure 5-11 shows how attributes affect the list's appearance in a browser.

Figure 5-11: The start and type attributes guide the appearance of a numbered list in a browser.

You have more control over your lists if you use CSS to define formatting. That's why the start and type attributes for list markup are *deprecated* (that is, abandoned as outmoded in the current version of HTML).

Bulleted lists

A *bulleted list* consists of one or more items each prefaced by a *bullet* (often a big dot; this book sometimes uses check marks as bullets).

You use this type of list if the items' order of presentation isn't necessary for understanding the information presented.

Formatting

A bulleted list requires the following:

- ✔ The unordered list element (`<ul>`) specifies a bulleted list.
- ✔ A list item element (`<li>`) marks each item in the list.
- ✔ The closing tag for the unordered list element (`</ul>`) indicates that the list has come to its end.

An *unordered list* (another name for bulleted list) with three items requires elements and content in the following order:

1. `<ul>`
2. `<li>`
3. Content for the first list item
4. `</li>`
5. `<li>`
6. Content for the second list item
7. `</li>`
8. `<li>`
9. Content for the third list item
10. `</li>`
11. `</ul>`

The following markup formats a three-item list as a bulleted list:

```
<!DOCTYPE html PUBLIC "-//W3C//DTD XHTML 1.0 Transitional//EN"
        "http://www.w3.org/TR/xhtml1/DTD/xhtml1-transitional.dtd">
<html xmlns="http://www.w3.org/1999/xhtml" xml:lang="en" lang="en">
  <head>
    <meta http-equiv="Content-Type" content="text/html; charset=ISO-8859-1" />
    <title>Bulleted Lists</title>
  </head>

  <body>
    <h1>Things to do today</h1>
    <ul>
      <li>Feed cat</li>
      <li>Wash car</li>
      <li>Grocery shopping</li>
    </ul>
  </body>
</html>
```

Figure 5-12 shows how a browser renders this with bullets.

Things to do today

- Feed cat
- Wash car
- Grocery shopping

Figure 5-12: An unordered list uses bullets instead of numbers to mark items.

Use CSS if you want to exert more control over the formatting of your lists, including the ability to use your own graphics as bullet symbols.

Definition lists

Definition lists group terms and definitions into a single list and require three different elements to complete the list:

- ✓ <dl>: Holds the list definitions (dl = definition list)
- ✓ <dt>: Defines a term in the list (dt = definition term)
- ✓ <dd>: Defines a definition for a term (dd = definition list definition)

You can have as many terms (defined by <dt>) in a list (<dl>) as you need. Each term can have one or more definitions (defined by <dd>).

Creating a definition list with two items requires elements and content in the following order:

1. <dl>
2. <dt>
3. First term name
4. </dt>
5. <dd>
6. Content for the definition of the first item
7. </dd>
8. <dt>
9. Second term name
10. </dt>

11. `<dd>`

12. Content for the definition of the second item

13. `</dd>`

14. `</dl>`

The following definition list includes three terms, one of which has two definitions:

```
<!DOCTYPE html PUBLIC "-//W3C//DTD XHTML 1.0 Transitional//EN"
        "http://www.w3.org/TR/xhtml1/DTD/xhtml1-transitional.dtd">
<html xmlns="http://www.w3.org/1999/xhtml" xml:lang="en" lang="en">
  <head>
    <meta http-equiv="Content-Type" content="text/html; charset=ISO-8859-1" />
    <title>Definition Lists</title>
  </head>

  <body>
    <h1>Markup Language Definitions</h1>
    <dl>
      <dt>SGML</dt>
        <dd>The Standard Generalized Markup Language</dd>
      <dt>HTML</dt>
        <dd>The Hypertext Markup Language</dd>
        <dd>The markup language you use to create Web pages.</dd>
      <dt>XML</dt>
        <dd>The Extensible Markup Language</dd>
    </dl>
  </body>
</html>
```

Figure 5-13 shows how a browser displays this HTML.

Figure 5-13: Definition lists group terms and their related definitions into one list.

If you think items in a list are too close together, you can use CSS styles to carefully control all aspects of list appearance, as shown in Chapter 9.

Note that definition lists often display differently inside different browsers, and they aren't always handled the same by search engines or text-to-speech translators. About.com has a nice discussion of definition lists at `http://webdesign.about.com/od/htmltags/a/aa112006.htm`. Alas, this means that definition lists may not be the best choice of formatting for lists you create (even lists of definitions). See the excellent coverage of this topic at `www.maxdesign.com.au/articles/definition` for a more detailed discussion.

Nesting lists

You can create subcategories by *nesting* lists within lists. Some common uses for nested lists include

- Site maps and other navigation tools
- Tables of content for online books and papers
- Outlines

You can combine any of the three kinds of lists to create *nested lists,* such as a multilevel table of contents or an outline that mixes numbered headings with bulleted list items as the lowest outline level.

The following example starts with a numbered list that defines a list of things to do for the day and uses three bulleted lists to break down those items further, into specific tasks:

```
<!DOCTYPE HTML PUBLIC "-//W3C//DTD HTML 4.01 Transitional//EN">

<html>
  <head>
    <meta http-equiv="Content-Type" content="text/html; charset=UTF-8">
    <title>Nested Lists</title>
  </head>

  <body>
    <h1>Things to do today</h1>
    <ol>
      <li>Feed cat
        <ul>
          <li>Rinse bowl</li>
          <li>Open cat food</li>
          <li>Mix dry and wet food in bowl</li>
          <li>Deliver on a silver platter to Pixel</li>
        </ul></li>
      <li>Wash car
        <ul>
          <li>Vacuum interior</li>
          <li>Wash exterior</li>
```

```
            <li>Wax exterior</li>
        </ul></li>
      <li>Grocery shopping
        <ul>
          <li>Plan meals</li>
          <li>Clean out fridge</li>
          <li>Make list</li>
          <li>Go to store</li>
        </ul></li>
    </ol>
  </body>
</html>
```

All nested lists follow the same markup pattern:

✔ Each list item in the top-level ordered list is followed by a complete second-level list.

✔ The second-level lists sit inside the top-level list, not in the list items.

Figure 5-14 shows how a browser reflects this nesting in its display.

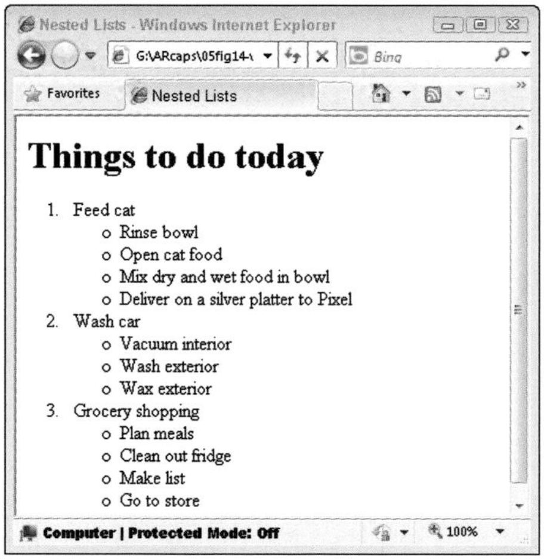

Things to do today

1. Feed cat
   o Rinse bowl
   o Open cat food
   o Mix dry and wet food in bowl
   o Deliver on a silver platter to Pixel
2. Wash car
   o Vacuum interior
   o Wash exterior
   o Wax exterior
3. Grocery shopping
   o Plan meals
   o Clean out fridge
   o Make list
   o Go to store

Figure 5-14: Nested lists combine lists for multilevel organization of information.

While you build nested lists, watch opening and closing tags carefully. *Close first what you opened last* is an important axiom. If you don't open and close tags properly, lists might not use consistent indents or numbers, or text might be indented incorrectly because a list somewhere was never properly closed.

Chapter 6

Linking to Online Resources

- -

In This Chapter

▶ Creating simple links

▶ Opening linked pages in new windows

▶ Setting up links to locations within a Web page

▶ Creating links to things other than Web pages

- -

*H*yperlinks, or simply *links,* connect (X)HTML pages and other resources on the Web. When you include a link on your page, you enable visitors to travel from your page to another Web site, another page on your site, or even another location on the same page. Without links, a page stands alone, disconnected from the rest of the Web. With links, that page becomes part of an almost boundless collection of information that is the World Wide Web.

Basic Links

To create a link, you need

- ✔ **The Web address** (called a Uniform Resource Locator; URL) for the Web site or file that's your link target. This usually starts with `http://`.

- ✔ **Some text** in your Web page to label or describe the link.

  Try to ensure that the text you use says something useful about the resource being linked.

- ✔ **An anchor element (`<a>`) with an `href` attribute** to bring it all together.

  The element to create links is called an *anchor element* because you use it to anchor a URL to some text on your page. When users view your page in a browser, they can click the text to activate the link and visit the page whose URL you specified in that link. You insert the full URL in the `href` attribute. This tells the link where to go.

You can think of the structure of a basic link as a cheeseburger (or your preferred vegan substitute). The URL is the cheese, the link text is the patty, and the anchor tags are the buns. Tasty, yes?

For example, if you have a Web page that describes HTML standards, you may want to refer Web surfers to the World Wide Web Consortium (W3C) — the organization that governs all things related to (X)HTML standards. A basic link to the W3C Web site, `www.w3.org`, looks like this:

```
<p>The <a href="http://www.w3.org">World Wide Web Consortium</a> is the
    standards body that oversees the ongoing development of the XHTML
    specification.</p>
```

You specify the link URL (`http://www.w3.org`) in the anchor element's `href` attribute. The text (`World Wide Web Consortium`) between the anchor element's open and close tags (`<a>` and `</a>`) labels or describes the link.

Figure 6-1 shows how a browser displays this bit of markup.

Figure 6-1: A paragraph with a link to the W3C.

You can also anchor URLs to images so that users can click an image to activate a link. For more about creating images that link, see Chapter 7. For a detailed discussion of the ins and outs of URLs, see Chapter 1.

Link options

You can link to a variety of online resources:

- ✔ Other (X)HTML pages (either on your Web site or on another Web site)
- ✔ Different locations on the same (X)HTML page
- ✔ Resources that aren't even (X)HTML pages at all, such as e-mail addresses, pictures, and text files

Anchor elements aren't block elements

Anchor elements are *inline elements* — that is, they apply to a few words or characters within a block of text (the text that you want to use as a link) instead of defining formatting for blocks of text. The anchor element typically sits inside a paragraph (<p>) or other block element, such as a paragraph or list item. When you create a link, you should always create it within a block element, such as a paragraph, list item, heading, or even a table cell. Turn to Chapter 5 for more information on block elements.

Although many Web browsers display anchors just fine even if you don't nest them in block elements, some browsers (such as the following) don't handle this breach of (X)HTML syntax very well:

- ✔ Text-only browsers for handheld devices or mobile phones
- ✔ Text-to-speech readers for the visually impaired

Text-based browsers rely on block elements to properly divide up the sections of your page. Without a block element, these browsers might display your links in the wrong places.

Link locations, captions, and destinations exert huge influence on how site visitors perceive links. Chapter 3 covers best practices for using links in your site design.

The kind of link you create is determined by where you link.

Absolute links

An *absolute link* uses a complete URL to connect browsers to a Web page or online resource.

Links that use a complete URL to point to a resource are called *absolute* because they provide a complete, standalone path to another Web resource. When you link to a page on someone else's Web site, the Web browser needs every bit of information in the URL to find the page. The browser starts with the domain in the URL and works its way through the path to a specific file.

When you link to files on someone else's site, you must always use absolute URLs in the `href` attribute of the anchor element. Here's an example:

```
http://www.website.com/directory/page.html
```

Relative links

A *relative link* uses a kind of shorthand to specify a URL for a resource you're pointing to.

Use the following guidelines with relative links in your (X)HTML pages:

- ✔ **Create relative links between resources in the same domain.**
- ✔ **Because both resources are in the same domain, omit domain information from the URL.**

  A *relative* URL uses the location of the resource you're linking from to identify the location of the resource you're linking to (for example, `page.html`).

A relative link is similar to telling someone that he or she needs to go to the Eastside Mall. If the person already knows where the Eastside Mall is, he or she doesn't need additional directions. Web browsers behave the same way.

If you use relative links on your site, your links still work if you change

- ✔ Servers
- ✔ Domain names

Simple links

You can take advantage of relative URLs when you create a link between pages on the same Web site. If you want to make a link from `http://www.mysite.com/home.html` to `http://www.mysite.com/about.html`, you can use this simplified, relative URL in an anchor element on `home.html`:

```
<p>Learn more <a href="about.html">about</a> our company.</p>
```

When a browser sees a link without a domain name, the browser assumes that the link is *relative* and uses the domain and path from the linking page to find the linked page. The preceding example works only if `home.html` and `about.html` are in the same directory, though.

Site links

As your site grows more complex and you organize your files into various folders, you can still use relative links. However, you must provide additional information in the relative URL to help the browser find files that don't reside in the same directory as the file from which you're linking.

Use `../` (two periods and a slash) before the filename to indicate that the browser should move up one level in the directory structure.

The markup for this process looks like this:

```
<a href="../docs/home.html>Documentation home</a>
```

The importance of http:// in (X)HTML links

Browsers make surfing the Web as easy as possible. If you type **www.sun.com**, **sun.com**, or often even just **sun** in your browser's address window, the browser obligingly brings up `http://www.oracle.com/US/Sun/index.html`. Although this technique works when you type URLs into your browser window, it doesn't work when you're writing markup.

The URLs that you use in your HTML markup must be *fully formed* (complete in every detail). Browsers won't interpret URLs that don't include the page protocol. If you forget the `http://`, your link may not work!

The notation in this anchor element instructs the browser to

1. **Move up one folder from the folder the linking document is stored in.**

2. **Find a folder called `docs`.**

3. **Find a file called `home.html`.**

When you create a relative link, the location of the file *to* which you link is always relative to the file *from* which you link. As you create a relative URL, trace the path a browser takes if it starts on the page you're linking from to get to the page to which you're linking. That path defines the URL you need.

Common mistakes

Every Web resource — site, page, or image — has a unique URL. Even one incorrect letter in a URL creates a *broken link,* which leads to an error page (usually the HTTP error `404 File or directory not found`).

URLs are so finicky that a simple typo breaks a link.

If a URL doesn't work, try these tactics:

- ✔ **Check the capitalization.** Some Web servers (Linux and Unix, most notably) are *case-sensitive* (they distinguish between capital and lower-case letters). For example, such servers treat the filenames `Bios.html` and `bios.html` as different files on the Web server. That means any browser looking for a particular URL *must* use uppercase and lower-case letters when necessary. Be sure that the capitalization in the link matches the capitalization of the URL.

To avoid problems with files on your Web site, follow a standard naming convention. Often, using only lowercase letters can simplify your life.

✔ **Check the extension.** `Bios.htm` and `Bios.html` are two different files. If your link's URL uses one extension and the actual filename uses another, your link won't work.

To avoid problems with extensions on your Web site, pick either `.html` or `.htm` *and stick to that extension.*

✔ **Check the filename.** For example, `bio.html` and `bios.html` are two different files.

✔ **Copy and paste.** Avoid retyping a URL if you can copy it. The best and most foolproof way to create a URL that works is as follows:

    a. Load a page in your browser.

    b. Copy the URL from the browser's address or link text box.

    c. Paste the URL into your (X)HTML markup.

The copy-and-paste method for grabbing URLs presumes that you're grabbing them from a Web site somewhere. If you open a local file on your PC in a browser, you'll see something that looks like this: `file:\\\I:\H4D6e\ html_letter.html`. Here's how to decipher it all:

✔ `file:\\\` is an Internet Explorer convention used to identify the document as a file in your local file system.

✔ `I:\` is a drive letter.

✔ `H4D6e\` is a folder or directory on that drive.

✔ `html_letter.html` — the rightmost text element, in this case — is the name of the HTML file you opened.

You can't use URLs like this on a Web site, so please — don't try to!

Most of us have had a letter returned to us at least once marked undeliverable because of an incomplete or inaccurate address. When the address isn't correct, the post office has no way of knowing how to locate the intended recipient. The same is true for URLs. Without a fully formed URL, Web servers don't know how to locate the target Web page. URLs generally take the following form:

✔ **Protocol identifier followed by a colon (:)** — This is generally either `http` for Hypertext Transport Protocol, `https` for secure-server sites, or `ftp` for file transfer sites.

✔ **Hostname** — This is generally either a domain name such as `edtittel. com` or an IP address. The hostname is always preceded by two slashes (`//`).

✔ **Directory path** — Directory paths are preceded by a forward slash (`/`), and they direct the user to the specific Web page being sought.

Thus, the form of a fully formed URL is `<protocolidentifier>://` `<hostname>/<directorypath>` or `http://www.mywebsite.com/ mywebpage`.

Customizing Links

You can customize links to

✔ Open linked documents in new windows

✔ Link to specific locations *within* a Web page of your own

✔ Link to items other than (X)HTML pages, such as

- Portable Document Format (PDF) files

- Compressed files

- Word processing documents

New windows

The Web works because you can link pages on your Web site to pages on other people's Web sites by using a simple anchor element. When you link to someone else's site, though, you send users away from your own site.

To keep users on your site, HTML can open the linked page in a new window or in a new tab inside the same browser window. (Internet Explorer, Firefox, Chrome, and other browsers open new tabs. You can set Internet Explorer and other browser preferences to open in a new window instead of a new tab if you prefer.) The simple addition of the `target` attribute to an anchor element opens that link in a new browser window (or tab) instead of opening it in the current window:

```
<p>The <a href="http://www.w3.org" target="_blank">World Wide Web Consortium</a>
is the standards body that oversees the ongoing development of the XHTML
specification.</p>
```

When you give a `target` attribute a `_blank` value, this tells the browser to

1. **Keep the linking page open in the current window.**
2. **Open the linked page in a new window or tab.**

Whatever document type (DTD) you use (Strict or Transitional) may make your code invalid if you add a target to an anchor. If you're using the strict DTD, then a new window, or any use of the `target` attribute, will make your markup invalid. If you know which document type you're using before you add targets to an anchor, this can save you hours of time (not to mention the headaches!) later when your markup won't validate and you're trying to figure out why! DTDs are addressed in detail in Chapter 4, so scope it out for more information.

The result of using the `target="_blank"` attribute is shown in Figure 6-2.

Figure 6-2: Use the `target` attribute to open a new Internet Explorer window for a linked file.

Pop-up windows irritate some users. Use this technique with care — and sparingly. Also, using the `target` attribute won't validate with the XHTML Strict DTD (it works fine with Transitional, though).

You can use JavaScript to control the size, location, and appearance of pop-up windows as well as to put buttons on them to help users close them quickly. Chapter 13 covers pop-up windows in more detail — including JavaScript details.

Locations in Web pages

Locations within Web pages can be marked for direct access by links on

- The same page
- The same Web site
- Other Web sites

Keep these considerations in mind when adding links to Web pages:

- Several short pages may present information more conveniently for readers than one long page with internal links.

  Links within large pages work nicely for quick access to directories, tables of contents, and glossaries.

- *Intradocument* linking works best on your own Web site, where you can create and control the markup.

  When you link to spots on someone else's Web site, you're at its manager's mercy because that person controls linkable spots. Your links will break if the site designer removes or renames any spot to which you link.

Naming link locations

To identify and create a location within a page for direct access from other links, use an empty anchor element with the name attribute, like this:

```
<a name="top"></a>
```

The anchor element that marks the spot doesn't affect the appearance of any surrounding content. You can mark spots wherever you need them without worrying about how your pages look (or change) as a result.

Linking to named locations

As we mention earlier, you can mark locations for direct access by links

- Within the same page
- Within the same Web site
- On other Web sites

Within the same page

Links can help users navigate a single Web page. Intradocument hyperlinks include such familiar features as

- ✔ Back to Top links
- ✔ Tables of contents

An *intradocument hyperlink,* also known as a named document link, uses a URL like this:

```
<a href="#top">Back to top</a>
```

The pound sign (#) indicates that you're pointing to a spot on the same page, not on another page.

Listing 6-1 shows how two anchor elements combine to link to a spot on the same page. (Documents that use intradocument links are usually longer. This document is short so you can easily see how to use the top anchor element.)

Listing 6-1:   Intradocument Hyperlinks

```
<!DOCTYPE html PUBLIC "-//W3C//DTD XHTML 1.0 Transitional//EN"
        "http://www.w3.org/TR/xhtml1/DTD/xhtml1-transitional.dtd">
<html xmlns="http://www.w3.org/1999/xhtml" lang="en" xml:lang="en">

  <head>
    <meta http-equiv="Content-Type" content="text/html; charset=ISO-8859-1" />
    <title>Intradocument hyperlinks at work</title>
  </head>

  <body>
    <h1><a name="top"></a>Web-Based Training</h1>

    <p>Given the importance of the Web to businesses and other organizations,
        individuals who seek to improve job skills, or fulfill essential job
        functions, are turning to HTML and XML for training. We believe this
        provides an outstanding opportunity for participation in an active and
        lucrative adult and continuing education market.</p>

    <p><a href="#top">Back to top</a></p>

  </body>
</html>
```

Figure 6-3 shows how this HTML markup appears in a Web browser. If the user clicks the Back to Top link, the browser jumps back to the `top` spot — marked by `<a name="top"></a>`. The text for this example is short, but you can see how it works by resizing your browser window to display only two or three words per line of text.

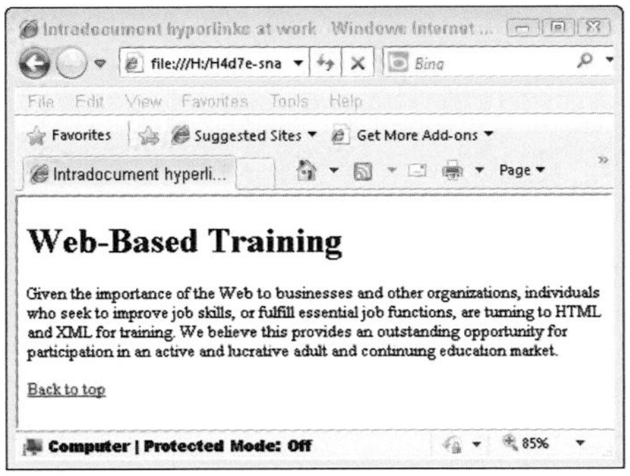

Figure 6-3: Use anchor elements to mark and link spots on a page.

Within the same Web site

You can combine intradocument and interdocument links to send visitors to a spot on a different Web page on your site. Thus, to link to a spot named `descriptions` on a page named `home.html` on your site, use this markup:

```
<p>Review the <a href="home.html#descriptions">document descriptions</a>
   to find the documentation for your particular product.</p>
```

On other Web sites

If you know that a page on another site has spots marked, you can use an absolute URL to point to a particular spot on that page, like this:

```
<p>Find out how to
<a href="http://www.yourcompany.com/training/online.htm#register">
register</a> for upcoming training courses led by our instructors.</p>
```

Be sure to check all links regularly to catch and fix the broken ones.

The Open Directory Project provides a laundry list of free and commercial tools you can use to make finding and fixing broken links easier:

```
http://www.dmoz.org/Computers/Software/Internet/Site_Management/Link_Management/
```

Non-HTML resources

Links can connect to virtually any kind of file, such as

- Word processing documents
- Spreadsheets
- PDFs
- Compressed files
- Multimedia

Two great uses for non-HTML links are for software and PDF download pages.

File downloads

Non-Web files must nevertheless be accessed via the Internet, so they possess unique URLs, just like HTML pages. Any file on a Web server (regardless of its type) can be linked using a URL.

For instance, if you want your users to download a PDF file named `doc.pdf` and a Zip archive called `software.zip` from a Web page, you use this HTML:

```
<h1>Download the new version of our software</h1>
<p><a href="software.zip">Software</a></p>
<p><a href="doc.pdf">Documentation</a></p>
```

You can't know how any user's browser will respond to a click on a link that leads to a non-Web file. The browser may

- Prompt the user to save the file
- Display the file without downloading it (common for PDFs)
- Display an error message (if the browser can't handle or doesn't recognize the type of file involved)

To help users download files successfully, you should provide your users with

- As much information as possible about the file formats in use
- Any special tools they need to work with the files
  - *Compressed files:* To work with the contents of a Zip file, the users need a compression utility, such as WinZip or ZipIt, if their operating systems do not natively support Zip files.
  - *PDFs:* To view a PDF file, users need the free Adobe Acrobat Reader.

You can make download markup more user-friendly by adding supporting text and links, like this:

```
<h1>Download our new software</h1>
<p> <a href="software.zip">Software</a> <\p>
   <p><b>Note:</b>
    You need a zip utility such as
<a href="http://www.7-zip.org">7Zip</a> (Windows) or
<a href="http://www.maczipit.com">ZipIt</a> (Macintosh)
   to open this file.</p>
<p><a href="doc.pdf">Documentation</a> <\p>
   <p><b>Note:</b>You need the free
<a href="http://get.adobe.com/reader/">Adobe Reader</a>
   to view this file.</p>
```

Figure 6-4 shows how a browser renders this HTML — and the dialog box it displays when you click the Software link.

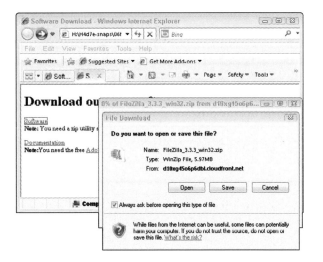

Figure 6-4: This browser prompts you to save or view the Zip file.

E-mail addresses

A link to an e-mail address can automatically open a new e-mail addressed to exactly the right person.

This is a great way to help users send you e-mail with comments and requests.

An e-mail link uses the standard anchor element and an `href` attribute. The value of the `href` attribute is the receiving e-mail address, prefaced with `mailto:`.

```
<p>Send us your
  <a href="mailto:comments@mysite.com">comments</a>.</p>
```

The user's browser configuration controls how the browser handles an e-mail link. Most browsers follow these two basic steps automatically:

1. Open a new message window in the default e-mail program.

2. Insert the address from the `href` attribute into the To field of the message.

Unfortunately, Web page `mailto:` links are a prime source of e-mail addresses for spammers. Creating a form to receive feedback is often a better idea; better still, use JavaScript encryption on the e-mail address. (For more info, see Steven Chapman's great article, "Hiding Your Email Address," at `http://javascript.about.com/library/blemail1.htm`.) We generally tend to provide our e-mail addresses in the form: `jeff at conquest media dot com`, knowing that people are smart enough to substitute @ for at and . for `dot`, but that address-harvesters usually aren't that canny. If you do elect to use a form instead, be aware that this too can present security issues — always be sure to check your input, or take steps to avoid so-called SQL injection attacks. For more info, see Colin Mackay's article, "SQL Injection Attacks and Some Tips on How to Prevent Them," at `www.codeproject.com/KB/database/SQLInjectionAttacks.aspx`.

Chapter 7

Finding and Using Images

In This Chapter

▶ Determining the right format for your images

▶ Adding images to Web pages

▶ Creating images and image maps that trigger links

*W*eb-page designers use images to deliver important information, direct site navigation, and contribute to the overall look and feel of a Web page. However, you have to use images properly, or you risk reducing their effectiveness.

When used well, images are a key element of page design. When used poorly, though, they can make a page unreadable, unintelligible, or inaccessible.

This chapter is a crash course in using images on Web pages. You find out which image formats are Web-friendly and how to use (X)HTML elements to add images to your Web pages. You also discover how to attach links to an image and how to create image maps for a Web page.

The Role of Images in a Web Page

Images in Web sites may be logos or clickable navigation aids, or they may display content; they can also make a page look prettier or serve to unify or illustrate a page's theme. A perfect example of the many different ways images can enhance and contribute to Web pages is the White House home page at `www.whitehouse.gov`, shown in Figure 7-1, where the White House logo, photos, and even the Great Seal of the United States are used to good effect.

Figure 7-1: The White House Web page uses images in a variety of ways.

Creating Web-Friendly Images

You can create and save graphics in many ways, but only a few formats are actually appropriate for images you intend to use on the Web. As you create Web-friendly images, you must pay attention to file formats and sizes.

Often, graphics file formats are specific to operating systems or software applications. Because you can't predict what a visitor's computer and software will be (other than he or she will use some sort of Web browser), you need images that anyone can view with any browser. This means you need to use *cross-platform* file formats that users can view with any version of Microsoft Windows, the Mac OS, or Linux.

These three compressed graphics formats are best for general use on the Web:

✔ **Graphics Interchange Format (GIF):** Images saved as GIFs often are smaller than those saved in other file formats. GIF supports up to 256 colors only, so if you try to save an image created with millions of colors as a GIF, you lose image quality. GIF is the best format for less-complex, nonphotographic images, such as line art and clip art.

✔ **Joint Photographic Experts Group (JPEG):** The JPEG file format supports 24-bit color (millions of colors) and complex images, such as photographs. JPEG is cross-platform and application-independent. A good image editing tool can help you tweak the compression so you can strike an optimum balance between the image's quality and its file size.

✔ **Portable Network Graphics (PNG):** PNG is the latest cross-platform and application-independent image file format. It was developed to bring together the best aspects of GIF and JPEG. PNG has the same compression as GIF but supports 24-bit color (and even 32-bit color) like JPEG.

Any good graphics editing tool, such as those mentioned in Chapter 23, allows you to save images in any of these formats. Experiment with them to see how converting a graphic from one format to another changes its appearance and file size, and then choose whichever format produces the best results.

Table 7-1 shows guidelines for choosing a file format for images by type.

Table 7-1	Choosing the Right File Format for an Image	
File Format	**Best Used For**	**Watch Out**
GIF	Line art and other images with few colors and less detail	Don't use this format if you have a complex image or photo.
JPEG	Photos and other images with millions of colors and lots of detail	Don't use with line art. This format compromises too much quality when you compress the file.
PNG	Photos and other images with millions of colors and lots of detail	Don't use with line art. PNG offers the best balance between quality and file size.

Optimizing images

As you build graphics for your Web page, maintain a healthy balance between file quality and file size. If you poke around with your favorite search engine, you can find good tutorials on trimming image file sizes and optimizing entire sites for fast download. For tips and tricks to help you build pages that download quickly, review these handy resources:

✔ Optimizing images: www.yourhtmlsource.com/optimisation/image optimisation.html

✔ Optimizing Web graphics: www.websiteoptimization.com/speed/12

TIP

For a complete overview of graphics formats, visit

- W3C's "Graphics on the Web" article at `www.w3.org/Graphics`
- Quackit.com's Web Graphics Tutorial at `www.quackit.com/web_graphics/tutorial`

Adding an Image to a Web Page

When an image is ready for the Web, you need to use the correct markup to add it to your page, but you need to know where to store your image as well.

Image location

You can store images for your Web site in several places. Image storage works best if it uses *relative* URLs — stored somewhere on the Web site with your other (X)HTML files. You can store images in the same root as your (X)HTML files, which gets confusing if you have a lot of files, or you can create a `graphics` or `images` directory in the root file for your Web site.

REMEMBER

Relative links connect resources from the same Web site. You use absolute links between resources on two different Web sites. Turn to Chapter 6 for a complete discussion of the differences between relative and absolute links.

Here are three compelling reasons to store images on your own site:

- **Control:** When images are stored on your site, you keep complete control over them. You know your images aren't going to disappear or change, and you can work to optimize them.
- **Speed:** If you link to images on someone else's site, you never know when that site may go down or respond unbelievably slowly. Linking to images on someone else's site also causes the other site's owner to pay for bandwidth required to display it on your pages — on another site!
- **Copyright:** If you link to images on another site to display them on your pages, you may violate copyright laws. If you must do this, obtain permission from the copyright holder to store and display images on your Web site.

Using the <img /> element

The image (`<img />`) element is an *empty element* (sometimes called a *singleton tag*) that you place on the page where you want your image to go.

REMEMBER

An empty element uses only one tag, with neither a distinct opening nor a distinct closing tag.

The following markup places an image named `07fg02-cd.jpg`, which is saved in the same directory as the (X)HTML file, between two paragraphs:

```
<!DOCTYPE html PUBLIC "-//W3C//DTD XHTML 1.0 Transitional//EN"
                      "http://www.w3.org/TR/xhtml1/DTD/xhtml1-transitional.dtd">
<html xmlns="http://www.w3.org/1999/xhtml" lang="en" xml:lang="en">
<head>
  <meta http-equiv="Content-Type" content="text/html; charset=ISO-8859-1" />
   <title>Optical Disks at Work</title>
</head>
  <body>
  <h1>CD/DVD as a Storage Medium</h1>
  <p>CD-ROMs and DVDs have become a standard storage option in today's computing
     world because they are inexpensive and easy to use.</p>
  <img src="07fg02-cd.jpg" alt="line drawing of optical disk"/>
  <p>To read from a CD or DVD, you only need a standard CD-ROM drive, but to
     create CDs or DVDs, you need a DVD burner (all DVD burners can read
     and write CDs as well).</p>
  </body>
</html>
```

A Web browser replaces the `<img />` element with the image file provided as the value for the `src` attribute, as shown in Figure 7-2.

Figure 7-2: Use the `<img />` element to place graphics in a Web page.

The `src` attribute is like the `href` attribute that you use with an anchor (`<a>`) element. The `src` attribute specifies the location for the image you want to display on your page. The preceding example points to an image file in the same folder as the HTML file referencing it.

Adding alternative and title text

Alternative text describes an image so those who can't see the images for some reason can access that text to learn more about the image. Adding alternative text (often referred to by HTMLers as "alt text") is a good practice because it accounts for

- ✔ Visually impaired users who may not be able to see images and must rely on alternative text for a text-to-speech reader to read to them

- ✔ Users who access the Web site from a phone browser with limited graphics capabilities

- ✔ Users with slow modem connections who don't display images

Some search engines and cataloguing tools use alternative text to index images.

Most of your users will see your images, but be prepared for those who won't. The (X)HTML specifications require that you provide alternative text to describe each image on a Web page. Use the `alt` attribute with the `<img />` element to add this information to your markup, like this:

```
<!DOCTYPE html PUBLIC "-//W3C//DTD XHTML 1.0 Transitional//EN"
                     "http://www.w3.org/TR/xhtml1/DTD/xhtml1-transitional.dtd">
<html xmlns="http://www.w3.org/1999/xhtml" lang="en" xml:lang="en">
<head>
  <meta http-equiv="Content-Type" content="text/html; charset=ISO-8859-1" />
  <title>Inside the Orchestra</title>
</head>

<body>
  <p>Among the different sections of the orchestra you will find:</p>
  <p><img src="07fg03-violin.jpg" alt="violin" title="violin" /> Strings</p>
  <p><img src="07fg03-trumpet.jpg" alt="trumpet" title="trumpet" /> Brass</p>
  <p><img src="07fg03-woodwinds.jpg" alt="clarinet and saxophone"
      title="clarinet and saxophone"/> Woodwinds</p>
</body>
</html>
```

When browsers don't display an image (or can't, as in text-only browsers such as Lynx), they display the alternative text instead, as shown in Figure 7-3. (We turned images off in Internet Explorer to produce the screenshot.)

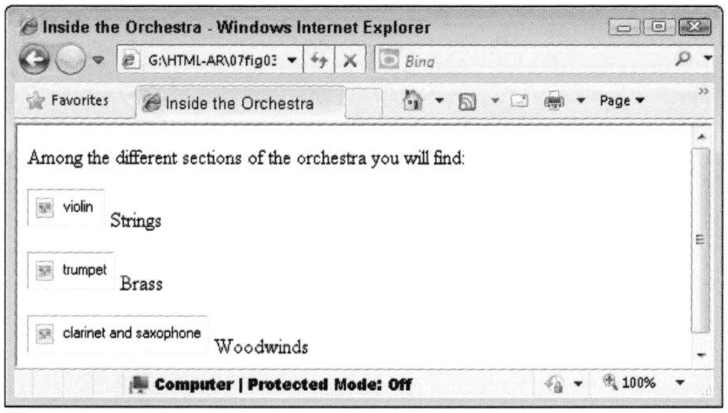

Figure 7-3: When a browser doesn't show an image, it shows alternative text.

When browsers show an image, browsers — including Internet Explorer, Firefox, Chrome, Safari, and Opera — show title text as pop-up tips when you hover your mouse pointer over an image for a few seconds, as shown in Figure 7-4. This requires adding a `title` attribute to each `<img />` element, which is why it's also included in the preceding markup. ***Note:*** `alt` text is required for a page to validate, but `title` text is not required.

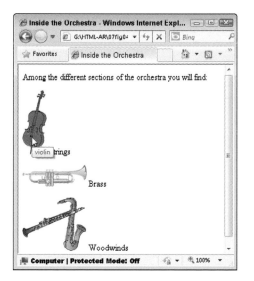

Figure 7-4: A browser displays title text as a pop-up tip.

This means you can use alternative text to describe the image to those who can't see it and/or title text to provide useful (or amusing) information about the same image.

The W3C's Web Accessibility Initiative (WAI) includes helpful tips for creating useful and usable alternatives to visual content at `www.w3.org/TR/WCAG10-TECHS/#gl-provide-equivalents`.

Specifying image size

You can use the `height` and `width` attributes with the `<img />` element to let the browser know just how tall and wide an image is (in pixels; px):

```
<p><img src="07fg03-trumpet.jpg"
     width="50" height="70" alt="trumpet" />Brass</p>
```

Most browsers download the HTML and text associated with a page before they download the page graphics. Instead of making users wait for the whole page to download, browsers typically display the text first and then fill in graphics as they become available. If you tell the browser how big a graphic is, the browser can reserve a spot for it in the page display. This speeds the process of adding graphics to the Web page.

You can check the width and height of an image in pixels in any image editing program, or in the image viewers built into Windows and the Mac OS. (You might be able simply to view the properties of the image in either Windows or the Mac OS to see its height and width.)

Another good use of the `height` and `width` attributes is to create colored lines on a page by using just a small colored square. For example, this markup adds a 10-x-10-px blue box to a Web page:

```
<img src="07fg05-blue-box.gif" alt="blue box" height="10" width="10" />
```

Use the `<img />` element `height` and `width` attributes to set image height and width. Thus we use these values to create a 10-x-10-px blue box in a browser window (shown at the top of Figure 7-5) even though the original image is 600 x 600 px. In general, it's safe to reduce image dimensions using these attributes although you'll always want to check the results carefully during testing. With any kind of aspect sensitive image, you want to maintain its aspect ratio by dividing the original dimensions by some common value.

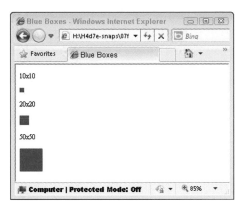

Figure 7-5: A series of small blue boxes.

Figure 7-5 also shows boxes with dimensions of 20 x 20 and 50 x 50 px. Here are the changes to the values for `height` and `width` in the markup to produce the other two boxes:

```
<img src="07fg05-blue-box.gif" alt="blue box" height="20" width="20" />
<img src="07fg05-blue-box.gif" alt="blue box" height="50" width="50" />
```

Using this technique, you can turn a single image like the blue box (only 2.39K in size) into a variety of lines — and even boxes:

  ✔ This can ensure that all dividers and other border elements on your page use the same color because they're all based on the same graphic.

  ✔ If you decide you want to change all your blue lines to green, you just change the image. Every line you created changes colors.

When you specify an image's height and width that are different from the image's actual height and width, you rely on the browser to scale the image display. This works great for single-color images (such as the blue box), but it doesn't work well for images with multiple colors or images that contain actual photos. The browser doesn't size images well, and you wind up with a distorted picture. Figure 7-6 shows how badly a browser handles enlarging a trumpet image when the markup multiplies the image height by four and its width by two (note the resemblance to a flugelhorn!):

```
<p><img src="07fg03-trumpet.jpg" width="200" height="124" alt="trumpet"
Title = "trumpet" />Brass</p>
```

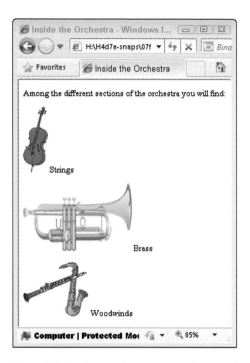

Figure 7-6: Don't use a browser to resize complex images; use a graphics editor.

If you need several sizes for the same image — as for a logo or navigation button — use a large image as the master for that graphic, and make smaller versions; doing so gives you better control over the final look and feel of each image.

Image borders and alignment

The image element supports a `border` attribute, and numerous options for aligning images are supported in (X)HTML markup, but they are deprecated in favor of working with CSS. Although you can use these controls if you must, we cover them only in passing in our discussion of deprecated markup in Chapter 8, and explain how to use CSS to control image borders, positioning, alignment, spacing, text flow, and more in Chapter 10. In case we haven't made this sufficiently clear already, we strongly urge you to use CSS for borders, positioning, and alignment for both text and images, and let (X)HTML do the job it does best: represent and point to actual content.

Images That Link

Web pages often use images for navigation. They're prettier than plain-text links, and you can add both form and function on your page with one element.

Triggering links

To create an image that triggers a link, you substitute an <img /> element in place of text to which you would anchor your link. This markup links text:

```
<p><a href="http://www.w3.org">Visit the W3C</a></p>
```

This markup replaces the text Visit the W3C with an appropriate icon:

```
<p><a href="http://www.w3.org"><img src="w3.jpg"
     alt="Visit the W3C Web Site" title = "Visit the W3C Web Site"
     height="75" width="131" border="2" /></a>

</p>
```

The preceding markup creates a linked image to http://www.w3.org. In the preceding example, the alternative text now reads Visit the W3C Web Site so users who can't see the image know where the link goes. When a user moves the mouse pointer over the image, the cursor changes from an arrow into a pointing hand (or any icon the browser uses for a link).

We include a 2px border around this image as a visual cue to let users know it also serves as a link. The border appears as a light blue outline (as shown in Figure 7-7) until the link is followed. After that, the blue outline turns purple to let users know this link has been visited.

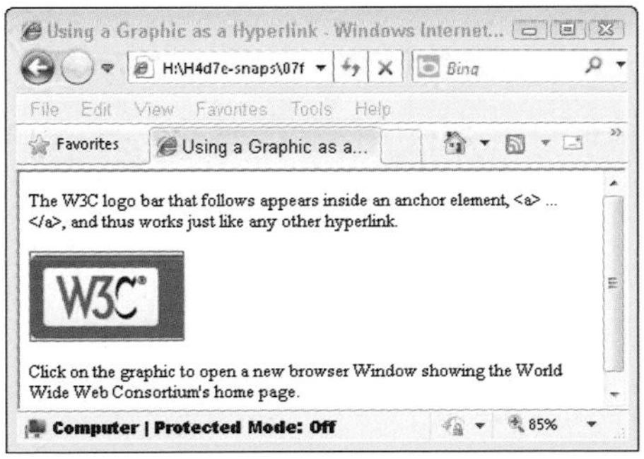

Figure 7-7: Combine image and anchor elements to create a linked image.

A quick click of the image launches the W3C Web site. It's as simple as that.

As shown earlier in the chapter, you should set the border of any image you use in a link to 0 if you want to keep the browser from surrounding your image with a blue line. Without the line, however, users need other visual (or alternative text) clues so they know that an image is a link. Be sure images that serve as links scream to the user (tastefully of course) "I'm a link!" In all cases, if the automatic outline is eliminated, you should build an outline into the graphic itself or add a caption that indicates that the image serves as a link.

Building image maps

When you use an `<img />` element with an anchor element to create a linking image, you can attach only one link to that image. To create a larger image that connects links to different regions on the page, you need an *image map*.

To create an image map, you need two things:

- **An image** with distinct areas obvious to users

  For example, an image of a park might show a playground, a picnic area, and a pond area.

- **Markup** to map the different regions on the map to different URLs

Elements and attributes

Use the `<img />` element to add the map image into your page, just as you would any other image. In addition, include the `usemap` attribute to let the browser know that image map information should go with that image. The value of the `usemap` attribute is the name of your map.

You use two elements and a collection of attributes to define the image map:

- `<map>` holds the map information. The `<map>` element uses the `name` attribute to identify the map. The value of `name` should match the value of `usemap` in the `<img />` element that goes with the map.

- `<area />` links specific parts of the map to URLs. The `<area />` element takes these attributes to define the specifics for each section of the map:

    - `shape`: Specifies the shape of the region (a clickable hot spot that makes the image map work). You can choose from `rect` (rectangle), `circle`, and `poly` (a triangle or polygon).

- `coords`: Defines the region's coordinates.

  A rectangle's coordinates include the left, right, top, and bottom points.

  A circle's coordinates include the x and y coordinates for the center of the circle as well as the circle's radius.

  A polygon's coordinates are a collection of x and y coordinates for every vertex in the polygon.

  You can use an image map editor like Mapedit from `www.boutell.com/mapedit`, or a graphics editor such as PaintShop Photo Pro from `www.corel.com`, to determine image coordinates; Mapedit also records them for you.

- `href`: Specifies the URL to which the region links (can be absolute or relative).

- `alt`: Provides alternative text for the image region.

Markup

The following defines a three-region map called `NavMap` linked to the graphics file named `07fg07-navmap.gif`:

```
<img src="07fg09-navmap.gif" width="302" height="30" usemap="#NavMap" border="0"
        />
<map name="NavMap" />
  <area shape="rect" coords="0,0,99,30" href="home.html" alt="Home"
        title="Home" />
  <area shape="rect" coords="102,0,202,30" href="about.html" alt="About"
        title="About" />
  <area shape="rect" coords="202,0,301,30" href="products.html"
        alt="Products" title="Products" />
</map>
```

Figure 7-8 shows how a browser displays this markup.

When the mouse sits over a region in the map, the cursor turns into a pointing hand (just as it changes over any other hyperlink). So take advantage of the title text to include useful information about the link and to make the map more accessible to the visually impaired, too.

A common use for image maps is to turn maps of places (states, countries, cities, and such) into linkable maps. About.com's image map tutorial at `http://webdesign.about.com/od/imagemaps/a/aabg051899a.htm` provides more details on building image maps by hand. HTML Goodies has a great collection of image map tutorials and information at `www.htmlgoodies.com/tutorials/image_maps/index.php`. For a more fully fleshed HTML file that implements the preceding image map example, see this book's Web site at `www.dummieshtml.com/examples/ch07/07fg09-validx.html`.

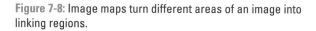

Figure 7-8: Image maps turn different areas of an image into linking regions.

Creating image maps by hand can be tricky. Use an image editor to identify each point in your map, and *then* create the proper markup for it. Most (X)HTML tools include utilities to help you make image maps. If you take advantage of such a tool, you can create image maps quickly and with few errors. Find out more about (X)HTML tools in Chapter 23.

Exercise caution when using image maps. If you're creating a visual aid (something like a map with links to different countries shown therein, for example), using an image map makes perfect sense. On the other hand, you should never use a graphic with image maps for your main navigation. (Well, you *could,* but you wouldn't like the results!) Always use (X)HTML and CSS for your main Web site navigation, or if you must use a graphical image map, include a text-based alternative along with that map so that visually impaired visitors to your site can also navigate successfully by using the alternate controls instead.

In general, the best thing for navigation is to use text for button labels, and to let CSS handle the work involved in making buttons look good. This comes in for further discussion in Chapter 20 on CSS3, but you could simply use CSS 2.1 to make some pretty good looking buttons as well.

Part III

Taking Precise Control over Web Pages and Styles

In this part . . .

Here, we introduce and describe Cascading Style
Sheets (CSS), a powerful markup language designed
to supplement (X)HTML and to manage the way pages
look inside a Web browser. (X)HTML can reference CSS
by including either an external style sheet or inline CSS
markup within an (X)HTML document.

You start by familiarizing yourself with the many and various capabilities of CSS, by looking at different kinds of
style sheets, and by getting acquainted with the rules for
handling multiple style sheets when they're applied to a
single Web page (that's where the *Cascading* in CSS comes
from). Of course, you also find out how to build and use
CSS for such things as creating visual layouts, positioning individual items, and handling fonts. Because CSS
also provides controls for modifying how color and text
appears on the page, we show you how to deal with these
capabilities, too.

Chapter 8

Deprecated (X)HTML Markup

. . . .

In This Chapter

▶ Understanding deprecation

▶ Finding deprecated markup

▶ Running down the deprecated elements

▶ Listing the deprecated attributes

▶ Cleaning up after deprecated markup

. . . .

*B*y definition, to *deprecate* means either "to express disapproval of, to deplore" or "to declare something obsolete or superseded." When (X)HTML talk turns to deprecated markup — and you'll find this term applied to both markup elements and attributes — however deplorable such markup may be, rest assured that the term is used in the second sense! That is, using deprecated markup is not recommended because the World Wide Web Consortium (W3C) is convinced that it won't be around forever, and because using deprecated markup leads to all kinds of unsavory coding habits, bad behavior, and possible jail time (just kidding on the last bit).

To understand why markup is deprecated, you need to think about the fundamental role of (X)HTML and how CSS plays into a thoroughly modern view of the Web. First and foremost, (X)HTML's job is to capture and deliver content including both graphical and textual information, plus pointers galore (hyperlinks put the "hyper" in hypertext, after all).

Early implementations of HTML included plenty of presentation controls as well as content elements and linking mechanisms. Over time, Web designers came to understand that separating content from presentation was highly desirable. CSS has come to take over the presentation role much more capably and effectively than HTML ever could. As you look at the deprecated markup elements and attributes covered in this chapter, you'll see that the vast majority deal with presentation controls best turned over to CSS, along with historical remnants of now-obsolete tools, technologies, and page design approaches.

Sure, you can find plenty of sites that use deprecated markup, and you may even find some deprecated markup in your own work here and there. Use this markup at your own risk, though, and do yourself a favor: As old pages give way to new, take the time and expend the effort to get that nasty old deprecated markup out of your pages!

And Now, A Word from Our Sponsor

If you look at the current HTML 4 specification at the W3C Website (available at `www.w3.org/TR/REC-html40/conform.html`), you'll find the following language used to explain deprecated and obsolete markup:

Deprecated

A deprecated element or attribute is one that has been outdated by newer constructs. Deprecated elements are defined in the reference manual in appropriate locations, but are clearly marked as deprecated. Deprecated elements may become obsolete in future versions of HTML.

User agents should continue to support deprecated elements for reasons of backward compatibility.

Definitions of elements and attributes clearly indicate which are deprecated.

This specification includes examples that illustrate how to avoid using deprecated elements. In most cases these depend on user agent support for style sheets. In general, authors should use style sheets to achieve stylistic and formatting effects rather than HTML presentational attributes. HTML presentational attributes have been deprecated when style sheet alternatives exist. . . .

Obsolete

An obsolete element or attribute is one for which there is no guarantee of support by a user agent. Obsolete elements are no longer defined in the specification, but are listed for historical purposes in the changes section of the reference manual.

As you read through this language, the term "user agent" is a technical term for any program that reads and interprets (X)HTML markup. Primarily, this means a Web browser of some kind, although lots of other programs read markup, too (think search engine, validator, editor, and so forth). Note that most programs will support deprecated markup, but its use is best avoided through — you guessed it — style sheets, or CSS.

Obsolete markup may still hang around on certain old and moldy Web pages, but that markup doesn't work in newer Web browsers. We don't even cover it in this book. If your curiosity about such markup must be satiated, please read the older HTML specifications!

On the other hand, if you want to dig deeper into markup details, check out the latest HTML 4.01 specification at `www.w3.org/TR/html4/cover.html#minitoc`.

If you want to jump right to deprecation, it's covered in Appendix A of the HTML 4.01 specification. The real action, however, is in the sections named "Index of Elements" and "Index of Attributes." In fact, extract the items marked D for *deprecated* in those two indices, and that's the basic skeleton for the next two sections that follow.

Deprecated Elements

We present these deprecated elements in alphabetical order in Table 8-1. Where replacement markup or alternate techniques (can you say "CSS"?) exist, we point that out, too. If the type is `pair`, that means you need opening and closing tags for the element (for example, `<center>this</center>`); if the type is `empty`, that means there's only one tag for the element (for example, `<isindex … />`).

Table 8-1		Deprecated HTML Markup Elements	
Name	*Type*	*Description*	*Alternative*
applet	pair	Invoke Java applets	`Object`
basefont	pair	Base font size	CSS font controls
center	pair	Shorthand for `<div align="center">`	CSS text alignment controls
dir	pair	Directory list type	`<ul>` with CSS formatting
font	pair	Local font assignment	CSS `font-family`
isindex	empty	Single line input prompt	HTML forms markup
menu	pair	List type for menu options	`<ul>` with CSS formatting
s	pair	Strikethrough text	CSS `text-decoration`
strike	pair	Strikethrough text	CSS `text-decoration`
u	pair	Underline text	CSS `text-decoration`

As you look over Table 8-1, only two markup elements are nonpresentational:

✔ `applet`: The `applet` tag hearkens back to an era when the Java programming language represented the primary means for adding code elements directly into Web pages. Today, the `object` element allows page developers to work with all kinds of programming languages, including Java, through a single uniform (X)HTML element.

✔ `isindex`: The `isindex` element was designed to enable quick-and-dirty access to a single line of input text from users. Today, the various elements that go into HTML forms (covered in Chapter 14 of this book) are used instead.

Deprecated Attributes

Whereas only 10 elements are deprecated in (X)HTML, a great many more attributes are deprecated — 44 of them are shown in Table 8-2, in fact (of which 32 are unique, and the rest repeats). Indeed, some attributes appear more than once in this table because they have different meanings when associated with specific (X)HTML elements. We use the W3C shorthand for values that attributes take, and explain those type entries in a list that follows the table. Here, we don't discuss alternatives or replacements because CSS supersedes the vast majority of deprecated elements.

Table 8-2	Deprecated HTML Attributes		
Name	**Related Elements**	**Type**	**Description**
Align	Caption	%CAlign	Table caption alignment
Align	applet, iframe, img, input, object	%IAlign	Vertical or horizontal alignment
Align	Legend	%LAlign	Form fieldset control
Align	Table	%TAlign	Table position relative to window
Align	Hr	LCR	Horizontal rule alignment
Align	div,h1... h6,p	LCRJ	Text block alignment

Name	Related Elements	Type	Description
Align	col, colgroup, tbody, td, tfoot, th, thead, tr	LCRJ	Table alignment
Alink	Body	%Color	Color for selected (high-lighted) links
Alt	Applet	%Text	Short description for applet function
Archive	Applet	CDATA	Comma separated java archive (.jar) list
background	Body	%URI	Image file for document background
Bgcolor	table, tr, td, th	%Color	Table element back-ground color
Bgcolor	Body	%Color	General document back-ground color
Border	img, object	%Pixels	Width for link border
Clear	Br	LRAN	Control of text flow after line break
Code	Applet	CDATA	Applet Java class file
codebase	Applet	%URI	Base location for classid, data, and archive files
Color	basefont, font	%Color	Text color
Compact	dir, dl, menu, ol, ul	*self	Reduced interword spacing
Face	basefont, font	CDATA	Comma-separated list of font names
Height	td, th	%Length	Table cell height
Height	Applet	%Length	Initial height for applet window
Hspace	applet, img, object	%Pixels	Horizontal gutter around box
Language	Script	CDATA	Predefined script lan-guage name

(continued)

Table 8-2 *(continued)*

Name	Related Elements	Type	Description
Link	Body	%Color	Color for links in document body
Name	Applet	CDATA	Provides id so applets can find each other
Noshade	Hr	*self	Turn off dropshadow on horizontal rule
Nowrap	td, th	*self	Suppress word wrap in table cells
Object	Applet	CDATA	Serialized applet file (read in pieces)
Prompt	Isindex	%text	Prompt message to solicit input
Size	Hr	%Pixels	Size of horizontal rule
Size	Font	CDATA	Various positive integer values for font size
Size	Basefont	CDATA	Base font size for all font elements
Start	Ol	Number	Starting value for numbered list
Text	Body	%Color	Document text color
Type	li, ol, ul	ListStyle	List item, numbering, and bullet styles
Value	Li	Number	Reset list sequence number
Version	Html	CDATA	HTML version number for DTD in use
Vlink	Body	%Color	Color for visited links
Vspace	applet, img, object	%Pixels	Vertical gutter around box
Width	Hr	%Length	Horizontal rule width
Width	td, th	%Length	Table cell width
Width	Applet	%Length	Initial width of applet window/box
Width	Pre	Number	Width of preformatted text area in characters

The following list describes the attribute type abbreviations and values in Table 8-2:

- %CAlign: Column alignment in table
- CDATA: SGML (Standard Generalized Markup Language) data type for general character data
- %Color: Color name or hexcode
- %IAlign: Alignment for iframes: top, middle, bottom, left, right
- %LAlign: Alignment for legends: top, bottom, left, right
- LCR: Left, Center, Right
- LCRJ: Left, Center, Right, Justified
- %Length: Length in pixels or percentages, or relative length
- ListStyle: List item styles, list bullet styles, list numbering styles
- LRAN: Left, All, Right, None
- Number: A string of one or more digits (values from 0 to 9)
- %Pixel: Integer representing length in pixels
- *self: Attribute name repeated as value (compact="compact")
- %TAlign: Alignment for table cells: left, center, right, justify, char
- %Text: Character data
- %URI: Uniform Resource Identifier, usually a URL

iframe is an HTML construct that functions like a window frame within a Web page but is used to insert one HTML document inside another, where the iFrame occupies only a specified area and scrolls like any other static page element. Content in an iFrame scrolls only within the specified display area if it is larger than the iFrame window itself. Unlike typical HTML frames used to divide the browser window into multiple display areas, an iFrame serves to insert an external element — often, an advertisement or an external text block — into a specific area on a Web page.

How to Handle Deprecated Markup

The short, sweet admonition of how to handle deprecated markup in your code is, "Get rid of it!" In practice, though, replacing the vast majority of deprecated elements and attributes will come quite naturally upon developing familiarity — and hopefully, even comfort — with Cascading Style Sheets (CSS). After you learn how to position items on a page, and to work with margins and padding, you can dispense entirely with most of the items in Table 8-2, and many of those in Table 8-1 as well.

A more serious question might be voiced as "What do I do when an (X)HTML editing tool uses deprecated markup?" If a third-party tool is generating markup on your behalf, at your behest, and to help you realize your page designs, we urge you to find and use tools that don't use deprecated markup. It's the only way to be sure your pages can stand the test of time. Fortunately, the tools that we recommend in Chapter 23 — as well as a great many more (X)HTML editors and development environments — have already eliminated deprecated markup, so hopefully you won't have to worry about it, either.

In general, when it comes to dealing with deprecated markup, you must decide what to do with the markup you need to remove from the Web page currently under consideration. In many cases, you'll simply remove HTML presentational markup and replace it with a CSS equivalent. Thus, for example, if you wanted text for a paragraph to be justified, you would take the markup shown in the next code snippet (commented to help you tell things apart) and replace it with the markup shown in the following snippet:

```
<!-- This markup uses the deprecated align="justify" code -->
<p align="justify">This sample paragraph needs enough text to be
at least three lines long, to show the effects of justification
at work. In fact, the longer the better, which is why we've
stretched this example out as far as we can make it go.</p>

<!-- This markup uses in-line style for a quick&dirty contrast -->
<p style="text-align: justify;">This sample paragraph needs enough
text to be at least three lines long, to show the effects of
justification at work. In fact, the longer the better, which is why
we've stretched this example out as far as we can make it go.</p>
```

Not all replacements for deprecated markup are quite so simple and straightforward as the one just shown. Interestingly, all of the presentation markup replacements are generally just that easy, but some other things have no real counterparts (or don't have counterparts yet, though HTML5 and CSS3 will remedy a few such things). That's why some planning and thought are often required when deciding what to do to remove deprecated markup. A bit of redesign or rework is often necessary to put things back together properly.

Chapter 9

Introducing Cascading Style Sheets

In This Chapter

▶ Understanding CSS

▶ Creating style rules

▶ Linking style rules to Web pages

▶ Introducing CSS properties

▶ Understanding inheritance and the style cascade

The goal of *Cascading Style Sheets* (CSS) is to separate a Web page's style from its structure, to make it easier to maintain Web pages you created. The structural elements of a page, such as headings (<h1> through <h6>) and body text, don't affect how those elements look. By applying styles to those elements, though, you can specify an element's layout on the page and add design attributes (such as fonts, colors, and text indentation).

Style sheets give you precise control over how structural elements appear on a Web page. Better yet, you can create one style sheet for an entire Web site to keep the layout and look of your content consistent from page to page. And here's the icing on this cake: Style sheets are easy to build and even easier to integrate into Web pages. In fact, with style sheets, you can

✔ Add style markup to individual (X)HTML elements (called *inline style*).

✔ Create sequences of style instructions in the head of an (X)HTML document (called an *internal style sheet*).

✔ Refer to a separate standalone style sheet via a link or other reference (called an *external style sheet*) inside your (X)HTML document.

In short, there are lots of ways to add style to a Web page!

As more Web sites transition to XHTML, the goal of the markup powers-that-be is to eventually *deprecate* (make obsolete) all formatting markup, such as the `<font>` element, from HTML's collection of elements. Someday, all presentation will belong to CSS. We cover this stale, old deprecated markup in Chapter 8 of this book.

When you want tight control over the display of your Web pages, style sheets are the way to go:

- Generally, style sheets give you more flexibility than markup can.
- Future HTML and XHTML elements will no longer include display-oriented attributes.

Most modern browsers handle CSS well. However, older browsers — such as Internet Explorer 4.0 and Netscape Navigator — have trouble displaying CSS correctly. Earlier browsers can't display CSS at all. If many of your site's users still use one or more of these obsolete browsers, test your pages inside those browsers; make sure your site's users can read your pages.

Advantages of Style Sheets

HTML's formatting capabilities are limited, to say the least. When you design a page layout in HTML, you're limited to tables, font controls, and a few inline styles, such as bold and italic. *Style sheets* supply lots of tools to format Web pages with precise controls. With style sheets, you can

- **Control every aspect of page display.** Specify the amount of space between lines, character spacing, page margins, image placement, and more. You can also specify positioning of elements on your pages.
- **Apply changes globally.** Ensure consistent design across an entire Web site by applying the same style sheet to every Web page.

You can modify the look and feel of an entire site by changing just one document (the style sheet) instead of the markup on every page. Need to change the look for a heading? Redefine that heading's style attributes in the style sheet and save the sheet. The heading's look changes throughout your site. You can imagine one page after rapidly adopting the new look in a "cascade" of changes (hence the name) although that moniker is just a metaphor because the cascade is instantaneous.

- **Instruct browsers to control appearance.** Provide Web browsers with more information about how you want your pages to appear than you can communicate using HTML.
- **Create dynamic pages.** Use JavaScript or another scripting language along with style sheets to create text and other content that moves, appears, or hides in response to user actions.

What CSS can do for a Web page

The gist of how style sheets work is as follows:

1. You define rules in a style sheet that specify how you want content that is described by a set of markup to appear.

   For example, you could specify that every first-level heading (`<h1>`) be displayed in purple Garamond 24-point type with a yellow background (not that you *would,* but you could).

2. You link style rules and markup.

3. The browser does the rest.

With the current specification, CSS2.1, you can

- ✔ Specify font type, size, color, and effects.
- ✔ Set background colors and images.
- ✔ Control many aspects of text layout, including alignment and spacing.
- ✔ Set margins and borders.
- ✔ Control list display.
- ✔ Define table layout and display.
- ✔ Automatically generate content for standard page elements, such as counters and footers.
- ✔ Control cursor display.
- ✔ Define aural style sheets for text-to-speech readers.

CSS3: Next-generation style sheets

The next generation of CSS — CSS3, that is — is a collection of *modules* that address different aspects of Web-page formatting, such as fonts, background colors, lists, and text colors. The first of these modules became standards (officially called *Candidate Recommendations*) in mid-2004. As of mid-2010, though, the majority of CSS3 modules haven't reached Candidate Recommendations status, and few browsers implement CSS3 features. In short, you don't need to worry about CSS3 — at least, not yet.

The W3C devotes an entire section of its Web site to CSS at `www.w3.org/Style/CSS/current-work`. You can find general CSS information there, as well as keep up with the status of CSS3. The site links to good CSS references and tutorials, and includes information on software packages that can make your style sheet endeavors easier.

What you can do with CSS

You have a healthy collection of properties to work with as you write your style rules. You can control just about every aspect of a page's display — from borders to font sizes and everything in-between:

- **Background properties** control the background colors associated with blocks of text and with images. You can also use these properties to attach background colors to your page or to individual elements, such as horizontal rules.

- **Border properties** control borders associated with a page, lists, tables, images, and block elements (such as paragraphs). You can specify border width, color, style, and distance from element content.

- **Classification properties** control how elements (such as images) flow on the page relative to other elements. You can use these properties to integrate images and tables with the text on your page.

- **List properties** control how lists appear on your page, such as

  - Managing list markers
  - Using images in place of bullets

- **Margin properties** control the margins of the page and margins around block elements, tables, and images. These properties extend ultimate control over the white space on your page.

- **Padding properties** control the amount of white space around any block element on the page. When you use these with margin and border properties, you can create complex layouts.

- **Positioning properties** control where elements sit on the page; you can use them to put elements in specific places on the page.

- **Size properties** control how much space (in height and width) your elements (both text and images) take up on your page. They're especially handy for limiting the size of text boxes and images.

- **Table properties** control the layout of tables. You can use them to control cell spacing and other table-layout specifics.

- **Text properties** control how text appears on a page. You can set such properties as font size, font family, height, text color, letter and line spacing, alignment, and white space. These properties give you more control over text with style sheets than the `font` HTML element can.

Entire books and Web sites are devoted to the fine details of using each and every property in these categories. We suggest one of these references:

✔ *CSS Web Design For Dummies* by Richard Mansfield.

✔ Westciv's CSS2 reference on the Web at `www.westciv.com/style_master/academy/css_tutorial/index.html`.

Although CSS syntax is straightforward, combining CSS styles with markup to fine-tune a page layout can get a little complicated. To become a CSS guru, you just need to

✔ Know how the different properties work.

✔ Experiment, to observe how browsers handle CSS.

✔ Practice, to learn how to convey your message on the Web using CSS.

Property measurement values

Many HTML properties use measurement values. We tell you which measurement values go with which properties throughout this book. Standard property measurements dictate the size of a property in two ways.

Absolute value measurements can dictate a specific length or height using one of these values:

✔ **Inches,** such as `.5in`

✔ **Centimeters,** such as `3cm`

✔ **Millimeters,** such as `4mm`

✔ **Picas,** such as `1pc`

   There are six picas in an inch.

✔ **Points,** such as `16pt`

   There are 12 points in a pica.

✔ **Pixels,** such as `13px` (these match up to individual dots on your computer display).

Relative value measurements base length or height on a *parent element* value in the document:

✔ `p%`: A percentage of the current `font-size` value, such as `150%`.

   For example, you can define a font size of `80%` for all paragraphs. If your document body is defined with a 15-pt font, the font size of the paragraphs is 12 pt (80% of 15).

- ✔ ex: A value that is relative to the x-height of the current font. An *x-height* is the equivalent of the height of the lowercase character of a font, such as 1.5ex.

- ✔ em: A value that is relative to the current font size, such as 2em. For any given typeface, 1 em is equivalent to its point size. (Thus, a 16pt font has an em size of 16pt: Get it?)

  In fact, both 1em and 100% equal the current size.

Be careful when using these values; certain properties support only some measurement values — length values, say, but not relative values. Don't let this jargon scare you. Just define the size in a value you're familiar with. If that doesn't work, try something else.

CSS Structure and Syntax

A style sheet is made of *style rules.* Each style rule has two parts:

- ✔ **Selector:** Specifies the markup element to which style rules apply
- ✔ **Declaration:** Specifies how content described by the markup looks

You use a set of punctuation marks and special characters to define a style rule. The syntax for a style rule always follows this pattern:

```
selector {declaration;}
```

A semicolon always follows each declaration to make it easier for computers to distinguish them. A single selector can include one or more declarations, as we explain later in this chapter. Furthermore, each declaration breaks down into two sub-items:

- ✔ **Properties** are aspects of how the computer displays text and graphics (for example, font size or background color).
- ✔ **Values** provide data to specify how you want text and images to look on your page (for example, a 24pt font size or a yellow background).

You separate the property from the value in a declaration with a colon.

Each declaration ends with a semicolon.

```
selector {property: value;}
```

For example, these three style rules set the colors for first-, second-, and third-level headings:

```
h1 {color: teal;}
h2 {color: maroon;}
h3 {color: black;}
```

The CSS specification lists exactly which properties you can work with in your style rules and different values they can take. Most are pretty self-explanatory (color and border, for example). See "What you can do with CSS," earlier in this chapter, for a quick rundown of properties included in the CSS2 specification.

Style sheets override a browser's internal display rules; your style declarations affect the final appearance of the page in the user's browser. This means that you can control how your content looks and create a more consistent and appropriate experience for visitors.

For example, the following style rules specify font sizes (in percentages, relative to the base font) for first-, second-, and third-level headings:

```
h1 {font-size: 300%;}
h2 {font-size: 200%;}
h3 {font-size: 150%;}
```

Figure 9-1 shows a simple HTML page with all three heading levels (plus some body text) without the style sheet applied. The browser uses its default settings to display the headings in different font sizes.

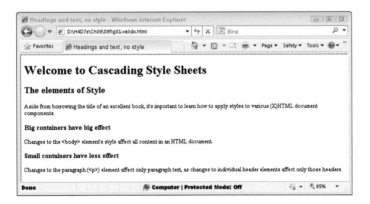

Figure 9-1: An HTML page without style specifications.

Figure 9-2 shows the same Web page with a style sheet applied. Things look very different because the body text is changed to a sans serif font, header titles are set for different colors, paragraph text is italic, and heading sizes are magnified beyond their usual settings.

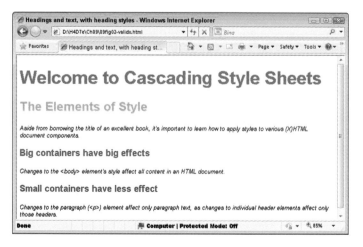

Figure 9-2: An HTML page with style specifications in effect.

Users can change their preferences so that their browsers ignore your style sheets (although most users will use your sheets). Test Web pages with style sheets turned off to be sure they look good (or acceptable) without your style sheets.

For detailed instructions on disabling or altering style sheets, see Jim Hatcher's discussion "Reading Web Pages without CSS" at www.jimthatcher.com/webcourseb.htm. The instructions vary by Web browser, but you can use accessibility plug-ins to manage or disable style sheets.

Selectors and declarations

You probably want a style rule to affect the display of more than one property for any given selector. You can create several style rules for a single selector, each with one declaration, like this:

```
h1 {color: teal;}
h1 {font-family: Arial;}
h1 {font-size: 36px;}
```

Font family

When assigning values to the `font-family` property, you can use a list of comma-separated font names. These names must match fonts available to a user's Web browser. If a font name includes spaces — such as Times New Roman — enclose it in quotation marks.

In the preceding rule, the browser knows to use Verdana first; if that's not available, it looks for Times New Roman, and then uses a generic serif font as its last option. Chapter 11 covers fonts in CSS.

```
h1 {font-family: Verdana, "Times New
      Roman", serif;}
```

However, such a large collection of style rules can be hard to manage. CSS allows you to combine several declarations in a *single* style rule that affects multiple display characteristics for a single selector, like this:

```
h1 {color: teal;
    font-family: Arial;
    font-size: 36px;}
```

All the declarations for the `h1` selector are within the same set of brackets (`{}`) and are separated by semicolons (`;`). You can put as many declarations as you want in a style rule; just end each declaration with a semicolon.

The semicolon at the end of the last declaration is optional. Some people include it to be consistent and end every declaration with a semicolon, but it's not necessary. We use it both ways throughout this book, but when you stop to think about it, it's a good idea to be consistent and *always* use a semicolon for each and every declaration.

From a purely technical standpoint, white space is irrelevant in style sheets (just as it is in HTML), but you should use a consistent spacing scheme to make it easy to read and edit your style sheets. One exception to this white space rule occurs when you declare multiple font names in the font-family declaration. See the "Font family" sidebar for more information.

You can make the same set of declarations apply to a collection of selectors, too: You just separate the selectors with commas. The following style rule applies the declarations for text color, font family, and font size to the `h1`, `h2`, and `h3` selectors:

```
h1, h2, h3 {color: teal;
            font-family: Arial;
            font-size: 300%;}
```

Sample style rules in this section show that style sheet syntax relies heavily on punctuation. When a style rule doesn't work exactly as you expect, make sure that you're not using a semicolon where you need a colon, or a parenthesis where you need a curly bracket. Watch out for commas and semicolons, too! Validation tools help catch these lapses: Use them.

The W3C CSS validation service at `http://jigsaw.w3.org/css-validator` helps find problems in your style sheets.

Working with style classes

Sometimes you need style rules that apply only to specific instances of an HTML markup element. For example, if you want a style rule that applies only to paragraphs that hold copyright information, you need a way to tell the browser that a rule has a limited scope.

To target a style rule closely, combine the `class` attribute with a markup element. The following examples show HTML for two kinds of paragraphs:

- ✔ A regular paragraph (without a `class` attribute)

    ```
    <p>This is a regular paragraph.</p>
    ```
- ✔ A `class` attribute with the value of `copyright`

    ```
    <p class="copyright">This is a paragraph of class copyright &copy; 2011.
            </p>
    ```

To create a style rule that applies only to the copyright paragraph, follow the paragraph selector in the style rule with

- ✔ A period (`.`)
- ✔ The value of the `class` attribute, such as `copyright`

The resulting rule looks like this:

```
p.copyright {font-family: Arial;
             font-size: 12px;
             color: white;
             background: teal;}
```

This style rule specifies that all paragraphs of class `copyright` display white text on a teal background in 12px Arial font. Figure 9-3 shows how a browser applies this style only to a paragraph where class equals `copyright`.

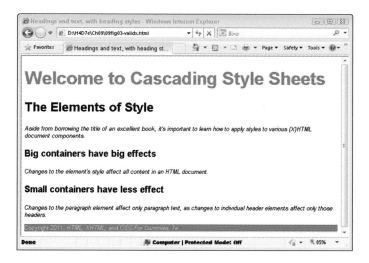

Figure 9-3: Classes can target your style rules more precisely.

You can also create style-rule classes that aren't associated with any element, like the following example:

```
.warning {font-family: Arial;
          font-size: 14px;
          background: blue;
          color: white;}
```

You can use this style class with any element by adding `class="warning"` to that element. Figure 9-4 shows how a browser applies the warning style to the paragraph and heading, but not to the block quote, in this HTML:

```
<p>This is a paragraph without the warning class applied.</p>
<blockquote>This is a block quote without a defined class.</blockquote>
<h1 class="warning">Warnings</h1>
<p class="warning">This is a paragraph with the warning class applied.</p>
```

You can also use the `span` element to selectively apply custom styles to inline content (or to create arbitrary content containers that extend from the opening <span> tag to its closing </span> counterpart):

```
<p>This is a paragraph without the <span class="warning">warning class</span>
   applied only to the words "warning class."</p>
```

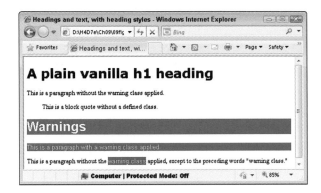

Figure 9-4: You can use classes to create style rules that work with any element.

Working with style IDs

You can also use the `id="name"` attribute with style markup when you want to create rules that apply only to certain instances of markup elements. Say you want to define a style that applies only to the first paragraph on each Web page so that it gets handled differently from other ordinary paragraphs, which might also have their own style settings.

To do this, you create an ID selector in your style definitions (either in the head of an (X)HTML document in an internal style sheet, or in a standalone CSS-only external style sheet), like this:

```
#first-graph {font-style: bold;
              text-indent: -0.25in;}
```

Then, whenever you write markup for a Web page, you craft the (X)HTML each initial paragraph as follows:

```
<p id="first-graph">The initial paragraph on will feature an 0.15 inch
   "hanging indent" and the typeface will be in heavy bold.</p>
<p>Subsequent paragraphs will use whatever style you have (or haven't) defined
   for the base paragraph style. In this case, this means ragged right
   justification and plain, unbolded text.</p>
```

Figure 9-5 illustrates how the Web page looks when using ID selectors to apply CSS definitions. ID selectors are useful because they can apply to all kinds of different markup elements (they're not tied to a single element as with class definitions) and they apply only when and as they're used. Very handy!

Pay attention to inheritance!

When you build complex style sheets to guide the appearance of every aspect of a page, keep inheritance in mind. For instance, if you set margins for a page in a body style rule, all margins you set for every other element on the page are based on margins set for the body. If you know how your style rules work together, you can use inheritance to minimize style rule repetition and create a cohesive display for your page.

This chapter covers basic CSS syntax, but you can fine-tune your style rules with advanced techniques. A complete overview of CSS syntax rules is available in the "CSS Structure and Rules" tutorial by the Web Design Group at `www.htmlhelp.com/reference/css/structure.html`.

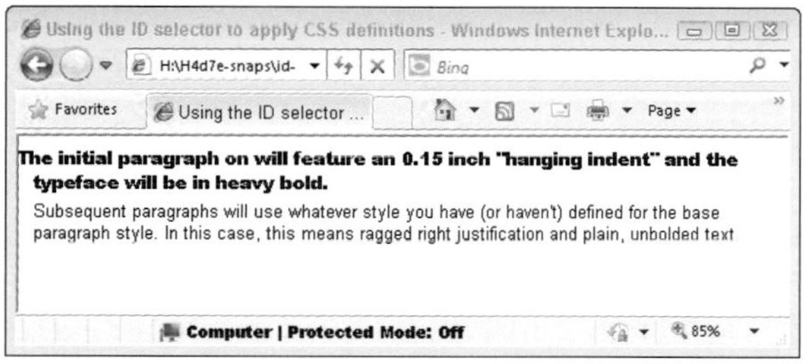

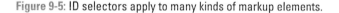

Figure 9-5: ID selectors apply to many kinds of markup elements.

Inheriting styles

A basic concept in HTML (and markup in general) is nesting tags:

- Every valid HTML document nests within `<html>` and `</html>` tags.

- Everything a browser displays in a window is nested within `<body>` and `</body>` tags. (That's just the beginning, really.)

The CSS specification recognizes that you often nest one element inside another and wants to be sure that styles associated with the parent element find their way to the child element. This mechanism is called *inheritance*.

When you assign a style to an element, the same style applies to all elements nested inside that element. For example, a style rule for the body element that sets page background, text color, font size, font family, and margins looks like this:

```
body {background: teal;
      color: white;
      font-size: 18px;
      font-family: Garamond;
      margin-left: 72px;
      margin-right: 72px;
      margin-top: 72px;}
```

To set style rules for the entire document, set them in the body element. Changing the font for the entire page, for example, is much easier to do that way; it beats changing every single element, one at a time.

When you link the following HTML to the preceding style rule, which applies only to the body element, that formatting is inherited by all subordinate elements:

```
<body>
  <p>This paragraph inherits the page styles.</p>
  <h1>As does this heading</h1>
  <ul>
      <li>As do the items in this list</li>
      <li>Item</li>
      <li>Item</li>
  </ul>
</body>
```

Using Different Kinds of Style Sheets

When you finish creating your style rules, you're ready to connect them to your HTML page using one of these options:

- **Insert style information into your document.** You can either

  - Use the `<style>` element to build a style sheet into a Web page.

    This is an *internal style sheet*.

  - Use the `style` attribute to add style information directly to a tag.

    This is an *inline style*.

- **Use an external style sheet.** You can either

  - Use the `<link>` tag to link your Web page to an external style sheet.

  - Use the CSS `@import` statement to import an external style sheet into the Web page.

Internal style sheets

An internal style sheet lives in your HTML page. Just add style rules to the
`<style>` element in the document header. You can include as many (or as
few) style rules as you want in an internal style sheet. (See Listing 9-1.)

Listing 9-1: Adding an Internal Style Sheet to an HTML Document

```
<!DOCTYPE html PUBLIC "-//W3C//DTD XHTML 1.0 Transitional//EN"
        "http://www.w3.org/TR/xhtml1/DTD/xhtml1-transitional.dtd">
<html xmlns="http://www.w3.org/1999/xhtml">
<head>
  <title>Internal Style Sheet Example</title>
  <style type="text/css">
    body {background: black;
          color: white;
          font-size: 16px;
          font-family: Garamond;
          margin-left: 72px;
          margin-right: 72px;
          margin-top: 72px;}

    h1, h2, h3 {color: teal;
                font-family: Arial;
                font-size: 36px;}

    p.copyright {font-family: Arial;
                 font-size: 12px;
                 font-color: white;
                 background: black;}

    .warning {font-family: Arial;
              font-size: 16px;
              font-color: orange;}
  </style>
</head>
<body>

<!-- Document content goes here -->

</body>
</html>
```

The benefit of using an internal style sheet is convenience: Your style rules
are on the same page as your markup, so you can tweak both quickly. And
if you want the same style rules to control the appearance of more than one
HTML page, move those styles from individual Web pages to an external style
sheet.

Use inline styles carefully

You can attach individual style rules, called an *inline style,* to individual elements in an HTML document. An inline style rule attached to an element looks like this:

```
<p style="color: green;">Green text.</p>
```

Adding style rules to an element isn't really the best approach. We generally recommend that you choose *either* internal *or* (preferably) external style sheets for your rules instead of attaching the rules to individual elements in your document. Here are a few reasons:

- Your style rules get mixed up in the page and are hard to find.

- You must place the entire rule in the value of the style attribute, which makes complex rules hard to write and edit.

- You lose all the benefits that come with grouping selectors and reusing style rules in external style sheets.

External style sheets

An external style sheet holds all your style rules in a separate text document that you can reference from any HTML file on your site. You must maintain a separate style sheet file, but an external style sheet offers benefits for overall site maintenance. If your site's pages use the same style sheet, you can change any formatting characteristic on all pages with a change to the style sheet.

We recommend using external style sheets on your sites.

Linking

To reference an external style sheet, use the link element in the Web page header, like this:

```
<html>
<head>
  <title>External Style Sheet Example</title>
  <link rel="stylesheet" type="text/css" href="styles.css" />
<head>
<body>

<!-- Document content goes here -->

</body>
</html>
```

The `href` attribute in the `<link>` element can take either

- ✏ A relative link (a style sheet on your own site)
- ✏ An absolute link (a style sheet that doesn't reside on your own site)

Usually, you shouldn't use a style sheet that doesn't reside on your Web site because you want control of your site's look and feel.

To quickly add style to your Web page (or to experiment to see how browsers handle different styles), use an absolute URL to point to one of the W3C's Core Style sheets. Read more about them at `www.w3.org/StyleSheets/Core`.

Chapter 6 covers the difference between relative and absolute links.

Importing

The `@import` statement instructs the browser to load an external style sheet and use its styles. You use it within the `<style>` element but before any of the individual style rules, like so:

```
<style>
   @import "http://www.somesite.edu/stylesheet.css";
</style>
```

Style rules in an imported style sheet take precedence over any rules that come before the `@import` statement. So, if you have multiple external style sheets referenced with more than one `@import` statement on your page, rules apply from the later style sheets (the ones farther down the page).

Understanding the Cascade

Multiple style sheets can affect page elements and build upon each other. It's like inheriting styles within a Web page. This is the *cascading* part of CSS.

Take this real-world example of a Web site for a university English department. The English department is part of the School of Humanities, which is one school in the university. Each of these entities — the university, the school, and the English department — has its own style sheet.

1. The university's style sheet provides style rules for all pages in the site.

2. The school's style sheet links to the university's style sheet (using an `@import` statement), and adds more style rules specific to the look the school wants for its own site.

 3. The English department's style sheet links to the school's style sheet.

 Thus, the department's pages both *have their own style rules* and *inherit the style rules from both the school's and the university's style sheets.*

But what if multiple style sheets define rules for the same element? What if, for example, all three style sheets specify a rule for the h1 element? In that case, the nearest rule to the page or element you're working on wins:

 ✐ If an h1 rule exists on the department's style sheet, it takes precedence over the school and university h1 styles.

 ✐ If an individual page within the department applies a style rule to h1 in a <style> tag, that rule applies.

Chapter 10

Using Cascading Style Sheets

In This Chapter

▶ Getting a handle on using CSS

▶ Positioning objects on a page

▶ Creating font rules

▶ Creating style sheets for print

▶ Understanding aural style sheets

*U*nderstanding the structure and syntax of CSS is easy. Learning about the properties that CSS can apply to (X)HTML documents takes a little more time and effort, though. However, where the learning curve really gets interesting is when it comes to learning how to use CSS to take a plain or ordinary Web page and kick it up a notch. This chapter deals with how to put CSS to work, rather than focusing on its structure and inner workings.

If you need a refresher of CSS style rules and properties, read Chapter 9 (a high-level overview of CSS and how it works). Then you can return to this chapter and put CSS into action.

Now it's time to make a page and give it some style!

To use CSS efficiently, follow these general guidelines:

▸ When you test how a page looks, use internal styles so you can tweak to your heart's delight. (This chapter shows internal style sheets, but Chapter 9 covers internal and external style sheets in greater detail.)

▸ When your test page looks just right, move those internal styles to an external sheet, and then apply them throughout your site, or to as many pages in that site as make sense.

Managing Layout and Positioning

You can use CSS to lay out your pages so that images and blocks of text

- Appear exactly where you want them to
- Fit exactly within the amount of space you want them to occupy

After you create styles within a document, you can create an external style sheet to apply the same styles to any page.

Listing 10-1 shows a Web page without any defined styles. This basic page is shown in Figure 10-1.

Listing 10-1:   A Fairly Dull Page

```
<!DOCTYPE html PUBLIC "-//W3C//DTD XHTML 1.0 Transitional//EN"
    "http://www.w3.org/TR/xhtml1/DTD/xhtml1-transitional.dtd">
<html xmlns="http://www.w3.org/1999/xhtml" lang="en" xml:lang="en">
<head>
  <title>Pixel's Page</title>
  <meta http-equiv="Content-Type" content="text/html; charset=ISO-8859-1" />
</head>
 <body>
  <h1>I'm Pixel the Cat. Welcome to my page.</h1>
  <div id="navBar">
    <p>Links of interest:</p>
      <p><a href="http://www.google.com/">Google</a></p>
      <p><a href="http://www.amazon.com/">Amazon</a></p>
      <p><a href="http://www.bing.com/">Bing</a></p>
  </div>
  <img src="/images/pixel1.jpg" alt="The Cat" width="320" height="240"
   id="theCat" />
 </body>
</html>
```

Creating links for your Web pages is covered in detail in Chapter 6. There, you'll find everything you need to know about creating great links. For questions regarding Cascading Style Sheets and the power they can bring to your Web site content, turn to Chapter 9.

The cat looks great, but the page certainly doesn't show off his possibilities. The addition of some styles improves this page immensely. Here's how!

Figure 10-1: This style-free page doesn't maximize this cat's possibilities.

Visual layouts

Instead of the links appearing above the image, as they do in Figure 10-1, we want them on the left, a typical location for navigation tools. The following markup floats the text for the search site links to the left of the image (see Figure 10-2):

```
<style type="text/css">
  #navBar {
    background-color: #CCC;
    border-bottom: #999;
    border-left: #999;
    border-width: 0 0 thin thin;
    border-style: none none groove groove;
    display: block;
    float: left;
    margin: 0 0 0 10px;
    padding: 0 10px 0 10px;
    width: 107px;
  line-height: 0.2em;
  }
</style>
```

Figure 10-2: The navigation bar now looks more like standard left-hand navigation.

In the preceding rules, we

- Added a `<style>` element
- Defined the `navBar` id inside the `<style>` element
- Used the `navBar` id to instruct the content to float to the left of images, which causes them to appear in the same part of the page to the left, rather than above the graphic

This rule says that anything on the page that belongs to the `navBar` id (as shown in Figure 10-2) should display with

- A light-gray background
- A thin, grooved-line border at bottom and left, in a darker gray
- No top or right border
- A block that floats to the left (so everything else on the page moves right, as with the image in Figure 10-2)
- A left margin of 10 pixels (px)
- Padding at top and bottom of 10px each
- A navbar area 100px wide

You'll note that we also set the line-height at 0.2em. This ensures that menu line entries are compact, without too much white space between individual elements.

Note that several properties in the declaration, called *shorthand properties,* take multiple values, such as margin and padding. Shorthand properties collect values from multiple related CSS properties (such as margin-height, margin-width, and so forth). See our online materials for a complete list. Those values correspond to settings for the top, right, bottom, and left edges of the navbar's box. margin creates an empty zone around the box, and padding defines the space between the edges or borders of the box and the content inside the box. Here are the rules that explain how to associate values with properties that deal with margins, borders, padding, and so forth:

- ✔ If all the sides have the same value, a single value works.

- ✔ If *any* side is different from the others, *every* side needs a separate value. It's okay to set some or all of these values to 0 (zero) as you see fit; this can often help to ensure that pages display consistently across a wider range of browsers (and browser versions).

To remember what's what, think of the edges of an element box in clockwise order, starting with the top edge: top, right, bottom, and then left. Notice that we define margins and padding using px (pixels) rather than pt (points) or em (default character m's width) as our unit of measure. This is a deliberate departure from best practices that we recommend elsewhere in this book (Chapter 11). That's because margins and padding usually involve small increments or values and because those things relate very strongly to individual actual displays within specific browsers. Experiment with these values to get them just right, and be sure to check them on as many different browsers and platforms as you can to ensure that visitors to your Web site see what you intended.

Positioning

CSS provides several ways to specify exactly where an element should appear on a page. These controls use various kinds of positioning based on the relationships between an element's box and its parent element's box to help page designers put page elements where they want them to go. The kinds of properties involved are discussed in the following sections.

Location

You can control the horizontal and vertical locations of an image. However, when you use absolute positioning with any page element, you specify exactly where that element must sit, relative to the upper-left corner of the browser window. Thus, instead of letting it be drawn automatically to the right of the navigation bar, you can place an image down and to the left, as in Figure 10-3. But absolutely positioned items always percolate to the top layer when items overlap, which is why Pixel's picture shows up on top. We change this default order later in the chapter.

```
#theCat {position: absolute; top: 120px; left: 107px;}
```

Figure 10-3: The image is more striking in this location.

You might be wondering why the `navbar` rule (defined in the listing in the earlier section, "Visual layouts") and the `theCat` rule (in the code snippet immediately preceding Figure 10-3) both start with a *pound symbol* (also known as a *hash mark* or *octothorpe*). That's because the pound symbol applies to an `id` attribute. You use a period to start a class rule, and it will apply to every instance of that class wherever it appears on a page. Thus, although you can apply either a `class` or an `id` to specific elements, the difference between these two is that a `class` can be used repeatedly. Comparatively, an `id` can appear only once on a page. You can't have anything else on the page that uses `theCat` as its `id`. The difference, quite simply, is that a `class` lets you refer to every instance of some (X)HTML element with a single reference, but an `id` can address only a single instance for an element.

Overlapping

Two objects *can* be assigned to the same position in a Web page. Although this may sound like a problem, overlap can produce interesting design effects — as you'll see with our navbar and photo in code and screenshots that follow. When overlap occurs, the browser must determine the display order and which objects to show and which ones to hide.

Using `z-index`, added to any rule, tells CSS how you want any object stacked over and under other objects that occupy the same space on the page:

- ✔ Lower numbers move down the stack.
- ✔ Higher numbers move up the stack.
- ✔ The default value for `z-index` is `auto`, which means it's the same as for its parent element.

Giving `theCat` a `z-index` value of `-1` automatically puts it behind everything else on the page (as shown in Figure 10-4) for which the `z-index` isn't set (see the HTML source for Figure 10-4 on the book's Web site for the details).

Figure 10-4: The cat is peeking out from behind the navigation bar.

Changing Fonts for Visual Interest and Better Readability

You can make a page more interesting by replacing old, boring, default fonts. Start by specifying a generic body font as well as setting some other default rules, such as background color and text color.

Body text

Here's an example that sets the style for text within the body element:

```
body {font-family: verdana, geneva, arial, helvetica, sans-serif;
      font-size: 1em; line-height: 1.33em; background-color: white;
      color: teal;}
```

Because the body element holds all content for any Web page, this affects everything on the page. The preceding rule instructs the browser to show all text that appears within the body element as follows:

✔ The text is rendered using one of the fonts listed. We placed Verdana at the head of the list because it's the preferred choice, and browsers check for available fonts in the order listed. *Note:* A generic font — in this case, sans-serif — almost always appears last in such lists because the browser can almost always supply such a font itself.

You can list more than one font. The browser uses the first font from your list that's available in the browser. For example, the browser looks for fonts from our list in this order:

1. Verdana

2. Geneva

3. Arial

4. Helvetica

5. The browser's default sans serif font

✔ 1.33em line height

The lines are spaced as though the fonts are 1em high, so there's more vertical space between lines.

Figure 10-5 shows that

✔ All changes apply to the entire page, including the navigation bar.

✔ The font-family changes in the h1 heading.

Because headers have specific defaults for font-size and line-height, another rule is needed to modify them.

In shooting Figure 10-5, the HTML used for our screen capture includes an additional tweak for Internet Explorer (IE). That's because a bug in Internet Explorer for Windows that doesn't occur in other browsers causes heading (h1) text to get truncated at the top. (Try the source (X)HTML for Figure 10-5 in IE to see what we mean; we had to add CSS markup that set line-height: 105%; for h1 to create this display.) Unfortunately, CSS rendering can be unpredictable enough that you must test style rules in various browsers to see how they look — and then tweak accordingly.

Figure 10-5: The fonts are nicer, but they could still use a little more work.

Headings

If we explicitly assign style properties to the h1 element, display results are more predictable. Here's a sample set of styles:

```
h1 {font-family: "trebuchet ms", verdana, geneva, arial, helvetica, sans-serif;
    font-size: 2em; line-height: w.167em;}
```

Figure 10-6 shows a first-level heading using the font family and type size that we want: 2em Trebuchet MS, with a 2⅙ em line height. If we didn't have the Trebuchet MS font on our system, the heading would appear in Verdana.

When a font name includes spaces (like trebuchet ms or times new roman), the full name must be within quotation marks. (See Chapter 11 for more information.)

Hyperlinks

We think that having the hyperlinks underlined — which is normal — makes the menu look a little cluttered. Luckily, we can turn underlines off with CSS, but we still want the hyperlinks to look like hyperlinks, so we tell CSS to

- ✔ Make links bold.
- ✔ Make underlines appear when the cursor is over a link.
- ✔ Show links in specific colors.

Figure 10-6: Declaring a rule for `h1` makes it appear just how we like it.

The following style rules define how a browser should display hyperlinks:

```
a {text-decoration: none; font-weight: bold}
a:link {color: blue}
a:visited {color: #93C}
a:hover {text-decoration: underline}
```

What's going on here? Starting from the top, we're setting two rules for the `<a>` tag that apply to all links on the page:

- ✔ **The `text-decoration` declaration sets its value to `none`.**

  This gets rid of the underlining for all the links.
- ✔ **The `font-weight` declaration has a value of `bold`.**

  This makes all the links on the page appear in bold.

The remaining rules in the preceding code are *pseudo class selectors*. Their most common usage is to modify how links appear in their different states. (For more information on pseudo classes, see Chapter 11.) Here we change the color when a link has been visited. We also turn on underlining when the mouse pointer hovers over link text to identify hyperlinks when the cursor is in clicking range. Figure 10-7 shows how the page appears when the previous style rules are applied.

Figure 10-7: The final version of our page.

Externalizing Style Sheets

When the final page is the way you want it, you're ready to cut and paste your tested, approved, internal style sheet into an external style sheet. The benefits of using an external style sheet are that

- ✔ Every page of the site can use the whole style sheet with the addition of only one line of code to each page.
- ✔ Changes can be made site-wide with one change in the external style sheet.

To create an external style sheet from a well-tested internal style sheet, follow these steps:

1. **Copy all text that sits between the `<style>` and `</style>` tags.**

2. **Paste that text into its own new document.**

   This text should include only CSS markup, without any HTML tags or markup.

3. **Append a `.css` suffix to the document's name (for example, `myStyles.css`) when saving.**

   The suffix shows at a glance that it's a CSS file.

So you have your external style sheet. Time now to link your HTML file to said external style sheet. You have two options available to you:

> ✔ **Use the `<link>` tag.**
>
> All CSS-capable browsers understand the `link` tag.
>
> ✔ **Use the `<style>` tag with the `@import` keyword.**
>
> Only newer browsers understand the `<style>` and `@import` combination.

See Chapter 9 for more on these two methods.

Sometimes style sheets can get complicated and long. That's when the `@import` keyword comes in handiest: You can create a master stylesheet and then use multiple `@import` statements to bring in individual stylesheets for headers, footers, body copy, menus, and so forth. Each `@import` references a subsidiary style sheet for one of those various categories for page content. This is probably overkill for most small-scale or personal Web sites, but as sites get "big and hairy," this technique can be very helpful.

Using CSS with Multimedia

You can specify how you want your Web pages to look or behave on different *media types* depending on the medium.

Table 10-1 lists all the media types and their uses.

Table 10-1	Recognized Media Types
Media Type	**Description**
`All`	Suitable for all devices
`aural`	For speech synthesizers
`braille`	For Braille tactile-feedback devices
`embossed`	For paged Braille printers
`handheld`	For handheld devices (such as those with a small screen, monochrome monitor, and limited bandwidth)
`print`	For paged, opaque material and for documents viewed onscreen but in Print Preview mode
`projection`	For projected presentations, such as projectors or transparencies
`screen`	For color computer screens
`Tty`	For media that use a fixed-pitch character grid, such as teletypes, terminals, or portable devices with limited display capabilities
`Tv`	For television-type devices (such as those with low resolution, color capability, limited-scrollability screens, and some sound available)

CSS can make changes to customize how the same pages

✔ **Render onscreen**

✔ **Print**

> A nifty color background might make your page a mess when it's printed on a black-and-white laser printer, but proper use of print-media styles can keep this sort of thing from happening!

✔ **Sound when read out loud**

Visual media styles

Table 10-2 lists the CSS properties that you're most likely to use in a typical Web page. Our online content for this book includes brief descriptions of the most commonly used CSS properties and (X)HTML tags and attributes.

Table 10-2	Visual Media Styles		
Property	*Values*	*Default Value*	*Description*
`Background-color`	Any color, by name or hex code	`transparent`	Background color of the associated element
`Background-image`	URL	`none`	Image URL as background for element
`Color`	Any color, by name or hex code	Up to you!	Color of the foreground text
`font-family`	Any named font, `cursive` `fantasy` `monospace` `sans-serif` `serif`	Up to you! (Stick to common fonts.)	Font for rendering related element content
`font-size`	Number + unit, `xx-small` `x-small` `small smaller` `medium large` `larger` `x-large` `xx-large` `% Length` (px, em, cm)	`medium`	Size of the font for rendering related element content

(continued)

Table 10-2 (continued)

Property	Values	Default Value	Description
font-weight	normal bold bolder lighter 100 200 300 400 500 600 700 800 900	normal 400 is the same as normal 700 is the same as bold	Weight (how bold or light) the font should appear
line-height	Normal **number + unit** % Length (px, em, cm)	normal	Vertical spacing between lines of text
text-align	left right center justify	Up to you; normal text direction	Determines how text on the page gets aligned
text-decoration	None underline overline line-through blink	none	Special text effects
list-style-image	**URL**	none	URL for an image to display as a list bullet
list-style-position	Inside outside	outside	Wrap list text inside or outside bullet points
list-style-type	Disc circle square decimal decimal-leading-zero lower-alpha upper-alpha none armenian georgian lower-greek lower-latin lower-roman upper-latin upper-roman	disc	Bullet type on lists

Property	Values	Default Value	Description
Display	block inline none	inline	Format of a defined section for a block element
Top	Number and unit auto	auto	Absolute positioning: sets top edge of element above/ below top edge of containing element; relative positioning: sets top edge of an element above/below its normal position
Right	Percentage number + unit auto	Auto	Absolute positioning: sets right edge of element to width next to right edge of containing element; relative positioning: sets right edge of element to width next to right edge of its normal position
Bottom	Percentage number + unit auto	Auto	Absolute positioning: sets bottom edge of element below bottom edge of its containing element; relative positioning: sets bottom edge of below its normal position

(continued)

Table 10-2 *(continued)*

Property	Values	Default Value	Description
Left	Percentage number + unit auto	Auto	Absolute positioning: sets left edge of element to right of left edge of its containing element; relative positioning: sets top edge of above/below its normal position
Position	Static absolute relative fixed	static	Method by which element box is laid out, relative to positioning context
Visibility	Collapse visible hidden inherit	inherit	Indicates whether object will display on the page
z-index	Number auto	Auto	Stacking order for objects (–1 always puts object at the very back)
border-style	none dotted dashed solid double groove ridge inset outset	Not defined	Style displayed for object borders. Can be broken out into border-top-style, border-right-style, border-bottom-style, and border-left-style

Property	*Values*	*Default Value*	*Description*
`border-width`	`Thin medium thick` Number	Not defined	Width of border around an object. Can be broken out into `border-top-width`, `border-right-width`, `border-bottom-width, and border-left-width`
`border-color`	Any color, by name or hex code `transparent`	Not defined	Color of object's border. Can be broken out into `border-top-color`, `border-right-color`, `border-bottom-color, and border-left-color`
`Border`	`Border-width` + `border-style` + `border-color`	Not defined	Combined features for border around object. Can be broken out into `border-top`, `border-right`, `border-bottom,` and `border-left`
`Float`	`left right none`	`none`	Specifies whether object should float to one side or other for document

(continued)

Table 10-2 *(continued)*

Property	Values	Default Value	Description
Height	Number + unit auto	Auto	Display height for object
Width	Number + unit auto	Auto	Display width for object
Margin	Number + unit auto	Not defined	Display margins for object. Can be broken out into margin-top, margin-right, margin-bottom, and margin-left
Padding	Number + unit auto	Not defined	Display blank space around object. Can be broken out into padding-top, padding-right, padding-bottom, and padding-left
Cursor	Auto cross-hair default pointer move text help URL e-resize n-resize ne-resize nw-resize progress s-resize se-resize sw-resize w-resize inherit	Auto	Cursor appearance in browser window

Some browsers don't support all CSS properties. If you're using CSS features, test your pages with the browsers that you expect your visitors will use. Use the CSS features that work on as many browsers as possible, and ignore the rest.

If you want to take an extremely thorough guide to CSS everywhere you go, put it on your iPod! Westciv's free podGuide is a folder of small text files. Download the zipped file and follow the instructions on how to install it, and you have complete documentation with you at all times. (You also win the title of "World's Biggest CSS Geek.") The podGuide is online at www.westciv.com/news/podguide.html.

Paged media styles

CSS can customize how a page looks when it's printed. We recommend these guidelines:

✔ **Replace sans serif fonts with serif fonts.**

Serif fonts are easier to read than sans serif fonts.

✔ **Insert advertisements that**

- Make sense when they aren't animated
- Are useful without clicking

In general, paged media styles help ensure that text looks as good when it's printed as it does in a Web browser. Paged media styles also help you hide irrelevant content when pages are printed (banners, ads, and so forth), thus reducing wasted paper and user frustration. See Table 10-3 for an explanation of paged media properties in CSS that you can use to help your users make the most when printing Web pages.

Table 10-3	Paged Media Styles		
Property	*Values*	*Default Value*	*Description*
orphans	Number	2	The minimum number of lines in a paragraph that must be left at the bottom of a page
page-break-after	Auto always avoid left right	auto	The page-breaking behavior after an element
page-break-before	Auto always avoid left right	auto	The page-breaking behavior before an element

(continued)

Table 10-3 *(continued)*

Property	Values	Default Value	Description
page-break-inside	Auto avoid	auto	The page-breaking behavior inside an element
widows	Number	2	The minimum number of lines in a paragraph that must be left at the top of a page

The example in Listing 10-2 uses these options for paged media styles:

✔ Make the output black text on a white background.

✔ Replace sans serif fonts with serif fonts.

Listing 10-2:   Adding a Print Style Sheet

```
<!DOCTYPE html PUBLIC "-//W3C//DTD XHTML 1.0 Transitional//EN"
    "http://www.w3.org/TR/xhtml1/DTD/xhtml1-transitional.dtd">
<html xmlns="http://www.w3.org/1999/xhtml" lang="en" xml:lang="en">
<head>
<title>This is my page</title>
<meta http-equiv="Content-Type" content="text/html; charset=ISO-8859-1" />
<style type="text/css">
    body {background-color: black; color: white; font-family: sans-serif;}

    @media print {
      body {background-color: white; color: black; font-family: serif}
    }
</style>
</head>
<body>
    This page will look very different when sent to the printer.
</body>
</html>
```

If you're now wondering why none of the properties in Table 10-3 were set but other properties were, it's because (in this example) their defaults worked fine. And just because those page properties can be set doesn't mean that you can't set other properties also — it isn't an either/or.

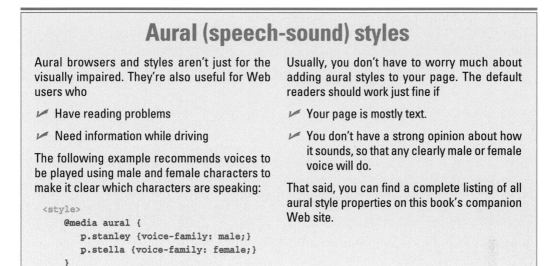

Aural (speech-sound) styles

Aural browsers and styles aren't just for the visually impaired. They're also useful for Web users who

✔ Have reading problems

✔ Need information while driving

The following example recommends voices to be played using male and female characters to make it clear which characters are speaking:

```
<style>
    @media aural {
        p.stanley {voice-family: male;}
        p.stella {voice-family: female;}
    }
</style>
```

Usually, you don't have to worry much about adding aural styles to your page. The default readers should work just fine if

✔ Your page is mostly text.

✔ You don't have a strong opinion about how it sounds, so that any clearly male or female voice will do.

That said, you can find a complete listing of all aural style properties on this book's companion Web site.

Chapter 11

Getting Creative with Colors and Fonts

. . . .

In This Chapter

▶ Using CSS to define text formatting

▶ Working with page colors and backgrounds

▶ Changing font display

▶ Adding text treatments

. . . .

*B*efore style sheets came along, Web designers had to rely on HTML markup to control backgrounds, colors, fonts, and text sizes on Web pages. With style sheets on the scene, however, designers could separate style information from content — meaning they could use Cascading Style Sheets (CSS) to control font, color, and other style information.

Why bother? Simple. When you use CSS, you get the following:

✔ Better control when updating or editing formatting information.

✔ No more HTML documents cluttered with `<font>` tags.

✔ More options for formatting text (such as defining line height, font weight, and text alignment) and for converting text to uppercase or lowercase characters.

(X)HTML still includes various formatting elements, such as `<tt>`, `<i>`, `<big>`, `<b>`, and `<small>`; however, all remaining formatting elements, such as `<font>`, are *deprecated*. That is, they're no longer recommended for use (although they still work, and most browsers recognize them). We don't think you should use them anymore, but that decision is yours to make. If you want to read more about deprecated formatting elements, we cover that in Chapter 8.

Color Values

(X)HTML defines color values in two ways:

- **Name:** You choose from a limited list.
- **Number:** Harder to remember, but you have many more options.

Color names

The HTML specification includes 16 color names that you can use to define colors in your pages. Table 11-1 shows these colors. The numbers that start with a hash mark (#) are in *hexadecimal* notation, a mix of the letters A–F (for 10–15) and the more typical 0–9 we all know and love from decimal numbers.

Table 11-1			Named Color Values in (X)HTML		
Name	*#RGB Code*	*Color*	*Name*	*#RGB Code*	*Color*
Black	#000000		Silver	#C0C0C0	
Gray	#808080		White	#FFFFFF	
Maroon	#800000		Red	#FF0000	
Purple	#800080		Fuchsia	#FF00FF	
Green	#008000		Lime	#00FF00	
Olive	#808000		Yellow	#FFFF00	
Navy	#000080		Blue	#0000FF	
Teal	#008080		Aqua	#00FFFF	

You can safely use color names in your CSS markup and be confident that browsers will recognize them and use the correct colors in your Web pages. You can also compare the colors that you see onscreen to those you see on this printed page to see how print and digital displays can sometimes differ. (In some cases, it may be the color balance on your screen that's off; in others, the color the printer tried to match on the page may not be precisely correct — it's not as easy as you might think!)

Visit `www.htmlhelp.com/reference/html40/values.html#color` to see how your browser displays these colors. If you can, view this page on two or three different computers to see how a different browser, operating system, graphics card, and monitor can subtly change the display.

The following CSS style declaration says that all text within <p> tags should be blue:

```
p {color: blue;}
```

If you're looking for burnt umber, chartreuse, or salmon, you're out of luck. This list is not a box of 64 crayons! You can, however, also find hex codes for Web-safe colors, along with color swatches, on the online Cheat Sheet at `http://www.dummies.com/how-to/content/html-xhtml-css-for-dummies-cheat-sheet.html`. These colors, though unnamed, are *Web-safe* because they reproduce pretty reliably on most color computer display devices and printers.

Color numbers

Color numbers allow you to use any color (even salmon) on your Wcb page.

Hexadecimal color codes

Hexadecimal notation uses six characters — a combination of numbers and letters — to define color. If you know a color's hexadecimal code (often called its *hex code* for short), you have all you need to use that color in your HTML page.

When you use hexadecimal code to define a color, you should always precede it with a pound sign (#). Otherwise, it may not display properly in some Web browsers.

The following CSS style declaration makes all text contained by <p> tags blue:

```
p {color: #0000FF;}
```

Finding any color's hex code

You can't just wave your magic wand and come up with the hex code for any color, but that doesn't mean that you can't find the hex code through less magical means. Color converters follow a precise formula that changes a color's standard RGB notation into hexadecimal notation. Because you have better things to do with your time than compute hex codes, you have several options for figuring out the code for your color of choice, including Web-safe colors shown on this book's online Cheat Sheet (www.dummies.com/cheatsheet/html). None of these make you use a calculator:

✔ **On the Web:** Some good sources for hexadecimal color charts are

>   http://www.webmonkey.com/2010/02/color_charts
>
>   www.colorschemer.com/online.html

You simply find a color you like and type the hex code listed next to it into your HTML.

✔ **Using image editing software:** Many image editing applications, such as Adobe Photoshop or Adobe Fireworks, display the hexadecimal notation for any color. Even the Microsoft Word color picker shows you hex codes for colors in an image. If you have an image you like that you want to use as a color source for your Web page, open the image in your favorite editor and find out what the colors' hex codes are.

RGB values

You can use two decimal RGB values to define color. These value types aren't as common as hexadecimal values, but they're just as effective:

✔ rgb(r,g,b): The r, g, and b are integers between 0 and 255 that (respectively) represent the red, green, and blue levels of the color.

✔ rgb(r%,g%,b%): The r%, g%, and b% represent (respectively) the percentage of red, green, and blue of the color.

Every color can be defined as a mixture of red, green, and blue (RGB). You can use either an RGB value or the equivalent hex code to describe a color's RGB value to a Web browser. For more information about hexadecimal notation, please visit the "Tutorial on Hexadecimal Color" at www.lts.com/class/hextoc.htm.

Color Definitions

You can define individual colors for any text on the Web page, as well as define a background color for the entire Web page or some portion thereof.

CSS uses the following properties to define colors:

✔ color defines the font color and is also used to define colors for links in their various states (link, active, focus, visited, and hover; see the upcoming section, "Links").

✔ background or background-color defines the background color for the entire page or defines the background for a particular element (for example, a background color for all first-level headings, similar to the idea of highlighting something in a Word document).

Text

You can change the color of text on your Web page with three steps:

1. **Determine the selector.**

   For example, will the color apply to all first-level headings, to all paragraphs, or to a specific paragraph?

2. **Use the color property.**

3. **Identify the color name or hexadecimal value.**

The basic syntax for the style declaration is

```
selector {color: value;}
```

Here is a collection of style declarations where we use the color property to assign text color to the body element (and hence, to all other subsidiary HTML elements that can occur in a document body, except where other specifications override that selection as with the h1 element):

```
body {color: olive; font-family: Verdana, sans-serif;
      background-color: #FFFFFF; font-size: 85%;}
hr {text-align: center;}
.navbar {font-size: 75%; text-align: center;}
h1 {color: #808000;}
p.chapternav {text-align: center;}
.footer {font-size: 80%;}
```

Note that in the preceding CSS rules, the color for all text on the page is defined by using a body selector. Color is applied to all text in the body of the document unless otherwise defined. To illustrate this at work, the first-level heading is defined as forest green, using hexadecimal notation.

Links

Pseudo classes allow you to define style rules based on information outside the document tree.

The most common CSS use of pseudo classes is to define a style rule for a given element in the *document tree* — a technical term that just means the browser builds a hierarchical representation for all elements in a document, much like a family tree, where every element has a parent and may contain a child. For example, `:link` is a pseudo class that defines style rules for any link that hasn't yet been visited.

The five common pseudo classes that you can use with hyperlinks are

- `:link` defines formatting for links that haven't been visited.
- `:visited` defines formatting for links that have been visited.
- `:focus` defines formatting for links that are selected by the keyboard (for example, by using the Tab key) and are about to be activated by using the Enter key.
- `:hover` defines formatting for links when the mouse cursor hovers over them.
- `:active` defines formatting for links when they are selected (clicked by the mouse, or activated by pressing Enter).

The pseudo class name is preceded by a colon (`:`).

Pseudo classes can be used with

- Elements (such as the `<a>` element that defines hyperlinks)
- Classes
- IDs

For example, to define the style rules for visited and unvisited links, use the following syntax:

- The following sets the color of any hyperlink pointing to an unvisited URL to red by using its hexadecimal value:

  ```
  a:link {color: #FF0000;}
  ```

- The following sets any hyperlink that points to a visited URL to appear in the named color `green`:

  ```
  a:visited {color: green;}
  ```

- The following designates unvisited links with a class of `internal` to appear in (named color) `yellow`: (See Chapter 9 for a discussion of CSS classes.)

  ```
  a.internal:link {color: yellow;}
  ```

Links can occupy multiple states at one time. For example, a link can be visited and hovered over at the same time. Always define link style rules in the following order: `:link`, `:visited`, `:visible`, `:focus`, `:hover`, `:active`.

CSS applies "last rule seen" to display your page. Thus, if you put the pseudo class selectors in the wrong order, your results may not be what you want. For example, if `visited` follows `hover` and the two have overlapping rules, hover effects apply only to links that haven't yet been visited.

The following CSS rules render the document with olive, as the color for links that haven't been visited, and with yellow, as the color of visited links:

```
body {color: #808000; font-family: Verdana, sans-serif; font-size: 85%;}
a:link {color: olive;}
a:visited {color: yellow;}
```

The CSS specification defines `:link` and `:visited` as mutually exclusive, and it's up to the browser application to determine when to change the state (visited versus unvisited) for any given link. For example, a browser might determine that a link is unvisited if you clear your history data.

Backgrounds

To change the background color for your Web page, or for a section of that page, follow these steps:

1. **Determine the selector.**

   For example, will the color apply to the entire background, or will it apply only to a specific section?

2. **Use the `background-color` or `background` property.**

3. **Identify the color name or hexadecimal value.**

The basic syntax for the style declaration is

```
selector {background-color: value;}
```

In the following collection of style declarations, the first style declaration uses the `background-color` property and sets it to light green by using hexadecimal notation:

```
body {color: #808000; font-family: Verdana, sans-serif;
      background-color: #EAF3DA; font-size: 85%;}
```

You can apply a background color to a block of text — for example, a paragraph — just like you define a background color for the entire page.

You use `background` as a shorthand property for all individual background properties, or use `background-color` to set just the color, like this:

```
selector {background: value value value;}
```

See Chapter 9 or "The Shorthand Property" section of Webmonkey's "Mulder's Stylesheets Tutorial" for more information at `www.webmonkey.com/2010/02/mulders_stylesheets_tutorial`.

Fonts

You can define individual font properties for different HTML elements with

- ✔ Individual CSS properties, such as `font-family`, `line-height`, and `font-size`
- ✔ A group of font properties in the catchall shorthand `font` property

Font family

To define the font face (a named and often copyrighted set of specific character designs, such as Times Roman, Arial, or Helvetica) by using the CSS `font-family` property:

1. Identify the selector for the style declaration.

For example, making p the selector defines a font family for all <p> tags.

2. Add the property name `font-family`.

Not all font families are supported by every browser. CSS allows you to specify multiple font families in case a browser doesn't support the font family you prefer. You can list multiple font family names, separated by commas. The browser uses the first name in the list available on the computer on which it's running. You can check out a list of Web-safe font families at FontTester.com at `www.fonttester.com/help/list_of_web_safe_fonts.html`.

3. Define a `value` for the property (the name of the font family).

Use single or double quotation marks around any font family names that include spaces.

To format all first-level headings to use the Verdana font, use a style declaration like this:

```
h1 {font-family: Verdana, Helvetica, sans-serif;}
```

In the preceding declaration, two more font families appear in case someone's browser doesn't support the Verdana font family.

We recommend including these font families in your style declarations:

- ✔ **Common:** At least one of these common font families:
    - Arial: ABCDEFGHIJKLMNOPQRSTUVWXYZ abcdefghijklmnopqrstuvwxyz
    - Helvetica: ABCDEFGHIJKLMNOPQRSTUVWXYZ abcdefghijklmnopqrstuvwxyz
    - Times New Roman: ABCDEFGHIJKLMNOPQRSTUVWXYZ abcdefghijklmnopqrstuvwxyz
    - Verdana: ABCDEFGHIJKLMNOPQRSTUVWXYZ abcdefghijklmnopqrstuvwxyz
- ✔ **Generic:** At least one of these generic font families:
    - Serif: ABCDEFGHIJKLMNOPQRSTUVWXYZ abcdefghijklmnopqrstuvwxyz
    - Sans serif: ABCDEFGHIJKLMNOPQRSTUVWXYZ abcdefghijklmnopqrstuvwxyz
    - Cursive: *ABCDEFGHIJKLMNOPQRSTUVWXYZ abcdefghijklmnopqrstuvwxyz*
    - Fantasy: ABCDEFGHIJKLMNOPQRSTUVWXYZ abcdefghijklmnopqrstuvwxyz
    - Monospace: ABCDEFGHIJKLMNOPQRSTUVWXYZ abcdefghijklmnopqrstuvwxyz

Different elements may be formatted using different font families. These rules define a different font family for hyperlinks (see Figure 11-1):

```
body {color: #808000; font-family: Arial, sans-serif; font-size: 85%;}
hr {text-align: center;}
a {font-family: Courier, "Courier New", monospace;}
```

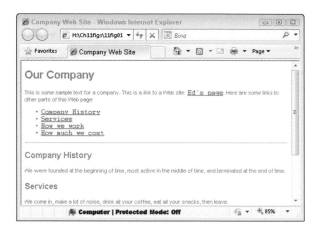

Figure 11-1: The font family for hyperlinks differs from the font family for the rest of the text.

Sizing

The following properties allow you to control the dimensions of your text.

Font size

The style declaration to specify the size of text is

```
selector {font-size: value;}
```

The value of the declaration can be

- ✔ **One of the standard font-property measurement values (listed in Chapter 9)**
- ✔ **One of these user-defined keywords:**

    xx-small, x-small, small, medium, large, x-large, or xx-large

    The value of each keyword is determined by the *browser,* not by the style rule.

The rules listed in upcoming subsections define

- ✔ A relative font value for all text
- ✔ An absolute value for the font size for all first-level headings

```
body {color: #808000; font-family: Arial, sans-serif; font-size: 85%;}
h1 {font-family: "trebuchet ms", verdana, geneva, arial, helvetica,
sans-serif; font-size: 2em; line-height: 2.5em; color: teal;}
```

Sizing text fonts with CSS

In addition to the font size names (`xx-small`, `x-small`, `small`, `medium`, `large`, `x-large`, or `xx-large`), you can also assign font sizes by using the following CSS units of measure: px (pixels), pt (points), or em (the m-height for the font in use, whatever it may be). Pixels depend on the size of an individual pixel on your user's display and will vary too much from screen to screen to be truly useful. Points are very small units of measure and may require too much experimentation to get just right. That

probably explains why em is the most widely used unit in sizing fonts in CSS nowadays, and why this approach is considered a best practice for sizing fonts using stylesheets. Choosing em units won't free you from experimentation, but it will make it quick and easy for you to size type relative to your underlying font. For more information on using these units, which take the form `font-size: 2em;` (to double font size) or `font-size: 0.8em;` (to reduce a font to 80 percent of the base), see Chapter 9.

The result appears in Figure 11-2.

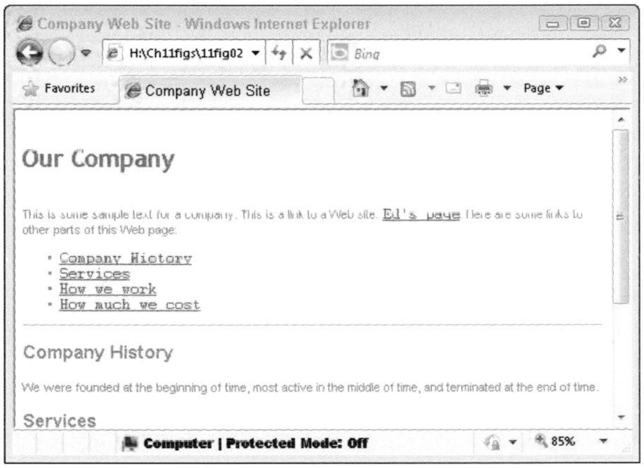

Figure 11-2: First-level headings are twice as big as the base font; font size for other text is relative.

Line height

The *line height* of a paragraph is the amount of space between each line within the paragraph.

Line height is like line spacing in a word processor.

To alter the amount of space between lines of a paragraph, use the line-height property:

```
selector {line-height: value;}
```

The value of the line-height property can be either

- ✔ One of the standard font property measurement values (listed in Chapter 9)
- ✔ A number that multiplies the element's font size, such as 1.5

We assign a quotation class to the first paragraph throughout this chapter so you can see the changes. This allows us to apply these styles to the first paragraph by using

```
<p class="quotation">
```

in the HTML document.

The following rules style the first paragraph in italics, indent that paragraph, and increase the line height to increase readability (see Figure 11-3):

```
body {color: #808000; font-family: Arial, sans-serif; font-size: 85%;}
    h1 {font-family: "trebuchet ms", verdana, geneva, arial, helvetica, sans-
            serif;
    font-size: 2em; line-height: 2.5em; color: teal;}
    .quotation {font-style: italic; text-indent: 2em; line-height: 150%;}
```

Character spacing

You can increase or reduce the amount of spacing between letters or words by using these properties:

- ✔ word-spacing: The style declaration for word-spacing is

    ```
    selector {word-spacing: value;}
    ```

    Designers call the space between words *tracking*.

- ✔ letter-spacing: The style declaration for letter-spacing is

    ```
    selector {letter-spacing: value;}
    ```

    Designers call the space between letters *kerning*.

The value of either spacing property must be a length defined by a standard font property measurement value (listed in Chapter 9).

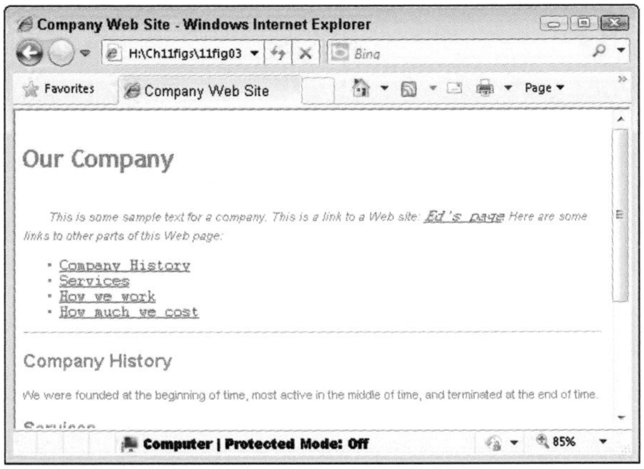

Figure 11-3: Any element that belongs to the quotation class gets the same formatting.

The following code increases the letter spacing (kerning) of the first paragraph (see Figure 11-4):

```
body {color: #808000; font-family: Arial, sans-serif; font-size: 85%;}
    h1 {font-family: "trebuchet ms", verdana, geneva, arial, helvetica, sans-
            serif;
    font-size: 2em; line-height: 2.5em; color: teal;}
    .quotation {font-style: italic; text-indent: 10pt; line-height: 150%;
            letter-spacing: 0.2em;}
```

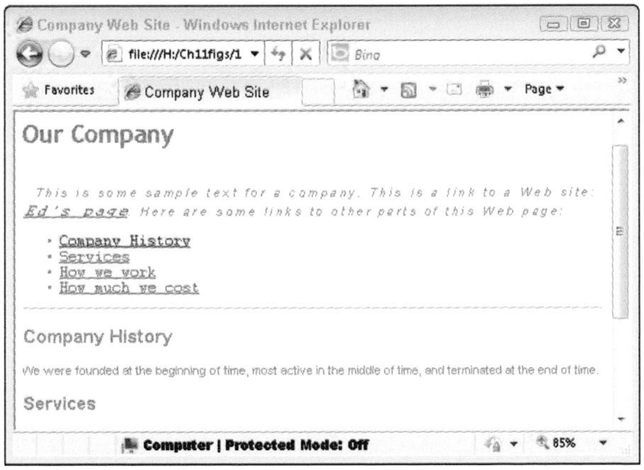

Figure 11-4: Kerning can be larger or smaller than the font's normal spacing.

Positioning Blocks of Text

Alignment properties allow you to control how the edges of text blocks line up against one another (otherwise known as "edge alignment").

Aligning text

Alignment determines whether the left and right sides of a text block are

- **Flush:** Starting or ending together
- **Ragged:** Starting or ending at different points

Syntax for text alignment

Alignment is defined with the `text-align` property. The style declaration to align text is as follows:

```
selector {text-align: value;}
```

The value of the `text-align` property must be one of the following keywords:

- `left`: Aligns the text to the left. The right side of the text block is ragged.
- `right`: Aligns the text to the right. The left side of the text block is ragged.
- `center`: Centers the text in the middle of the window. Both sides of the text block are ragged.
- `justify`: Aligns the text for both the left and right side. The spacing within the text in each line is adjusted so both sides of the text block are flush.

  Justifying text affects letter or word spacing in the paragraph. Test the results before displaying your Web pages to the world.

Markup for text alignment

The following example defines the alignment for the first-level heading and the first paragraph (see Figure 11-5):

```
body {color: #808000; font-family: Verdana, sans-serif; font-size: 85%;}
h1 {color: teal; font-family: "Trebuchet MS", Verdana, Geneva, Arial, Helvetica,
    sans-serif;
    font-size: 2em; line-height: 2.5em; color: teal; text-align: center}
.quotation {font-style: italic; text-indent: 2em; text-align: left;}
```

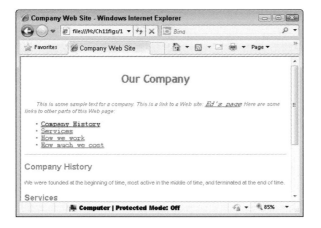

Figure 11-5: The first-level heading is centered; the first paragraph is indented and left-aligned.

Indenting text

You can define the amount of space that should precede the first line of a paragraph by using the text-indent property.

Using the text-indent property doesn't indent the whole paragraph — only the first line. To accomplish indenting a whole paragraph, you need to use CSS box properties, such as margin-left and margin-right (see Chapter 10).

Syntax for indenting text

The style declaration used to indent text is

```
selector {text-indent: value;}
```

Here, *value* must be one of the standard length-property measurement values (listed in Chapter 9).

Markup for indenting text

As seen in this chapter, the quotation class has a text-indent of 2em.

```
body {color: #808000; font-family: Verdana, sans-serif; font-size: 85%;}
.quotation {font-style: italic; text-indent: 2em;}
```

Text Treatments

CSS allows you to decorate your text by using boldface, italics, underline, overline, or line-through, and even allows your text to blink (when that's supported by browsers).

Embolden with bold

Using a boldface font is one of the more common text embellishments a designer uses. To apply boldface in HTML, use the <b> tag. However, CSS provides you with more control over the font weight of the bolded text.

Syntax for applying bold

This style declaration uses the font-weight property:

```
selector {font-weight: value;}
```

The value of the font-weight property may be one of the following:

- ✔ bold: Renders the text in an average bold weight
- ✔ bolder: Relative value that renders a font weight bolder than the current weight (possibly assigned by a parent element)
- ✔ lighter: Relative value that renders a font weight lighter than the current weight (possibly assigned by a parent element)
- ✔ normal: Removes any bold formatting
- ✔ One of these integer values: 100 (lightest), 200, 300, 400 (normal), 500, 600, 700 (standard bold), 800, 900 (darkest)

Markup for applying bold

The following example bolds hyperlinks (see Figure 11-6), turns the underline off, and changes the color to green once a link is visited (we did this to the Company History item to show you what it looks like):

```
body {color: black; font-family: Arial, sans-serif; font-size: 85%;}
a {font-weight: bold;}
a:link {color: olive; text-decoration: underline;}
a:visited {color: green; text-decoration: none;}
```

Emphasizing with italic

Italics are commonly used to set off quotations or to emphasize text. To apply italics in HTML, use the <i> tag. However, CSS provides you with more control over the font style of text through the font-style property.

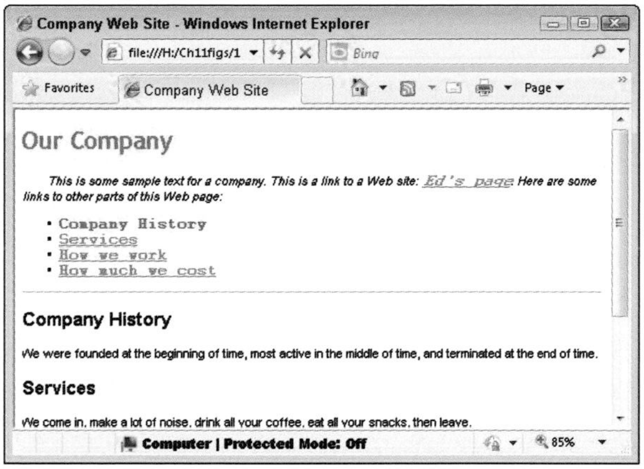

Figure 11-6: All hyperlinks are bolded.

Syntax for applying italic

This style declaration uses the `font-style` property:

```
selector {font-style: value;}
```

The value of the `font-style` property may be one of the following:

- ✔ `italic`: Renders the text in *italics* (a special font that usually slopes to the right)
- ✔ `oblique`: Renders the text as *oblique* (a different slanted version of a normal font; seldom if ever used for font definitions)
- ✔ `normal`: Removes any italic or oblique formatting

Markup for applying italic

The following example assigns an italic font style to the first-level heading:

```
body {color: #808000; font-family: Verdana, sans-serif; font-size: 85%;}
h1 {color: teal; font-family: "MS Trebuchet", Arial, Helvetica, sans-serif;
    text-transform: uppercase; font-style: italic; font-weight: 800;
    font-size: 2em; line-height: 30pt; text-align: center;}
```

Changing capitalization

You use the `text-transform` property to set capitalization in your document.

Syntax for changing capitalization

This style declaration uses the `text-transform` property:

```
selector {text-transform: value;}
```

The value of the `text-transform` property may be one of the following:

- ✔ `capitalize`: Capitalizes the first character in every word

- ✔ `uppercase`: Renders all letters of the text of the specified element in uppercase

- ✔ `lowercase`: Renders all letters of the text of the specified element in lowercase

- ✔ `none`: Keeps the value of the inherited element

Markup for changing capitalization

The following example renders the first-level heading in uppercase (shown in Figure 11-7):

```
body {color: black; font-family: Arial, sans-serif; font-size: 85%;}
    a {font-weight: bold;}
    a:link {color: olive; text-decoration: underline;}
    a:visited {color: green; text-decoration: none;}
    h1 {font-family: "Trebuchet MS", verdana, geneva, arial, helvetica, sans-
            serif;
    font-size: 2em; line-height: 2.5em; color: teal; text-transform: uppercase;
    text-align: center}
```

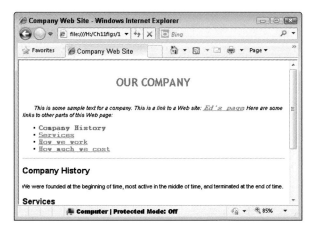

Figure 11-7: The first-level heading is rendered in all uppercase.

Getting fancy with the text-decoration property

The text-decoration property allows for text formatting that's a tad crazier. It isn't used often.

Syntax for text decoration

This style declaration uses the text-decoration property:

```
selector {text-decoration: value;}
```

The value of the text-decoration property may be one of the following:

- ✔ underline: Underlines text
- ✔ overline: Renders the text with a line over it
- ✔ line-through: Renders the text with a line through it
- ✔ blink: Blinks the text onscreen

  Are you *sure* you want blinking text?

  - blink isn't supported by all browsers.
  - blink can be dreadfully annoying and distracting.

- ✔ none: Removes any text decoration

Markup for text decoration

The following example changes the link when the mouse hovers over it. In this case, it turns off any underlining for a link:

```
body {color: #808000; font-family: Verdana, sans-serif; font-size: 85%;}
a:link {color: olive; text-decoration: underline;}
a:visited {color: olive; text-decoration: underline;}
a:hover {color: olive; text-decoration: none;}
```

The Catchall Font Property

Many font properties can be summarized in one style declaration by using the shorthand font property. When it's used, only one style rule is needed to define a combination of font properties:

```
selector {font: value value value;}
```

The value of the `font` property is a list of any values that correspond to the various font properties:

- ✔ The following values must be defined in the following order although they don't have to be consecutive:

  - `font-size` (required)

  - `line-height` (optional)

  - `font-family` (required)

    The `font-family` value list must end with a semicolon.

  Use commas to separate multiple font family names. For example, you can use the following style declaration to create a specific style for paragraph text that specifies font-size, line-height, and font-family in that (required) order:

  ```
  p {font: 1.5em bold 150% Arial, Helvetica, sans-serif;}
  ```

- ✔ The following values are optional and may occur in any order within the declaration. Individual values are separated by spaces:

  - `font-style`

  - `font-variant`

  - `font-weight`

For example, you can use the following style declaration to create a specific style for a first-level heading that mixes the optional values in among the required ones (font-style and font-weight before line-height and font-family in this case, with font-size and font-variant omitted):

```
h1 {font: italic bold 150% Arial, Helvetica, sans-serif;}
```

Part IV
Scripting and (X)HTML

The 5th Wave   By Rich Tennant

J. MONK OPTOMETRIST

"Games are an important part of my Web site. They cause eye strain."

In this part . . .

Here, we introduce and describe the types of scripting languages that work on Web pages, and dig lightly into JavaScript — by far the most popular of all Web-scripting languages. Scripting languages help static, unchanging Web pages become active, dynamic documents that can solicit and respond to user input.

Next, you dig more deeply into working with forms so you can understand how to solicit — and deal with — input from your users. The following chapter shows how to embed third-party services and information — such as Flickr, Twitter, Google Maps, and YouTube — to make your pages more dynamic and interesting while leveraging the work of others.

The next chapter shows you ways to put JavaScript to work in your Web pages. You pick up the basic concepts and techniques for creating dynamic HTML (sometimes called DHTML) and using client-side JavaScripts and prefabricated code to perform basic tasks, such as displaying date and time information, counting site visitors, or tabulating current statistics. Part IV concludes with an overview of Web-based content management systems (CMS), including WordPress, Joomla!, and Drupal.

Chapter 12

Top 20 CSS Properties

In This Chapter

▶ Digging into backgrounds and borders

▶ Fiddling with fonts, spacing, and positioning

▶ Managing text color and line-height

▶ Linking up with pseudo classes

▶ Making the most of online CSS resources

*A*s you can see in Chapters 9–11, there's an awful lot you can do with Cascading Style Sheet (CSS) markup to manage and control how Web pages behave inside users' browsers. In this chapter, we single out a small subset of 20 specific CSS properties that you're most likely to encounter — and use — on even fairly simple Web pages. Of course, we know this won't be enough for real Web-heads, or even aspiring ones, so this chapter also includes a tasty set of *nonpareil* CSS references where you can dig up more details and learn about other properties to your heart's content.

 Eric A. Meyer not only wrote the Foreword for this book, but he's also authored numerous gems of his own on the subject of CSS. Be sure to check out his many CSS-related titles, especially the invaluable *Smashing CSS: Professional Techniques for Modern Layout* (Wiley).

Background Properties

As a CSS concept, *background* refers to numerous properties (six in all) introduced with CSS 1.0 to manage what goes behind elements on display in a Web page. Table 12-1 lists all the background properties, after which we provide examples and details for two of the properties. To read more about background properties and other CSS markup, visit the "Best CSS Resources" section at the end of this chapter for additional information and useful tips.

Table 12-1	Background Properties
Property	*Description*
`background`	Shorthand placeholder for all background properties
`background-attachment`	Determines whether background image remains fixed or scrolls with the page
`background-color`	Sets background color for related element
`background-image`	Supplies background image for related element as URL
`background-position`	Sets starting position for background image
`background-repeat`	Determines how background image repeats on page

background-color

The `background-color` property allows you to establish a solid color for an element's background, including any associated padding and border settings that go with it. Colors may be assigned by name, as described and illustrated on the online Cheat Sheet at `www.dummies.com/cheatsheet/html` (aqua, black, blue, fuchsia, and so forth) or by hex code number. (Color values and hex code numbers are discussed in more detail in Chapter 11.)

In the code for the Web page displayed in Figure 12-1, we set the text color for the `body` element to olive (`#808000`) for text. We then define a basic style rule for the default level one (`h1`) heading shown at the top with a gray `background-color`, and black text. The second heading uses a class instance named `alt-h1` to set large margins, padding, and borders to create a large silver background area around the text and an indent to the left.

 Visit the Web site for this book at `www.dummieshtml.com`, and then check the listings for Chapter 12 for easy access to all source code used to produce screenshots in this book (find links for figures by number: 12-1, 12-2, and so on).

background-image

Use the `background-image` property to use an image instead of a solid color as the background for an element. We take the code from Figure 12-1, make `alt-h1` text italic, and replace `background-color: silver;` with `background-image: url(texture.jpg);`, where a photographic texture is the background (see Figure 12-2).

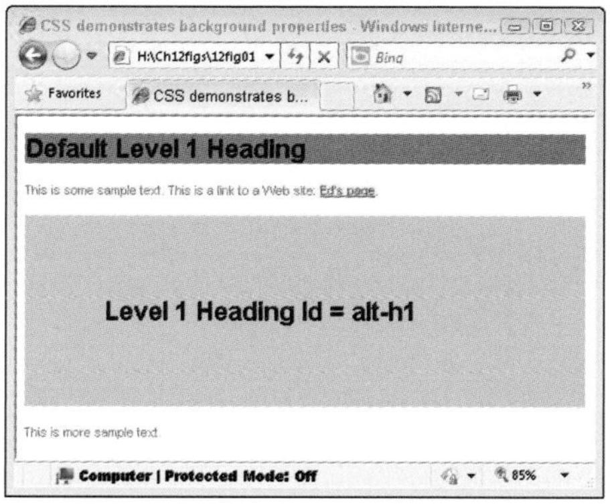

![Screenshot of a browser window titled "CSS demonstrates background properties" showing a Default Level 1 Heading, sample text with a link, and a gray box containing "Level 1 Heading id = alt-h1", followed by "This is more sample text."]

Figure 12-1: A general style rule defines `h1` appearance, further refined by instance `alt-h1`.

When using images as background, repetitive textures or relatively quiet abstract images work best, particularly if you want users to be able to read foreground text.

![Screenshot of a browser window titled "CSS demonstrates background properties" showing a Default Level 1 Heading, sample text, and a box with a photographic diagonal-slash texture background containing "Level 1 Heading id = alt-h1".]

Figure 12-2: This time, the `alt-h1` instance picks up a photo as the background.

Border and Outline Properties

Borders and outlines define the edges and help to make boundaries around elements visible. You'll find all kinds of controls for individual edges as well as for color, style, and width. To keep the jargon straight, a *border* falls just inside the edge of an element box, whereas an *outline* includes that edge. Table 12-2 lists the various border and outline properties along with a description of what they do.

Table 12-2	Border and Outline Properties
Property	*Description*
border	Shorthand for all border properties
border-bottom	Sets all bottom border properties
border-bottom-color	Sets bottom border color
border-bottom-style	Sets bottom border style
border-bottom-width	Sets bottom border width
border-color	Sets color for all four borders
border-left	Sets all left border properties
border-left-color	Sets left border color
border-left-style	Sets left border style
border-left-width	Sets left border width
border-right	Sets all right border properties
border-right-color	Sets right border color
border-right-style	Sets right border style
border-right-width	Sets right border width
border-style	Sets style for all four borders
border-top	Sets all top border properties
border-top-color	Sets top border color
border-top-style	Sets top border style
border-top-width	Sets top border width
border-width	Sets width for all four borders
outline	Sets all outline properties
outline-color	Sets outline color
outline-style	Sets outline style
outline-width	Sets outline width

border

For CSS, `border` is a *shorthand property:* That is, it combines width, style, and color in a single declaration. Each of these three components applies to the top, right, bottom, and left edges of an element box, in that order. Here's a mnemonic: We use TRBL — that's right, *trouble* — as shorthand for the order of top, right, bottom, and left.

This single CSS property actually permits as many as 12 subsidiary properties to be set at the same time. In the example shown in Figure 12-3, we surround paragraphs with thin dashed purple lines, thereby addressing width (thin), color (purple), and style (dashed) in a single declaration. Although you can control settings for each such characteristic per edge (in TRBL order), it's seldom necessary to do so.

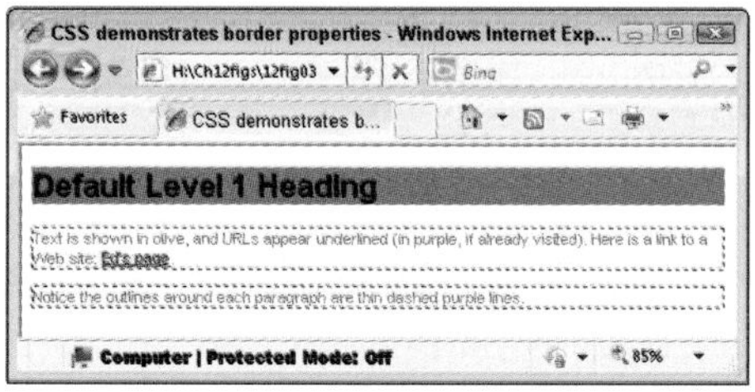

Figure 12-3: Paragraphs get a thin purple dashed outline on this page.

Feel free to explore other border and outline properties as you see fit. There are quite a few of them, so give yourself some time to learn and play.

Dimension

Dimension properties define size information — namely, height and width — to control where elements are placed on a Web page. In addition to basic height and width, maximum and minimum values for such properties can also be set. Sometimes called "min-max" properties, using these can be helpful to ensure that display areas are always at least as large as some minimum value to make sure visual information doesn't get lost. Min-max can be especially useful when text or images must float on a page. (Also check out the CSS `overflow`, `overflow-clip`, `clip`, and `visibility` properties later in this chapter, in Chapter 20, and on `www.dummieshtml.com` to see how to handle odd, unexpected, or unwanted floating behavior.) Table 12-3 provides a listing of dimension properties.

Table 12-3	Dimension Properties
Property	**Description**
height	Sets element height
max-height	Sets maximum element height
max-width	Sets maximum element width
min-height	Sets minimum element height
min-width	Sets minimum element width
width	Sets element width

height and width

We handle both height and width in a single example, where the image (img) element is sized to occupy 10 percent of a paragraph for each of these properties. This resizes the image to occupy no more than 10 percent of the horizontal dimension of the browser's display window, where height is maintained to preserve the original aspect ratio (see Figure 12-4). Height and width can also be specified using various absolute units of measure (pixels, points, picas, ems, and so forth). Min-max values make sure that elements never get too big or too small.

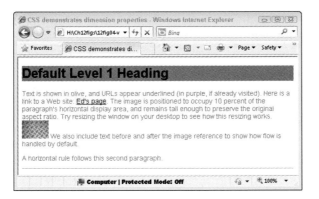

Figure 12-4: Use height and width properties to set element size and preserve aspect ratio.

These properties are best played within an editor, along with resizing your browser window, to best understand how things work.

Fonts and Font Properties

CSS not only allows you to manage font properties galore, it also allows you to associate fonts with specific (X)HTML elements, and even define arbitrary sequences of fonts to use for those elements.

If you want to reference a font whose name includes any embedded spaces, enclose that name in double quotation marks (*not* smart quotes) so that browsers can identify and use them if available on their host machines.

As you can see in Table 12-4, the shortcut `font` property covers a huge range of values, so dig into this carefully and master to use it!

Table 12-4	Font Properties
Property	*Description*
font	Shortcut for all font properties
font-family	Sets font family (generic or by name)
font-size	Sets font size (using typical units of measure)
font-style	Sets font style (normal, italic, oblique)
font-variant	Turns small caps on or off (small-caps, normal)
font-weight	Sets font weight (bold, bolder, lighter, 100-900)

font-family

Use the `font-family` property to select fonts by name from your users' installed collection. You can assign multiple comma-separated values (CVSs) to this property in CSS markup. The browser will use the first match it finds, starting from the leftmost specification. Always end a string of font specifications with a generic font name, such as `serif` or `sans-serif`, so that a local system can always use a default selection should all else fail (or be absent). In Figure 12-5, we select Arial as our level one heading font, and we use Lucida Console as our body (paragraph) font, but also show off a variety of fonts including also Arial Black, Book Antiqua, Tahoma, Times New Roman, Comic Sans, and Cooper Black.

Figure 12-5: Fonts on display include heavy black fonts (Cooper and Arial) plus other serif and sans serif choices.

font-weight

The font-weight property determines how light or heavy type is drawn on a page. In our example in Figure 12-6, we identify all the named font-weights as well as all the recognizable numeric font-weight values. Notice that you really can't tell much difference between bold and bolder, and that the numeric values don't show uniform gradations either. For most page designers, bold is bold enough, and numbers 200–500 and 600–900 appear interchangeable. Font designers often build black versions of font faces (for example, Arial Black or Cooper Black), which might be better used with its plain-vanilla counterpart (Arial or Cooper) to create heavier font weights or more weight variations.

font-size

The font-size property is the setting that manages how big or small a font looks onscreen. For truly small type, use points (pt) for sizing; most normal paragraph fonts are usually 10pt to 12pt. Fonts smaller than 6pt are hard to see onscreen. Sizing fonts in whole ems can get out of hand pretty quickly. You can use the source page for the example shown in Figure 12-7 to conduct your own font-sizing *experiments* pretty quickly, if you like.

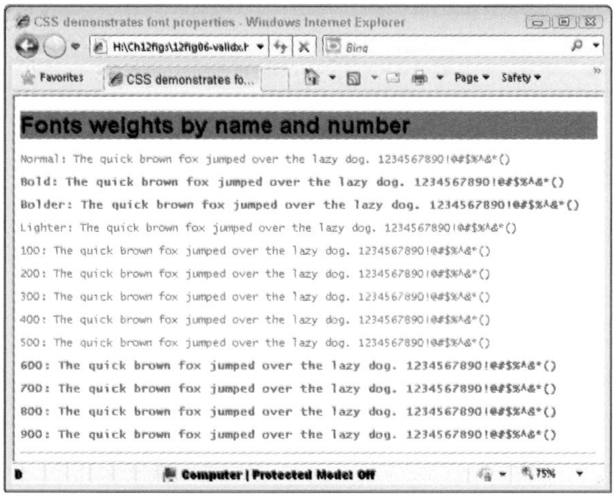

Figure 12-6: Although font weights are many, there isn't much difference onscreen.

Figure 12-7: Usable font sizes must be big enough to see, and small enough not to overwhelm the page.

Spacing Properties: Margin and Padding

Margins define space around the edges for block elements that background colors don't fill. *Padding* defines space around the edges for block elements that background colors do fill. Table 12-5 holds these properties. Although we discuss these two shorthand properties and their constituent properties separately in the text that follows, we combine them in a single example in Figure 12-8 to better compare and contrast them and also to show how they work together. We also include borders to show where element box outlines reside as well.

Table 12-5	Margin and Padding Properties
Property	*Description*
margin	Shortcut for all margin properties (TRBL)
margin-bottom	Sets element bottom margin
margin-left	Sets element left margin
margin-right	Sets element right margin
margin-top	Sets element top margin
padding	Shortcut for all padding properties (TRBL)
padding-bottom	Sets element bottom padding
padding-left	Sets element left padding
padding-right	Sets element right padding
padding-top	Sets element top padding

margin

Like padding, margin is a shortcut property, where the constituent values address TRBL (as we discuss earlier: top, right, bottom, and left) edges, in that order. If you supply a single value for margin, it applies to all four edges alike. Thus, for example, the CSS margin: 0.5em; is identical to margin-top: 0.5em; margin-right: 0.5em; margin-bottom: 0.5em; margin-left: 0.5em;.

padding

Like margin, padding is a shortcut property, where the constituent values address TRBL edges, in that order. If you supply a single value for padding, it applies to all four edges alike. Here again, the CSS padding: 0.5em; is identical to `padding-top: 0.5em; padding-right: 0.5em; padding-bottom: 0.5em; padding-left: 0.5em;`.

Close inspection of the figure shows that padding extends the text box around the element, including the background. Using `margin`, on the other hand, moves the edges of the text box away from the edge of the parent text box so that content is indented all the way around. The combination of the two (see the final pair of elements in Figure 12-8) extends the background around the elements (padding) and moves the edges to accommodate their margins.

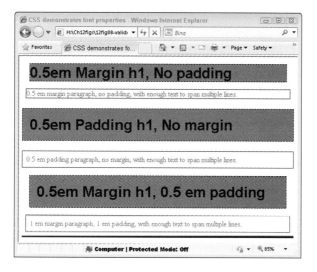

Figure 12-8: Margin and padding at work separately and together.

Positioning

Positioning controls (see Table 12-6) define where elements appear on a page, how elements relate to one another, and how text flows (or doesn't) around various elements. The TRBL properties (top, right, bottom, and left) come into play here, and elements may be positioned *absolutely* (with reference to the origin, or upper-left corner of the page) or *relatively* (with reference to whatever element encloses them).

HTML source code for all of the figures in this chapter (and the rest of the book) are available at `www.dummieshtml.com`. There, you can find the relevant source in the Chapter 12 section (labeled Figure 12-1, Figure 12-2, and so on).

Table 12-6	Positioning Properties
Property	*Description*
bottom	Sets bottom margin edge for positioned box
clear	Blocks element edges to other floating elements
clip	Clips absolutely positioned element
cursor	Selects type of cursor for display
display	Selects what box type an element should generate
float	Turns box float on or off
left	Sets left margin edge for positioned box
overflow	Controls how content overflows an element box
overlow-clip	Controls how content overflows an element box
position	Selects positioning type for an element
right	Sets right margin edge for a positioned box
top	Sets top margin edge for a positioned box
visibility	Turns element visibility on or off
z-index	Assigns stack order for an element (numeric)

float

Use float to direct how text flows around an element. Floating has been around ever since the days when various Web browsers provided nonstandard HTML "extensions" to permit page designers to "float" images to the right- or left-hand side of a Web page. CSS makes this standard, and applies it equally to text blocks (such as paragraphs or lists) and to images. float can take the values left, right, or none (the default) as we show in Figure 12-9.

Notice that both left and right float push atop the background for the h1 headings in Figure 12-9. (We show you how to fix this in the upcoming section, "clear.") This illustrates that managing float (and where img elements get placed in paragraphs) can be important. Our final paragraph with no float shows how graphics can plop onto the page wherever they're called: That's not ideal, either, even if it doesn't overlap with other elements on the page.

z-index

When you start positioning multiple elements on a page (as we did in Chapter 10 with a menu and a photograph), overlap can occur, and may sometimes even be desirable. The z-index adds a third dimension for positioning, along the lines of depth as in 3D coordinates (x, y, and z). On a Web page, the z-index value is purely relative. It's used to manage display order, so higher values sit "closer" to the front of the screen, and lower ones sit closer to the back. In other words, when drawing boxes in which elements sit, a browser gives precedence to those with higher numbers when some boxes with lower numbers occupy the same space. In Chapter 10, we show how to use z-index with a menu and a photo, and explain in the markup for Figure 10-4 that a negative z-index goes behind everything with a positive z-index. For a quick illustration, check it out!

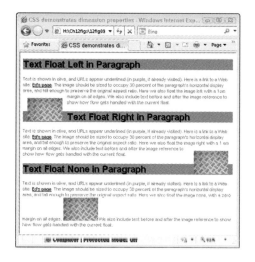

Figure 12-9: Float settings make it easy to move items inside text blocks, but also show why other positioning tools are absolutely necessary.

Exercise caution when using z-index, and make certain it's defined for your CSS menu (or anything else with dynamic properties that might overlap an embedded object when performing a function call). Furthermore, an undefined z-index can cause display issues when using CSS with Flash. Flash often includes a default z-index in its action-script that may conflict.

clear

To solve the problem illustrated in Figure 12-9, where the images floated into the heading backgrounds in the second and third paragraphs, using clear enables designers to prevent such impingement. clear can take these values: left, right, both, and none (the default). Because overlap occurs after an image and text flows from left to right, adding clear: right; to image markup fixes this problem, as shown in Figure 12-10.

Figure 12-10: Use clear to enforce the margin around an element.

cursor

Using the `cursor` property changes the appearance of the mouse cursor in a Web browser as it hovers over specific elements. Numerous values can be assigned to this property, so experiment to see how they look in various browsers and whether you can use them to good effect. Figure 12-11 uses four texture images, each with a different cursor so you can see how this looks for yourself onscreen. (It's hard to show dynamic behavior in a book, so we made a collage of screenshots from the same underlying page.)

CSS supports as many as 17 different cursor styles, so be sure to spend some time experimenting with different values that the `cursor` property can take.

Text

Some people might argue that text properties are the most important elements in the CSS collection. We don't want to fight about this, for sure, but instead recommend that you dig into Table 12-7 to see what's available for controlling text appearance and behavior while it's on display using CSS. We think you'll be amazed, but we hope you'll also be pleased.

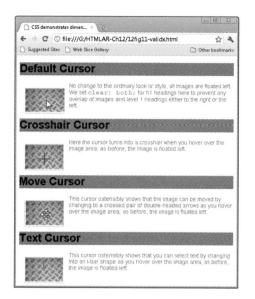

Figure 12-11: A composite of multiple screenshots shows various cursor styles.

Table 12-7	Text Properties
Property	**Description**
color	Sets text color of text (name or hex code)
direction	Specifies text/writing direction (ltr or rtl)
letter-spacing	Manages space between characters in text
line-height	Sets line height
text-align	Sets horizontal alignment (left, right, justify, center)
text-decoration	Specifies decoration added to text
text-indent	Sets indent for first line in a text-block
text-shadow	Sets text shadow effect added
text-transform	Controls text capitalization
vertical-align	Sets vertical element alignment
white-space	Manages space between words in text
word-spacing	Manages space between words in text

color

Use `color` to, um, establish color for text within elements, where colors may be assigned by using names or hex codes. (See the online Cheat Sheet at `http://www.dummies.com/how-to/content/html-xhtml-css-for-dummies-cheat-sheet.html` for a sizable list of such names and values.) We show this capability throughout Chapters 9–11, and this chapter as well, so we don't illustrate it here.

line-height

The `line-height` property sets the height for the inline boxes (those allocated for each line of text) in a text block of some kind. Use `line-height` as an easy way to expand or compress the space between lines of text, as the example in Figure 12-12 shows.

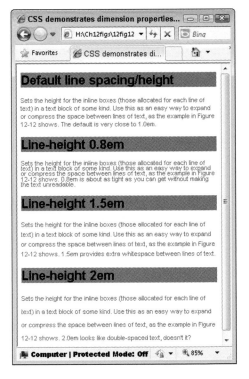

Figure 12-12: Various line heights show the effects of varying this property.

Pseudo Classes

Pseudo classes in CSS may seem a little strange at first: They take some getting used to because they modify (X)HTML elements. That explains why Table 12-8 starts each pseudo class name with a colon (it acts as a delimiter with the element it modifies, and it signals the presence of a CSS pseudo class). Generally, pseudo classes serve to make content on Web pages more dynamic and interactive, as you'll discover when you get comfortable with them.

Table 12-8	CSS Pseudo Classes
Pseudo Class	*Description*
:active	Adds a style to an activated element
:after	Adds content following an element
:before	Adds content preceding an element
:first-child	Adds a style to first child element inside another element
:first-letter	Adds a style to first character in a text sequence
:first-line	Adds a style to first line in a text sequence
:focus	Adds a style to element with keyboard input focus
:hover	Adds a style to element as you mouse over it
:lang	Adds a style to any element with a specific language attribute
:link	Adds a style to unvisited link
:visited	Adds a style to visited link

By far, the most widely used pseudo classes apply to (X)HTML links. In the example in the next section, we combine :hover, :link, and :visited to show how this works (and looks).

:hover, :link, and :visited

The pseudo classes :hover, :link, and :visited all apply to hyperlinks.

- :hover comes into play when the mouse cursor hovers over a hyperlink.
- :link applies style to a hyperlink that has not yet been visited.
- :visited applies style to a hyperlink that has been visited.

All these behaviors are readily visible in the code created for Figure 12-13.

In our example, we change `font-variant` for visited links to small caps, and use the `linethrough` (strikethrough) text decoration. Unvisited links use a larger font with an underline. When you hover over a link, it turns bold and red, and the cursor changes from a pointer to a hand.

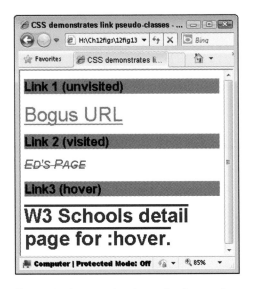

Figure 12-13: Link-related pseudo classes change the appearance of hyperlinks in response to visitation state and mouse activity.

Best CSS Resources

The following collection of Web sites offers some outstanding references on CSS and its proper use on well-crafted Web pages. The very first reference from W3Schools.com is terrific, and provided much of the raw material on which Tables 12-1 through 12-8 were based.

W3Schools.com

www.w3schools.com/css/css_reference.asp

This is a great online resource that offers CSS definitions and usage, related pages, browsers supported, examples, and even the ability to "try it yourself" in a controlled environment (beats fiddling HTML documents manually) at www.w3schools.com/css/tryit.asp?filename=trycss_background.

Firebug

http://getfirebug.com

This is by far the best browser resource for debugging and figuring out why in the world your CSS or HTML pages aren't behaving like you think they should. Using this Firefox plugin, you can select elements on a page and see which CSS properties are currently assigned, by file (if you have multiple style sheets) or even by specific line in the source document. You can also instruct this tool to temporarily add or ignore CSS declarations, which makes it very easy to experiment with and debug your CSS markup.

Eric Meyer's Reset

http://meyerweb.com/eric/tools/css/reset/reset.css

This URL above is a great example of a *reset style sheet*. A *reset style sheet* seeks to reduce browser inconsistencies for settings that include default line heights, margins, font sizes in headings, and so on. The general reasoning behind reset is discussed in Meyer's May 2007 blog post entitled "Reset Reloaded" (http://meyerweb.com/eric/thoughts/2007/05/01/reset-reloaded). Reset styles appear quite often in CSS frameworks, and Meyer's original "meyerweb reset" was incorporated into the Blueprint home page (www.blueprintcss.org), among many others. Reset style sheets are definitely worth learning about as well as applying to your own Web design efforts. If you click the preceding link, you'll see a text listing of the entire reset.css style sheet.

Spoon Browser Sandbox

www.spoon.net/browsers

Unfortunately, CSS sometimes displays differently in different browsers. To avoid designing what you think is a really great site only to discover that everything gets jumbled in some other browser you didn't try out, use this site. Right now, Spoon Browser Sandbox is PC-only, but it allows you to remotely launch Web browsers that aren't even installed on your computer. Use it to see what your pages look like in multiple versions of Internet Explorer, Firefox, Opera, Chrome, and Safari.

W3C CSS Validation Service

http://jigsaw.w3.org/css-validator

Check CSS and (X)HTML documents with style sheets with this fine, free, online tool. Point it at publicly accessible Web pages, upload files to it, or drop code into a text box to check its contents.

Web-Developer's Handbook

`www.alvit.de/handbook`

This site is almost overkill, featuring a really big directory of CSS links and general links related to Web design. Numerous sections on CSS cover daily reading, showcases and galleries, tools and services, specifications, and lots, lots more. Give yourself some time to chew through this compendium; there's an amazing amount of good stuff to masticate here!

YSlow

`https://addons.mozilla.org/en-US/firefox/addon/5369`

Drawing from a set of rules used on high-performance Web pages, YSlow analyzes Web pages to suggest ways to improve their performance. YSlow is a Firefox add-on for the Firebug Web development tool. It grades Web pages by using one of three predefined rulesets or a user-defined ruleset. In addition, YSlow also offers suggestions to improve page performance, summarizes page components, displays page statistics, and provides performance analyses such as Smush.it and JSLint.

Chapter 13

Scripting Web Pages

In This Chapter

▶ Exploring what JavaScript can do for your Web pages

▶ Arranging content

▶ Opening new windows

▶ Checking user input

▶ Exploring more uses for JavaScript

*W*hen used in conjunction with your HTML markup, *scripts* — small programs that you add to your Web page — help your Web pages respond to user actions. Scripts create the interactive and dynamic effects you see on the Web, such as images that automatically change when visitors move mouse pointers over them, additional browser windows that pop up when a page loads, and animated or interactive navigation bars.

Because scripts are mini-programs, they're often written in a programming language called JavaScript. If you're unfamiliar with the term, JavaScript may sound like a Hollywood screenplay doused with coffee. However, it is actually a scripting language built right into all popular Web browsers.

Fortunately, because of the Nobel Prize–worthy invention of "copy and paste," you don't need to be a technoguru to add scripting to your Web sites. The Web has many sites that feature canned JavaScript elements that you can freely copy and then paste right into your Web page. (Chapter 14 lists several of the best JavaScript sites.)

Many good Web page editors (such as Adobe Dreamweaver and Adobe Fireworks) include built-in tools to help you create scripts — even if you don't know anything about programming.

In this chapter, you explore how scripting works inside your Web page by dissecting three sample scripts written in JavaScript. If you're interested in learning more about JavaScript and how it works, please check out *JavaScript For Dummies,* 5th Edition, by Emily Vander Veer, for more information and to dive a little deeper into the JavaScript language itself.

Finding Out What JavaScript Can Do for Your Pages

Adding scripts to your Web site is much like those reality-TV makeover shows that transform a house or a person's appearance into something completely new and wonderful. The same is true with JavaScript. You can transform a plain, dull Web page into an interactive and dynamic Web extravaganza to bring joy to your visitors for years to come. (Okay, maybe we're exaggerating just a tad, but you get the point.)

For example, if you visit Dummies.com (`www.dummies.com`) and click the blue Search button next to the Start Exploring box without entering a term to search on, the browser displays a nice warning box that reminds you to enter a search term before you actually search, as shown in Figure 13-1.

Figure 13-1: The search term is empty — that is, missing.

A short script verifies whether you entered a search term before the engine runs the query:

- ✔ If you enter a search term, you don't see the warning.
- ✔ If you don't enter a search term, the script built into the page prompts the dialog box to appear.

JavaScript is not Java

In the late 1990s, the originators of the JavaScript scripting language wanted to ride the coattails of the massive popularity of the Java programming language, so they gave it a catchy name — JavaScript. However, when they made this decision, they also introduced a lot of confusion given the similarity of the two names. To clarify, the full-featured Java programming language *isn't* a scripting language on the Web. Java is a descendent of the C and C++ programming languages. Programmers can create Java applications that can run on Windows, Macintosh, Linux, and other computer platforms:

- On the client side, Java is used to create *applets* (small programs that download over the Net and run inside Web browsers). Because Java is designed to be cross-platform, these applets should run identically on any Java-enabled browser.

- On the server side, Java is used to create many Web-based applications.

This bit of scripting makes the page *dynamic,* which means that it adds programmed functionality to your Web pages, allowing them to respond to what users do on the page (for example, filling out a form or moving the mouse pointer over an image). When you add scripts to your page, the page interacts with users and changes its display or its behavior in response to what users do.

The page URL doesn't change, and another browser window doesn't open when you try to search on nothing. The page responds to what you do without sending a request back to the Web server for a new page. This is why the page is considered *dynamic.*

If you try this trick without using a script (that is, without dynamic functionality), the browser would send the empty search string back to the Web server. Then the server would return a warning page reminding the user to enter a search term. All the work would be done on the Web server instead of in the Web browser. This is slower because the request must first go to the server, and then the server must transmit the warning page back to your browser — and thus the server feels much less fluid to the user. It's much better to just click a button on the page and have an alert pop up instantly to help the user.

In the following sections, we showcase three common ways in which JavaScript can be used in your Web pages.

Don't worry about the details of the JavaScript code in the following examples. Just focus on how JavaScript scripts can be pasted into your Web page to work alongside your HTML markup.

Using JavaScript to Arrange Content Dynamically

JavaScript can be used with Cascading Style Sheets (CSS; covered in Chapters 9–12) to change the look of a page's content in response to a user action. Here's an example: Two writers share a blog named Backup Brain (www.backupbrain.com). One of the writers prefers small, sans serif type, and the other one finds it easier to read larger, serif type, so the blog has buttons that change the look of the site to match each person's preference. Of course, site visitors can use the buttons to switch the look of the type, too, and the site remembers the visitor's choice for future visits by setting a *cookie* (a small preference file written to the user's computer). Figure 13-2 shows the two looks for the page.

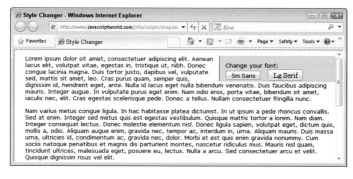

Figure 13-2: Change how text displays.

JavaScript and CSS create this effect by switching between two style sheets:

- The sans serif style sheet, sansStyle.css
- The serif style sheet, serifStyle.css

Listing 13-1 shows the source code for an example page that contains the switching mechanism shown in Figure 13-2:

- When a user clicks the Sm Sans button on the page, the styleSwitcher.js script referenced in the <head> element runs and switches the active style sheet to sansStyle.css. (.js is the file extension that's used with JavaScript files, as in the src value for the script element in Listing 13-1.)

- When the user clicks the Lg Serif button, the same script switches to the serifStyle.css style sheet.

Listing 13-1: Style Switching

```
<!DOCTYPE html PUBLIC "-//W3C//DTD XHTML 1.0 Transitional//EN"
        "http://www.w3.org/TR/xhtml1/DTD/xhtml1-transitional.dtd">
<html xmlns="http://www.w3.org/1999/xhtml" lang="en" xml:lang="en">
<head>
    <title>Style Changer</title>
    <meta http-equiv="Content-Type" content="text/html; charset=ISO-8859-1" />
    <link href="simpleStyle.css" rel="stylesheet" rev="stylesheet" />
    <link href="sansStyle.css" rel="stylesheet" rev="stylesheet"
        title="default" />
    <link href="serifStyle.css" rel="alternate stylesheet"
        rev="alternate stylesheet" title="serif" />
    <style type="text/css" media="all">@import url("complexStyle.css");</style>
    <script src="styleSwitcher.js" language="javascript1.5"
        type="text/javascript"></script>
</head>
<body>
<div class="navBar">
<br />Change your font:
<form action="none">
    <input type="button" class="typeBtn" value="Sm Sans"
        onclick="setActiveStylesheet('default')" />
    <input type="button" class="typeBtn2" value="Lg Serif"
        onclick="setActiveStylesheet('serif')" />
</form>
</div>

<div class="content" id="headContent">
<p>Replace this paragraph with your own content.</p>
</div>
</body>
</html>
```

You can see the example page for yourself at www.javascriptworld.com/
js5e/scripts/chap16/ex6/index.html.

This example relies on several different files (HTML, CSS, and JavaScript).
You can download all these files, if you'd like, from www.javascriptworld.
com/js5e/scripts/index.html.

The Font Style Changer files appear in the Chapter 16.

Working with Browser Windows

JavaScript can tell your browser to open and close windows.

You've probably seen an annoying version of this trick: advertising pop-up
windows that appear when you try to leave a site. (Let's not go there.) This
technology can be used for good as well as evil, though. For example, you
can *preview* a set of big image files with small thumbnail versions. Clicking a
thumbnail image can perform such actions as

- Opening a window with a larger version of the image.
- Opening a page with a text link that opens a window with an illustration
  of that text, as shown in Figure 13-3.

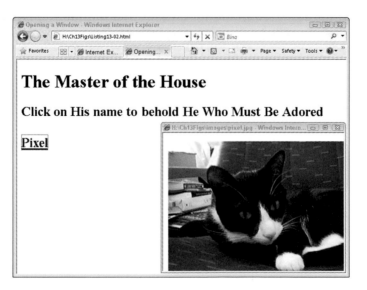

Figure 13-3: When you click the link, a pop-up window appears with
a picture in it.

The code required to do this sort of pop-up window is fairly straightforward, as Listing 13-2 shows with its invocation of the window.open function.

Listing 13-2: Pop-up Windows

```html
<!DOCTYPE html PUBLIC "-//W3C//DTD XHTML 1.0 Transitional//EN"
        "http://www.w3.org/TR/xhtml1/DTD/xhtml1-transitional.dtd">
<html xmlns="http://www.w3.org/1999/xhtml">
<head>
    <title>Opening a Window</title>
    <script language="Javascript" type="text/javascript">

    function newWindow() {
        catWindow = window.open("images/pixel2.jpg", "catWin",
            "width=330,height=250")
    }
    </script>
</head>
<body bgcolor="#FFFFFF">
    <h1>The Master of the House</h1>
    <h2>Click on His name to behold He Who Must Be Adored<br /><br />
    <a href="javascript:newWindow()">Pixel</a></h2>
</body>
</html>
```

Pop-up windows are no longer a best practice and should be used with caution. Overuse of pop-up windows can backfire on you. Many Web sites use pop-up windows to deliver ads, so users are becoming desensitized (or hostile) to them and simply ignore them (or install software that prevents them). Also, some Web browsers — such as Firefox, Safari, and Internet Explorer — automatically block pop-up windows by default these days. Before you add a pop-up window to your site, be sure that it's absolutely necessary. Then, alert your visitors that you'll be using pop-ups so they can instruct their Web browsers to permit them to appear.

Soliciting and Verifying User Input

A common use for JavaScript is to verify that users have filled out all the required fields in a form before the browser actually submits the form to the form processing program on the Web server. Listing 13-3 places a form-checking function, checkSubmit, in the <script> element of the HTML page and references it in the onsubmit attribute of the <form> element.

Listing 13-3: Form Validation

```
<!DOCTYPE html PUBLIC "-//W3C//DTD XHTML 1.0 Transitional//EN"
        "http://www.w3.org/TR/xhtml1/DTD/xhtml1-transitional.dtd">
<html xmlns="http://www.w3.org/1999/xhtml" lang="en" xml:lang="en">
<head>
  <title>Linking scripts to HTML pages</title>
  <meta http-equiv="Content-Type" content="text/html; charset=ISO-8859-1" />
  <script type="text/javascript" language="javascript">
    function checkSubmit ( thisForm ) {
      if ( thisForm.FirstName.value == '' ) {
            alert('Please enter your First Name.');
            return false;
      }

      if ( thisForm.LastName.value == '' ) {
            alert('Please enter your Last Name.');
            return false;
      }

      return true;
    }
</script>
</head>

<body>
  <form method="post" action="/cgi-bin/form_processor.cgi"
        onsubmit="return checkSubmit(this);">
  <p>
    First Name: <input type="text" name="FirstName" /><br />
    Last Name: <input type="text" name="LastName" /><br />
    <input type="submit" />
  </p>
  </form>
</body>
</html>
```

This script performs one of two operations if either form field isn't filled in when the user clicks the Submit button:

- It instructs the browser to display a warning to let the user know that he forgot to fill in a field.
- It returns a value of `false` to the browser, which prevents the browser from submitting the form to the form processing application.

If the fields are filled in correctly, the browser displays no alerts and returns a value of `true`, which tells the browser that the form is ready for the Web server. Figure 13-4 shows how the browser displays an alert if the first name field is empty.

Figure 13-4: A good use of JavaScript is to validate form data.

Although this example only verifies whether users filled out the form fields, you can create more advanced scripts that check for specific data formats, such as using @ signs in e-mail addresses and using only numbers in phone number fields.

When you create forms that include required fields, we recommend that you always include JavaScript field validation to catch missing data before the script finds its way back to the server. Visitors get frustrated when they take the time to fill out a form only to be told to click the Back button to provide missing information. When you use JavaScript, the script catches any missing information before the form page disappears, which allows users to quickly make changes and try to submit again.

But Wait . . . There's More!

You can do much more with JavaScript. The following list highlights several common uses of the scripting language:

- Detect whether a user has a browser plug-in installed that handles multimedia content
- Build slide shows of images
- Automatically redirect the user to a different Web page
- Add conditional logic to your page so that if the user performs a certain action, other actions are triggered
- Create, position, and scroll new browser windows
- Create navigation bars and change the menus on those bars dynamically
- Automatically put the current date and time on your page
- Combine JavaScript and CSS to animate page elements

An innovative use of JavaScript occurs in *Gmail,* the free Web-based e-mail service from Google, which you can find at www.gmail.com. Gmail uses JavaScript to load an entire e-mail user interface into the user's browser, which makes Gmail much more responsive to user actions than most other Web-based mail programs. Gmail uses JavaScript to keep to an absolute minimum the number of times the page has to fetch additional information from the servers. By doing much of the processing in the user's browser, the Gmail Web application feels more like an e-mail program that runs on your computer. Figure 13-5 shows the JavaScript-powered Gmail interface. It's a great example of the power of JavaScript.

Figure 13-5: The Gmail interface is powered by JavaScript.

Server-side scripting

JavaScript is a scripting language that runs inside the browser, but there are other scripting languages that run on the server side, such as Perl, ASP (Active Server Pages), PHP (PHP Hypertext Preprocessor, an (X)HTML embedded scripting language), Python, .NET, and others. Programs written in these languages reside on the server and are called by the Web page, usually in response to a form filled out by the user. People who write these Web pages may include snippets of code that pass bits of information from the HTML page to the program on

the server. When called, the program runs and then returns a result of some sort to the user.

Amazon (www.amazon.com) runs a familiar e-commerce Web application that runs mostly on the server side, using server scripts. Web pages displayed by the browser when you visit Amazon result from processing server-side scripts, all of which take place before the page ever hits your browser. If you'd like more information on JavaScript and what it can do for you, check out *JavaScript For Dummies, Quick Reference* by Emily A. Vander Veer.

Chapter 14

Working with Forms

In This Chapter

▶ Using forms in your Web pages

▶ Creating forms

▶ Working with form data

▶ Designing easy-to-use forms

▶ Making forms easy with a form framework

*M*ost of the HTML you write helps you display content and information for your users. Sometimes, however, you want a Web page to gather information from users instead of giving static information to them. HTML *form markup elements* give you a healthy collection of tags and attributes for creating forms to collect information from visitors to your site.

This chapter covers the many different uses for forms. It also shows you how to use form markup tags to create just the right form for soliciting information from your users, reviews your options for working with the data you receive, and gives you some tips for creating easy-to-use forms that really help your users provide the information you're looking for.

Uses for Forms

The Web contains millions of forms, but every form is driven by the same set of markup tags. Web forms can be short or long, simple or complex, and they have myriad uses. But forms all fall into one of two broad categories:

- ✔ **Search forms** that let users search a site or the entire Web
- ✔ **Data collection forms** that provide information for online shopping, technical support, site preferences, and personalization

Before you create any form markup, you need to determine what kind of data your visitors will search for on your site and/or what kind of data you need to collect from visitors. Your data drives the form elements that you use as well as how you put them together on a page.

Search forms

Search forms help you give visitors information.

The following search forms are from the friendly folks at the Internal Revenue Service (IRS). The difference between these search forms is the data the IRS site needs from you for its search:

- The IRS home page (shown in Figure 14-1) is a simple, multifaceted search form featuring various layout areas to help visitors easily search for tax forms and publications, online services, filing and payment information, task-oriented instructions, and general information. This type of page can produce dozens of relevant responses. Visitors can both

  - Choose the best option.

  - Look at more than one option.

Figure 14-1: The IRS home page offers easy access to forms, publications, and information.

- A more complicated search form, such as the Get Refund Status page (as shown in Figure 14-2), produces only one specific response: namely, IRS records for the status of your income tax refund. Because this page demands detailed information — and after all, because the IRS doesn't want you to see anyone else's refund — it serves dual purposes:

  - Finding data that visitors need

  - Hiding data that visitors shouldn't see

Figure 14-2: Something like a refund status search form is a little more complex.

Searches come in all shapes and sizes, so the search forms that drive those searches come in all shapes and sizes, too. A short keyword search might do the trick, or you might need a more sophisticated search method.

Data collection forms

Data collection forms receive information you want to process or save. When you create a form that collects information, the information you need is what drives the structure and complexity of the form:

- **Just a little:** If you need just a little information, the form may be short and (relatively) sweet.

  Example: The Library of Congress (LoC) uses a form to collect information from teachers to subscribe to a free electronic newsletter, as shown in Figure 14-3. The LoC doesn't need much information to set up the subscription, so the form is short and simple.

- **Lots:** If you need a lot of information, your form may be several pages long.

  Example: RateGenius uses long and detailed forms to gather the information it needs to help customers get the best possible loan rate. The page in Figure 14-4 is just the first of several that a visitor must fill out to provide all the necessary information.

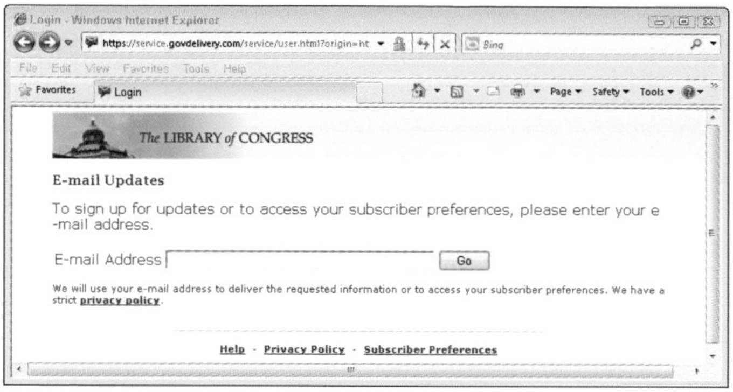

Figure 14-3: A free subscription form collects basic information.

Figure 14-4: Some sites use many detailed forms to collect necessary data.

Creating Forms

HTML forms can present information to users, using text and images. But it can also proffer various types of text input fields (in-line, single line, or multiple lines) as well as various types of data selection tools, such as radio buttons (which let you pick one option from a group), pick lists (which let you fill in a value from a pre-defined set of options), or check boxes (which enable you to pick zero, one, or more values from a predefined set of inputs). All in all, HTML form markup tags and attributes help you

- ✔ Define the overall form structure.
- ✔ Tell the Web browser how to handle the form data.
- ✔ Create input objects, such as text fields and drop-down lists.

Every form has the same basic structure. Also, which input elements you use depends upon the data you're presenting and collecting.

Structure

The form element is a content (and input) container, and it works much like the paragraph (p) element (which contains paragraph text) or the division (div) element (which contains various types of sub-elements in a logical document section). Thus, all input elements associated with a single form are

- ✔ Contained within a <form> tag
- ✔ Processed by the same form handler

A *form handler* is a program on the Web server (or a simple mailto: URL) that manages the data a user sends to you through the form. A Web browser can only gather information through forms; it doesn't know what to do with the information after it has it. You must provide some other mechanism to actually *do* something useful with the data you collect in any form. (This chapter covers form handlers in detail later in the "Processing Data" section.)

Attributes

You always use these two key attributes with the <form> tag:

- ✔ action: The URL of the form handler
- ✔ method: How you want the form data to be sent to the form handler

    Your form handler dictates which of these values to use for method (your hosting or service provider probably has a document that describes how to invoke your local Web server's form handler, including those oh-so-necessary details — and probably some examples, too):

    - get sends the form data to the form handler on the URL.
    - post sends the form data in the HyperText Transfer Protocol (HTTP) header.

Webmonkey offers a good overview of the difference between get and post in its "Add HTML Forms to Your Site" article at www.webmonkey. com/2010/02/add_html_forms_to_your_site.

Markup

The markup in Listing 14-1 creates a form that uses the post method to send user-entered information to a form handler (guestbook.php) to be processed on the Web server.

Listing 14-1:   A Simple Form Processed by a Form Handler

```
<!DOCTYPE html PUBLIC "-//W3C//DTD XHTML 1.0 Transitional//EN"
        "http://www.w3.org/TR/xhtml1/DTD/xhtml1-transitional.dtd">
<html xmlns="http://www.w3.org/1999/xhtml">
<head>
    <title>Forms</title>
    <meta http-equiv="Content-Type" content="text/html; charset=ISO-8859-1" />
</head>
<body>
    <form action="cgi-bin/guestbook.php" method="post">

    <!-- form input elements go here -->

    </form>
</body>
</html>
```

The value of the action attribute is a URL, so you can use absolute or relative URLs to point to a form handler on your server. Absolute and relative URLs are covered in more detail in Chapter 6.

Input tags

The tags you use to solicit input from your site visitors make up the bulk of any form. HTML supports a variety of different input options — from text fields to radio buttons and from files to images.

Every input control associates some value with a name:

  ✔ When you create the control, you give it a name.

  ✔ The control sends back a value based on what the user does in the form.

For example, if you create a text field that collects a user's first name, you might name the field firstname. When the user types her first name in the field and submits the form, the value associated with firstname is whatever name the user typed in the field.

The whole point of a form is to gather values associated with input controls, so how you set the name and value for each control is important. The following sections explain how you should work with names and values for each of the input controls.

The input element (and by extension, the empty <input ... /> tag) is the major player when it comes to using HTML forms to solicit user input. Inside the input element is where you define the kinds of input you want to collect, and how you package and present the input fields and cues you present to users so they can give you what you're asking for.

Input fields

You can use a variety of input fields in your forms, such as text, password, radio buttons/check boxes, hidden, and more. Not all fields require values for name and type attributes (for example, text box or password fields), but it's a good idea to provide users with explanatory labels and examples of input data any time they might have questions about formats — as when pondering whether or not to include dashes or spaces in credit card or telephone numbers. Check boxes and radio buttons, on the other hand, require such information so they can be properly labeled when the browser shows users what selections are available.

For input elements that require a user to select an option (a check box or radio button) rather than typing something into a field, you define both the name and the value. When the user selects a check box or a radio button and then clicks the Submit button, the form returns the name and value assigned to the element.

We discuss these two types of input fields in the upcoming section, "Check boxes and radio buttons."

Text fields

Text fields are single-line fields in which users type information. When you need to offer the user the opportunity to fill in more than one line, you use a text box, as we discuss in the upcoming section, "Multiline text boxes."

Here's how to create a single-line text field:

1. **Define the input type as a text field by using the `<input />` element with the `type` attribute set to `text`.**

   ```
   <input type="text" />
   ```

2. **Then use the `name` attribute to give the input field a name.**

   ```
   <input type="text" name="firstname" />
   ```

   The user supplies the value when she types in the field.

The following markup creates two text input fields — one for a first name and one for a last name:

```
<form action="cgi-bin/guestbook.php" method="post">
<ul style="list-style-type: none;">
  <li>First Name: <input type="text" name="firstname" /></li>
  <li>Last Name: <input type="text" name="lastname" /></li>
</ul>
</form>
```

In addition to the <input /> elements, the preceding markup includes list (<ul> and <li>) elements and some text to label each of the fields. By themselves, most form elements don't give the user many clues about the type of information you want them to enter. Lists are covered in more detail in Chapter 5.

You must use HTML block and inline elements to format the appearance of your form and also to supply the necessary text. Figure 14-5 shows how a browser displays this kind of HTML. (To see the HTML source that produced this figure, visit our Web site at www.dummieshtml.com, pick Chapter 14, and look at the source code for Figure 14-5.)

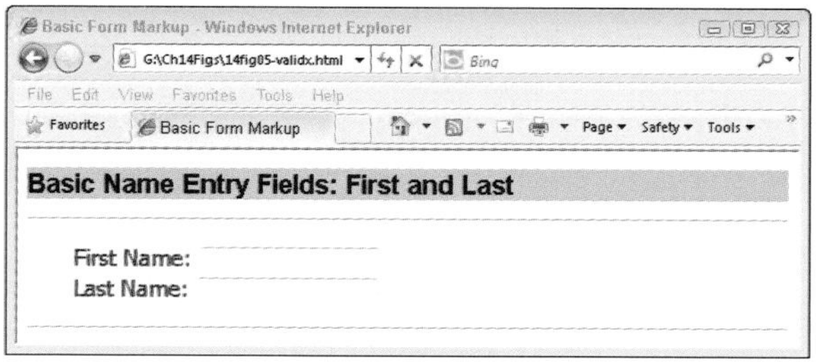

Figure 14-5: Text entry fields in a form.

You can control the size of a text field with these attributes:

- size: The length (in characters) of the text field
- maxlength: The maximum number of characters the user can type into the field

The following markup creates a form that sets both fields to a size of 30 (characters long) and a maxlength of 25 (characters long). Even though each field will be about 30 characters long, a user can type only 25 characters into each field, as shown in Figure 14-6. (Setting the size attribute greater than `maxlength` ensures that the text field will always have some white space between the user input and the end of the field box on display; you don't have to do this yourself, but we find it visually pleasing.)

```
<form action="cgi-bin/guestbook.php" method="post">
<ul style="list-style-type: none;">
  <li>First Name: <input type="text" name="firstname" size="30"
      maxlength="25" /></li>
  <li>Last Name: <input type="text" name="lastname" size="30"
      maxlength="25" /></li>
</ul>
</form>
```

Figure 14-6: You can specify the length and maximum number of characters for a text field.

Password fields

A *password field* is a special text field that doesn't display what the user types. Each keystroke is represented on the screen by a placeholder character, such as an asterisk or bullet, so that someone looking over the user's shoulder can't see sensitive information.

You create a password field by using the `<input />` element with the `type` attribute set to `password`, as follows:

```
<form action="cgi-bin/guestbook.php" method="post">
<ul style="list-style-type: none;">
  <li>First Name: <input type="text" name="firstname" size="30"
      maxlength="25" /></li>
  <li>Last Name: <input type="text" name="lastname" size="30"
      maxlength="25" /></li>
  <li>Password: <input type="password" name="psswd" size="30"
      maxlength="25" /></li>
</ul>
</form>
```

Password fields are programmed like text fields.

Figure 14-7 shows how a browser replaces what you type with bullets. ***Note:*** Depending on the browser's default settings, some browsers will replace the text with asterisks or some other character.

Figure 14-7: Password fields mask the text a user enters.

Check boxes and radio buttons

If only a finite set of possible values is available to the user, you can give him a collection of options to choose from:

- **Check boxes:** Choose more than one option.
- **Radio buttons:** Choose only one option.

    Radio buttons differ from check boxes in an important way: Users can select a single radio button from a set of options but can select any number of check boxes (including none, one, or more than one).

If many choices are available (more than half-a-dozen or so), use a drop-down list instead of radio buttons or check boxes. We show you how to create those in the upcoming section, "Drop-down list fields."

To create radio buttons and check boxes, you

1. **Use the `<input />` element with the `type` attribute set to `radio` or `checkbox`.**

2. **Create each option with these attributes:**
    - `name`: Give the option a name.
    - `value`: Specify what value is returned if the user selects the option.

You can also use the `checked` attribute (with a value of `checked`) to specify that an option should be already selected when the browser displays the form. This is a good way to specify a default selection in a list.

The following markup shows how to format check box and radio button options:

```
<form action="cgi-bin/guestbook.cgi" method="post">
<p>What are some of your favorite foods?</p>
<ul style="list-style-type: none;">
  <li><input type="checkbox" name="food" value="pizza" checked="checked" />
    Pizza</li>
  <li><input type="checkbox" name="food" value="icecream" />Ice Cream</li>
  <li><input type="checkbox" name="food" value="eggsham" />Green Eggs
      and Ham</li>
</ul>

<p>What is your gender?</p>
<ul style="list-style-type: none;">
  <li><input type="radio" name="gender" value="male" />Male</li>
  <li><input type="radio" name="gender" value="female" checked="checked" />
    Female</li>
</ul>
</form>
```

In the preceding code, each set of options uses the same name for each input control but gives a different value to each option. You give each item in a set of options the same name to let the browser know they're part of a set. Figure 14-8 shows how a browser displays this markup, where we also checked the box for Pizza and left the default check next to Ice Cream as-is. If you want to, in fact, you can check as many boxes as you like by default in the page markup, simply by including `checked="checked"` in each `<input ... />` element you choose to check in advance.

Hidden fields

A *hidden field* gives you a way to collect name and value information that the user can't see along with the rest of the form data. Hidden fields are useful for keeping track of information associated with the form, such as its version or name.

If your Internet service provider (ISP) provides a generic application for a guest book or feedback form, you might have to put your name and e-mail address in the form's hidden fields so that the data goes specifically to you.

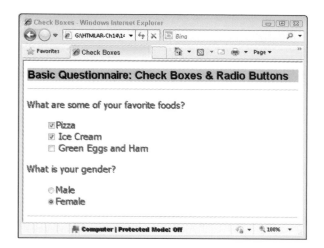

Figure 14-8: Check boxes and radio buttons offer choices.

To create a hidden field, you

⮕ Use the `<input />` element with its `type` attribute set to `hidden`.

⮕ Supply the name and value pair you want to send to the form handler.

Here's an example of markup for a hidden field:

```
<form action="cgi-bin/guestbook.php" method="post">
<input type="hidden" name="e-mail" value="me@mysite.com" />
<ul style="list-style-type: none;">
  <li>First Name: <input type="text" name="firstname" size="30"
      maxlength="25" /></li>
  <li>Last Name: <input type="text" name="lastname" size="30"
      maxlength="25" /></li>
  <li>Password: <input type="password" name="psswd" size="30"
      maxlength="25" /></li>
</ul>
</form>
```

As a general rule, using your e-mail address in a hidden field is just asking for your address to be picked up by spammers. If your ISP says that this is how you should do your feedback form, ask for suggestions as to how you can minimize the damage. Surfers to your page can't see your e-mail address, but spammers' spiders can read the underlying tags. At a minimum, you would hope that your ISP supports one of the many JavaScript encryption tools available to obscure e-mail addresses from harvesters.

File upload fields

A form can receive documents and other files, such as images, from users. When the user submits the form, the browser grabs a copy of the file and sends it with the other form data. To create this file upload field

- ✔ Use the <input /> element with the type attribute set to file.

  The file itself is the form field value.

- ✔ Use the name attribute to give the control a name.

Here's an example of markup for a file upload field:

```
<form action="cgi-bin/guestbook.php" method="post">
<p>Please submit your resume in Microsoft Word or plain text format:<br />
    <input type="file" name="resume" />
</p>
</form>
```

Browsers render a file upload field with a Browse button that allows a user to navigate a local hard drive and select a file to send, as shown in Figure 14-9.

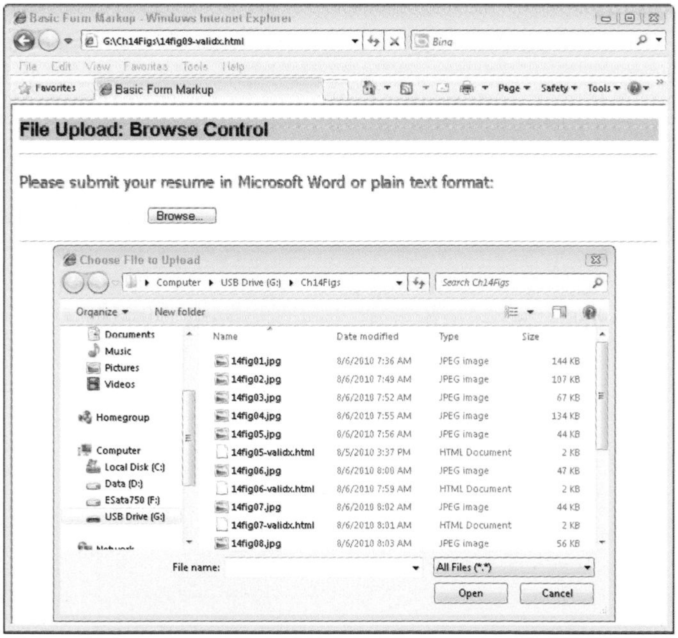

Figure 14-9: A file upload field.

When you accept users' files through a form, you may receive files that are either huge or perhaps virus-infected. Consult with whomever is programming your form handler to discuss options to protect the system where files get saved. Several barriers can help minimize your risks, including

- Virus-scanning software
- Restrictions on file size
- Restrictions on file type

Drop-down list fields

Drop-down lists are a great way to give users lots of options in a small amount of screen space. You use two different tags to create a drop-down list:

- `<select>` creates the list.

  Use a `name` attribute with the `<select>` element to name your list.

- A collection of `<option>` elements identifies individual list options.

  The `value` attribute assigns a unique value for each `<option>` element.

Here's a markup example for a drop-down list:

```
<form action="cgi-bin/guestbook.cgi" method="post">
<p>What is your favorite food?</p>
  <select name="food">
    <option value="pizza">Pizza</option>
    <option value="icecream">Ice Cream</option>
    <option value="eggsham">Green Eggs and Ham</option>
  </select>
</form>
```

The browser turns this markup into a drop-down list with three items, as shown in Figure 14-10.

You can also enable users to select more than one item from a drop-down list by changing the default settings of your list:

- If you want your users to be able to choose more than one option (by holding down the Ctrl [Windows] or ⌘ [Mac] key while clicking options in the list), add the `multiple` attribute to the `<select>` tag. The value of `multiple` is `multiple`.

  Because of XHTML rules, standalone attributes cannot stand alone; therefore, the value is the same as the name for the attribute.

✔ By default, the browser displays only one option until the user clicks the drop-down menu arrow to display the rest of the list. Use the `size` attribute with the `<select>` tag to specify how many options to show.

If you specify fewer than the total number of options, the browser includes a scroll bar with the drop-down list.

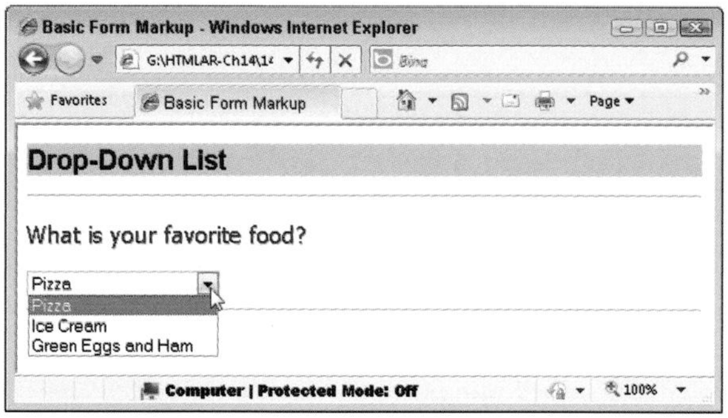

Figure 14-10: A drop-down list.

You can specify that one of the options in the drop-down list be already selected when the browser loads the page, just as you can specify a check box or radio button to be checked. Simply add the `selected` attribute to have a value of `selected` for the `<option>` tag you want as the default. Use this when one choice is very likely, but don't worry — users can override your default selection quickly and easily.

The following markup example

✔ Allows the user to choose more than one option from the list

✔ Displays two options

✔ Selects the third option in the list by default

```
<form action="cgi-bin/guestbook.cgi" method="post">
<p>What are some of your favorite foods?</p>
<select name="food" size="2" multiple="multiple">
 <option value="pizza">Pizza</option>
 <option value="icecream">Ice Cream</option>
 <option value="eggsham" selected="selected">Green Eggs and Ham</option>
</select>
</form>
```

Figure 14-11 shows how adding these attributes modifies the appearance of the list in a browser.

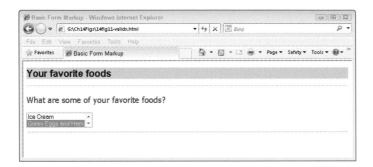

Figure 14-11: A drop-down list with modifications.

Multiline text boxes

If a single-line text field doesn't offer enough room for a response, create a text box instead of a text field:

- ✔ The <textarea> element defines the box and its parameters.
- ✔ The rows attribute specifies the height of the box in rows based on the font in the text box.
- ✔ The cols attribute specifies the width of the box in columns based on the font in the text box.

The text that the user types into the box provides the value, so you need only give the box a name with the name attribute:

```
<form action="cgi-bin/guestbook.cgi" method="post">
   <p> Please include any comments here.</p>
   <textarea rows="10" cols="40" name="comments">
...comments here...
   </textarea>
</form>
```

Any text you include between the <textarea> and </textarea> tags appears in the text box in the browser, as shown in Figure 14-12 (and contrary to expectation, default text does not appear flush left in a text box: It's slightly offset to the right, but not centered, either). The user then enters information in the text box and overwrites your text.

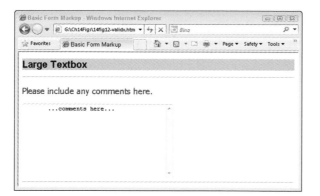

Figure 14-12: A text box.

Submit and Reset buttons

Submit and Reset buttons help the user tell the browser what to do with the form. You can create buttons to either submit or reset your form, using the `<input />` element with the following `type` and `value` attributes:

- **Submit**

  Visitors have to tell a browser when they're done with a form and want to send the contents. You create a button to submit the form to you by using the following markup:

  ```
  <input type="submit" value="Submit" />
  ```

  You don't use the `name` attribute for the Submit and Reset buttons. Instead, you use the `value` attribute to specify how the browser labels the buttons for display.

- **Reset**

  Visitors need to clear the form if they want to start all over again or decide not to fill it out. You create a button to reset (clear) the form by using the following markup:

  ```
  <input type="reset" value="Clear" />
  ```

You can set the value to anything you want to appear on the button. In our example, we set ours to `Clear`. Of course, you can use something that's more appropriate to your Web site if you'd like.

Listing 14-2 shows an example of markup to create Submit and Reset buttons named Send and Clear, respectively:

Listing 14-2: A Complete Multi-Part Form

```
<!DOCTYPE html PUBLIC "-//W3C//DTD XHTML 1.0 Transitional//EN"
        "http://www.w3.org/TR/xhtml1/DTD/xhtml1-transitional.dtd">
<html xmlns="http://www.w3.org/1999/xhtml" lang="en" xml:lang="en">
<head>
    <title>Basic Form Markup</title>
    <meta http-equiv="Content-Type" content="text/html; charset=ISO-8859-1" />
    <style type="text/css">
      h1 {background-color: silver;
          color: black;
          font-size: 1.2em;
          font-family: Arial, Verdana, sans-serif;}
      hr {color: blue;
          width: thick;}
      body {font-size: 12pt;
            color: brown;
            font-family: Tahoma, Bodoni, sans-serif;
            line-height: 0.8em;}
    </style>

</head>
<body>
  <h1>Multi-Part Form</h1>
  <hr />
    <div>
      <form action="cgi-bin/guestbook.cgi" method="post">
        <h1>Name and Password</h1>
          <p>First Name: <input type="text" name="firstname" size="30"
             maxlength="25" /></p>
          <p>Last Name: <input type="text" name="lastname" size="30"
             maxlength="25" /></p>
          <p>Password: <input type="password" name="psswd" size="30"
             maxlength="25" /></p>
        <h1>Favorite Foods</h1>
          <p>What are some of your favorite foods?</p>
          <p><input type="checkbox" name="food" value="pizza"
             checked="checked" />Pizza</p>
          <p><input type="checkbox" name="food" value="icecream" />
             Ice Cream</p>
          <p><input type="checkbox" name="food" value="eggsham" />
             Green Eggs and Ham</p>
        <h1>Gender Information</h1>
          <p>What is your gender?</p>
          <p><input type="radio" name="gender" value="male" />Male</p>
          <p><input type="radio" name="gender" value="female" />Female</p>

        <p style="line-height: 2em; margin: 2em;">
```

```
        <input type="submit" value="Send" />
        <input type="reset" value="Clear" />
    </p>
  </form>
  </div>
  <hr />
</body>
</html>
```

Figure 14-13 shows how a browser renders these buttons in a form.

Figure 14-13: Submit and reset buttons labeled as Send and Clear.

Customizing Submit and Reset buttons

If you don't like the default Submit and Reset buttons that a browser creates, you can monkey with the CSS style definitions to your heart's content, as we did here:

```
input {background-color: teal;
        font-family: Lucida Console, Arial, sans-serif;
        padding: 6px;
        margin: 0.2em;
        font-size: 1.2em;
        color: white;
        border-left-color: gray;
        border-top-color: gray;
        border-bottom-color: black;
        border-right-color: black;
        border-style: double;
        font-weight: bold;}
```

In about ten minutes of fooling around, we created the snazzy-looking buttons you see in Figure 14-14.

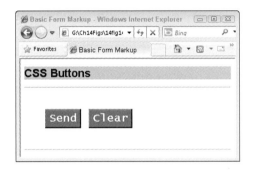

Figure 14-14: A little creative CSS goes a long way toward snazzing up your buttons.

On the other hand, if you desire something more sophisticated, you can substitute your own graphical buttons by using

- ✔ The <input /> element with a type of image.
- ✔ An src attribute that specifies the image's location.
- ✔ A value that defines the result of the field:
  - For an image that submits the form, set value to submit.
  - For an image that clears the form, set value to reset.

Use the alt attribute to provide alternative text for browsers that don't show images (or for users who can't see them). This will allow you to use fancy buttons with rounded corners, dropshadows, and other cool effects like those available at www.buttongenerator.com.

The following markup creates customized Submit and Reset buttons:

```
<p>
    <input type="image" value="submit" src="submit_button.gif" alt="Submit" />
    <input type="image" value="reset" src="reset_button.gif" alt="Clear" />
</p>
```

Form validation

No matter how brilliant your site's visitors may be, there's always a chance that they'll enter data you aren't expecting. JavaScript to the rescue!

Form validation is the process of checking data the user enters before it's put into your database. Check the data with both JavaScript and Common Gateway Interface (CGI) scripts on your server.

JavaScript

You can validate entries in JavaScript before data goes to the server. This means that visitors don't wait for your server to check the data. They're told quickly (before they click Submit, if you want) if there's a problem.

If you want to use JavaScript in your forms and on your Web site, you can read more about it in Chapter 13 of this book, or online at

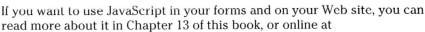

- www.w3schools.com/js/default.asp
- www.quirksmode.org/js/forms.html
- http://www.webmonkey.com/2010/02/javascript_tutorial

CGI

You need to validate your form data on the server side because users can surf with JavaScript turned off. (They'll have a slower validation process.) Find out more about CGI in the next section and at

- www.4guysfromrolla.com/webtech/LearnMore/Validation.asp
- www.cgi101.com/book

Processing Data

Getting form data is really only half the form battle. You create form elements to get data from users, but then you have to do something with that data. Of course, your form and your data are unique every time, so no single, generic form handler can manage the data for every form. Before you can find (or write) a program that handles your form data, you must know what you want to do with it. For example:

- ✔ If you just want to receive comments from a Web form by e-mail, you might need only a simple `mailto:` URL.

- ✔ If a form gathers information from users to display in a guest book, you

  - Add the data to a text file or a small database that holds the entries.

  - Create a Web page that displays the guest-book entries.

- ✔ If you want to use a shopping cart, you need programs and a database that can handle inventory, customer order information, shipping data, and cost calculations.

Your Web-hosting provider — whether it's an internal IT group or an ISP to which you pay a monthly fee — has the final say in what kind of applications you can use on your Web site to handle form data. If you want to use forms on your site, be sure that your hosting provider supports the applications you need to run on the server to process form input data (which will normally use the `post` or `get` method that we discuss earlier in this chapter). Chapter 3 includes more information on finding the right ISP to host your pages.

Processing forms on your pages

Typically, form data is processed in some way or another by some kind of program running on a Web server. It might be a CGI script written in some programming language such as Perl, Java, or AppleScript, or a different handler program written using PHP, Apache, Java Server Pages (JSP), ASP, or other programs that run on Web servers to process user input. These programs make data from your form useful by

- ✔ Putting it into a database or sharing it with some other kind of program

- ✔ Creating customized HTML based on the data

- ✔ Writing the data to a flat file

  Flat file is computer-geek speak for a plain, unadorned text file, or one that uses commas or tab characters on individual lines of text to separate field values (also known as CSV for *comma-separated values* or TSV for *tab-separated values*).

You don't have to be a programmer to make the most of forms. Many ISPs support (and provide) scripts for processing common forms, such as guest books, comment forms, and even shopping carts. Your ISP may give you

- ✔ All the information you need to get an input-processing program up and running

- ✔ HTML to include in your pages so they can interact with that program

You can tweak the markup that manages how the form appears in the canned HTML you get from an ISP, but don't change the form itself — especially the `form` tag names and values. The Web-server program uses these to make the entire process work.

Several online script repositories provide free scripts that you can download and use along with your forms. Many of these also come with some generic HTML you can dress up and tweak to fit your Web site. You simply drop the program that processes the form into the folder on your site that holds programs (sometimes called `cgi-bin`, often something else), add the HTML to your page, and you're good to go. Some choice places on the Web to find scripts you can download and put to work immediately are

- ✔ **Matt's Script archive:** `www.scriptarchive.com/nms.html`

- ✔ **The CGI Resource Index:** `http://cgi.resourceindex.com`

- ✔ **ScriptSearch.com:** `www.scriptsearch.com`

If you want to use programs that aren't provided by your ISP on your Web site, you need complete access to your site's scripts or processing programs folder (sometimes named `cgi-bin`). Every ISP setup is different, so read your documentation to find out

- ✔ **Whether your ISP allows you to use programs or scripts in your Web pages**

- ✔ **Which languages the ISP supports**

    Perl and PHP are generally safe bets, but it's best to be sure.

Sending form data by e-mail

You can opt to receive your form data from e-mail instead of using a script or other utility to process a form's data. You get just a collection of name-and-value pairs tucked into a text file sent to your e-mail address, but that isn't necessarily a bad thing. You can include a short contact form on your Web site that asks people to send you feedback (a feature that always looks professional); then you can simply include, in the `action` URL, the e-mail address where you want the data sent:

```
<form action="mailto:me@mysite.com" action="post">
```

Many spam companies grab e-mail addresses by trolling Web sites for `mailto:` URLs. Consider setting up a special e-mail account just for comments so that your regular e-mail address won't get pulled onto spam mailing lists. On the other hand, you can also use JavaScript-based e-mail address encryption tools that will garble and disguise the contents of such addresses — as long as they can be un-encrypted on the receiving end, that is!

Designing User-Friendly Forms

Designing *useful* forms is a different undertaking from designing *easy-to-use* forms. Your form may gather the data that you need, but if your form is difficult for visitors to use, they may abandon it before they're done.

As you use the markup elements from this chapter, along with the other elements that drive page layout, keep the following guidelines in mind:

- **Provide textual cues for all your forms.** Be clear about
  - Information you want
  - Format you need

  For example, tell users details such as whether
  - Dates must be entered as `mm/dd/yy` (versus `mm/dd/yyyy`).
  - The number of characters a field can take is limited.

    As you learned earlier in this chapter, character length can be limited by using the `maxlength` attribute.

- **Use field width and character limits to provide visual clues.** For example, if users should enter a phone number as *xxx-xxx-xxxx,* consider creating three text fields — one for each part of the phone number.

- **Group similar fields.** A logical grouping of fields makes filling out a form easier. It's confusing if you ask for the visitor's first name, then birthday, and then last name.

- **Break long forms into easy-to-manage sections.** Forms in short chunks are less intimidating and more likely to be completed.

  Major online retailers (such as Amazon.com — `www.amazon.com`) use this method to get the detail they need for orders without making the process too painful.

- **Mark required fields clearly.** If some parts of your form *can't* be left blank when users submit the form, mark those fields clearly.

You can identify required fields by

- Making them bold
- Using a different color
- Placing an asterisk beside them

✔ **Tell users what kind of information they need for the form.** If users need any information in their hands before they fill out your form, a *form gateway* page can detail everything users should have before they start filling out the form.

The RateGenius page (shown in Figure 14-15) lays out clearly for visitors about to fill out a long form exactly what information to prepare before starting.

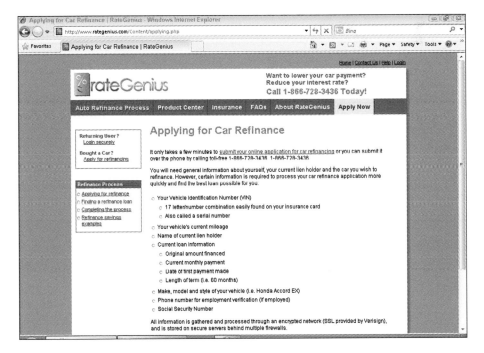

Figure 14-15: A form gateway page helps users prepare to fill out a long form.

The series of forms that RateGenius uses to gather information for car loans and loan refinancing are excellent examples of long forms that collect a variety of different kinds of data by using all the available form markup elements. Visit www.rategenius.com to review its form techniques.

Other Noteworthy Forms-Related Markup

Table 14-1 lists other forms-related (X)HTML markup attributes that you might find in HTML files.

Table 14-1	Other Forms-Related (X)HTML Attributes		
Name	*Function/Value Equals*	*Value Types*	*Related Element(s)*
Accept	Lists acceptable MIME types for file upload	CS Media types	`<form>` `<input />`
Accept-charset	Lists character encodings	character set encodings	`<form>`
Checked	Preselects option for select lists	`"checked"`	`<input />`
MIMDisabled	Disables form elements	`"disabled"`	`<button>` `<input>` `<optgroup>` `<option>` `<select>` `<textarea>`
Enctype	Specifies encoding method for form input data	Media type	`<form>`
For	Points to ID reference from other attributes	Idref	`<label>`
Label	Identifies a group of options in a form	Text	`<optgroup>`
Label	Specifies an option name in a form	Text	`<option>`
Method	HTTP method to use when submitting a form	`{"get"| "put"}`	`<form>`
Multiple	Permits selection of multiple options in a form	`"multiple"`	`<select>`

Name	*Function/Value Equals*	*Value Types*	*Related Element(s)*
Name	Names a specific form control	CDATA	`<button>` `<textarea>`
Name	Names a specific form input field	CDATA	`<select>`
Name	Names a form for script access	CDATA	`<form>`
Readonly	Blocks editing of text fields within a form	`"readonly"`	`<input />` `<textarea`
Size	Specifies number of lines of text to display for a drop-down menu	Number	`<select>`
Tabindex	Defines tabbing order for form fields	Number	`<a><area />` `<button>` `<input />` `<object>` `<select>` `<textarea>`
Type	Defines button function in a form	`{"button" | "reset" | "submit"}`	`<button>`
Type	Specifies type of input required for form input field	`{"button" | "checkbox" | "file" | "hidden" | "image" | "password" | "radio" | "reset" | "submit" | "text"}`	`<input />`
Value	Supplies a value to send to the server when clicked	CDATA	`<button>`
Value	Associates values with radio buttons and check boxes	CDATA	`<input />`

Key for the Value Types Column in Table 14-1:

- **CDATA:** SGML character data type permits all keyboard characters to be used

- **CS Media Types:** Case-sensitive type names such as "text/html" "image/gif" or "text/css"

- **Character set encodings:** Usually UTF-8, ISO-LATIN-1, or ISO-8859-1; for a more complete list, see `www.w3schools.com/TAGS/ref_character sets.asp`

- **MIME:** Abbreviation for Multi-part Internet Mail Extensions, a standard method to encode various document and data types for e-mail attachments and for HTTP; for more info see `http://en.wikipedia.org/wiki/MIME`.

Form Frameworks

Form frameworks basically put all the building blocks for building, validating, and processing forms data together into a single coherent collection of tools and code. When you learn how to use a framework, it's trivial to build complex robust forms of your own — at least, as long as that framework is available on your Web server!

- **Wufoo (`http://wufoo.com`):** Wufoo is an HTML form builder that helps you to create contact forms, online surveys, and invitations so you can collect data, registrations, and online payments you need without writing a single line of code. Quick and easy!

- **jQuery Validation Plugins (`http://docs.jquery.com/Plugins/Validation`):** Even though jQuery makes it easy to write your own validation plugins, there are still a lot of subtleties you must worry about. For example, you need a standard library of validation methods (think of e-mails, URLs, and credit card numbers). You need to place error messages into Web documents, and then show and hide them when appropriate. You want to react to more than just a submit event, like `keyup` or `blur`. You may need different ways to specify validation rules, based on the server-side environment in use for a particular project. And after all, you don't want to reinvent the wheel, do you?

- **Validatious (`http://validatious.org/learn/examples`):** Validatious offers easy form validation with unobtrusive JavaScript support, using a predefined CSS class named `validate`. This makes validations simply a matter of adding validator names to form elements, such as `input`, `select`, `textarea`, and so forth. It's not a complete forms framework but does make the validation part — often the trickiest for newbies and professionals alike — smooth and straightforward.

In addition, many Web-oriented development environments, such as Visual Studio, Web Expressions, ASP.NET, and so forth also include extensive form design and processing components. These work like frameworks, too, but generally require you to work within their overall environments to take advantage of their often awesome capabilities.

CAPTCHA This!

CAPTCHA stands for *completely automated public turing test to tell computers and humans apart* — in other words, it's a way of interacting on the Web that permits developers to assume (with great assurance) that the entity typing input on the other end of a remote connection is a person and not a program. CAPTCHA is an important technique used to verify that a person is providing input (especially, updating sensitive or valuable information) to a Web form or other user input mechanism. The reason for this technology is to stymie spammers and phishers from creating bogus e-mail addresses and Web accounts that they can then use to pursue their own malicious ends. You may not need to use CAPTCHA on your Web pages, but you need to know what it is and why it's important.

Basically, CAPTCHA works by bending text in wavy lines and overlaying extra strokes or black marks, so that while humans can read the copy they must enter at the keyboard to prove their intelligence is at work, computer programs generally can't decipher and regurgitate the text involved. The standard example from www.captcha.net appears as Figure 14-16 with the words "overlooks inquiry" subjected to the aforementioned treatment.

Figure 14-16: The CAPTCHA example from the home page at www.captcha.net.

The Web site at www.captcha.net explains the technology in more detail, and goes on to describe how you can use it to add another level of authentication to your Web pages. It's not necessary for simple forms, but any time you let users set up accounts, manage account info, or access sensitive data (personally identifiable information, or PII, such as Social Security numbers, credit card numbers, account numbers, and so forth, are prime targets for such protection), it's a good idea to put CAPTCHA in the way of would-be evildoers.

Chapter 15

Bring the Best of the Web to Your Web Site

In This Chapter

▶ Understanding what embedding can do for your page content (and your workload)

▶ Embedding Twitter feeds, Flickr photos, and Google maps

▶ Making the most of multiple embeddings via mashups

▶ Mashing up maps and restaurant reviews, plus maps and Twitter feeds

*T*o this point in the book, we cover a lot of the basics with HTML, XHTML, and CSS on how to create your own Web site. Before you rush off and start creating oodles of content, though, you might first want to find out whether anything like what you want already exists. The great thing about the Internet is that lots of excellent content is already out there, ripe for (proper) reuse. With some practice, you can easily "grab" this content and use it on your Web site. Harnessing the power of such services can save tons of time and effort you would otherwise have to expend on your own, reinventing well-worn wheels. After all, nobody wants to reinvent the wheel: Sure, it's okay improve upon it, but no need to start over from scratch.

For example, if you want to give a friend directions to your house, you could spend lots of time painstakingly drawing or photographing your entire neighborhood. Next, you could put all those images together and figure out how to display them effectively. After all that work, you'd finally be ready to put everything together inside a graphical interface so your site can provide directions. That's a big chunk of time working on a solution that might be inaccurate owing to changes in the landscape by the time you finish, if you finish at all. Sure, you can do all that, but who wants to? Numerous existing solutions are readily available to handle this for you (such as Google or Bing Maps, or perhaps MapQuest). Sometimes, getting things done is more about embedding other content that works for your site so you can use your precious time, energy, and money more wisely.

Bringing the best of Web content to your site is an easy way to harness the power of services that others have already created and want to make available to you. And that means more than maps, including photo galleries, lists of local restaurants with reviews, content-categorized videos with comments, and countless combinations of two or more such things. This chapter is about grabbing and using such stuff on your Web pages, not just to make your life easier but also to add valuable information to your site, all the while leaving the hard work of keeping things current to somebody else. Trust us: It just doesn't get any better than that on the Web!

What's Up with Content Embedding?

When we talk about *content embedding,* we aren't talking about stealing or breaking any sort of other Internet taboos. Rather, we simply mean following established rules provided by other companies, individuals, or organizations that specifically allow others — like you, for instance — to present their work on your site without requiring you to reinvent their particular wheels. In other words, embedding seeks to take advantage of news, services, and information (maps at Google, Bing, or MapQuest are great examples) that are freely offered to the public for access and reuse.

The really neat thing about content embedding is that if you look around carefully, you can find lots of cool elements that you are invited — nay, encouraged — to use on your own site. These things save time and effort, but that's not all: They also help you to design and deliver a more dynamic Web site that does some of the hard maintenance and upkeep work for you, without forcing you to spend every waking moment working on it!

In the sections that follow, you find examples to help you better understand what's involved in embedding content in a Web page, how it works, and what it looks like.

Using a Twitter widget

If you still haven't heard of (or been on) Twitter, we'd like to congratulate you on waking up out of your long nap or coma, and welcome you to the 21st century. Yes, hover boards haven't yet been invented yet, but Twitter and other social media services are taking over the Internet.

In a nutshell, Twitter is a communications tool interface inside which users update their status or posts in the form of tiny messages (140 characters or less) called *tweets.* Individual collections of tweets from a particular sender are called Twitter feeds, and Internet users generally sign up to follow one or more such feeds to catch all the tweets that each feed contains.

Certain Twitter posters can (and many do) continually post trivial information (what they ate for breakfast or what they're wearing), which may not be too helpful (or interesting) to some readers. Others Twitter posters, though — like us, for instance — use Twitter to help build community, answer questions, interact with readers, stay in touch with friends, and so forth. (And no lectures, please, on spelling, grammar, punctuation, and cryptic shorthand. After all, 140 characters is 140 characters.)

Depending on how Twitter is used (as with many technologies), it can add value to a Web site. A perfect example involves embedding your own (or even someone else's) Twitter feed on your site. This feed updates automatically with new tweets without requiring you to do any manual updating, saving, or uploading. Even better, Twitter offers custom widgets so you can embed feeds on a page quite easily.

As with our earlier map example, one example is to embed our own Twitter feed for this book into an HTML page. Then, whenever we issue a tweet, that message not only displays within Twitter, it also automatically updates our Web page with zero additional effort on our part.

First, we must craft a Twitter profile widget to describe our feed, and share it with the world. This happens at `http://twitter.com/goodies/widget_ profile`.

You can see a Twitter profile page illustrated in Figure 15-1, but first, briefly review the profile widget that resides at the preceding URL. To get this party started, start at the preceding Twitter link. (*Note:* If you already have a Twitter account, your username is supplied automatically. If you have no such account, you can easily change the name to whatever moniker you'd like to use on your Web page. By default, you'll see a base account named "Twitter" appear, unless you've already grabbed or used a name for yourself. You must, however, set up an account and login before you can see and use Twitter widgets, or the buttons that appear at the bottom of Figure 15-1.)

We don't cover everything in depth, but you can update Preferences, Appearance, and Dimensions for your Twitter feed widget to customize its look and feel on your Web page.

Second, after adjusting any or all of those items, click the Finish & Grab Code button also shown in Figure 15-1. (You can cut and paste that script into Notepad or your favorite text editor for safe keeping.)

Then, all you need to do is paste that code into the body section of an (X) HTML page, save the file, and pull up the page in any Web browser. Figure 15-2 shows the Twitter feed on the Web site for this book. It's really just that easy! Check it out at `www.dummieshtml.com/examples/ch15/twitter` (and view the source to see how we pasted the script right into the `body` section).

Figure 15-1: The dummieshtml profile widget page.

Figure 15-2: The dummieshtml Twitter feed page.

For more Twitter widgets, check out `http://twitter.com/about/resources/widgets`. There, you'll find various widgets that work on general Websites (My Website) and on Facebook. These include additional items such as a search widget, a faves widget, and a list widget to let users look for tweets, show off their favorites, or list specific tweet items on a page.

You can always check out our Twitter page to stay up to date with what we are doing with this book, or send us questions or comments.

Working with Flickr

In our opinion, and that of many other experts and aficionados, Flickr is one of the best online photo management and sharing applications around. One of its greatest features is that you can easily upload and aggregate photos, create your own slide shows, or even share your photos in an automated slide show. Why are we telling you all this? Because you can also embed Flickr photos into your own Web pages.

Yahoo! owns Flickr so all you need is a Yahoo! ID and password to log in. If you don't have one, you must create a Yahoo! Account before you can use Flickr. (Yahoo! Accounts are free and available to the general public, with no hidden gotchas involved.) We skip over the account stuff and assume that you can log in without our help. Then, after you log in and upload some photos, you can view your photostream, as shown in Figure 15-3.

Click Slideshow, the hyperlinked gray text at the upper-right corner of the Flickr window, right under the Search box (see Figure 15-3). Upon clicking this item, you go to a new page that displays larger scaled versions of photos from the photostream. These photos auto advance through the entire collection but also provide various controls. For example, you can jump around those photos by clicking on any thumbnail image, pause the slide show at any time, or make the images show in full screen mode.

Undoubtedly, this is good stuff. Given a gaggle of snaps, you can send a link to your friends and family so they can enjoy them, too. But here, our concern is to explain how to embed a Flickr photostream on your site. As with Twitter, that process is both simple and easy. Here's how you do it:

1. **Click the Share This menu item at the top right.**

    Make certain you do this while the slide show is playing.

2. **Click the Copy to Clipboard button under the Grab the Embedded HTML text box.**

3. **Open your target Web page and paste the `object` element from the Clipboard inside the `body` section of that page.**

    It's easy! Check it out at `www.dummieshtml.com/examples/ch15/flickr`.

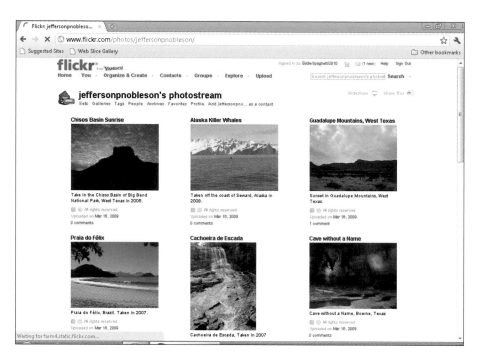

Figure 15-3: A Flickr photostream page.

If you look at the markup for that page, you'll see that we customized some of the HTML to fit the overall design for that page, and you can easily do likewise for yourself. In our case, we created a `div` section with an `id` value of `"content"` so that we could set up a background color and margin controls.

The real value of embedding Flickr on a page is that every time you upload a new photo to Flickr into your photostream, it automatically displays in the gallery on your new HTML page as well!

Creating a map

Another good example to illustrate the power of embedding content is a simple map. Say that Ed is having a party, and he creates a Web site for the party information and to give some of his out of town friends a map of Austin, TX, in case they get lost. He can do something like what's shown in Figure 15-4 (also available at `www.dummieshtml.com/examples/ch15/map-image.html`).

In our initial discussion in this chapter, we explain how you could spend hours drawing a new map, such as the one we drew of Austin (and a not very good one at that). We exported that image onto a static Web page using the `<img src>` element. Visitors to this page saw a crude map of Austin with zero interactivity, as shown in Figure 15-4.

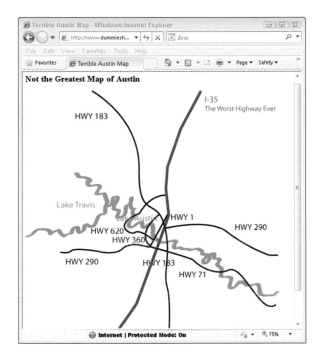

Figure 15-4: You could use a quick-and-dirty hand-drawn map.

As a more powerful alternative (check out `www.dummieshtml.com/examples/ch15/map-google.html`), we can sign up for a Google Maps API key, and follow the steps in its free tutorial to create a sample map. (For brevity, we'll skip those steps here.) After creating the sample map, we can customize the map's latitude and longitude for Austin. This is absolutely essential because, by default, Google pulls up a map from Australia! That's very much the long way around for Ed's party.

Visitors to this page can view four different map versions: a 2D map, a satellite view, a hybrid map (satellite overlaid with 2D), or terrain views of Austin. They can also use the map interface to pan left, right, up, or down, as well as zoom in or out to whatever level of detail they like (from the tiniest nooks and crannies to the whole continent).

If you look at the code, you'll notice some new elements. In this example, the latest Google Maps API (Version 3, also known as V3) now uses HTML 5. For more information on HTML 5, check out Chapter 19: It won't tell you everything, but it will tell you enough to understand what's going on here.

For more information on creating your own Google map, visit `http://code.google.com/apis/maps/documentation/javascript/tutorial.html`.

For those of you who don't already know the latitude and longitude for your chosen location (who does?), plenty of Web sites can provide this information. We prefer `http://stevemorse.org/jcal/latlon.php`.

Other embeddings to check out

The preceding examples represent only a few services you can freely and enthusiastically embed onto your Web site. That's just the beginning, though: You could also include literally hundreds of others, should you wish to do so. In fact, here are a few more "best of the Web" items that we recommend visiting:

- **YouTube** (`www.youtube.com`) for online video streaming
- **Picasa** (`http://picasa.google.com`) for online photo management
- **Scribd** (`www.scribd.com`) for sharing Web documents
- **SlideShare** (`www.slideshare.net`) for uploading and sharing presentations
- **AddThis** (`http://addthis.com`) for sharing content on your Web site

Honestly, we certainly can't cover even the very best of the best of the Web in depth given the many, many sites that qualify for this status. Some would argue that each of these services deserves a book the size of this one to fully master its concepts and capabilities. Here, our goal is just to show you what's possible, and to let you know there's a world of other similar things out there on the Web.

Mashups: Two or More Sites

In the music industry, a *mashup* is a song or composition created by blending two or more songs to create something new and different. For example, in 2004, the critically acclaimed *The Grey Album* from DJ Danger Mouse distinguished itself by combining samples from The Beatles' *White Album* and vocals from rapper Jay-Z's *The Black Album.* Neither of these artists had ever worked together, nor do they share a common musical genre, nor is there even any historical overlap between the two works. Nevertheless, DJ Danger Mouse took each of these albums, put them together, and used them to create something interesting and new.

Returning to the topic for this book — namely, Web development — a mashup is something like what's found in the music industry except that samples and vocals are replaced with data or functionality from two (or more) external services to create something new and interesting online.

In short, mashups provide a way to combine and extend various individual Web site services to create new functionality that didn't exist before. Why would anybody want to do this? Some might say "Just because you can" or "Just for the thrill." Others might enjoy tackling the same kind of challenge on the Web that DJ Danger Mouse took on in the studio in 2004.

In writing this book, we make the assumption that you're learning your way around HTML and CSS. Consequently, we don't expect you to be able to use every line of code in every mashup. However, we do think you need to know that mashups exist, and that they are a popular and growing portion of the Web. Our goal here is to help you understand what mashups are, and to expose you to just a little about how mashups work.

As you progress with your coding skills, you can tackle projects like building your own mashups. The real beauty of mashups stems from the trend that more and more applications and Web sites keep opening (a least a portion of) their services through special application programming interfaces (APIs) for embedding and reuse on other sites. Even better, whole online communities, tutorials, and documentation explain how to access APIs and the data and services they deliver from the best of the Web's providers. (Just remember: Some services are better than others, and some APIs and tools are easier to work with than others, too. The best of the best is just that because both the services and the tools you use to access them are pretty darn good indeed.)

Again, please don't feel overwhelmed. For the moment, be happy understanding that mashups exist and are pretty darn cool. To get a better idea why we think this is worth knowing, check out some of the following examples.

Creating a Yelp/Google Maps mashup

In the earlier section, "Creating a map," we walk you through building a Google map for some out-of-town friends attending a party in Austin. If you've never been to Austin, one particular food item worth discussing (at least briefly) is breakfast tacos. Depending on where you live, you may not have heard of these delectable treats. For those who don't know, in its simplest form, a breakfast taco holds beloved breakfast items (eggs, potatoes, bacon, and so forth), plus salsa (mild, hot, green, or whatever), rolled up inside a tortilla (whole wheat, white, or corn are common, but other variations can and do pop up). Now that we think about it, a breakfast taco is a great subject here because you could say it's a food mashup!

Say those out-of-town guests will benefit from a list of breakfast taco restaurants during their visit for the party. In case they're not inclined to trust our culinary judgment, we can create a mashup that lets them see what a whole bunch of people in Austin think about various breakfast taco restaurants all over town. Here's a search at Yelp that proffers this kind of info: `www.yelp.com/search?find_desc=breakfast+tacos&ns=1&find_loc=Austin%2C+TX`.

We could send our friends a link to Yelp, which provides 600-plus results (at the moment) with reviews and comments from real people. This helpful info is bound to provide our friends with lots of opinions and data on the breakfast taco restaurants in Austin.

The Yelp list also includes addresses and phone numbers to help our friends find each and every location. By itself, though, this Yelp list alone doesn't actually show where each restaurant is located. Adding this capability is what mashups are about, and what gives them their value. So we do that very thing and give our friends a map to go along with the address so they don't get lost (or too terribly hungry) while on their quest for breakfast tacos.

In Figure 15-5, notice the little map on the right side of that page for a perfect example of a mashup. Here, Yelp is presenting its data (Yelp already stores the address for each location) on a Google Map of Austin. Just as in the previous section's map, our friends can zoom and pan this map, but here, they also get Yelp overlays for each location from Yelp's own site data. The combination is better than either part by itself, see?

Clicking the Mo' Map hyperlink expands the tiny default map to show location data better. Click Less Map to see a smaller map but with more restaurant info (the default view). Pretty neat, isn't it? It may not be revolutionary, but if you hover ahead on a few of the markers on the map, you see information about each location from Yelp by using the Google Map. Double-click any such marker, and you jump to the Yelp detail page for the corresponding location. In all these ways, Yelp has "mashed up" its breakfast taco data (locations, reviews, comments, addresses, hours, and so forth) and made it all accessible through a Google Map to create the best of both worlds.

At this point, you're probably saying: "Gee, that's great but this is Yelp's work. I'm sure they have great programmers who simply rolled up their sleeves and figured this out for themselves." That's true, but you can take a similar approach to build something for yourself.

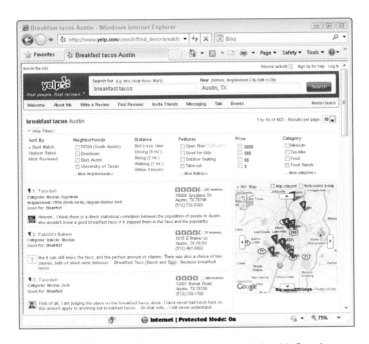

Figure 15-5: Yelp mashes its location and review info with Google Maps for a tasty combo.

We decided to expand on this idea (as shown in Figure 15-6) in a Web site that author Jeff Noble and his friend Ron Norman created just for grins. Taking the same approach as Yelp, they accessed its API (remember, that's application programming interface, fancy talk for programming links that let services talk to one another through a Web page) to display Yelp information about breakfast taco joints inside a Google satellite map. The results are displayed in Figure 15-6 below or check it out online at www. breakfasttacomap.com.

Notice how we updated the map markers with little breakfast taco icons? You can do this, too! All sorts of neat customizations are possible when you make your own mashups. No salsa needed, either!

For more information, check out these resources:

- **The Google Maps JavaScript API V3** at http://code.google.com/apis/maps/documentation/javascript/examples/index.html
- **Yelp for Developers** at www.yelp.com/developers/documentation

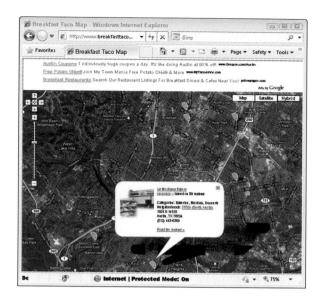

Figure 15-6: Homemade breakfast taco map mashup

Crafting a Twitter/Google Maps mashup

In earlier sections, we covered how to embed a single map as well as how to embed data from Yelp into a Google Maps mashup. We even covered embedding Twitter in a page before that, so now let's create a Twitter/map mashup, too.

For example, you might want to build a mashup that displays a map of Round Rock, Texas (which is where author Ed Tittel lives), that shows locations for people's tweets and what they said, as a way to keep up with what's going on around town. We've also said that the beauty of mashups and embedded content comes by *not* reinventing the wheel. And, in fact, that's what brings the work of map guru Adam DuVander and his interesting Twitter/map mashup into this discussion. Check it out at `http://mapscripting.com/twitter`.

In our example (see Figure 15-7), Adam automatically loads a Google map with your current location (or your current Internet service provider's location, as the case may be for people living out in the sticks) and recent tweets from that area, helpfully circled on the map. In Figure 15-7, we clicked on one map marker to display a tweet from someone in the Austin area with an electrical problem by searching on the word *half.*

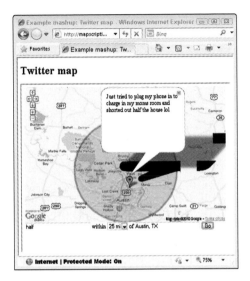

Figure 15-7: You can search by topic and location.

To add more capability, Adam includes controls on this map/tweet mashup. Using these controls, visitors can search around other locations for all tweets (the location controls enable distance selections underneath the map, or by location at the lower right). You can also search for a specific tweet topic, as we did in Figure 15-7 where we were looking for Half Price Books (a popular used book store in our area), using the tweet search box at the lower left of the mashup where we entered the word "half" to pull up any mentions of the store.

Here again, we recognize that Adam is an expert, and illustrations like his tweet/map mashup are meant to inspire and to show you what's possible. If you build on the basics presented in this book, you too can one day use your XHTML, CSS, and JavaScript skills to build cool mashups like this one.

For more information on building your own maps, we urge you to dig into Adam's online book: *Map Scripting 101,* available at http://mapscripting.com/book. To see other mapping mashups by Adam, visit http://mapscripting.com/example-maps. For still more mashup info, visit this Web page entitled "How to make your own Web mashup" available at www.programmableweb.com/howto.

Chapter 16

Fun with Client-Side Scripts

In This Chapter

▶ Using image and text rollovers

▶ Adding dynamic content

▶ Using Web cookies

▶ Showing pop-up windows

*I*f you're the outdoor type, you can get an adrenaline rush by climbing a mountain, mountain biking, or perhaps inventing a new sport, such as parafishing or sewer snorkeling. If you are reading this book, chances are you're sitting in front of your computer trying to create a Web site. If so, we have a different idea for a Web adrenaline rush: Dynamic HTML!

Dynamic HTML, also known as *DHTML,* is techie talk for a useful and powerful set of technologies. It's the combination of HTML, Cascading Style Sheets (CSS), the Document Object Model (the DOM), and JavaScript. If you use these four technologies together, you're creating DHTML.

DHTML is like a printed document in which the DOM acts as the nouns, JavaScript as the verbs, CSS as the adjectives, and HTML as the paper itself. The individual parts are useful, but it's in combination that they become truly powerful. If you can put them all together, you can speak DHTML.

In this chapter, we explore how to use DHTML and its component technologies to bring active content to your Web pages. Specifically, we explore how to create rollovers, add dynamic content to your page, display pop-up windows, and tap into the power of cookies.

Adding Rollovers to Your Pages

If you're new to HTML, a rollover probably sounds like a pet trick. In actuality, though, a rollover is perhaps the most common use of DHTML on the Web. It's an instruction that brings your Web page to life when a mouse pointer hovers over an image or text. In the past, it was common to address rollovers with JavaScript/HTML/CSS solutions, but now all you really need is CSS. With that observation in mind, it's time to start the fun!

Text rollovers with CSS

For years, the only option available for creating a rollover was to create button images and then "activate" them with JavaScript. However, now that CSS has gained acceptance in newer browser versions, here's an alternative way to create rollovers without using images at all.

Text rollovers have advantages and disadvantages when compared with JavaScript image rollovers:

- ✔ **Good news:** Text is faster and more meaningful to search engines, and it's always easier to add plain text to a page than it is to create two images and add them both to a page, with an image rollover. Plus, you don't need to worry about preloading, tracking, and maintaining images.

- ✔ **Bad news:** Although you can control the text font, style, and border for your image using CSS, you currently can't do all the nifty visual tricks that you can do to images using a program like Adobe Photoshop (or some reasonable facsimile thereof). These tricks include visual effects such as anti-aliasing, drop shadows, and animation. (You can, however, apply such visual effects using HTML 5 and CSS3, which we discuss in Chapters 19 and 20, respectively.) In addition, this method works only in reasonably current browsers. If your target viewing audience uses a browser released in this century, that should be fine.

Figure 16-1 shows a plain-Jane Web page with two rollover text links: *Home* and *About Me.* Moving the cursor over one of the images, as shown in Figure 16-2, causes the rolled-over version of the text to display white text on a black background, instead of teal-on-white for unvisited links and gray-on-white for visited links. Listing 16-1 displays the HTML and CSS required for this rollover effect.

Figure 16-1: A page with text rollovers handled with CSS.

Figure 16-2: Moving the cursor over the link text changes the text and background colors.

The link text still shows up onscreen regardless of whether you visited the linked page. Figure 16-3 shows how the page appears after you visit this site's home page. Although that text is grayed out, it's still a link, so rolling over it still produces the same effect shown in Figure 16-2.

Listing 16-1:   A Text Rollover with CSS

```
<!DOCTYPE html PUBLIC "-//W3C//DTD XHTML 1.0 Transitional//EN"
      "http://www.w3.org/TR/xhtml1/DTD/xhtml1-transitional.dtd">
<html xmlns="http://www.w3.org/1999/xhtml">
<head>
    <title>CSS Text Rollover</title>
    <meta http-equiv="Content-Type" content="text/html; charset=ISO-8859-1" />
    <style type="text/css">
        h4 {font: 18pt geneva, sans-serif; margin: 0; color: teal;
            background: white;}
        a {text-decoration: none;}
        div#navbar {width: 200px;}
        div#navbar a {display: block; margin: 0; padding: 0.3em;}
        div#navbar a:link {color: #008080; background-color: transparent;}
        div#navbar a:visited {color: #C0C0C0; background-color: transparent;}
        div#navbar a:hover {background: black; color: white;}
    </style>
</head>
<body>
<div id="navbar">
    <h4><a href="index.html">Home</a></h4>
    <h4><a href="aboutMe.html">About Me</a></h4>
</div>
</body>
</html>
```

In this example, we change the text from teal-on-white to white-on-black when the cursor hovers over the link; that way, it's easy for you to see what's going on in the screenshots. You may want to use a different approach on your site (or a different color scheme). The link goes gray after being visited.

Figure 16-3: After you visit a page, the link text color shows that the page was visited.

Adding this type of navigation to your site couldn't be simpler:

1. Within the `<head>` tags, add the preceding code (from Listing 16-1) inside and including the `<style>` and `</style>` tags.

2. Add links inside individual `<h4>` tags.

3. Make sure that the entire menu is inside a `<div>` tag with an `id` attribute of `navbar`.

If you add the CSS to your site via a link to a site-wide external style sheet (see Chapters 9 and 10 for more information on style sheets), you can add, change, or delete menu-bar links on your site at any time without having to touch a single line of CSS or JavaScript. You simply add or modify your `<a href>` tags. Slick, huh?

Image rollovers with CSS

With text rollovers under your belt, kick things up a notch and move on to image rollovers. Say you have a basic image that you want to change to some different image when a visitor to your Web site rolls over its display frame. In the past, you needed JavaScript to handle the mechanics for image rollovers. Lucky for you, this can all easily be done with CSS now. Check out this sample page where you can mess with Jeff's head (literally) `www.dummieshtml.com/examples/ch16/image%20rollover`.

Here, we use some CSS trickery to apparently take one image and replace it with another. Actually, it's really a single image that was created by stacking two separate images together, one next to the other. We use some format tricks to handle the rollover behavior using CSS by shifting our frame of reference to the right as we hover over that image.

Figure 16-4 shows the sample image (notice how it's really two images). Figure 16-5 shows the Web page of the formatted image with part of the image hidden from view. Hovering the cursor over the black-and-white part of the image, as shown in Figure 16-6, causes the rolled-over version of the image to display (it's in color). Listing 16-2 displays the HTML and CSS that we use to produce this rollover effect.

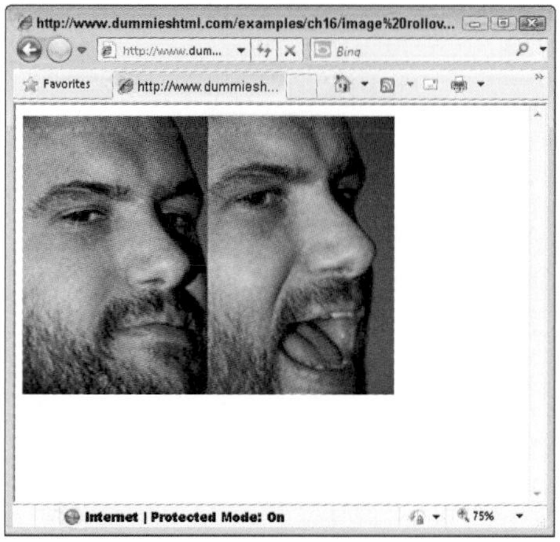

Figure 16-4: One image composed of two pictures of intrepid author, Jeff Noble.

Figure 16-5: The page showing the base (black-and-white) image of Jeff.

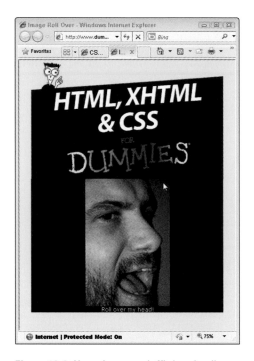

Figure 16-6: Hovering over Jeff's head calls up the color image of Jeff as a rollover.

Listing 16-2:   HTML and CSS Creating a Rollover Effect

```
<!DOCTYPE html PUBLIC "-//W3C//DTD XHTML 1.0 Transitional//EN"
      "http://www.w3.org/TR/xhtml1/DTD/xhtml1-transitional.dtd">
<html xmlns="http://www.w3.org/1999/xhtml">
<head>
    <meta http-equiv="Content-Type" content="text/html; charset=UTF-8" />
    <title>Image Roll Over</title>
    <style type="text/css">
      body{margin: 0px; padding: 0px;
          background-image:url(images/background-page.gif);}
      #top{width: 580px; height: 351px; background-image:url(images/header.gif)}
      #container{margin: 0px auto; width: 580px}
      #content{ background-color:#001021; margin-left: 6px; margin-right: 5px;}
      .jeffPhoto {width: 251px; height: 376px;
                background-image:url(images/jeff.jpg);margin: 0px auto;}
      .jeffPhoto:hover{ background-position: -251px 0px}
      .caption{color:#FFF; width: 251px; margin: 0px auto; text-align:center;
              font-family:Verdana, Geneva, sans-serif}
    </style>
</head>
```

```
<body>
    <div id="container">
    <div id="top"></div>
    <div id="content">
    <div class="jeffPhoto"></div>
    <div class="caption">Roll over my head!</div>
    </div>
    </div>
</body>
</html>
```

It's the trick with the background position on the hover that switches the image over from the black-and-white part on the left to the color part on the right. By changing the first value to -251px, the image shifts all the way to the right edge, which shows us the right-hand "half" (in color).

Custom button rollovers with CSS

When you're familiar with text and image rollovers, you can really ramp up your Web site by combining aspects of both to create your own custom buttons.

In the old days, people often created buttons using images with text on them. This method worked, but it also required creating a bunch of individual graphics with rollovers. This not only takes a long time to build and maintain, but images also take time to load when visitors come to your site.

No more! You can create standard buttons using CSS to change their presentation, as we show in Chapter 12. While this works, it doesn't provide the push that takes your site's power level up to "11" (as the special amplifiers did for that famous but fictional rock band, Spinal Tap). A snazzier way to create buttons is to use a CSS "Sliding Doors" technique, which involves using multiple images that scale with the width of your HTML text.

We challenge you to take your new-found skills and attempt this technique on your own. We defer to Janko Jovanovic, a true master of fancy buttons for the sliding doors technique. Be sure to check out his tutorial and try it yourself. You may even be able to improve it using your new skills! Visit "Janko At Warp Speed" at www.jankoatwarpspeed.com/post/2008/04/30/make-fancy-buttons-using-css-sliding-doors-technique.aspx.

Working with Cookies

Every time we start talking about cookies, we're tempted to grab a glass of milk and get ready for dipping. Then we remind ourselves that Web cookies, as useful as they can be, are actually tasteless. (We imagine they'd taste more like chicken than cookies made from the Toll House recipe.) Although they may not be tasty, you may find cookies helpful as you create your Web site.

A *cookie* allows you to store information on visitors' computers that you can revisit later. Cookies offer a powerful way to maintain "state" within Web pages. The code in Listing 16-3 reads and writes two cookies as a visitor loads the page:

- ✔ pageHit contains a count of the number of times the visitor has loaded the page.

- ✔ pageVisit contains the last date and time the visitor visited.

Figure 16-7 shows how the page appears on the initial visit, and Figure 16-8 shows how it looks on subsequent visits.

Figure 16-7: This cookie knows you've never been to this page before.

Figure 16-8: These cookies know not only that you've been here before, but when.

Listing 16-3: Cookie-handling Script

```
<!DOCTYPE html PUBLIC "-//W3C//DTD XHTML 1.0 Transitional//EN"
        "http://www.w3.org/TR/xhtml1/DTD/xhtml1-transitional.dtd">
<html xmlns="http://www.w3.org/1999/xhtml">
<head>
    <title>Cookie Demo</title>
    <meta http-equiv="Content-Type" content="text/html; charset=ISO-8859-1" />
    <script type="text/javascript" language="javascript">
<!--
    now = new Date
    expireDate = new Date
    expireDate.setMonth(expireDate.getMonth()+6)

    hitCt = parseInt(cookieVal("pageHit"))
    hitCt++
    lastVisit = cookieVal("pageVisit")
    if (lastVisit == 0) {
        lastVisit = ""
    }

    document.cookie = "pageHit="+hitCt+";expires=" + expireDate.toGMTString()
    document.cookie = "pageVisit="+now+";expires=" + expireDate.toGMTString()

    function cookieVal(cookieName) {
        thisCookie = document.cookie.split("; ")
         for (i=0; i<thisCookie.length; i++) {
             if (cookieName == thisCookie[i].split("=")[0]) {
                 return thisCookie[i].split("=")[1]
             }
         }
        return 0
    }
-->
    </script>
</head>
<body>
<h2>
    <script type="text/javascript" language="javascript">
<!--
    document.write("You have visited this page " + hitCt + " times.")
    if (lastVisit != "") {
        document.write("<br />Your last visit was " + lastVisit)
    }
-->
    </script>
</h2>
</body>
</html>
```

Unlike preceding examples, Listing 16-3 has a `<script>` section in both the head and the body:

- ✔ Cookies are read and written in the header script when the page loads.
- ✔ The body script dynamically writes out the contents of the page itself.

Follow these steps to add the cookie-handling script to your page:

1. **Copy both `<script>` sections and put them into the appropriate parts of your page.**

2. **Change the `<body>` section to contain the text that you want the page to display.**

   The lines inside the `document.write()` statements write the text out to the document on the fly.

A cookie has an *expiration date,* after which it's no longer available. This example creates cookies that expire in six months. If you want your cookies to live longer (or not so long), adjust the JavaScript code near the top that sets a value for `expireDate`. Thus, the following example increases the current expiration date by six months:

```
expireDate.setMonth(expireDate.getMonth()+6)
```

Working with jQuery and FancyBox Lightbox

In days of yore, it was commonplace to use browser pop-ups to present additional information about your Web site. In fact, we even used this technique in the last edition of this book. Owing to overuse at some unscrupulous Web sites, plus their annoying in-your-face nature, pop-ups are now mostly blocked by major browsers . . . and that's probably a good thing!

Instead of pop-ups, we now recommend using lightboxes. This may sound like a weapon out of Star Wars or a tool used by photographers (that last guess is close). In this case, however, a *lightbox* is a tool that displays images, HTML content, and multimedia atop of a Web page.

Dozens of different lightboxes are available on the Internet. Please use your favorite search engine to check those out if you want to know more. Here, we only discuss jQuery and FancyBox.

If you're unfamiliar with jQuery, think of it as a popular JavaScript library that you can reference without writing much real code yourself. (We don't dig much into jQuery in this book, but you need only do a Web search on this term to find more information than you can read in an entire Sunday afternoon.) jQuery can be extended for many different uses — say for example, a lightbox — by no coincidence whatsover!

To create a lightbox, such as the one at `www.dummieshtml.com/examples/ch16/lightbox`, follow these steps:

1. **Download FancyBox at `http://fancybox.googlecode.com/files/jquery.fancybox-1.3.1.zip`.**

   The FancyBox home page is shown in Figure 16-9.

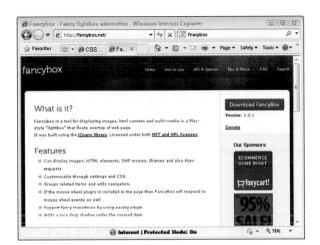

Figure 16-9: The FancyBox home page.

2. **Unzip its files into your Web site folder.**

3. **Create a blank HTML page, and then add the necessary JavaScript files along with the Fancy Box CSS File (see Figure 16-10).**

4. **Include the following code in that document (inside the `head` part):**

```
<script type="text/javascript"
  src="http://ajax.googleapis.com/ajax/libs/jquery/1.4/jquery.min.js">
</script>
<script type="text/javascript"
      src="fancybox/jquery.fancybox-1.3.1.pack.js"></script>
<link rel="stylesheet" href="fancybox/jquery.fancybox-1.3.1.css"
    type="text/css" media="screen" />
```

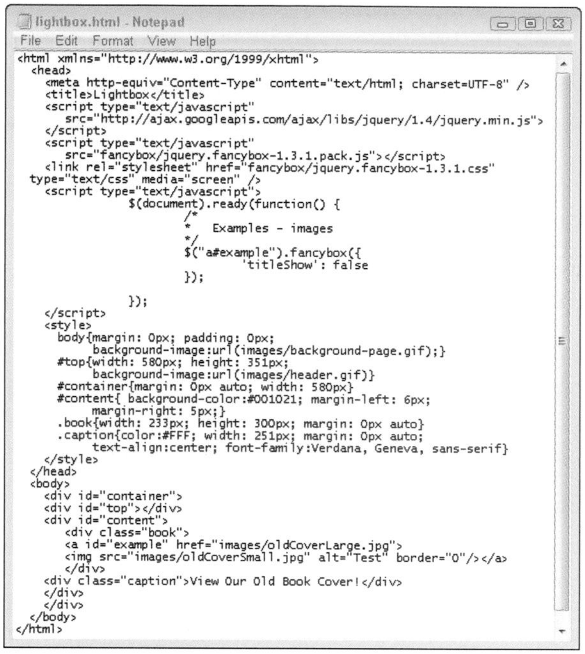

Figure 16-10: HTML source code for our lightbox example.

5. Create a link to launch the lightbox.

In this example (see Figure 16-11), we use a small image to launch a larger one.

```
<a id="example" href="images/oldCoverLarge.jpg">
<img src="images/oldCoverSmall.jpg" alt="Our Old Book Cover"
    border="0" /></a>
```

Figure 16-11 shows how the lightbox looks on the Web page when completed. You can also view it online at www.dummieshtml.com/examples/ch16/lightbox.

Here's the magic part: We add some JavaScript to enable the lightbox to work with jQuery.

6. Enter the following code into the head section of your document:

```
<script type="text/javascript">
$(document).ready(function() {
    $("a#example").fancybox({
            'titleShow': true
    });
});
</script>
```

Figure 16-11: The lightbox example from the HTML For Dummies Web site.

This example is intended to showcase what's possible using these tools. Check out the sample code on our site and give it a shot! (You can also visit www.dummieshtml.com/examples/ch16/lightbox, and then choose View⇨Source in Internet Explorer or View⇨Page Source in Firefox.)

For additional resources for this example, visit the following sites:

- **jQuery:** http://docs.jquery.com/How_jQuery_Works
- **FancyBox:** http://fancybox.net/howto

To find alternative lightbox plugins, check the following sites:

- **6 Lightbox Plugins for WordPress:** http://franklinbishop.net/6-lightbox-plugins-for-wordpress
- **jQuery lightBox:** http://leandrovieira.com/projects/jquery/lightbox

You can find more about JavaScript libraries at the following sites:

- **jQuery:** www.jquery.com
- **script.aculo.us:** http://script.aculo.us
- **MooTools:** http://mootools.net

If you try to follow along with the various techniques we illustrate in these chapters, you'll realize that we didn't describe every single step in complete detail. You will need to load image files into the various environments (Flickr, for example), and in general, you must make sure that file paths and other resource references are absolutely correct (or images and objects won't show up where they should). Our skeleton approach is designed to help you understand what you must do in general. If you need more help in completing the steps, drop us an e-mail (etittel@yahoo.com, jeff@conquestmedia.com) or send us a tweet (@dummieshtml), and we'll add a step-by-step tutorial to the Web site.

Chapter 17

Content Management Systems

In This Chapter

▶ Understanding the differences between content management systems and HTML

▶ Introducing WordPress, Drupal, and Joomla!

▶ Customizing CSS using content management systems

A content management system (CMS) is a Web application designed to make life easy for nontechnical users to add, edit, and (wait for it . . .) *manage* a Web site. A CMS is like a Web site on steroids: bigger, stronger, and with more abilities. However, a CMS might be overkill for what many folks need — and there are side effects.

Well, that's it for us: You can now put this book down and just use a CMS instead of HTML. Cue the music and thanks very much: The End. Alas, if only that were true. Many people start with HTML, XHTML, and CSS, and eventually graduate to their very own CMS Web site, whereas others jump directly into CMS and move ahead from there. It really just depends on what makes you comfortable and happy. Regardless of whether you start out with or graduate to a CMS, learning HTML, XHTML, and CSS will help (not hurt) as you prepare for life with a CMS (if you choose that option).

Comparing CMS Sites to HTML Sites

Table 17-1 describes a few ways in which a CMS-based site compares with a basic HTML Web site.

Table 17-1 HTML-Only and CMS-Based Web Sites Compared	
CMS-Based Site	*HTML-Only Site*
Edit anywhere using a Web browser and an Internet link	Edit local files and upload to a Web server
HTML, XHTML, and CSS knowledge not required, but helpful for customization	HTML, XHTML, and CSS required unless using a WYSIWYG editing tool (such as Dreamweaver)
Access can be restricted on a per-user basis	Anyone with write access to the right server folder can add, change, or delete HTML files
Hard to set up unless assisted by Web host	Easy to set up
Easy to update, lots of automation support	Easy to update, little or no automation support
Requires a database to store information	A database is possible but not required

Popular CMS Sites and Programs

There are probably more CMS options available than pages in this book. Supporters of any particular CMS are a lot like most of the mixed martial arts fans that we know — all of them think whoever or whatever they support is the absolute best and no amount of arguing can change that — until one party takes the other party out! We don't cover any particular CMS in depth in this chapter. Rather, we identify three of the most popular CMS choices available — WordPress, Drupal, and Joomla! — and introduce them with some high-level exploration. For those who might want to find out more about any or all of these systems, whole books are dedicated to each. We recommend checking them out so you can pick one to explore further on your own, without any threat of someone putting you into the infamous "kimura hold."

If it looks like we're avoiding in-depth coverage of these CMS options, this is a case where looks do not deceive. There's no way we can cover everything about CMS systems and capabilities in a single chapter, nor can we provide much useful information or detail about any single CMS in the same space. However, we can tell you what makes them useful, interesting, and popular, so that's what we do instead.

Lots of Web hosts offer the CMS systems we cover briefly here — namely, WordPress, Drupal, and Joomla! — to their customers (often for free; sometimes, for a slightly higher monthly fee). For the companion site for this book, we were able to set up the sample sites we use as examples in the following sections using all three of these CMS options for no extra cost. Hmmm . . . something else you might want to think about using when selecting a Web hosting provider, especially if you find one or more of these CMS offerings appealing.

WordPress

WordPress is widely known as a blogging system but has evolved into a full-blown CMS. It's offered as a multi-platform CMS in a hosted solution from its developers (www.wordpress.com) and in a self-hosted solution (www.wordpress.org). The differences between these two varieties of WordPress are minor, and your choice will depend on your intentions and the amount of control you will need over your site.

For the most part, the hosted solution involves an easier setup and requires neither a download nor an installation to some specific Web server. On the other hand, the self-hosted solution offers many more customization options and confers complete control to its operators. Either way, a basic setup is free (and the self-hosted version is open source, so you can download, install, modify, and share the WordPress code for free). With a user community in the millions, thousands of optional features are available with plugins and themes that you can use to extend WordPress and add to its already formidable list of features and functions. (Most plugins and themes are free, though some commercial products also play on this field.)

WordPress distinguishes itself from other CMS because it is

- ✔ Extremely easy to use
- ✔ Highly extensible
- ✔ Home to strong and passionate user and developer communities

Our companion site for this book (www.dummieshtml.com) is built atop a WordPress self-hosted solution for which we've done a fair amount of custom CSS development.

Drupal

Drupal is an open source CMS. According to the Drupal Web site (www.drupal.org), Drupal is a "free software package that allows an individual or community of users to easily publish, manage, and organize a wide variety of content on a Web site." Drupal is known to most as a solid and well-thought-out CMS, but it is hampered with a somewhat difficult installation, and its management interface can also be a bit confusing. Like WordPress, Drupal offers additional modules that you can add to a Web site to extend its functionality. Also like WordPress, thousands of these modules are available for you to download and install.

Drupal's strengths include the following:

- It's free
- It supports highly flexible layout and page creation capabilities
- It's also highly extensible

There is no hosted version of Drupal available at a single centralized site, but you can download Drupal from `www.drupal.org` and install it anywhere you might like!

Joomla!

In discussing this CMS, we drop the exclamation point from its proper name, Joomla!, following the same convention in other books. We think this makes the name more readable, if less emphatic.

Joomla is an open source CMS that gives its users total control over the Web sites under its management. Joomla is extremely powerful and offers "out of the box" features that include user (account) management, multi-language support, template management, and an integrated help and support system. As with WordPress and Drupal, Joomla supports a plethora of add-on features (called extensions) that you can download and install.

Joomla is known for the following characteristics:

- It's free
- It's easy for site designers and operators to use to set up individual Web sites
- It's highly extensible, and it offers a comprehensive set of management and support tools

You can download Joomla from `www.joomla.org`. However, Joomla's great power also puts the burden of great responsibility on its operators (who run the servers on which Joomla is used to set up and manage individual Web sites), if not also on its operators (who build and manage those individual sites).

Customizing CSS on a CMS

Sure, reading about CMS is nice and all that, but this is an HTML (plus XHTML and CSS) book, so we have to dive in a little deeper. Here again, we won't swim all the way down to the bottom of this pool — we just cover some areas within the individual CMS packages introduced in the previous section and explain how you might go about updating the HTML/CSS in each one.

Each of the three systems — namely, WordPress, Drupal, and Joomla — uses different methods to edit CSS. However, for all the systems, changing the "theme" is the key to accessing and managing page presentation for the sites under their control.

WordPress and CSS

Installing and managing themes in WordPress is easy. With the CSS skills we provide you in this book, you should find it even easier to update and tweak the look and feel for any predefined theme you might like. In fact, you can use what you know to create your own themes, using a predefined WordPress theme as your point of departure.

First, log in to your site's WordPress administration view. Then, from the main dashboard, click the Appearance link in the panel to the left (the one with a small icon that looks like some sections on a page). This screen shows your current theme and how to activate other themes, and lets you install new ones, as shown in Figure 17-1.

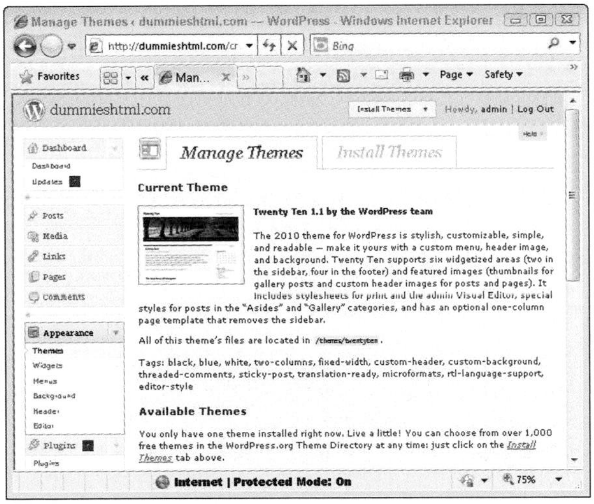

Figure 17-1: Basic theme management in WordPress.

To edit the current theme, click the Editor link in the Appearance panel. The main stylesheet contents open in a text input area in the main screen. Alternatively, you can select the style you want to work on under the Styles category on the right side of the page.

After you handle these preliminaries, all you must do to update the CSS is to choose some element in the current stylesheet, modify it, and then click the Update File button (under the input area). This saves your changes and makes them part of the theme, so be prepared to spend some time tweaking and tuning to get things just right.

In our simple example, we want to increase the font size for the body text in our Web site (this actually requires changing a stylesheet entry named #content, so be sure to make your changes for that element in particular). To do this, we scroll to the #content element, then bump the font size up from .76em to 1em, and then click the Update File button. See Figure 17-2 for the before (top) and after (bottom) results of changing the font size.

When you're working on style sheets from any of these CMSs, you may find it easier to grab them and import them to your local machine, where you can use a CSS-savvy editor (or at least a text editor with search-and-replace functionality) instead of the waaaay-too-basic text editing any of these systems gives you.

You can also update the CSS in WordPress using an entirely different method. Here's how:

1. **Log in to your Web site with an FTP client.**

   (See Chapter 23 for information on FTP clients.)

2. **Navigate to the CSS folder (usually found in /www/wp-content/ themes).**

3. **Select your current theme folder.**

4. **Download the main stylesheet.**

   Be careful — there may be multiple styles with a .css file extension.

5. **Modify the file using a Web site editor.**

   (For recommendations, see Chapter 23.)

6. **Upload the main stylesheet file back to the location from which you downloaded it.**

For more information about updating CSS and tons of other features about WordPress, we suggest latching on to a copy of *WordPress For Dummies,* 3rd Edition, by Lisa Sabin-Wilson.

Figure 17-2: Before (top) and after (bottom) changing the font size on the WordPress site.

Drupal and CSS

Themes in Drupal are a bit more involved and require more effort to update than in WordPress. Even so, we think the process is pretty fascinating!

First, you must know which theme is designated as the default Drupal theme. To make this determination, follow these steps:

1. **Log in to your Drupal administration page.**

2. **In the Administrator panel, choose Site Building⇨Themes.**

3. **On the Themes page, scroll down to find the name of the theme that's currently enabled. (Look for the selected check box in the Enabled column, as shown in Figure 17-3.)**

   Remember this name.

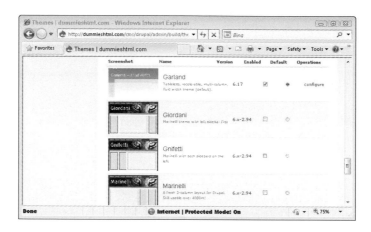

Figure 17-3: The Themes page in Drupal shows that the Garland theme is selected.

4. **Log in to your Web site with an FTP client and navigate to the CSS folder.**

   This folder is usually found in the `/httpdocs/themes` folder; for our site, the directory specification is `.../cms/drupal/themes/garland`, where Garland is the name for our default theme.

5. **Select your current theme folder and download the main stylesheet (it lives in a file named `style.css`).**

   In this example, we want to make the body text in our Web site bigger, so we open up the main stylesheet. (Be careful — you'll find many files that end in `.css` in any theme directory.)

6. **Modify that file in a Web editor.**

   We opened the `style.css` file with a Web site editor, and then found the `<body>` tag and changed the `font-size` from `12px` to `16px`.

7. **Upload the edited file back to the same location.**

Figure 17-4 shows the original page (top) and the edited page (bottom).

For more information about Drupal, we suggest checking out *Drupal For Dummies* by Lynn Beighley.

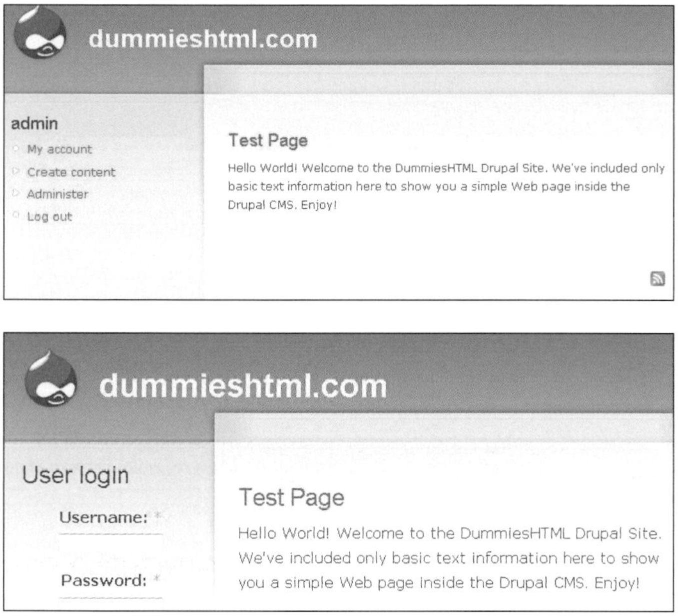

Figure 17-4: Before (top) and after (bottom) with Drupal and a font size enlargement.

Joomla and CSS

While not as quite as user friendly as WordPress, editing themes in Joomla is much easier than in Drupal — but at least, it's not FTP based!

To edit a theme using CSS in Joomla, follow these steps:

1. **Log in to Joomla.**

2. **On the Administration page, choose Extensions➪Template Manager.**

   The template manager is where you select your (drum roll please) template — which is a lot like selecting a theme in WordPress or Drupal.

   You see a list of installed templates, and the default template in effect for your Web site is tagged with a yellow star in the Default column, as shown in Figure 17-5.

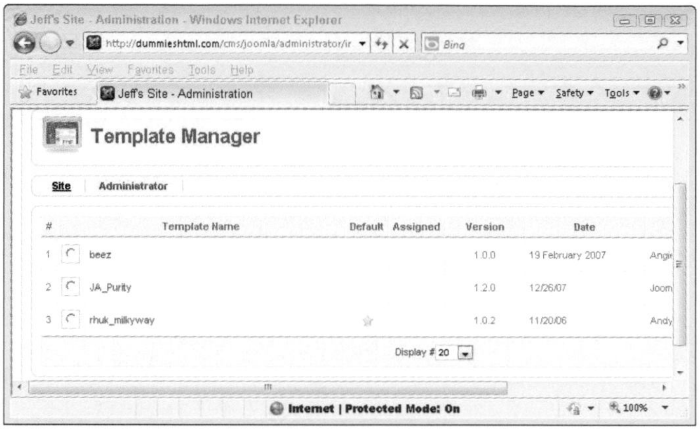

Figure 17-5: The Joomla Template Manager marks the current template with a yellow star.

3. **Click the template name that's designated with the star (that is, you'll want to click the left-most column in the table of entries) for an overview of that template.**

4. **Click the Edit CSS icon at the upper right.**

   A list of CSS files appears.

5. **To edit any of these files, click the radio button on the left to select a particular file, and then click the Edit icon above the table on the right.**

   In this example, we want to make the body text in our Web site bigger, so we click the radio button to the left of the main CSS template called template.css. Then we click the Edit icon above the table. The CSS for the selected template file opens in a text input box.

6. **Edit the CSS code in the text input box.**

   For example, we scrolled to the <body> tag and changed font-size from 12px to 16px.

7. **Click the Save icon above the text input box to commit your changes to the template file.**

   That's it! See Figure 17-6 to view the site before (top) and after (bottom) changing the font size.

For more information about Joomla, we suggest checking out *Joomla! For Dummies* by Steven Holzner and Nancy Conner.

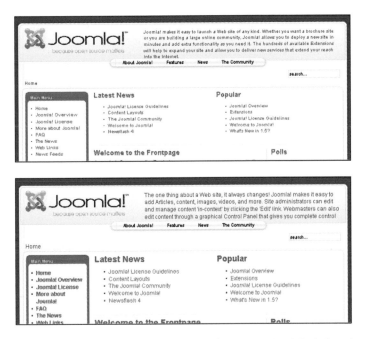

Figure 17-6: Before (top) and after (bottom) changing the default Joomla body font size.

Pssst! Hey Buddy! Wanna See Some CMS?

As exciting as this section heading may seem, the reality actually both exceeds its floridity and promise. We built three sample sites for each of the CMS options we cover in this chapter (WordPress, Drupal, and Joomla), so you can drop by the companion site for this book (in the CMS section, if you must know) to visit any or all of them.

Don't get your hopes up too high, though — we're permitting you read-only access to these offerings, so you can look but you can't touch. As the protagonist himself said to Robin Hood in *Shrek 1:* "Hey, that's my princess. Go find your own!"

Here are the URLs for the various CMS versions:

- http://dummieshtml.com/cms/wordpress
- http://dummieshtml.com/cms/drupal
- http://dummieshtml.com/cms/joomla

Part V

The Future of (X)HTML

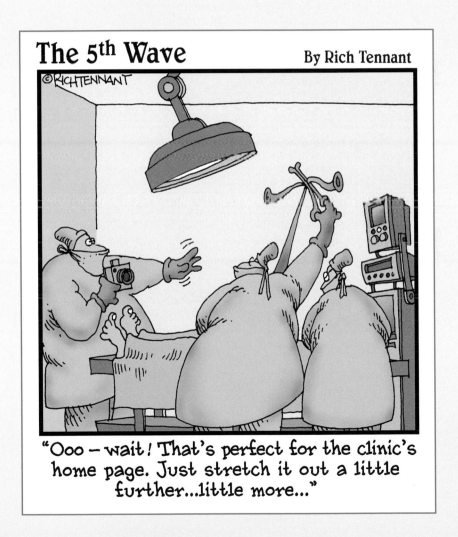

The 5th Wave   By Rich Tennant

"Ooo — wait! That's perfect for the clinic's home page. Just stretch it out a little further...little more..."

In this part . . .

Here, we look at several looming and important developments in (X)HTML that aren't quite completely cooked. While you must know about these works in progress, incorporate them into your work very carefully (if at all) and plan to weather the inevitable changes that time will bring to them.

We introduce you to (X)HTML for mobile devices, a "markup dialect" especially tailored to work well (and look good) on such mobile devices as smartphones, GPSs, and iPads. After that, we give you an overview of HTML5, a very cool and emerging remake of HTML to improve work and life for Web developers and Web users. Part V concludes with a look at the Cascading Style Sheet Language Level 3 (better known as CSS3), which builds on existing CSS capabilities to bring cool looks and dynamic behaviors to the Web pages it graces.

One word of warning: Different Web browsers offer differing degrees of support for all the topics we cover in this part. Depending on the browser you use, be prepared to read about things you can't see, or to find things working differently than the way we describe them. Currently, not all browsers can handle or display all this stuff properly.

Chapter 18

Mobile Web Design

In This Chapter

▶ Understanding mobile access devices and their special display environments

▶ Making the most of limited screen real estate

▶ Learning best practices and principles for mobile Web site design

▶ Building usable, friendly mobile Web sites

*T*here's no doubt today that mobile devices have gone mainstream. Today's marketplace boasts a wide array of products, many competing manufacturers, and oodles of innovative features. However, before we wax too eloquent, we should clarify that we aren't talking about ski mobiles, mobile homes, or even Mobile, Alabama. For this book, the mobile Web serves those portable multi-use phones and other devices (such as the iPad or a Wi-Fi-connected portable GPS) that are so easy to carry around and integrate into our everyday lives.

Mobile devices are unbeatable for quick access to directions and maps, to check out product reviews or comparisons, to find contact information, or to simply surf the Internet while on the go. Because of this, we think understanding mobile Web design is important, too. That way, you can utilize your new skills and knowledge to account for the many unique challenges that mobile access can pose, and perhaps build a better Web site as a result.

Understanding Different Mobile Devices

Unfortunately, the more you look around at the different types of mobile devices, the more it seems like there's no ready way to categorize them all or no single approach to implement Web pages in their limited display space.

For example, you typically find mobile devices categorized by one or more of the following characteristics:

✔ Input device (touchscreen, stylus, keyboard, or touchpad)

✔ Operating system (Symbian, Windows Mobile, Apple iOS, Android)

✔ Processor and memory

✔ Screen size

✔ Internet access

✔ Connectivity (Bluetooth, USB)

✔ Other cool features (camera, video, ringtones, games)

This list could go on and on . . . you get the idea that there are almost as many ways to profile mobile devices as there are mobile devices themselves.

On the most basic level, the safest and easiest way to classify mobile devices is by smartphone versus feature phone. A smartphone is usually characterized by its computerlike features, such as an operating system integrated into the phone, a more powerful processor and memory, the capability to install and run custom applications, wireless access, color display, advanced input capabilities, and higher costs (more expensive to buy and costlier to use, in fact). The iPhone, shown in Figure 18-1, is one of the most popular smartphones.

Figure 18-1: Apple iPhone.

Feature phones usually incorporate less powerful processors and memory, have a basic and proprietary operating system, offer limited application possibilities (if any), and, of course, cost less (feature phones often cost less than half of what smartphones do and, with more limited data handling capabilities, often cost about half as much for monthly service as well). A typical example of a feature phone is the Nokia phone shown in Figure 18-2.

Figure 18-2: Standard Nokia feature phone.

Here's the bad news: Not only do these types of phones differ in features and prices, they also display Web sites differently. Feature phones have extremely limited CSS and JavaScript support, if they have any such support at all. However, before you throw your hands up in the air (and wave them like you just don't care), we recommend learning more about mobile Web site design in the following sections. Feature phones aren't all bad, nor are smartphones all good. For both types of devices, some Web site compromises will prove necessary.

Optimizing Mobile Web Site Design

When you start thinking about how to design mobile version(s) of your Web site, and produce the best possible results for visitors who employ mobile devices to visit your pages, you need to ponder the unique challenges that the mobile Web can pose for your site's design and implementation.

Considerations to keep in mind when you design sites for the mobile Web include:

- ✔ **Limited screen real estate:** Mobile designs must fit on small screens (for example, 320 x 240 pixels).

- ✔ **Low bandwidth:** Limit images and text to ensure that pages load quickly even at slow connection speeds (2G data rates seldom exceed 500 Kbps; even 3G rates under 600 Kbps are common).

- ✔ **Interface limitations:** Create links and other navigation options that are easy to click with a (fat) finger, stylus, or other limited input options.

- ✔ **Limited processing power and memory:** Large files and scripts that require fast processors don't work well (or at all) on many mobile devices.

- ✔ **Distracted users:** Mobile device users often are on the go or multitasking, so aim for stark, simple designs with extremely easy navigation.

- ✔ **Urgent need for information:** Many people turn to the mobile Web because they must, because they're lost or late, or because they *really* need to know who won the Super Bowl in 1987 to win a bet.

- ✔ **Time and place:** Mobile device users' actions are likely affected by where they are, the time of day, and even whether it's raining or not. Be sure to include location-specific information, such as maps, and consider adding geographic location features, like those incorporated into the new HTML5 specification (such as the geolocation API).

The Geolocation API Specification is available at www.w3.org/TR/geolocation-API. You might also want to check out this nifty HTML 5 Geolocation Demo, too: http://maxheapsize.com/static/html5gcolocationdemo.html. Maxheap.com isn't viewable using

Internet Explorer because it requires a GeoLocation-aware browser to work. You'll need to use FireFox3.1b3, or greater, or perhaps Safari or Chrome, to view the Maxheap.com demo.

Designing for small screens

If every mobile phone had the same screen size, we might not have had to write about mobile Web design for this book. While there are many other considerations to think about when creating mobile Web sites or pages, limited display real estate is one of the most important to keep in mind.

Creating a single design with a fixed width doesn't work if you want to take best advantage of real estate available on each screen. Also, remember that many smartphones can be rotated, so the user may view your page in both landscape and portrait views!

Optimizing for low bandwidth

Smaller screen size isn't the only thing that limits how well you can display images and multimedia on a cellphone; limited bandwidth also figures importantly when designing and building a Web site for mobile access. And although a growing number of mobile users can take advantage of faster 3G and 4G mobile networks, many mobile device users are still hampered by connections best described as painfully slow.

The same challenges with limited bandwidth that throttled early Web design and access for pioneering users in the early to mid-1990s now slow the mobile Internet. It lags far behind high-speed DSL and cable modem connections from a desktop or notebook computer.

While you design a mobile version of your site, the following tips will help your site provide tolerable service for visitors with low-bandwidth connections:

- ✔ **Be ruthless with images and multimedia files.** Limit your mobile site to a precious few images to help tell your story and add visual interest. Keep things small and simple.

- ✔ **Replace banners and button images with text links.** These work on any device and consume only minimal storage space and bandwidth.

- ✔ **Be careful when including multimedia.** For example, don't put video or audio files on the front page of a mobile site. Instead, link to multimedia files so they're optional for mobile browsers. Also, include warnings about file size and the way the media displays on different devices.

- ✔ **Keep the total size of your front page to 7K or less for low-end mobile devices.** Yes, you read that right, 7K — that's one tiny image and a few links, and no more.

Navigating on mobile devices

Mobile visitors are most likely to interact with their devices by

- Touching the screen with a finger
- Tapping the screen with a stylus
- Entering information using buttons, a wheel, or a teeny-tiny keypad

That means you need to

- **Make links easy to see and click.** If you design multiple versions of your site, be sure to optimize for the input options on each device. If visitors use a stylus, they can click links relatively close together, but if they use a touchscreen, put enough space between links to make it easy to tap them with a fat fingertip.

- **Limit the total number of links, especially on the low-end version of your site.** Help people move through your site by leading them from one short list of links to another until they reach the content that serves them best.

- **Organize link levels.** Don't include too many levels with your links, and consider adding breadcrumbs to help users find their way back through your site. *Breadcrumbs* are a list of links, usually at the top of a page, that help users identify where they are in the structure of the site. The links to each section and subsection are ahead of the current page in the site's structure, from the home page all the way down to the current page (which is accessible through the browser's address box).

- **Use a navigation menu, not a navigation bar.** Although most desktop Web sites include a navigation bar that links to all main sections in a site at the top of every page, that's generally not the best use for real estate on a small screen. Instead, consider including one link at the top of every page with a name like Menu, and then link it to a navigation bar.

  Including a list of links to all the main pages of your site on every page may not be worth the download time, but creating a small site map and including a link to that page from every other page on the site provides a similar option without lots of extra overhead. Use this strategy to include a list of links at the bottom of each page, too, with a Menu link up top that jumps visitors to the links at the bottom.

- **Consider back and forward buttons.** Back and forward buttons help users move through many pages of content or images.

- **Link from one site version to another.** It's always a good practice to include a link on the front page of your mobile site to the desktop version and vice versa. Visitors to your mobile site may already be familiar with your desktop version and prefer to visit that full site, especially if they are using an iPhone or Droid.

Designing for distracted surfers

When people visit a mobile site, they're often doing something else at the same time, and they're often under pressure to find information quickly.

Here are a few quick tips to make your mobile site easier for distracted visitors to use:

- ✔ Make key information, such as your address and phone number, easy to find right away.

- ✔ Make all links big and easy to click.

- ✔ Use text and contrasting background colors so the text is easy to read, even in low light (or on a display that's hard to read in strong sunlight).

Surfing the Web on many mobile devices

To appreciate the challenges of the mobile Web, surf to your Web site on a mobile phone. However, don't stop at one phone, especially if you have an iPhone or Android. The iPhone and Android may get all the headlines (and a majority of the traffic on the mobile Web), but they're not the only phones likely to visit your site. Those same sites viewed on a BlackBerry or, worse, a Razr, may be completely unreadable.

Although you can test your mobile site using online emulators, such as the high-end testing site at DeviceAnywhere (`www.deviceanywhere.com`), the best way is to hold a device in your hand so you can see how your site feels and looks on that phone.

Visit a mobile phone store and be really nice to the salespeople while you test your sites on their phones. Better yet, compare notes with friends and family. Ask people to visit your Web site on different phones and watch what they do, how they find their way around (or where they get lost), and how hard it is for them to get to the information they need when they interact with your site.

Best Practices for Mobile Web Sites

In the following sections, we explore some best practices to help you name your mobile Web site to make it easy for mobile device users to type your site's name. We also describe some common ways in which you may want to make use of a mobile version of your Web site.

Set up mobile Web addresses

So that everyone with a mobile phone can easily get to the URL of your mobile site (by typing as little as possible), set up multiple mobile addresses and direct them all to the mobile version of your site.

Until a clear winner appears in the mobile URL game, use all the most common addresses to increase the odds that your visitors find you on their first try.

The following are typical mobile URLs in common use on the mobile Web:

- ✔ m.*yourdomain*.com: Recommended for ease of typing
- ✔ wap.*yourdomain*.com: This is a common address for sites created using the WML (Wireless Markup Language)
- ✔ *yourdomain*.com/mobile: Common alternative because of easy server setup
- ✔ *yourdomain*.com/i: For versions built specifically for the iPhone
- ✔ *yourdomain*.mobi: Requires registering a .mobi version of your domain name, which many sites don't seem to bother with

Whatever you do, drop the www. — no one should ever have to type those three letters and that dot again on the modern Web.

Create a virtual demo or showcase

Consider what's most important to your audience. If you don't have a physical location but want to use your mobile site to showcase your work, create a portfolio that displays well on the small screen. Then, the next time you're at a party or business event, your mobile phone will be everything you (or your sales and marketing staff) need to present an impromptu demo of your products or services anywhere, anytime.

Location, location, location

Mobile Web surfers can be anywhere, including in front of your restaurant, office, or store, or worse, lost on the road trying to find you.

When you consider how to design a mobile version of your Web site, consider not just how to make things smaller but also how to present the information most likely to be useful to someone using a mobile device, wherever he or she might be. And while you're at it, make it quick, easy to find, and easy to use, too.

One of the most common uses of mobile phones is still the most obvious — making phone calls. Be sure your phone number is easy to find on the first screen of any mobile site, and include your street address and links to maps for those who might be lost and trying to make their way to your location.

Include a link to a Google map on your home page. This makes it easy to find you. For best results, link to Google Maps for Mobile at `www.google.com/mobile/maps`.

Both Yahoo! and Google let you prioritize searches for local matches on their mobile sites. Take the time to optimize your mobile site and be sure to include location-specific keywords: the names of the cities, states, or even local neighborhoods that you serve.

Don't make users type or click too much

Even on the best mobile devices, typing and clicking links can be a challenge. Always make links big and easy to click for mobile visitors, and don't overload any page with too many options.

The best approach is to lead users through a series of simple choices, limiting options to no more than five to seven big links at any stage. Directing visitors to increasingly specific sets of links is best until users can choose the information they want or need.

Avoid drop-down lists, or anything else that uses AJAX or JavaScript around links. That's because many mobile devices don't support these Web technologies, therefore making these links impossible to use.

Some information, such as contact information, should never be more than one click away. In nearly all cases, including your phone number on the main page of your mobile site is good practice — after all, you know your visitor has a phone handy!

Mobile Frameworks

After reading our various lists of mobile design considerations earlier in this chapter, you may feel inclined to jump into your modified DeLorean and head back to simpler times with Marty McFly. However, before you hit 88 mph and activate the flux capacitor, you might want to check out some interesting new approaches to Web and application development based on HTML, CSS, and JavaScript. Just like Doc Brown in *Back to the Future,* the following frameworks aren't perfect, but they do provide a good indication of what the future is likely to hold when it comes to mobile Web design and related technologies.

Sencha Touch

www.sencha.com/products/touch

Sencha Touch is the First HTML5 Mobile App Framework that allows you to develop Web apps that look and feel native on Apple iOS and Google Android touchscreen devices.

Visit the Get Started with Sencha Touch page at http://dev.sencha.com/deploy/touch/getting-started.html to find out more about using Sencha Touch to develop Web apps.

To try some demos, as shown in Figure 18-3, visit www.sencha.com/products/touch/demos.php.

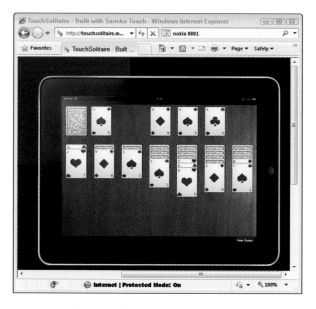

Figure 18-3: Sencha Touch demo on an iPad.

jQTouch

www.jqtouch.com

jQTouch is a beta jQuery plugin for mobile Web development on the iPhone, iPod Touch, and "other forward-thinking devices."

Visit the Getting Started page at http://github.com/senchalabs/jQTouch/wiki/gettingstarted to find out more about developing Mobile Web sites with jQTouch.

To view the jQTouch demo for the iPhone, shown in Figure 18-4, go to www.jqtouch.com/preview/demos/main.

Figure 18-4: jQTouch demo on a simulated iPhone.

Additional Resources

For additional information, we highly recommend checking out *Mobile Web Design For Dummies* by Janine Warner and David LaFontaine. It covers all the popular cellphone and smartphone platforms, and the tools needed for mobile design, with particular emphasis on XHTML and CSS.

The W3C mobileOK Checker (shown in Figure 18-5) is a free service from the World Wide Web Consortium that helps check the level of mobile-friendliness in Web documents and, in particular, determine whether a Web document is "mobile okay." Visit the mobileOK Checker at http://validator.w3.org/mobile.

Figure 18-5: The W3C mobileOK Checker.

Chapter 19

Party On with HTML5

In This Chapter

▶ Understanding HTML5 and what it could mean for your Web site

▶ Making the Web more interoperable with HTML5

▶ Simplifying markup with HTML5

▶ Losing deprecated elements and attributes with HTML5

▶ Adding snazzy new input types with HTML5

▶ Watching HTML5 at work

*C*hances are good that you've heard of HTML5, the most widely hyped markup development to hit the Web in a long, long time. Everybody seems to have an opinion about it. Some folks tout HTML5 as a magic elixir to relieve all the pains and annoyances from existing Web problems, while others are more skeptical and want to reserve judgment until there's more substance upon which to base an evaluation. One thing's for sure: HTML5 promises to give authors more flexibility and greater interoperability by introducing enhancements to form controls, APIs, multimedia, structure, and semantics. Before moving into those topics, we cover the basics first.

HTML5 is the latest iteration of the HyperText Markup Language (HTML) from the World Wide Web Consortium. Go ahead, try saying that three times quickly, and you will understand why it's better known as the W3C. (The W3C was established in October 1994 to lead the World Wide Web to its full potential by developing common protocols and services to promote its evolution and ensure its interoperability. Essentially, the W3C is an international group of experts that helps to set the rules the rest of us must follow to design Web sites.)

The W3C developed HTML5 to address issues with previous versions (this means HTML4 and XHTML — which we cover in this book) to simplify and enhance authoring of Web pages. Another noteworthy aspect of HTML5 is that it attempts to bridge the gap between the experience Web users obtain from previous versions and the interactions they'd like to achieve, especially considering the tools and techniques available to Web designers and developers to help users reach those goals. Today's world is different from what it was when earlier HTML implementations and a host of other supporting environments appeared. HTML5 seeks to catch up the markup and its surrounding Web and browser environment with the dynamic, interactive, and media-rich environment that users expect to find and use online.

HTML5 Highlights: Why It's Important

To begin, let's get something straight: HTML5 incorporates and continues to use nearly all the markup associated with HTML4 and XHTML. Everything in this book — for the most part — is as relevant to HTML5 as it is to older versions. In fact, this observation applies even after HTML5 gets past its draft and candidate recommendation stages, and achieves full-blown status as an official W3C standard. And guess what: It's nearly guaranteed that all the elements and attributes deprecated in HTML4 and XHTML (documented in Chapter 8) will *not* be part of HTML5. The HTML5 specification tells it like this: "The majority of presentational features from previous versions of HTML are no longer allowed."

Don't hold your breath waiting for a finalized version of HTML5. Best guesses as to when that might happen fall between 2020 and 2022, with a candidate recommendation expected no sooner than 2012. Despite the long wait for a finalized version, many aspects of the HTML5 draft specification (the most recent draft posted August 27, 2010, at the W3C site) are already quite stable, and developers and browser makers are adding HTML5 features to their offerings. To look over the latest version of the HTML5 specification, visit `http://dev.w3.org/html5/spec/Overview.html`. (The address is case sensitive, so make certain you type **Overview** and not **overview** when entering the URL; otherwise, you'll get a File Not Found error message.)

A short quote from Section 1.4 in the latest HTML5 specification is helpful when it comes to understanding why HTML5 has proven itself necessary to many Web designers and developers:

> The WHATWG [the working group formed to pursue the development of HTML5 when the W3C initially chose not to participate] was based on several core principles, in particular that technologies need to be backwards compatible, that specifications and implementations need to match even if this means changing the specification rather than the implementations, and that specifications need to be detailed enough that implementations can achieve complete interoperability without reverse-engineering each other.

The original members of the WHATWG group — namely, Apple Computer, Mozilla (the organization behind the Mozilla Web browser and Firefox), and Opera (the company behind the terrific Opera Web browser) — have been joined by representatives from companies like Google and Microsoft in efforts to develop HTML5, under the renewed auspices of the W3C since 2007. HTML5 is chugging along and is already showing up in pages you can visit. It will become more widespread, and will start making sense to browsers that you and your site's visitors are likely to use, no later than 2012 or 2013 at the outside. Heck, we even show you an HTML5 page on our companion Web site for this book!

What makes HTML5 attractive is that it seeks to eliminate any need for proprietary Web technologies — such as Adobe Flash (discussed in the next section) — by offering equivalent standards-based functionality that is free, open, and designed to look and act the same inside all compliant Web browsers. The technology areas that HTML5 seeks to address in particular include animation, rich media (streaming video, music, live video, and so forth), simplified and enhanced markup, forms and user interactions, and various application hooks (APIs) for all kinds of things. The following section takes a closer look at a specific item in this grab bag of topics.

HTML5 and Flash

On today's Web, Adobe Flash is a major tool in the content developer's arsenal, particularly when he or she wants to build something highly animated, interactive, or visually complex. It's true that the Adobe Flash player is free to any Web user who wants to download a browser plugin for Internet Explorer, Firefox, Safari, Chrome, or Opera, but it's not available to any and all browsers. Alas, the tools that developers use to create Flash content are by no means free: They embody proprietary technology that belongs to Adobe, and developers who want to exercise that technology must pay for that privilege. Developers spend thousands or even tens of thousands of dollars on Adobe technologies they use to build their Web sites.

To some extent, HTML5 seeks to break the Web out of what's sometimes called the "proprietary trap" that some Web technologies impose on content development. A leading notion that drives HTML5 development, as the quote from the specification in the preceding section shows, is a desire for multiple implementations (from different builders, different vendors, and, presumably, different owners) to work together without difficulty or restriction, including a need to license proprietary tools or technologies.

What do we think is going to happen? We think some of the features for which developers must turn to Flash and other proprietary technologies will gradually appear in HTML5, but Flash won't go away any time soon. It's hard to say exactly how things will turn out, but we guess that Flash will stick around for some time, losing market share as HTML5 takes over basic animation and interaction, but continuing on in other, more complicated Web arenas, like online gaming (where users accept proprietary technologies).

The Adobe-Apple controversy heats up

Some vendors — most notably, Apple — have taken a hard line regarding Adobe Flash and won't allow it onto their platforms, period. Although the iPhone and iPad are themselves no paragons of openness, Apple's participation in the HTML5 initiative is meant to bring interoperability and rich media to those devices without requiring Apple to support (or use) Flash technology. Apple's exclusion of Flash from its products has led to speculation and rumor that HTML5 is "in" and Flash is "out." Adobe, as you can imagine, hasn't responded warmly to Apple's exclusion of Flash, and the resulting negative attention to the Flash product lead to a media feud between Apple and Adobe. Adobe plans to release a mobile device version of Flash in late 2010 to prove that Flash is here to stay.

The insults and finger pointing from Apple and Adobe in flashy (pun intended) press conferences and slickly worded public relations memos don't seem to presage an end to the Adobe-Apple debacle anytime soon. Both companies make relevant points, but whatever eventually happens, we would like to point out that such companies exist to make money selling proprietary products.

This situation leaves us lacking something we desperately want: legitimately installed Flash on an iPhone or iPad. Perhaps we can get some help from the Feds. (Or maybe Adobe and Apple can settle this in Judge Judy's court or on a reality TV show where the victor is granted The Future of the Web award.) Okay, these are all terrible ideas, but you get the point. It's a difficult, tricky situation with no immediate consumer gains in sight.

Here's the kicker: Even if Flash does go away (and that's a long shot), the advancement of the Web doesn't stop with HTML5. HTML5 is no perfect solution. It's sure to have its faults, even if we're just guessing as to what they might be right now. Just as with the versions that preceded it — which means HTML4 and XHTML — there will be something new that we will all debate in the future to take its place (HTML6 anyone?) . . . and that's the way it should be.

Simplified and Enhanced HTML5 Markup

One interesting development that's underway in HTML5 is an attempt to simplify and normalize the way markup is expressed. This means leaving some old, gnarly roots behind (see the following section that explains how HTML's roots in Standard Generalized Markup Language, or SGML, are fading into the background), and taking complex expressions and making them shorter and easier to specify (as you see in the later section, "Simplified character encoding"). Finally, there will be some interesting markup additions to HTML5, as we describe in a series of tables in sections that deal with new markup and input types on their way in, and old deprecated elements and attributes on their way out.

Simplified doctype

The SGML document type, or `doctype`, declaration is usually the first text element in any HTML document; it even precedes the opening `<html>` tag. However, a `doctype` declaration itself is not HTML: Rather it's an instruction to the Web browser about the version of markup language in which a page is written. In fact, the `doctype` statement harkens back to the SGML and its document type definitions, or DTDs. SGML originated at IBM in the 1970s with Charles Goldfarb and his crew. Today, SGML still serves as the inspiration for and parent to both HTML and XML.

In this book, we use the following `doctype` declarations for the transitional versions of HTML4 and XHTML, respectively (there are other declarations for strict and frameset DTD versions as well, covered in Chapter 4):

```
<!DOCTYPE HTML PUBLIC "-//W3C//DTD HTML 4.01 Transitional//EN"
   "http://www.w3.org/TR/html4/loose.dtd">
<!DOCTYPE html PUBLIC "-//W3C//DTD XHTML 1.0 Transitional//EN"
   "http://www.w3.org/TR/xhtml1/DTD/xhtml1-transitional.dtd">
```

The `doctype` declaration for HTML5 looks like this instead

```
<!DOCTYPE HTML>
```

Tell us: Which one is easier to remember and reproduce? *Hint:* It's neither the HTML 4.01 nor the XHTML 1.0 DTD references reproduced above! With its SGML heritage no longer on display, HTML5 is more svelte and simple.

Simplified character encoding

When you create any HTML document, a browser (or other software) that parses that document so it can show it to you (or do something else with it, like add it to a search database, validate its syntax and structure, or whatever) must be able to interpret its contents. Without explicitly specifying a character encoding for an HTML document, you take the risk that characters in your content might be interpreted incorrectly.

Though this doesn't happen terribly often, interpretation errors could cause the text on your page to look mangled when it shows up in a browser (or other software). Before you pooh-pooh this notion, stop to consider that there are more than a dozen encodings for the ISO-Latin-1 character set traditionally used for Web pages (denoted `ISO-8859-1` through `ISO-8859-15`). Many other encodings are allowed besides those, too, including UTF-8, UTF-16, and more. For the record, UTF-8 is recommended in the HTML5 draft specification, and it's designated as the default character set that authoring tools should use automatically when creating new documents.

In previous versions of HTML and XHTML, character-encoding statements appear inside the document head and look like this (the value for the `charset` attribute may change, but this statement remains exactly the same):

```
<meta http-equiv="Content-Type" content="text/html; charset=UTF-8" />
```

In XML documents, character encoding appears in the `xml` element that kicks off all such items and takes the form:

```
<?xml version="1.0" encoding="UTF-8" standalone="no"?>
```

In HTML5, this declaration uses the following short string, which draws on XML's simplicity while sticking with traditional HTML terminology:

```
<meta charset="UTF-8">
```

Here again, the value for the `charset` attribute may change (though it probably won't differ very often), but the statement otherwise stays the same.

In HTML5, you can set a document's character encoding in three ways. We prefer the markup shown in the preceding HTML snippet, thanks to its brevity and simplicity. For backward compatibility — a big deal for HTML5, by the way — the old methods for HTML4 and XHTML still work. It's possible to insert a Unicode Byte Order Mark (BOM) at the start of a file to identify an encoding. (This is something that an editing or content creation tool does on a content creator's behalf, unless that content creator decides to edit a document file using a bit-level editor. It's unlikely that you'll encounter this method.) Our advice: Use the short, revised `meta` markup shown above.

The HTML5 specification requires all `meta` elements to appear within the first 512 bytes of a document. This makes it a best practice to place character encoding (and other `meta`) elements right after the `<head>` tag, as close to the start of the document as they can get!

What's New and Improved in HTML5

Whenever HTML goes into a new version (so far, we've seen the specification go from major version numbers 2 to 4, and we are now getting to know 5), there's always new stuff involved. In the sections that follow, we lay out new elements and attributes that are on the HTML5 drawing board. Most of these are likely to survive into the official standard, but a handful or so may not get that far. Only time, and the foibles of the W3C's standards-making process, will tell.

Elements new in HTML5

HTML5 adds some exciting new elements that did not exist in previous versions. Here are the highlights, with all 25 new elements listed in alphabetical order along with brief descriptions:

- ✔ <article> — an independent piece of content, such as a blog entry or news article

- ✔ <aside> — a piece of content that relates only slightly to the rest of a page

- ✔ <audio> — provides a standard way to handle audio information for multimedia content (this also ties into the new APIs that HTML5 makes available, but Web browsers will also include a built-in default audio interface as well)

- ✔ <canvas> — used to render bitmap graphics on the fly, for graphs, games, or other dynamic elements (this also ties into the new APIs that HTML5 makes available)

- ✔ <command> — a command that a user can invoke inside the page or document

- ✔ <datalist> — use this with a new list attribute for the input element to create lists of elements for pull-down menus in combo boxes

- ✔ <details> — additional information or controls available to users on demand

- ✔ <embed> — used for plug-in content, to reference external code and capabilities

- ✔ <figcaption> — provides a caption for a figure element in HTML5 (optional)

- ✔ <figure> — a standalone piece of flow content, which may be a static graphic or a multimedia content element, referenced as a single unit inside a document's main flow

- ✔ <footer> — the concluding information for a section; can contain author, copyright, or other information used to identify content and control its re-use

- ✔ <header> — a collection of introductory or navigational aids at the start of any page

- ✔ <hgroup> — a header for a section, or a collection of pages

- ✔ <keygen> — a user accessible control for generating private, public key pairs for security and encryption purposes

- ✔ `<mark>` — a run of text in a document marked or highlighted for easy reference, owing to its relevance to or citation in some other document

- ✔ `<meter>` — a visual indicator for some measurement (disk usage, for example)

- ✔ `<nav>` — a section of a document that provides navigation aids and information

- ✔ `<output>` — some type of output, perhaps from a script-based calculation or API-based program call

- ✔ `<progress>` — a visual meter for task completion (downloading a file, performing some series of calculations or operations)

- ✔ `<ruby>`, `<rt>`, `<rp>` — markup designed to accommodate annotations created in the Ruby (also known as "Ruby on Rails") Web programming language

- ✔ `<section>` — a generic document or application section, which may be used with h1–h6 elements to delineate document structure

- ✔ `<summary>` — a summary, legend, or caption for `details` information

- ✔ `<time>` — a value for representing a date and/or a time

- ✔ `<video>` — provides a standard way to handle video information for multimedia content (also ties into the new APIs that HTML5 makes available, and likewise browsers will offer a built-in, default video interface as well)

- ✔ `<wbr>` — denotes a possible or potential line break point for text flow

To learn more about these new elements, visit this portion of the HTML5 specification: `http://dev.w3.org/html5/html4-differences`.

Attributes new in HTML5

A variety of new attributes are introduced for HTML5, some for improved consistency with other, pre-existing HTML elements, and others to add new (or extend existing) functionality. As in the previous section, we present these attributes in alphabetical order in the following two sections.

New element-specific attributes for HTML5

For the following list, we follow the attribute name with the HTML5 element (or elements) in parentheses to which that attribute applies. Here are the new element-specific attributes for HTML5:

- ✔ async (script) — influences script loading and execution, allowing these activities to proceed asynchronously (not in lockstep, and not at a specific time)

- ✔ autocomplete (input) — supplies known or guessed input values in data fields

- ✔ autofocus (input, select, textarea, button) — provides a declarative way to focus a form control during page load (user can turn it off if desired; does not apply to input when the hidden attribute is enabled)

- ✔ charset (meta) — widely supported outside the spec in many tools for HTML4, a better way to specify character encoding for HTML5

- ✔ disabled (fieldset) — disables all descendant controls in a field set when specified

- ✔ form (input, output, select, textarea, button, fieldset) — allows controls to be associated with a form, so that elements can appear anywhere on a page, not just inside a form element

- ✔ formaction (input, button) — identifies special handling for forms (overrides action, attribute for the form element)

- ✔ formenctype (input, button) — identifies special handling for forms (overrides enctype attribute for the form element)

- ✔ formmethod (input, button) — identifies special handling for forms (overrides method attribute for the form element)

- ✔ formnovalidate (input, button) — identifies special handling for forms (overrides novalidate attribute for the form element)

- ✔ formtarget (input, button) — identifies special handling for forms (overrides target attribute for the form element)

- ✔ hreflang (area) — added for consistency to match a and link elements

- ✔ label (menu) — allows element to transform into a menu as in a typical GUI, and to provide context menus working with the global context menu attribute

- ✔ manifest (html) — points to an application cache manifest for use with the API for offline Web applications

- ✔ max (input) — specifies a maximum value when input values fall within some range

- ✔ media (a, area) — added for consistency with the link element

- ✔ min (input) — specifies a minimum value when input values fall within some range

- ✔ multiple (input) — indicates that multiple input, comma-separated input values are allowed

- ✔ novalidate (input) — used to disable form validation upon submission

- ✔ pattern (input) — specifies some specific pattern for input values (for example *nnn-nnn-nnnn* indicates the pattern for U.S. telephone numbers, where *n* is an integer from 0 to 9)

- ✔ ping (a, area) — specifies a space-separated list of URLs to ping when a hyperlink is followed; allows browsers (or other agent programs) to inform users which URLs will be pinged, and gives users a way to turn ping off if desired

- ✔ placeholder (input, textarea) — presents a hint to aid users with data entry

- ✔ rel (area) — added for consistency to match a and link elements

- ✔ required (input, textarea) — indicates that users must supply a value to submit a form (does not apply to input if type is hidden, image, or a button type such as submit)

- ✔ reversed (ol) — used to indicate that list order is descending (from higher to lower numbered values)

- ✔ sandbox (iframe) — works with seamless and srcdoc attributes to sandbox frame content and keep it from interacting with the external runtime environment

- ✔ scoped (style) — allows scoped style sheets to be enabled, where style rules within a scoped style element apply only to the local document tree

- ✔ seamless (iframe) — works with sandbox and srcdoc attributes to sandbox frame content and keep it from interacting with the external runtime environment

- ✔ sizes (link) — used in conjunction with the icon relationship (set using the rel attribute) to set the size of a referenced icon (supports use of different icon sizes)

- ✔ srcdoc (iframe) — works with sandbox and seamless attributes to sandbox frame content and keep it from interacting with the external runtime environment

- ✔ start (ol) — no longer deprecated (not presentational)

- ✔ step (input) — specifies a minimum increment between pairs of input values

- ✔ target (base, a, area) — added to base, and no longer deprecated for a and area (helpful in conjunction with iframe element)

- ✔ type (menu) — allows element to transform into a menu as in a typical GUI, and to provide context menus working with the global contextmenu attribute

- ✔ value (li) — no longer deprecated (not presentational)

Global HTML5 Attributes

Not all of these global attributes are new (we mark new ones with an asterisk in the following list), but we include every last one of them because they're important to know and because there aren't that many of them:

- ✔ `aria-*` — collection attributes useful for instructing assistive technologies for readers with visual or audio impairments

- ✔ `class` — an identifier for element instances throughout an entire HTML document

- ✔ `contenteditable*` — indicates that element content is editable, so that users can change element contents and subsidiary markup therein

- ✔ `contextmenu*` — points to a context menu provided by the content creator

- ✔ `data-*` — a collection of user defined attributes where the prefix lets users create their own attributes to avoid clashes with future HTML versions (such attributes may not be used to extend user agent/browser functionality: they're non-standard)

- ✔ `dir` — establish text direction for element content display

- ✔ `draggable*` — works with HTML5's new drag-and-drop element content manipulation API

- ✔ `hidden*` — indicates an element is not relevant to current page content (change as needed to hide/display elements, or take them out of or put them into play)

- ✔ `id` — an identifier for a single element instance somewhere in an HTML document

- ✔ `lang` — identifies the language in which element content is expressed

- ✔ `role*` — collection attributes useful for instructing assistive technologies for readers with visual or audio impairments

- ✔ `spellcheck*` — lets content developers hint whether or not element content may be checked for spelling

- ✔ `style` — use to add inline style rules within an HTML document body

- ✔ `tabindex` — indicates the order in which fields or other user-accessible information in an HTML document may be accessed using the Tab key

- ✔ `title` — provides a text label for any HTML element instance

Deprecated elements gone from HTML5

In the following list, we indicate whether an element is purely presentational and its job has been passed off to CSS; whether that element usage had a negative impact on usability or accessibility of page content for users; or whether it is being dropped because that markup was used only rarely.

The following elements have been dropped from HTML5. Here again, we present these elements in alphabetical order:

- ✔ acronym (rarely used) — created confusion with the abbr (abbreviation) element; authors should use only the abbr element going forward

- ✔ applet (rarely used) — obsolete, the generic object element replaces this Java-specific reference

- ✔ basefont (presentational) — establish base document font; use CSS font-family rules instead

- ✔ big (presentational) — establish a larger font size in a document, use CSS font-size rules instead

- ✔ center (presentational) — center content in a document, use CSS text-align rules instead

- ✔ dir (rarely used) — creates directory lists, use unordered lists (ul) instead

- ✔ font (presentational) — sets running or in-line document fonts, use CSS font-family rules instead

- ✔ frame (negative usage) — breaks up the browser display area into sub-areas called frames, no longer used (or recommended)

- ✔ frameset (negative usage) — manages the relationship between specific URLs and frame areas for frame display, no longer used (or recommended)

- ✔ isindex (rarely used) — obsolete, general form input mechanisms provide a more capable and general purpose replacement

- ✔ noframes (negative usage) — provides display instructions for browsers that cannot render frames, no longer used (or recommended; does not work with XML anyway)

- ✔ s (presentational) — demarks strikethrough text, use CSS text-decoration rules instead

- ✔ strike (presentational) — demarks strikethrough text, use CSS text-decoration rules instead

- ✔ tt (presentational) — demarks monospace text as from a teletype machine, use CSS font-family rules instead and select a monospace font

- ✔ u (presentational) — demarks underlined text, use CSS text-decoration rules instead

Absent and removed HTML5 attributes

The attributes described in Table 19-1 are no longer present in HTML5 because they've been disallowed because of disuse or a negative impact on the user experience.

Table 19-1	Disallowed HTML5 Attributes
Attribute	**Parent Element**
rev, charset	link, a
shape, cords	a
longdesc	img, iframe
target	link
nohref	area
profile	head
version	html
name	img (use id instead)
scheme	meta
archive, classid, codebase, codetype, declare, standby	object
valuetype, type	param
axis, abbr	td, th
scope	td

The attributes described in Table 19-2 are deprecated and removed from HTML5 primarily because they addressed presentational functions now delegated to CSS.

Table 19-2	Deprecated HTML5 Attributes
Attribute	**Parent HTML Element**
Align	caption, iframe, img, input, object, legend, table, hr, div, h1, h2, h3, h4, h5, h6, p, col, colgroup, tbody, td, tfoot, th, thead, tr
alink, link, text, and vlink	body
background	body
bgcolor	table, tr, td, th, body
border	table, object
cellpadding, cellspacing	table
char, charoff	col, colgroup, tbody, td, tfoot, th, thead, tr
clear	br

(continued)

Table 19-2 *(continued)*

Attribute	Parent HTML Element
compact	dl, menu, ol, ul
frame	table
frameborder	iframe
height	td, th
hspace, vspace	img, object
marginheight	iframe
noshade	hr
nowrap	td, th
rules	table
scrolling	iframe
size	hr
type	li, ol, ul
valign	col, colgroup, tbody, td, tfoot, th, thead, tr
width	hr, table, td, th, col, colgroup, pre

Find a complete list of disallowed (22 total) and presentational (also no longer supported, 29 total) attributes no longer in the HTML5 picture in the *HTML5 Differences from HTML4* document's "Absent Attributes" section at www.w3.org/TR/HTML5-diff/#absent-attributes.

New Input Types in HTML5

The impetus for these new input types is to permit *user agents* (Web browsers as far as most of us are concerned, though other programs can interpret and render or analyze HTML markup) to solicit input and provide a user interface inside Web pages. This is how content designers can gain easy access to standard capabilities for ready re-use, such as a calendar-oriented date picker or integration with an address book to access name, street address, e-mail address, phone numbers, and so forth. These Application Program Interfaces (APIs for short) can interact with related systems or services, obtain input, and submit data in a carefully defined format to a Web server. This approach gives users a better experience because their input can be checked and validated before sending it on to the server. Generally, this also means faster handling because pre-checked input requires less processing on the server side and less time devoted to waiting for feedback from the server.

These new input types differ from various new HTML5 elements mentioned earlier in this chapter because they apply only to the input element (they aren't independent markup elements). These input types identify specific kinds of input data and, generally, play the same role for HTML5 input data that data types play for variables in conventional programming languages (they tell you what kind of data they can represent). Table 19-3 spells out these new options.

Table 19-3		HTML5 Input Types	
Keyword	*State*	*Control*	*Description*
color	Color	A color well	An sRGB color with 8-bit red, green, and blue components
date	Date	A date control	A date (year, month, day) with no time zone
datetime	Date and Time	A date and time control	A date and time (year, month, day, hour, minute, second, fraction of a second) with the time zone set to UTC
datetime-local	Local Date and Time	A date and time control	A date and time (year, month, day, hour, minute, second, fraction of a second) with no time zone
email	E-mail	A text field	An e-mail address or list of e-mail addresses
month	Month	A month control	A date consisting of a year and a month with no time zone
number	Number	A text field or spinner control	A numerical value
range	Range	A slider control or similar	A numerical value, with the extra semantic that the exact value is not important
search	Search	Search field	Text with no line breaks
tel	Telephone	A text field	Text with no line breaks
time	Time	A time control	A time (hour, minute, seconds, fractional seconds) with no time zone
url	URL	A text field	An absolute IRI
week	Week	A week control	Date consisting of a week-year number and a week number with no time zone

HTML5 Web APIs

An *API* defines rules for communication and interaction with other programs from inside a specific program. For most people, the Web APIs of greatest import for HTML5 are those that are called from inside HTML documents, to invoke special functionality for things like playing audio, playing video, and interacting with other applications, and that help to add to the Web browser user interface (dragging and dropping objects in Web pages, for example).

Here's a list of APIs that HTML5 incorporates with the intent of providing "help in creating Web applications" (this quote comes directly from the "APIs" section in the "W3C HTML5 Differences from HTML4" document cited two sections earlier):

- Video and audio playback API, for use with the new `video` and `audio` elements
- Access to offline Web applications through a special API
- An API designed for Web applications to register themselves to receive certain protocols and media types
- An API to permit page visitors to edit content and markup in concert with the new global `contenteditable` attribute.
- A drag-and-drop API used with the `draggable` attribute to permit users to drag and drop items onto Web pages to provide input
- An API that exposes browser history data and that permits pages to add to that data to prevent breaking the Back button.

Mostly, these APIs are where the significant action is for HTML5 (think about the Adobe Flash controversy we covered earlier in this chapter) and where change is nearly inevitable between the draft version and whatever more final form(s) HTML5 takes. APIs are the keys to user interaction and dynamic page behavior, and they will figure heavily into future uses for (and applications of) the Web and the Internet, especially in an era when many people are coming to believe that the Web and the Internet are more interchangeable than otherwise.

Limits to HTML5 Access and Use

Most Web browsers support HTML5 features in some form or fashion, with varying degrees of support and enthusiasm. Currently, Apple Safari and Google Chrome appear to be leading the way, followed by Mozilla Firefox, and then Opera, with Microsoft Internet Explorer dead last among the Top 5. This is entirely understandable, because not all these companies can release products overnight.

To us, what's absolutely fascinating is that in the preceding list, the most popular browsers — namely, Mozilla Firefox and Internet Explorer — do not support as many HTML5 features as do their less popular, less widely adopted competitors. Although HTML5 is meant to degrade nicely (this is Web-speak for "keeps working even in the face of missing markup elements and attributes"), it's vexing for Web designers and developers to figure out which features work in what browsers.

Likewise, it's annoying for Web site visitors to miss out on cool HTML5 features because of the browser they choose to employ. For instance, Internet Explorer 8 does not recognize the `canvas` element, and these two don't play together at all right now. Most seasoned Web observers believe that this somewhat fragmentary state of affairs is only transitory and that when Internet Explorer 9 is released, it will address this and other HTML5-related shortcomings. The same is no doubt also true for Firefox.

In the short term, we recommend trying out HTML5 Shiv, a JavaScript script you can include on your HTML5 Web pages that helps browsers (such as Internet Explorer) work properly with HTML5. Our special thanks to Remy Sharp for creating this script, and for making it available to the world through the Google Code project. Download HTML5 Shiv from `http://HTML5shiv.googlecode.com/svn/trunk/html5.js`. (The address is case sensitive, so make certain you type in the URL exactly as presented or you'll receive an error code.)

The HTML5 Shiv page is at `http://code.google.com/p/html5shiv`, where you need to copy and paste a three-line script from that page to a target Web page as follows:

```
<!--[if lt IE 9]>
<script src="http://html5shiv.googlecode.com/svn/trunk/html5.js"></script>
<![endif]-->
```

To extend our discussion of HTML5 browser support, one of the most limiting and confusing aspects of HTML5 is the purported date for a finalized specification (in W3C terms this is a "recommended specification"). Everyone wants to know whether HTML5 is ready or not. However, there's widespread disagreement on this topic within the industry. The existence of Web sites like those shown in Figure 19-1 perfectly illustrates the degree of madness and mayhem that surrounds HTML5's fitness of purpose and suitability for use.

Here's how nutty things are when it comes to timing HTML5. On one hand, Web software developers and designers agree that all the important features of and functions in HTML5 will be supported by 2012. On the other hand, the W3C (which owns and controls the HTML5 standard) estimates the delivery date for an HTML5 recommendation — that is, a final, finished, and official specification — at 2022. This looks like a complete disconnect — or perhaps the opening salvoes in a bargaining round between hostile and suspicious parties purportedly seeking agreement — but it's no joke!

Figure 19-1: Two different — and diametrically opposed — views on HTML5.

By our estimates, we will all be zipping around on hover boards by the next decade. We suspect that in the delivery of HTML5, as in reaching a difficult bargain, the actual date will fall somewhere between the 2012 date that industry insiders predict and the 2022 date that the W3C is currently pushing forward. Does that mean we must all wait for a recommended HTML5 speci-fication from the W3C to start using HTML5? Heck, no: We will all probably start using HTML5 on or before 2012, and the industry will move through many other tools and technologies by the time 2022 rolls around.

Additional HTML5 Resources

Assuming you'd like to read more about HTML5, here are some nice resources we've found helpful. If you're still jonesing for more about HTML5, use your favorite search engine to search for *HTML5 reference, HTML5 tutorial,* or *HTML5 introduction,* and you'll soon be up to your ears in reading material.

We recommend the following resources for more about all things HTML5:

- **A List Apart — A Preview of HTML5:** `http://www.alistapart.com/articles/previewofhtml5`

- **eWeek — 20 Essential Things to Know about the HTML5 Web Language:** `www.eweek.com/c/a/Application-Development/20-Essential-Things-to-Know-About-the-HTML5-Web-Language-329684`

- **W3Schoools HTML5 Tutorial (includes handy and complete reference guides, forms coverage, and lots, lots more):** `www.w3schools.com/HTML5`

Introducing HTML5

We've also put a couple of nice Web pages together for your examination on the companion site for this book. Dig into and explore these two pages. You can even supply their URLs to the W3C Markup Validation Service to see that it recognizes HTML5, and that our pages pass the validation test (though you will get a pro forma warning that the HTML5 Conformance Checker is still experimental and "may be unreliable, or not perfectly up to date with the latest development of some cutting-edge technologies").

Find the basic layout page shown in Figure 19-2 at www.dummieshtml.com/examples/ch19.

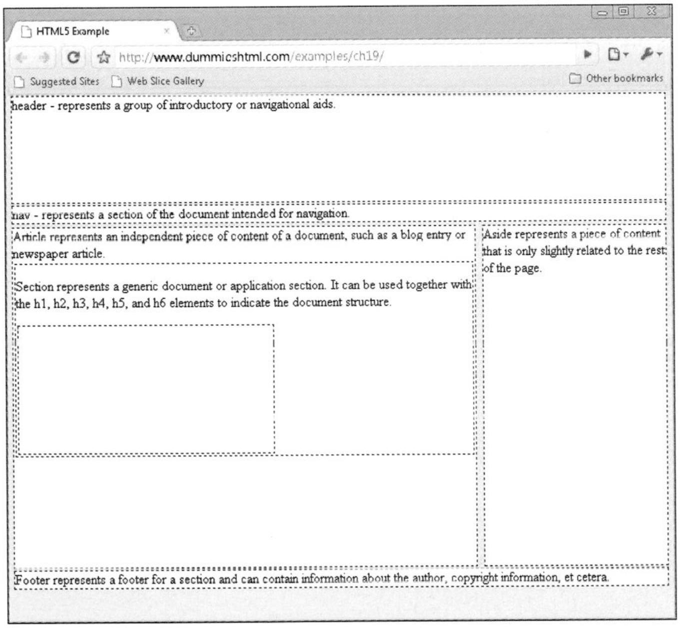

Figure 19-2: A simple sample HTML5 page with lots of new markup elements on display.

For those in need of some more serious demonstration, check out the use of the experimental RGraph HTML5 canvas graph library in the more complex HTML5 page (see Figure 19-3) available online at www.dummieshtml.com/examples/ch19/complete.html.

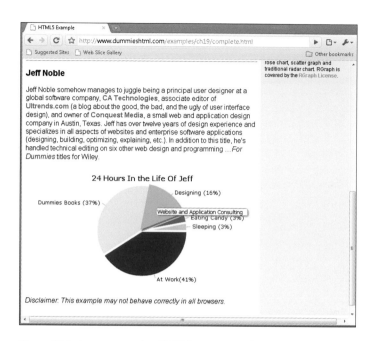

Figure 19-3: A more complex HTML5 page uses the canvas element to display a pie chart.

At the HTML5 gallery (`http://html5gallery.com`), you find pointers to more than 600 HTML5-based Web sites. If you want to see more, you only need to look. Enjoy!

Chapter 20

CSS3

In This Chapter

▶ Understanding what's important about CSS3

▶ Using new CSS3 properties for Web fonts, transitions, borders, and shadows

▶ Turning CSS3 loose with transitions and animation

▶ Finding the edge of the road: Where CSS3 stops

SS3 supports exciting new features that make some current styling techniques almost laughable. From fonts and borders to transitions and transforms, CSS3 is a wonderful collection of tools to make your Web pages over into something chic and downright stylish. We can't cover all these new CSS introductions (at least not in this book) but we can — and do — highlight some of the most interesting ones.

About the CSS3 "Standard"

Whereas both CSS1 and CSS2 were proposed, debated, and finally recommended as big, monolithic standards for Cascading Style Sheets, CSS3 is a collection of many individual modules. If you visit the CSS Level 3 (the formal name for what we and others blithely call CSS3 instead) works-in-progress page at the W3C Web site (www.w3.org/Style/CSS/current-work.html), you can count 45 modules in varying stages of completion. In Table 20-1, we lay these modules out with brief descriptions and use two-letter codes to describe their standardization status. CR stands for *Candidate Recommendation,* meaning the module is nearing standardization; LC stands for *Last Call* (for comments, prior to attaining CR status); N/A stands for *None,* no date or status available; and WD stands for *Working Draft* (standard and documentation still under discussion and development).

Table 20-1		CSS Level 3 Modules, Descriptions, and Standards Status
Name	*Status*	*Description*
Template Layout	WD	Describes a new method for positioning elements using constraints on their mutual alignment and flexibility of motion, where a layout grid defines the basic template
Aural Style Sheets	N/A	An audio module that includes properties to attach background sounds to elements, sound effects to state transitions (`hover`, `onclick`), and more
Backgrounds and Borders	CR	Describes background colors and images, and border styles, including background image stretch, images for borders, rounded corners, and shadows
Basic User Interface	CR	Features for styling interactive, dynamic Web page aspects, including form element appearance to denote state, plus cursors and colors for GUI use
Box Model	WD	Describes block-level content in normal flow, where document elements are laid out as rectangular boxes in sequence or nested orders that together comprise a horizontal or vertical (for Chinese and Japanese) flow
Extended Box Model	N/A	Provides extra control over positioning of floats and box sizing
Marquee	CR	Contains properties to control speed and direction of a marquee area, a scrolling mechanism that moves text through a region with no user intervention involved; used mostly on mobile devices
Cascading and Inheritance	WD	Describes how values are assigned to properties, where cascading describes how multiple style sheets are combined, and inheritance involves parent value assignments or initial value settings
Color	LC	Specifies color-related CSS controls, including transparency and notations for the `color` value-type
Fonts	WD	Properties to select and adjust fonts, including emboss and outline effects, kerning, smoothing, and anti-aliasing
Generated Content for Paged Media	WD	Advanced printing properties that go beyond the Paged Media module, including creating footnotes, cross-references, and generation of running headers from section titles

Name	Status	Description
Generated and Replaced Content	WD	Defines how to deposit content on a page before, after, or instead of some element, where content can be text or an image or some other external object
Hyperlink Presentation	WD	Properties to control how hyperlinks are presented, including controls on which hyperlinks are active, where targets are shown when a user traverses a link, and more
Introduction	WD	A summary of all CSS3 modules (can't be finished until all modules are complete so the W3C status table remains the place to look for CSS3 module and status info)
Line Layout	WD	Describes alignment of text and other boxes on a line; expands `vertical-align` property for CSS1/2 to support alignment of multiple script types, including non-Roman alphabets and ideographs
Lists	WD	Properties for styling lists, especially for bullet types, numbering systems, and use of images (especially for bullets) within list displays
Math	N/A	Properties for styling mathematical formulae, based on the "presentational" elements in the XML-based MathML application
Multi-column Layout	CR	New properties to flow content into flexibly defined columnar layouts
Namespaces	N/A	Explains how CSS selectors can be extended to select elements based on XML-derived namespaces that can distinguish among multiple uses of the same element name from one another across multiple style sheets
Object Model	N/A	The Document Object Model (DOM) specifies functions used in programming libraries and Web browsers to manipulate HTML, XML, and CSS documents; addresses functions for adding and deleting rules and changing properties in CSS style sheets, for APIs called the CSS Object Model or CSSOM
CSSOM View Module	WD	Tool APIs to enable authors to inspect and manipulate document view information, including position data for element layout boxes, width of script viewports, and element scrolling
Paged Media	WD	Extends print control properties from CSS2 with controls for running headers, footers, and page numbers

(continued)

Table 20-1 *(continued)*

Name	Status	Description
Positioning	N/A	Covers properties for absolute, fixed, and relative positioning of elements, to take them out of normal document flow and place them elsewhere on a page
Presentation Levels	WD	Tools for stepping forward and backward through multiple renderings of a document, especially useful for slide presentations, outline views, and so forth
Reader Media Type	WD	(Dropped in March 2008) Media type used in Media queries for screen, print, projection, and other device types to guide display and presentation handling
Ruby	CR	Properties to manipulate Ruby positions, for small annotations on top of or next to ideograms or words in Chinese and Japanese (often used to hint pronunciation or meaning for difficult ideograms)
Scoping	N/A	Controls to specify sub-trees within a document tree where identifiable sets of style rules apply
Grid Positioning	WD	Elements with columns establish an implicit grid; these CSS controls offer display of explicit grid lines and define a coordinate system for positioning floats, plus relative and absolute box placement
Speech	WD	Properties to specify how document gets rendered by a speech synthesizer, including settings for volume, voice, speed, pitch, cues, pauses, and more (takes over speech elements from CSS2 Aural module)
Style Attribute Syntax	LC	Rules for expressing CSS markup as part of HTML and other markup language attributes (SVG)
Syntax	WD	Generic, forward-compatible grammar which all levels of CSS must follow; value syntax restrictions for specific properties are addressed in other modules
Tables	N/A	Table layout controls, including rows, columns, cells, captions, borders, and alignment (same as in CSS2 but described in more detail in CSS3)
Text	WD	Text-related properties from CSS2 with new properties for dealing with text in different languages and scripts with special emphasis on International Layout; text properties are also covered in the Text Layout and Line Grid modules as well.

Name	Status	Description
Text Layout	N/A	Properties to control text direction into horizontal or vertical lines and the way in which they scan or flow
Line Grid	N/A	Describes text where symbols in a line are aligned to an invisible grid, so all symbols line up vertically, commonly used for text composed of ideographs as in Japanese
Values and Units	WD	Describes common values and units associated with CSS properties, along with describing how specified values from a stylesheet get processed into computed values or actual values at runtime
Web fonts	LC	Now merged with the Fonts module, describes how to download fonts for use within a document (also used within SVG, an XML-based stroke graphics rendering markup application)
Behavioral Extensions	WD	Defines the binding property from the XML-based XML Binding Language, or XBL, to CSS, for associating elements in a document with scripts, event handlers, and CSS
Flexible Box Layout	WD	Defines the `box` and `inline-box` keywords for the CSS `display` property, which causes an element to be displayed as a row or column of child elements, with controls over order and space distribution
Image Values	WD	Defines how properties can refer to images using URLs; common to all properties that can take images as a value
2D Transforms	WD	Defines properties to apply rotations, translations, or other visual transformations to an element box (same as in SVG)
3D Transformations	WD	Extends 2D transformations with 3D perspective transforms (joint project with SVG working group)
Transitions	WD	Properties to animate transitions between pseudo-classes, as when an element enters or leaves the hover state, with values for delay, and value transitions between pairs of values (old/new, on/off, and so on)
Animations	WD	Specifies properties that change their values during an animation, what sequence of values they take, and how long they hold each value

If you're interested in more information about current work on CSS3 (or other related efforts), please visit the W3C's Current Work page at www.w3.org/Style/CSS/current-work. There, you'll find a multi-colored status page (shown in Figure 20-1) that tells you where the various CSS modules are in the standards progression. (The Current column refers to CSS2/2.1, and the Upcoming column refers to CSS3.)

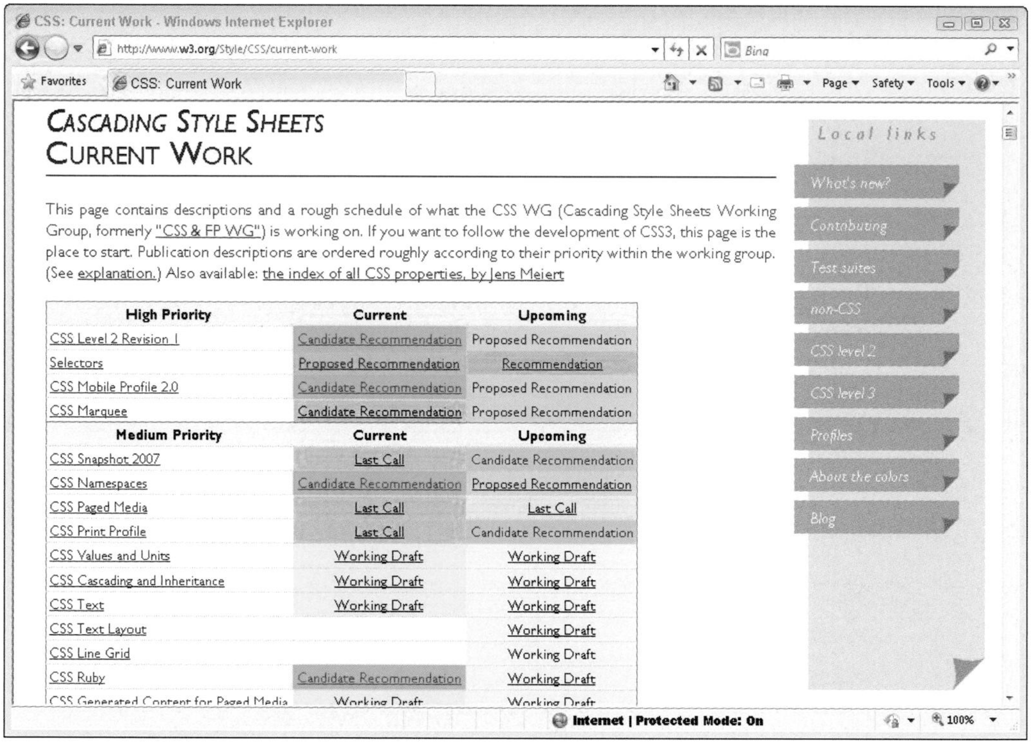

Figure 20-1: For standards, blue is best, and green is good!

CSS3 Highlights Hint at Riches Available

In the sections that follow, we explore some of the new CSS3 markup that is increasingly finding support in Web browsers. Unlike HTML5, there's no big controversy about when these modules will achieve Recommended, or "final and standard" status. But many of the Medium and Low Priority CSS modules are in the Working Draft state — which means essentially "under construction" — so it is likely to be at least three or four years before the whole slate advances to at least Candidate Recommendation status. Nevertheless, we think you'll find a lot to like here, and you'll want to start learning more about these style rules and their capabilities.

Fonts

Back in the bad old days on the Web, we had to create custom graphics to ensure that text on a Web page displayed exactly as we wished. Using CSS3, that's no longer the case. We think one of the most exciting additions to CSS3 comes from its new, improved font controls. The primary item of interest is the @font-face pseudo-class.

The @font-face *pseudo-class* (a type of style rule that can be invoked for an arbitrary part of a document, regardless of the element names, attributes, or content it contains) permits Web page designers to link to fonts that can be automatically activated when needed. This lets authors bypass the limitations inherent to *Web-safe fonts* (those that look good in browser windows and that are generally available on most systems) to support consistent and predictable rendering of pages whether or not specific fonts are available on some machine (in some browser).

@font-face lets you specify any font family you like, as long as you can point to some legitimate (licensed) source for a usable TrueType (.ttf) or OpenType (.otf) font file. The markup to invoke an external font will download that font to the user's machine if it is not already available there. The CSS syntax for this pseudo-class looks like this:

```
@font-face {
    Font-family: CABNDWebBold;
    Src: url(http://site/fonts/ CABNDWebBold.otf);}
h1,h2,h3,h4,h5,h6 {font-family: CABNDWebBold, sans-serif;}
```

In most cases, you'll download fonts to a directory of your choosing, rather than reference them at some other site, so owners can be sure that users adhere to font licensing agreements and requirements. If you browse to www. dummieshtml.com/examples/ch20/font-face and choose View⇨Source, you'll see that's just what we did for the CSS3 Fonts page (but this only works in Safari, Opera, and Chrome as we write this book). See Figure 20-2.

Technically, the @font-face property was originally part of CSS2, but only Internet Explorer recognized this style rule (until recently, no other browser supported it because Microsoft implemented it using a proprietary font format that no one else uses). Now, thanks to the introduction of the OpenType font files (.otf) to supplement Microsoft's TrueType font files (.ttf), @font-face has been resurrected for inclusion in CSS3 and also enjoys nearly universal browser support in the latest Opera, Chrome, Safari, and Firefox versions, as well as in Internet Explorer.

For a nice summary and some useful compatibility information (though it's not completely up to date), check out the @font-face overview at http://reference.sitepoint.com/css/at-fontface.

Figure 20-2: Putting @font-face to work.

Borders

CSS3 adds considerable excitement to drawing borders around boxes with some new border properties. In our humble opinions, the biggest boon in this area comes from rounded corners, which until recently had to be elaborately hand-crafted, using images that fit together like a puzzle (and with nearly as many pieces and parts involved as the jigsaw puzzles we put together on rainy days when we were young). Thankfully, round corners have come to CSS3's border-building tools, which should save us all a lot of time and effort.

You can do many great things with borders in CSS3, but the main property related to rounded corners is border-radius. If you browse to www. dummieshtml.com/examples/ch20/borders and choose View⇨Source, you'll see the following markup included in the <style> section:

```
.newRoundCorners {
    -moz-border-radius:15px;
    border-radius: 15px;
    text-align:center;
    }
```

This markup not only includes the standard CSS3 border-radius property, it also references a Mozilla/Firefox specific property named -moz-border-radius. When you approach the bleeding edge of Web markup and technology, you often find yourself learning how to invoke non-standard markup. For experimental kits and APIs related to HTML5 and CSS3, names preceded by dashes are a common way to invoke non-standard stuff within the markup. That's what's going on here to make sure that things look the same in Firefox as in Opera, Chrome, Safari, and IE. Visit our rounded corners example page at www.dummieshtml.com/examples/ch20/borders (see Figure 20-3).

We only show rounded corners at work in our example, but there are quite a few different border properties; border-image is another property worth checking out!

Figure 20-3: Rounded corners for element backgrounds are surprisingly easy to specify.

For a nice, example-loaded tutorial on working with all the various border-radius options (including illustrations that show how to manipulate corner curvature), visit www.css3.info/preview/rounded-border.

Backgrounds

Lining up multiple elements so that their backgrounds align perfectly and, likewise, mixing and matching multiple backgrounds can be difficult to achieve. It might take many lines of markup to get this job done right, especially working with CSS1 or CSS2. However, with CSS3, you can apply multiple backgrounds to a single element easily, and then use it to provide a backdrop for an element or a group of subsidiary elements. For example, on the backgrounds example page at www.dummieshtml.com/examples/ ch20/backgrounds/index.html, we combine three background images and apply them to one div.

The relevant CSS3 markup looks like this:

```
.customBackground {
    margin: 0px auto;
    width: 400px;
    height: 200px;
    border-radius: 10px;
    background:
    url(images/top.gif) top left repeat-x,
    url(images/bottom.gif) bottom left repeat-x,
    url(images/middle.gif) center repeat;
    }
```

The trick to this markup lies in the background specification, where we reference URLs for images for the three different backgrounds named top.gif, bottom.gif, and middle.gif, respectively. We use the repeat-x attribute to repeat the top and bottom horizontally. Using repeat means that middle. gif is repeated both horizontally and vertically. Top.gif applies the dark to medium blue shading at the top of the frame, bottom.gif does likewise from the bottom, and middle.gif supplies the dots. See Figure 20-4; visit the page at www.dummieshtml.com/examples/ch20/backgrounds/index.html.

CSS3.info strikes again in this case with its coverage of multiple backgrounds (particularly, check out its other background property coverage and excellent CSS3 coverage in general) at www.css3.info/preview/multiple-backgrounds.

Shadows

Shadows first appeared in CSS2, but they enjoyed only limited browser support and required various hacks to make them work properly. CSS3 lets designers apply and manage shadows for borders, images, and text in more or less the same way. Note that this is another case where some extensions are needed for the box shadow (around the div element) and image shadow (around our old book cover) to make sure things work and look the same for various browsers. Here you encounter the -webkit name that attaches to the compatibility kit for the Apple Safari Web browser for the first time, too. The relevant source code looks like this:

```
.boxShadow{
    height: 25px;
    background-color:#f25e1e;
    border: 5px solid #feb089;
    -moz-box-shadow: 3px 3px 5px #888;
    -webkit-box-shadow: 3px 3px 5px #888;
}
.textShadow{
    text-shadow: 2px 2px 7px #111;
}
.imageShadow{
    -moz-box-shadow: 3px 3px 5px #888;
    -webkit-box-shadow: 3px 3px 5px #888;
}
```

Figure 20-4: Here we artfully repeat three backgrounds to blend dots against two shaded backgrounds.

The `box-shadow` attribute works with element boxes (the rectangular region that surrounds any kind of HTML element as rendered) and with the boundary around the edge of a graphic. The `text-shadow` attribute creates a shadow around individual characters inside some kind of block element (a paragraph in the following example). See Figure 20-5, and visit our CSS3 shadows example at `www.dummieshtml.com/examples/ch20/shadows`.

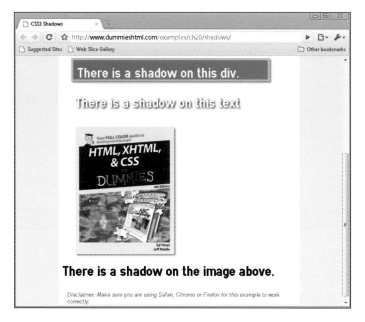

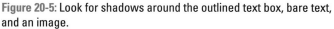

Figure 20-5: Look for shadows around the outlined text box, bare text, and an image.

Both of the shadow properties take three length values and a color as their attributes, as shown in `text-shadow: 2px 2px 7px #010101;` in the preceding code snippet. The three lengths take the following meanings (and the color defines the color for the shadow):

- **Shadow horizontal offset,** where a positive value falls to the right and a negative value falls to the left
- **Shadow vertical offset,** where a positive value falls below and a negative one falls above
- **Blur radius,** where if the value is zero (0), the shadow is sharp; the higher the value gets the more blurred the shadow will be

More kudos to CSS3.info for great tutorials on the box-shadow and text-shadow properties and attributes at www.css3.info/preview/box-shadow and www.css3.info/preview/text-shadow.

CSS3 Transitions and Animations

Transitions and animations provide nice visual effects to show changes in state or behavior for the former, and to liven up images for the latter. CSS3 makes working with both of these capabilities much easier than in previous versions. Where significant manual labor had been required to set up and run transitions or animations using CSS1 or CSS2, CSS3 simplifies and streamlines both of these considerably.

Transitions

Transitions within CSS offer an easy way to add extra polish to a Web site by instructing CSS to change values smoothly from an initial starting value to a final stopping value over a specified period of time. For example, when hovering over an item like a link or button, earlier versions of CSS only enabled switching colors, and the change always occurred instantly. Using CSS3, it's possible to transition from one color to another, showing the full range of colors in between. Our example shows a pretty dramatic and eye-twitch-inducing transition from blue to hot pink over a one-second period (but it only works for us in Chrome and Safari as we write this chapter; Internet Explorer, Opera, and Firefox show only an instant transition and square corners).

See this page in Figure 20-6 and at www.dummieshtml.com/examples/ch20/transitions/index.html.

A quick peek at the relevant CSS3 markup in the source code shows the following:

```
a.coolTransition{
    color:#FFF;
    background:#016ab0;
    padding:8px;
    -webkit-border-radius: 5px;
    -webkit-transition-property: color, background;
    -webkit-transition-duration: 1s, 1s;
    -webkit-transition-timing-function: linear, ease-in;
    }
a.coolTransition:hover{ color:#000;
    background: #f80e6a;}
```

Figure 20-6: When it works the way it should, you see a noticeable shift from blue to hot pink while you hover.

For a terrific tutorial on transitions and animations (covered in the next section), see the Web article entitled "Going Nuts with CSS Transitions" by Natalie Downs, where she explains and illustrates both topics with great discussion, explanation, and examples. Check it out at `http://24ways. org/2009/going-nuts-with-css-transitions`.

Animations

Animations within CSS3 provide a cool new way to add interaction with elements on a page that previous versions of CSS didn't support. Before CSS3, Web designers could only fake this sort of movement by using an animated gif or Adobe Flash, but no more. An easy example of CSS3 animation involves moving or rotating a document division (`div`) when hovering over its normal display area. In our example Web page, the cover art for the previous edition of this book spins clockwise as long as the cursor hovers on it. (Careful: Don't get too dizzy!). Check it out in Figure 20-7 and at `www.dummieshtml. com/examples/ch20/animations/index.html`.

Revisit Natalie Downs's "Going Nuts with CSS Transitions," where you'll find her "Throwing Polaroids at a Table" animation especially interesting and informative (don't forget to hover on as many photos as you can). Visit it directly at `http://media.24ways.org/2009/14/3/index.html`.

Figure 20-7: Hover on the cover and watch it spin!

Transform Your Content

Transforms allow elements that CSS renders to move around a page in either two- or three-dimensional space. Previous CSS versions couldn't support this kind of interaction at all, so transforms represent an exciting and interesting new feature in CSS3. In the following example, we transform a book that was left out in the library to return it back to its shelf (if only we could do this for our real books, too!). See Figure 20-8, and visit the page at `www.dummieshtml.com/examples/ch20/transforms/index.html`.

Visit Rich Bradshaw's interesting and profusely illustrated tutorial entitled "Using CSS3 Transitions, Transforms, and Animation" to get another look at CSS3's new dynamic side and capabilities (he even checks out your browser as you come to the site and tells you what features will and won't work for you inside its window). Be sure to check out the many cool examples at `http://css3.bradshawenterprises.com`.

Figure 20-8: Hover on the book cover image to return it to its shelf.

CSS3 Limitations

Many of CSS3's new features are great and have been a long time coming. However, as with any new and relatively untried technology, even with all its wonderful new capabilities, we recommend taking a cautious approach to deployment and use. Because CSS3 degrades nicely, it's not going to ruin an entire page layout, but not all browsers support all of CSS3's new features — especially the really cool ones like transforms, animations, and transitions.

For those browsers that do support some of these snazzy CSS3 features, there is far too often no single method or markup approach that applies to all browsers. This leads conscientious developers into creating multiple declarations just to make a shadow, transition, or whatever display correctly in each browser. This adds extra lines of code to your work, with at least two negative effects: more work for you to keep up with browser specifics, and more waiting for users while they download larger files to look at your pages.

As far as the @font-face pseudo-class is concerned, specifying a font face for your page displays is pretty neat. Nevertheless, be aware that there can be questions about the legality of including fonts that belong to others on your pages. First, be sure to check license terms and conditions when you download any .ttf or .otf files you wish to use. Second, check for multiple sources of permission to avoid unwanted and illegal propagation of stolen or cracked fonts. On the plus side, OpenType fonts are a step in the right direction and shouldn't be subject to legal action or difficulty. On the minus side, the potential for abuse of TrueType fonts is very real: Although it may be fun and easy to take and embed fonts we like, their creators should be recognized and fairly compensated where that's called for. Please don't steal fonts, either knowingly or by accident!

Finally, just because you can add a shadow, a border, and a border radius (for rounded corners), then choose a fancy font and layer multiple backgrounds behind the content in a document section or division, and then transform the entire element to dance around the screen doesn't mean you should. As with Photoshop, Flash, or any other Web tool, CSS3 can be misused, overused, and even abused if you don't keep communication as your primary goal, with all the cool stuff purely in a supporting role.

Finding More on CSS3

Many great resources are available online where you can get more information about CSS3, starting with the W3C's own CSS3 Road Map at www. w3.org/TR/css3-roadmap.

Don't forget the CSS3 specifications and other materials available at the W3C, too (we referenced those earlier in this chapter, but you can find most of what you'll need through the preceding Road Map link as well).

Two of our other favorite CSS3 sites are CSS3.info (www.css3.info) and CSS3.com (www.css3.com), both of which include tutorials, reference materials, rafts of examples, and other good stuff that can help you learn the details necessary to use CSS3 on your Web site. When you get to know CSS3, you can't help but want to put its cool capabilities to work.

Part VI
The Part of Tens

In this part . . .

Here, we point you toward some undeniably cool HTML tools, cover top do's and don'ts for HTML markup, and help you catch potential bugs and errors in your Web pages. We also bring some killer HTML, XHTML, and CSS specification and resource sites to your attention. Enjoy!

Chapter 21

Ten HTML Do's and Don'ts

*B*y themselves, HTML and XHTML are neither particularly complex nor overwhelmingly difficult. *HTML ain't rocket science,* as some high-tech wags (including a few rocket scientists) have put it. Nevertheless, important do's and don'ts can make or break the Web pages you build with HTML, XHTML, and CSS. Consider these humble admonishments as guidelines for making the most of your markup without losing touch with your users (or watching your page blow up on its launch pad).

If points we make throughout this book seem to crop up here, too — especially regarding proper and improper use of (X)HTML — it's no accident. Heed ye well the prescriptions and avoid ye the maledictions. But hey, they're your pages. You can do what you want. Your users will decide the ultimate outcome. (We'd *never* say, "We told you so.")

Don't Lose Sight of Your Content

Any Web site lives or dies by its content. That a site is meaningful, that it delivers information directly, easily, and efficiently, and that a user can reasonably expect to find something new and interesting there with each new visit — all are pluses. But all those things (and more) rest on solid, useful content that gives visitors a reason to come (and return) to your site.

So we return to the crucial question of payload: page content. Why? Well, as Darrell Royal (legendary football coach of the University of Texas Longhorns in the '60s and '70s) is rumored to have said to his players, "Dance with who brung ya." In normal English (as opposed to Texan), this means that you should stick with the people who've supported you all along, and give your loyalty to those who've given it to you.

We're not sure what this means for football, but for Web pages it means keeping faith with your users and keeping content paramount. If you don't have strong, solid, informative content, users quickly get that empty feeling that hits when Web pages are content-free. When that happens, they'll be off to richer hunting grounds on the Web, looking for content wherever it can be found.

To satisfy user hunger, put your most important content on your site's major pages. Save the frills and supplementary materials for secondary pages. The short statement of this principle for any kind of markup is "Tags are important, but what's between the tags — the content — is what really counts." Chapter 3 covers making your content the best it can be.

Do Structure Your Documents and Your Site

For users, a clear road map of your content is as important for a single home page as it is for an online encyclopedia. When longer or more complex documents grow into a full-fledged Web site, a road map becomes more important still. This map ideally takes the form of (you guessed it) a flow chart of page organization and links. If you like pictures with a purpose, the chart could appear in graphic form in an explicitly labeled site map.

We're strong advocates of top-down page design: Don't start writing content or placing tags until you understand what you want to say and how you want to organize your material. Start building your (X)HTML document or documents using paper and pencil (or your modeling tool of choice). Sketch out relationships within the content and among your pages. Know what and where you're building before rolling out the heavy equipment.

Good content flows from good organization. It helps you stay on track during page design, testing, delivery, and maintenance. Organization helps users find their way through your site. Need we say more? Well, yes: Don't forget that *organization changes over time.* Revisit and critique your organization and structure on a regular basis — and don't be afraid to change either one to keep up with changes in your Web site's content or focus.

Do Make the Most from the Least

Markup, scripting, and style sheets make much possible, but not all possibilities deserve implementation — Web sites can't live by snazzy graphics, special effects, and blinking marquees alone. Let your design and content drive the markup, the graphics, and interaction. With good design and content, your site will do its job without over-dazzling (or confusing) visitors.

More is not always better, especially when it comes to Web pages. Try to design and build your pages using minimal ornaments and simple layouts. Don't overload pages with graphics or cram in as many levels of headings as you can fit. Instead, do everything you can to make sure your content is easy to read and follow. Keep distractions and departures to a minimum, and make sure any hyperlinks you include add real value to your site.

Gratuitous links to useless information are nobody's friend; if you're tempted to link to a Webcam that shows a dripping faucet — resist, resist, resist!

Structure and images exist to *highlight* content. The more bells, whistles, and dinosaur yowls dominate a page, the more they distract visitors from content. Use structure and graphics sparingly, wisely, and carefully. Anything more impedes content delivery. Go easy on animations, links, and layout tags, or risk having your message (even your page) devoured by a hungry T. Rex.

Do Build Attractive Pages

When users visit Web pages with a consistent framework that focuses on content, they're likely to feel welcome. The important thing is to *supplement* content with graphics and links — don't overwhelm users with a surfeit of pictures and links. Making Web pages pretty and easy to navigate only adds to a site's basic appeal and makes your cybercampers even happier.

If you need inspiration, cruise the Web and look for layouts and graphics that work for you. If you take the time to analyze what you like, you can work from other people's design principles without having to steal details from their layouts or looks (which isn't a good idea anyway).

When designing Web documents, start with a basic, standard page layout. Pick a small, interesting set of graphical symbols or icons and adopt a consistent navigation style. Use graphics sparingly (yes, you've heard this before); make them as small as possible — limit size, number of colors, shading, and so on, while retaining visual appeal. After you build simple, consistent navigation tools, label them clearly and use them everywhere. Your pages can be both appealing and informative if you invest enough time and effort.

Don't Lose Track of Those Tags

If you start with solid markup and good content — and then plow through what you've built to make sure everything works the way it should (and communicates what it ought) — you're on your way to a great Web site. But after construction is over, testing begins. And only when testing produces positive results should you open your virtual doors to the public.

Although you're building documents, it's easy to forget to use closing tags, even when they're required (for example, the `</a>` that closes the opening anchor tag `<a>`). When you're testing Web pages, some browsers can compensate for such errors, leaving you with a false sense of security.

The Web is no place to depend on the kindness of strangers. Scrutinize your tags to head off possible problems from browsers that might not be quite so understanding (or lax, as the case may be). Validation (using `http://validator.w3.org`) is always a good idea, too!

As for claims that some HTML authoring tool vendors make ("You don't have to know any HTML!"), all we can say is, *"Uh-huh, suuurre. . . ."* HTML is a big part of what makes Web pages work; if you understand it, you can troubleshoot with minimal fuss. Also, only you can ensure that your pages' inner workings are correct and complete, whether you build them yourself or a program builds them for you.

We could go on and on about this, but we'll exercise some mercy and confine our remarks to the most pertinent items:

- **Keep track of tags yourself while you write or edit HTML by hand.** If you open a tag — be it an anchor, a text area, or whatever — create the closing tag for it right then and there, even if you have content to add. Most HTML editors do this for you.

- **Use a syntax checker to validate your work during the testing process.** Syntax checkers are automatic tools that find missing tags or errors. Use these syntax checkers whether you build pages by hand or with software. The W3C's (free) validator lives at `http://validator.w3.org`.

- **Test pages with as many browsers as you can.** This not only alerts you to missing tags, but can also reveal potential design flaws or browser issues (covered in the later section, "Do Avoid Browser Dependencies"). This exercise also emphasizes the need for alternate text. That's why we check our pages with Lynx (a character-only browser). Ask friends, colleagues, and co-workers to check out your work, and tell them to use as many browsers as they can, too. Please!

- **Always follow HTML document syntax and layout rules.** Just because browsers don't require elements such as `<html>`, `<head>`, and `<body>` doesn't mean you can omit them. It means browsers don't care whether you use them or not. But browsers per se are not your audience. Your users (and future browsers) may indeed care.

Although HTML isn't exactly a programming language, it makes sense to treat it like one. Following formats and syntax helps you avoid trouble, and careful testing and rechecking of your work ensures a high degree of quality, compliance with standards, and a relatively trouble-free Web site.

Do Avoid Browser Dependencies

When building Web pages, the temptation to view the Web only in terms of your favorite browser is hard to avoid. That's why you must recall that users view the Web in general (and your pages in particular) from many perspectives — and through many different browsers.

During the design and writing phases, you'll probably hop between HTML and a browser view of your work. At that point, you should switch among browsers and test your pages using different ones (including at least one text-only browser like Lynx). This helps you visualize your pages better, and also helps keep you focused on content. Using a text-only browser is also a great way to ensure that visually impaired visitors can still relate to your site.

Check out the Spoon Browser Sandbox page at www.spoon.net/browsers. It lets you emulate numerous browsers on a Windows PC, including multiple versions of IE, Firefox, Chrome, Safari, and Opera. Additionally, you can use free public Telnet servers with Lynx (a character-mode browser) installed. Otherwise, visit http://brainstormsandraves.com/articles/browsers/lynx for a good discussion of using Lynx when testing Web pages (you'll also find pointers to Lynx downloads for Windows, DOS, Mac OS, and other platforms there). There's even a free Firefox plugin for Lynx previews inside a pop-up window available at https://addons.mozilla.org/en-US/firefox/addon/1944.

During testing and maintenance, browse your pages from many points of view. Work from multiple platforms; try both graphical and character-mode browsers on each page. Testing takes time but repays that effort with pages that are easy for everyone to read and follow. It also helps viewers who come at your materials from many platforms, and helps your pages achieve true independence from any single viewpoint. Why limit your options?

If several pages on your site use the same basic (X)HTML, create one template for those pages. Test that template with as many browsers as you can. When you're sure the template is browser-independent, use it to create other pages. This helps every page look good, regardless of the browser that visitors use, and moves you closer to real HTML enlightenment.

Don't Make It Hard to Navigate Your Wild and Woolly Web

Users who view the splendor of your site don't want to be told *you can't get there from here.* Aids to navigation are vital amenities on a quality Web site. A *navigation bar* requires a consistent placement and use of controls to help users get from A to B. Judicious use of links, and careful observation of what constitutes a complete screen (or screenful) of text, help users minimize (or even avoid) scrolling. Text anchors make it easy to move to previous and next screens, as well as to the top, index, and bottom of any document. Just that easy, just that simple — or so it appears to the user.

We believe in *low scroll* pages: Users should have to scroll *no more than one* screenful from a point of focus or entry to find a navigation aid that lets them jump (not scroll) to their next point of interest. If users must scroll, vertical scrolling is okay, but horizontal scrolling is an absolute no-no!

We don't believe navigation bars are mandatory — nor that names for controls should always be the same. But we do believe that the more control you give users over their browsing, the better they like it. The longer a document gets, the more important controls become; they work best if they occur about every 30 lines (or in a set of always visible page controls).

Don't Think Revolution, Think Evolution

The tendency to sit on one's fundament, if not rest on one's laurels, after launching a Web site is nearly irresistible. It's okay to sit down, but it isn't okay to leave things alone for too long or to let them go stale from lack of attention and refreshment. If you stay interested in what's on your site after it's ready for prime time, your content probably won't go past its expiration date. Do what you can (and what you must) to stay on top of things, and you'll stay engaged — as should your site visitors!

Over time, Web pages change and grow. Keep a fresh eye on your work and keep recruiting fresh eyes from the ranks of those who haven't seen your work before to avoid what we call "organic acceptance."

This concept is best explained by the analogy of your face in the mirror: You see it every day; you know it too well, so you aren't as sensitive as someone else to how your face changes over time. Then you see yourself on video, or in a photograph, or through the eyes of an old friend. At that point, changes obvious to the world reveal themselves to you as you exclaim, "I've gone completely gray!" or "My spare tire could mount on a semi!"

Changes to Web pages are usually evolutionary, not revolutionary. They proceed in small daily steps; big leaps are rare. Nevertheless, you must stay sensitive to the underlying infrastructure and readability of your content as pages evolve. Maybe the lack of onscreen links to each section of your Product Catalog didn't matter when you had only three products — but now that you offer 25, they're a must. You've heard that form follows function; in Web terms, the structure of your site needs to follow changes in its content. If you regularly evaluate your site's effectiveness at communicating, you know when it's time to make changes, large or small.

This is why user feedback is crucial. If you don't get feedback through forms or other means, aggressively solicit some from your users. If you're not sure how you're doing, consider this: If you don't ask for feedback, how can you tell?

Don't Get Stuck in the Two-Dimensional-Text Trap

Because of centuries of printed material and the linear nature of books, our mindsets also need adjustment. The nonlinear potentials of hypermedia give new meaning to the term *document,* especially on the Web. It can be tempting to pack pages full of capabilities until they resemble a Pony Express dynamite shipment that gallops off in many directions at once. Be safe: Judge hypermedia by whether it

- ✔ Adds interest
- ✔ Expands on your content
- ✔ Makes a serious — and relevant — impact on users

Within these constraints, such material can vastly improve any user's experience of your site.

Stepping intelligently outside old-fashioned linear thinking about text can improve your users' experience of your site and make your information more accessible. That's why we encourage careful use of document indexes, cross-references, links to related documents, and other tools to help users navigate your site. Keep thinking about the impact of links as you look at other people's Web materials; it's the quickest way to escape the linear-text trap. (The printing press was high-tech for its day, but that *was* nearly 600 years ago!) If you're seeking a model for Web site behavior, don't use your new trifold four-color brochure, however eye-popping it may be; think about how customer-service people talk to new customers by phone. *("How can I help you today?")*

Don't Let Inertia Overcome You

When dealing with Web materials post-publication, it's only human to goof off after finishing a big job. Maintenance isn't as heroic or inspiring as creation, but involves most of the activity required to keep any document alive and well. Sites that aren't maintained often become ghost sites; users stop visiting when developers stop working on them. Never fear — a little work and attention to detail keep pages fresh. If you start with something valuable and keep adding value, a site's value appreciates over time — just like any other property. Start with something valuable and leave it alone and it soon becomes stale and loses value.

Consider your site from the viewpoint of a master aircraft mechanic: Correct maintenance is a real, vital, and on-going accomplishment, without which you risk a crash. A Web site, as a vehicle for important information, deserves regular attention; maintaining a Web site requires discipline and respect. (See `www.disobey.com/ghostsites/index.shtml` for a humorous look at ghost sites.)

Keeping up with change translates into creating (and adhering to) a regular maintenance schedule. Make it somebody's job to spend time on a site regularly; check to make sure the job's getting done. If people get tagged to handle regular site updates, changes, and improvements, they flog other participants to give them tasks when scheduled site maintenance rolls around. Pretty soon, everybody's involved in keeping information fresh — just as they should be. This keeps your visitors coming back for more!

Chapter 22

Ten Ways to Exterminate Web Bugs

In This Chapter

▶ Avoiding gaffes in markup and spelling

▶ Keeping links hot and fresh

▶ Gathering beta-testers to check, double-check, and triple-check your site

▶ Applying user feedback to your site

*A*fter you put the finishing touches on a set of pages (but before you go public on the Web for the entire world to see), it's time to put them through their paces. Testing remains the best way to ensure site quality and effectiveness.

Thorough testing *must* include content review, analysis of (X)HTML and CSS syntax and semantics, link checks, and various sanity checks to make doubly sure that what's built is what you really want. Read this chapter for some gems of testing wisdom (learned from a lifetime of Web adventures) as we seek to rid your Web pages of bugs, errors, and lurking infelicities. Out! Out! Darned Spot!

Make a List and Check It — Twice

A sense of urgency that things must work well and look good on a Web site never fails to goad you to keep your site humming along. That said, if you work from a visual diagram of how your site is (or should be) organized, you'll be well equipped to check structure, organization, and navigation. Likewise, put your pages through their paces regularly (or at least each time they change) with a spell checker, and you'll be able to avoid unwanted *tpyos*.

Your design should include a road map (often called a *site map*) that tells you what's where in every individual (X)HTML document and stylesheet in your site — and clues you into the relationships among its pages. If you're really smart, keep this map up to date as you move from design to implementation. (In our experience, things always change as you go down this path.) If you're merely as smart as the rest of us, don't berate yourself — update that map *now!* Be sure to include all intra- and inter-document links.

A site map provides the foundation for a test plan. Yep, that's right — effective testing isn't random. Use your site map to

- ✔ Investigate and check every page and every link systematically.
- ✔ Make sure everything works as you think it should — and that what you built has some relationship (however surprising) to your design.
- ✔ Define the list of things to check as you go through the testing process.
- ✔ Check everything (at least) twice. (Red suit and reindeer harness optional.)

Master Text Mechanics

By the time any collection of Web pages comes together, you're looking at thousands of words, if not more. Yet many Web pages are published without a spell check, which is why we suggest — no, *demand* — that you include a spell check as a step when testing and checking your materials. (Okay, we can't put a gun to your head, but you *know* it's for your own good.) Many (X)HTML tools, such as Expression Web, Kompozer, and Dreamweaver, include built-in spell checkers, the first spell-check tools you should use. These (X)HTML editors also know how to ignore markup and just check your text.

Even if you use (X)HTML tools only occasionally, and hack out most of your markup by hand, do a spell check before posting your documents to the Web. (For a handy illustration of why this step matters, keep a log of spelling and grammatical errors you find during your Web travels. Be sure to include a note on how those gaffes reflect on the people who created the pages involved. Get the message?)

You can use your favorite word processor to spell check your pages. Before you check them, add (X)HTML and CSS markup to your custom dictionary, and pretty soon the spell checker runs more smoothly — getting stuck only on URLs and odd strings that occasionally occur in Web documents.

If you prefer a different approach, try any of the many (X)HTML-based spell-checking services now available on the Web. We like the free Lite Edition of the CSE HTML Validator (www.htmlvalidator.com).

If CSE HTML Validator Lite's spell checker doesn't float your boat, visit a search engine, such as www.yahoo.com or www.google.com, and use *web page spell check* as a search string. Doing so lets you produce a list of spell-checking tools made for Web pages.

One way or another, persist until you root out all typos and misspellings. Your users may not thank you for your impeccable use of language — but if they don't trip over errors while exploring your work, they'll think more highly of your pages (and their creator), even if they don't know why.

Don't forget to put your eyeballs on the copy and thoroughly proofread the text, too. No spell checker in the world will recognize "It's time two go too the store" as badly mangled text, although you should catch that right away! Better yet, hire a professional editor or proofreader to help out during testing.

Lack of Live Links — A Loathsome Legacy

New content and active connections to current, relevant resources are the hallmarks of a well-tended Web site. You can't achieve these goals without regular (sometimes, constant) effort, so plan for ongoing activity. The rewards can be huge — starting with a genuine sense of user excitement at what new marvels and treasures reveal themselves on their next visit to your site. Such anticipation is impossible to fake (without doing what you'll have to do to keep things fresh in the first place). So please, keep it real, too!

We performed an unscientific, random-sample test to double-check our own suspicions; users told us that positive impressions of a particular site are proportional to the number of working links they find there. The moral of this survey: *Always check your links.* This is as true after you publish your pages as it is before they're made public. Nothing irritates users more than a link that produces the dreaded 404 File Not Found error instead of the good stuff they seek! Remember, too, that link checks are as indispensable to page maintenance as they are to testing.

If you're long on 21st-century street smarts, hire a robot to do this job for you: They work long hours (no coffee breaks), don't charge much, and check every last link in your site (and beyond, if you let them). The best thing about robots is that you schedule them to work at your pleasure: They always show up on time, always do a good job, and never complain (though we haven't found one that brings homemade cookies or remembers birthdays). All you must do is search online for phrases like *link checker.* You'll find lots to choose from!

To begin with, you might use the W3C Link Checker (`http://validator.w3.org/checklink`) because it's easy to use and less work to set up, too. Another good option is the Free Online Link Checker at `www.2bone.com/links/linkchecker.shtml`. The REL Link Checker Light is a free version of REL Software's commercial Web Link Validator, and good enough for smaller hobby, personal, or modest business sites (grab it from `www.relsoftware.com/rlc/downloads`). Finally, Xenu's Link Sleuth is another free package you can try out from `http://home.snafu.de/tilman/xenulink.html`.

If a URL points to one page that simply points to another (a pointer), you can't leave that link alone. Sure, it works, but for how long? And how annoying! Therefore, if your link-checking expedition shows a pointer that merely points to another pointer (yikes), do yourself (and your users) a favor by updating the URL to point *directly* to the real location. You save users time, reduce Internet traffic, and earn good cyberkarma.

When Old Links Must Linger

If you must leave a URL active after it's become outdated to give your users time to bookmark your new location, instruct browsers to jump straight from the old page to the new by including the following HTML command in the old doc's `<head>`:

```
<meta http-equiv="refresh" content="0"; url="newurlhere" />
```

This nifty line of code tells a browser that it should refresh the page. The delay before switching to the new page is specified by the value of the `content` attribute, and the destination URL is determined by the value of the `url` attribute. If you build such a page, also include a plain-vanilla link in its `<body>` section, so users with older browsers can follow that link manually, instead of automatically. You might also want to add text that tells visitors to update their bookmarks with the new URL. Getting there may not be half the fun, but it's the whole objective.

Make Your Content Mirror Your World

When it comes to content, the best way to keep things fresh is to keep up with the world in which your site resides. When things change, disappear, or pop up in that world, similar events should occur on your Web site. Because something new is always happening, and old ways or beliefs are always fading, reporting on what's new, and musing on what's fading from view, provide visitors a reason to keep coming back. What's more, if you can accurately and honestly reflect (and reflect upon) what's happening in your world of interest, you'll grab loyalty, respect, and continued patronage.

Look for Trouble in all the Right Places

There's an ongoing need for quality control in any kind of public content, but that need is particularly acute on the Web, where the whole world can stop by (and where success often follows the numbers of those who drop in *and return*). You must check your work while you're building the site and continue to check your work over time. This practice forces you to revisit your material with new and shifting perspectives, and to evaluate what's new and what's changed in the world around you. That's why testing and checking are never really over; they just come and go — preferably, on a regular schedule!

You and a limited group of handpicked users should thoroughly test your site before you share it with the rest of the world — and more than once. This process is called *beta testing,* and it's a bona fide, five-star *must* for a well-built Web site, especially if it's for business use. When the time comes to beta-test your site, bring in as rowdy and refractory a crowd as you can find. If you have picky customers (or colleagues who are pushy, opinionated, or argumentative), you might have found them a higher calling: Such people make ideal beta testers — that is, if you can get them to cooperate.

Don't wait until the very last minute to test your Web site. Sometimes the glitches found during the beta-test phase can take weeks to fix. Take heed: Test early and test often; you'll thank us in the end!

Beta testers will use your pages in ways you never imagined possible. They interpret your content to mean things you never intended in a million years. They drive you crazy and crawl all over your cherished beliefs and principles. And they do all this before your users do! Trust us, that's a blessing — even if it's in disguise.

These colleagues also find gotchas, big and small, that you never knew existed. They catch typos that spell checkers couldn't. They tell you things you left out and things that you should have omitted. They give you a fresh perspective on your Web pages, and they help you see them from extreme points of view.

The results of all this suffering, believe it or not, are positive. Your pages will be clearer, more direct, and more correct than they would have had you tested them by yourself. (If you don't believe us, of course, you *could* try skipping this step. And when real users start banging on your site, forgive us if we don't watch.)

Cover all the Bases with Peer Reviews

If you're creating a simple home page or a collection of facts and figures about your private obsession, this tip may not apply to you. Feel free to read it anyway — it just might come in handy down the road.

If your pages express views and content that represent an organization, chances are, oh, *about 100 percent* that you should run your pages through peer-and-management review before publishing them to the world. In fact, we recommend that you build reviews into each step along the way as you build your site — starting by getting knowledgeable feedback on such basic aspects as the overall design, writing copy for each page, and the final assembly of your pages into a functioning site. These reviews help you avoid potential stumbling blocks, such as unintentional off-color humor or unintended political statements. If you have any doubts about copyright matters, references, logo usage, or other important details, bring the legal department in. (If you don't have one, you may want to consider a little consulting help for this purpose. Paying to avoid legal trouble beforehand is always cheaper than paying to get out of such trouble after the fact.)

Building a sign-off process into reviews so you can prove that responsible parties reviewed and approved your materials is a good idea. We hope you don't have to be that formal about publishing your Web pages, but it's far, far better to be safe than sorry. (This process might best be called *covering your bases,* or perhaps it's really covering something else? You decide.)

Use the Best Tools of the Testing Trade

When you grind through your completed Web pages, checking your links and your HTML, remember that automated help is available. If you visit the W3C validator at `http://validator.w3.org`, you'll be well on your way to finding computerized assistance to make your HTML pure as air, clean as the driven snow, and standards-compliant as, ah, *really well-written HTML.* (Do we know how to mix a metaphor, or what?)

Likewise, using link checkers covered earlier in the chapter is smart; run them regularly to check links on your pages. These faithful servants tell you if something isn't current, and they tell you where to find links that need fixing.

Schedule Site Reviews

Every time you change or update your site, you should test its functionality, run a spell check, perform a beta test, and otherwise jump through important hoops to put your best foot forward online. But sometimes you'll make just a small change — a new phone number or address, a single product listing, a change of name or title to reflect a promotion — and you won't go through the whole formal testing process for "just one little thing."

That's perfectly understandable — but one thing inevitably leads to another, and so on. Plus, if you solicit feedback, chances are good that you'll learn something that points out a problem you'd never noticed or considered before. Schedule periodic site reviews, even if you've made no big changes or updates since the last review. Information grows stale, things change, and tiny errors have a way of creeping in as one small change succeeds another.

If there's any code on your site (JavaScript, Active Server Pages, Java Server Pages, or whatever), you'll want to give it a thorough workout and inspection, too. A pool-shooting buddy of ours who works in quality control for a major technology company was recently assigned to review a Web site built to provide real-time security and error information to developers who use its products. He told me that it was obvious the developers didn't try everything, in every possible combination, at the same time — with a rueful shake of his head — and that when he did so, he broke things they didn't know could be broken. Better to do this yourself (or hire somebody to do it for you) and fix it in advance than to pay the price of public humiliation.

Just as you take your car in for an oil change or replace your air-conditioning filter, plan to check your Web site regularly. Most big organizations we talk to do this every three months or so; others do it more often. Although you might think you have no bugs to catch, errors to fix, or outdated information to refresh, you'll often be surprised by what a review turns up. Make this part of your routine, and your surprises will be less painful — and require less work to remedy!

Foster User Feedback

Who better to tell you what works and what doesn't than those who use (and hopefully, depend on) your site? Who better to say what's not needed and what's missing? But if you want user feedback to foster site growth and evolution, you must not only ask for it, you have to encourage it to flow freely and honestly in your direction, then act on that feedback to keep those well-springs working.

Even after you publish your site, testing never ends. (Are you having flash-backs to high school or college yet? We sure are.) You may not think of user feedback as a form (or consequence) of testing, but it represents the best reality check your Web pages are ever likely to get, which is why doing every-thing you can — including offering prizes or other tangibles — to get users to fill out HTML forms on your Web site is a good idea.

This reality check is also why reading *all* feedback you get is a must. Go out and solicit as much feedback as you can handle. (Don't worry; you'll soon have more.) But carefully consider all feedback that you read — and implement the ideas that actually bid fair to improve your Web offerings. Oh, and it's a really good idea to respond to feedback with personal e-mail, to make sure your users know you're reading what they're saying. If you don't have time to do that, make some!

The most finicky and picky of users can be an incredible asset: Who better to pick over your newest pages and to point out the small, subtle errors or flaws they so revel in finding? Your pages will have contributed mightily to the advance of society by actually finding a legitimate use for the universal delight in nitpicking. Your users can develop a real stake in boosting your site's success, too. Working with users gets them more involved, and helps guide the content of your Web pages (if not the rest of your professional or obsessional life). Who could ask for more? Put it this way: You may yet find out, and it could be very helpful.

If You Give to Them, They'll Give to You!

Sometimes, simply asking for feedback or providing surveys for users to fill out doesn't produce the results you want — either in quality or in volume. Remember the days when you'd occasionally get a dollar bill in the mail to encourage you to fill out a form? It's hard to deliver cold, hard cash via the Internet, but a little creativity on your part should make it easy for you to offer your users something of value in exchange for their time and input. It could be an extra month on a subscription, discounts on products or services, or some kind of freebie by mail. (Maybe you can finally unload those stuffed Gila monsters you bought for that trade show last year. . . .)

There's another way you can give back to your users that might not cost you too much. An offer to send participants the results of your survey, or to otherwise share what you learn, may be all the incentive participants need to take the time to tell you what they think, or to answer your questions. Just remember that you're asking your users to give of their time and energy, so it's only polite to offer something in return.

Chapter 23

Ten Cool HTML Tools and Technologies

In This Chapter

▶ Identifying your HTML toolbox needs

▶ Discovering your favorite HTML editor

▶ Adding a graphics application to your toolbox

▶ Authoring systems for the Web

▶ Understanding essential utilities for Web publishing

*H*TML documents are made of plain text, which means you can build one using a no-frills text editor like Notepad. Once upon a time, that was all Web authors used. But as the Web has evolved, so have the tools used to create Web pages. Nowadays, Web authoring is complex enough that a simple text editor doesn't cut it unless

✔ You don't care (much) about graphics and HTML validation.

✔ You're on a quick in-and-out mission to make small changes to an existing HTML document.

After you gain more experience with HTML, you'll build your own HTML toolbox. This chapter is designed to help you stock that toolbox. In fact, some of these tools may already be on your system, quietly waiting to help you create amazing Web pages.

When you go shopping for items for your HTML toolbox, look for good buys. Students and educators often qualify for big discounts on major-brand software, if they use a search engine to look for "educational software discount." But careful shopping can save anybody money on just about any software purchase. Try comparison-shopping at sites such as CNET Shopper (http://shopper.cnet.com) or PC Magazine (http://www.pcmag.com/shop).

WYSIWYG HTML Editors

WYSIWYG (what you see is what you get) editors do everything but your laundry. Lots of WYSIWYG (pronounced "wiz-eee-wig") editors offer code views like the helper editors do (see the following section), plus a lot more.

A WYSIWYG editor creates markup for you while you create and lay out Web page content on your monitor (often by dragging and dropping visual elements or working through GUI menus and options), shielding your delicate eyes from bare markup along the way. These tools are like word processors or page-layout programs; they do lots of work for you.

WYSIWYG editors make your work easier and save hours of endless coding — you have a life, right? — but you should only use WYSIWYG editors during the design stage. For example, you can use a WYSIWYG editor to create a complex table in under a minute during initial design work. Later, when the site is live, you would then use an HTML helper editor to refine and tweak your HTML markup directly.

Dreamweaver

Dreamweaver is the best WYSIWYG Web development tool for Macintosh and PC systems. Many (if not most) Web developers use Dreamweaver. Dreamweaver is an all-in-one product that supports

- Web site creation
- Maintenance
- Content management

The current version, Adobe Dreamweaver CS5, belongs to a suite of products — Adobe Creative Suite 5, usually abbreviated CS5 — that work together to provide a full spectrum of Internet solutions. Adobe CS5 comes in many flavors and includes such components as InDesign, Photoshop, Illustrator, Acrobat Professional, Dreamweaver, Fireworks, Contribute, After Effects Professional, Premiere Pro, Soundbooth, Encore, and even OnLocation. For a mere $2,600 or so, you can buy the Adobe Creative Suite 5 Design Premium Collection and get all of these things in a single (very expensive) box!

Dreamweaver features an easy-to-follow GUI so you can style Web pages using CSS without even knowing what a style rule is! Many of the benefits of Dreamweaver stem from its sleek user interface and its respect for clean HTML. You can find more information on Dreamweaver by visiting the Adobe Web site at www.adobe.com/products/dreamweaver.

If you're too low on funds for a top-of-the-line WYSIWYG HTML editor like Dreamweaver CS5 (suggested retail price is about $400, but discounts of up to $200 are available), there are other possibilities. You can ponder the suggestions in the next section or go a-searching on the Web (the search string "WYSIWYG HTML editor" should do nicely).

Other WYSIWYG editors

WYSIWYG editors generate allegiances that can seem as pointless as the enmity between owners of Ford and Chevy trucks. The following editors have many fans, and both produce great Web pages:

- **Kompozer** is a Web page editor that offers text and WYSIWYG editors, along with color coding, automatic code completion, HTML validation, nice site management chops, and more good stuff. Plus, it's free. Check it out at http://kompozer.net.

- **Microsoft Expression Web 4** is a Windows-based Web package that offers a code editor (text) and a visual editor (WYSIWYG), along with scripting tools, great graphics support, search engine optimization (SEO) tools, and more. It retails for $149, but, if you shop around, you can find it for under $100. Check it out at www.microsoft.com/expression/products/web_overview.aspx.

Helper HTML Editors

An HTML helper works the way it sounds. It helps you create HTML, but it doesn't do all the markup work for you. HTML is displayed "raw" — tags and all. You can reach right into the code and tweak it (provided you have *HTML, XHTML & CSS For Dummies*). This is often called a "code view" or "markup view."

Good helpers save time and lighten your load. Functions like these make HTML development easier and more fun:

- Tags are a different color than content.
- The spell checker knows tags aren't misspelled words.

Use a helper editor when you're building complex tables or multilevel lists. The more complex your markup, the more help a helper editor can provide!

Aptana Studio

Aptana Studio is a full-blown development tool that supports JavaScript, Personal Home Page (PHP), CSS, and HTML. Aptana also provides a very full-featured HTML editor that's well suited for beginners and professionals. Aptana requires some HTML knowledge to use but assists you at every step.

We like the Aptana interface and its many facilities. You can

- ✔ Automatically sync directories with your FTP server.

- ✔ Incorporate all kinds of cool plugins (Aptana is based on Eclipse, a well known and widely used integrated development environment, or IDE). Aptana makes it easy to work with other languages, such as Ruby on Rails, jQuery, Python, and more, using widely available plugins.

- ✔ Create, edit, and validate CSS, JavaScript, HTML, and PHP.

- ✔ Automatic code completion and text coloring capabilities to separate HTML, CSS, JavaScript, and so forth.

- ✔ Take advantage of a huge collection of documentation and tutorials and active community support and interaction.

 Aptana is an open source project, which means it's free. You can download Aptana from www.aptana.com. If you're not inclined to tackle a do-it-yourself type of Web development environment, check out our other contenders in the following section.

Other helper editors

You can find lots of great HTML helper editors. Here's our slate of alternatives:

- ✔ **Komodo Edit** is a classy, highly functional software package that gets high ratings from everyday users and experts. It's not WYSIWIG, but it gets the job done. Komodo includes lots of great features and functions, including built-in validators for CSS, HTML, and accessibility features; color coding and tag completion for HTML and XML; multi-file search and replace; and support for Web-related languages, such as Perl, Python, Tcl, PHP, JavaScript, and much more.

  - • Komodo Edit is a free, scaled-down version of the $295 Komodo IDE product from ActiveState.com. Unless you also develop software, Komodo Edit should meet your needs well and completely.

  - • Download the free version from www.activestate.com/komodo-edit/downloads. Supports Windows, Mac OS X, and Linux.

- ✔ **HTML-Kit** is a compact Windows tool with

  - Menu-driven support for both HTML and Cascading Style Sheets (CSS) markup

  - A nice preview window for a browser's-eye view of your markup

  If you want to download HTML-Kit, go to www.chami.com/html-kit. You can download a free version or register your copy for $65 and obtain a bunch of extra tools, including a spiffy table designer, a log analyzer, and a nifty graphical (X)HTML/XML editor that lets you view and navigate all those documents through their syntactical structure.

- ✔ **Open Source Notepad++** offers useful and functional support for HTML and CSS, among lots of other languages and markup. Find it at http://notepad-plus-plus.org.

Inexpensive Graphics Editors

Graphics applications are beasts. They can do marvelous things, but learning how to use them can be overwhelming at first. Even scaled-down toolsets (such as Photoshop Elements) take time and genuine effort to learn and use properly and effectively.

If you aren't artistically inclined, consider paying someone else to do your graphics work. Graphics applications can be pricey and complicated. But you should have some kind of high-function (if not high-end) graphics program to tweak images should you need to. Our highest rating goes to Adobe Photoshop, but considering its cost and the average newbie HTML hacker's budget, we discuss a lower-cost alternative first.

At around $100 (with discounts as low as $60), Adobe Photoshop Elements 9 is an affordable PC- and Mac-based starter version of the full-blown Photoshop (the gold standard for graphics). You can do almost anything with Photoshop Elements that you might need for beginner- and intermediate-level graphics editing.

This product is for you if you want to add images to your site but you don't want to work with graphics all the time, or use fancy special effects. To learn more about Photoshop Elements, visit www.adobe.com/products/photoshopelwin.

If you're really on a tight budget, check out these graphic editors:

- **Paint Shop Pro Photo X3:** This PC-only graphics editor is a good buy because it does nearly everything that Photoshop does and costs less than Photoshop Elements. You'll need to shop around to find the lowest price, though (Corel charges $80 or $90 for this package).

- **GIMP:** If you're really on a shoestring budget, check out the free GNU Image Manipulation Program, better known as GIMP. It's an open source package whose functionality rivals that of Photoshop without the expensive price tag. GIMP supports a user-customizable interface, offers all kinds of sophisticated image and photo enhancements, and includes digital retouching, broad device support, and tons of graphics file formats. It works with Linux, Windows, Mac OS X, Sun OpenSolaris, and the FreeBSD operating systems, too. Check it out at www.gimp.org and then download it!

Professional Graphics Editors

If you work with photographs or other high-resolution, high-quality images or artwork, you may need one of these Web graphics tools.

Adobe Photoshop

If it weren't so darned expensive, we'd grant top honors to Photoshop CS5. Alas, $699 is too high for many novices' budgets. Wondering whether to upgrade from Photoshop Elements? Adobe mentions these capabilities among its top reasons to upgrade:

- **Improved file browser:** Shows and tells you more about more kinds of graphics files and gives you more powerful search tools.

- **Shadow/Highlight correction:** Powerful built-in tools add or manipulate shadows and highlights in images.

- **More powerful color controls:** Color palettes and color-matching tools with detailed controls that Elements lacks.

- **Text on a path:** Full-blown Photoshop lets you define any kind of path graphically and then instructs your text to follow that path. This capability supports fancy layouts that Elements can't match.

If you need to use sophisticated visual effects, edits, or tweaks on high-resolution photorealistic images, full-blown Photoshop is your best bet. For basic Web sites, however, Photoshop is overkill — it can do just about anything to photos or images of all kinds, which of course is why it's the most popular professional graphics editing tool.

Like its little brother Photoshop Elements, full-blown Photoshop works with both Macintosh and PC operating systems. The current version is Adobe Photoshop CS5. It's included in all of Adobe's product suites.

Photoshop CS5 add-ons and plugins provide specialized functions — such as complex textures or special graphics effects. This extensibility is nice because graphics professionals who need such capabilities can buy them (most cost $100 and up, with $300 a pretty typical price) and add them without muss or fuss. But those who don't need them don't have to pay extra for the base-level software.

Adobe Fireworks

Fireworks is a graphics program designed specifically for Web use, so it offers lots of nice features and functions for that purpose. The current version is Adobe Fireworks CS5. Fireworks has one killer feature — it lets you save portable network graphics (PNG) files with layers defined that work more or less the same way that Photoshop Document (PSD) files do.

Fireworks is tightly integrated with other Adobe products and therefore is of potentially great interest if you're using (or considering) Dreamweaver. Simply put, this combination of Adobe products makes it very easy to add graphical spice to Web pages.

For more information about Fireworks and related Adobe products, check out www.adobe.com/products/fireworks.

W3C Link Checker

A broken link on your site can be embarrassing. To spare your users the dreaded 404 Object Not Found error message, use a link checker to make sure your links are correctly formatted before and after you publish on the Web. Many HTML editors and Web servers include built-in local link checkers, and they may even scour the Web to check external links.

Other Web sites may change or disappear after you publish your site. Regularly check your site's links to make sure they still work. The worst broken link is one that points to a page on your *own* site which is no longer there.

The W3C link-checking tool is free, easy to use, and works surprisingly quickly (thanks to HP, we guess, for the servers they donate to support the W3C). Here's how it works: You drop a URL in for a document you want to check, and the tool comes back to you with information about the links it finds on that page. It will even do recursive checking, if you click the Check Linked Documents check box on the submission page. Try this champion link checker for yourself at `http://validator.w3.org/checklink`.

You can also download a version of this tool that you can run on your own machine from `http://validator.w3.org/docs/checklink.html`. You have a couple of download options:

- ✔ Grab a compiled version for your computer and operating system and run it as-is.
- ✔ Grab the source code and tweak it for your needs and situation.

Other Link Checkers

The following programs are pretty good link checkers. They just need the application of a little elbow grease to learn and to use. Better yet, their price is right: free!

- ✔ **LinkScan/QuickCheck:** LinkScan offers a real-time, single-page, link check and a free evaluation software package that can handle sites with up to 500,000 documents. It creates an annotated, color-coded listing of each HTML or XHTML document it parses, and makes it easy to find broken or suspect links, missing image files, and so forth.

  Check it out at `www.elsop.com/quick`.

- ✔ **SourceForge LinkChecker:** LinkChecker offers free, complex, and sophisticated link-checking services, including color-coded output, support for lots of protocols and services, all kinds of URL filters and link-checking controls, cookie checks, HTML and CSS syntax checks, and lots more.

  To find out more, take a look at `http://linkchecker.sourceforge.net/`.

HTML Validators

Validation compares a document to a set of document rules — a Document Type Definition (DTD), an XML Schema, or whatever other rules explicitly describe its syntax and structure. Simply put, validation checks the actual markup and content against the rules that govern it and flags any deviations it finds.

Typically, a document author follows this process:

1. **Create an HTML document in an HTML editor.**

   For example, imaging this step results in a file called `mypage.htm`.

2. **Submit `mypage.htm` to an HTML or XHTML validation site for inspection and validation.**

   If any problems or syntax errors are detected, the validator reports such errors in an annotated version of the original HTML document.

3. **If the validator reports errors, the author corrects those errors and resubmits the document for validation.**

Sometimes, breaking HTML rules is the only way for your page to look right in older Web browsers. But document rules exist for a reason: Nonstandard or incorrect HTML markup often produces odd or unpredictable results.

Browsers usually forgive markup errors. Most browsers identify HTML pages without an `<html>` element. But someday, markup languages may be so complex and precise that browsers won't be able to guess whether you're publishing in HTML or another markup language. Get the markup right from the beginning and save yourself a bunch of trouble later.

HTML validation is built into many HTML editors, including Dreamweaver, and all of the other WYSIWIG and HTML Helper tools we mention at the outset of this chapter. You can find validators at

- ✔ **W3C validator:** The W3C has a free, Web-based validation system available at `http://validator.w3.org`. It will provide copious output about what errors or inconsistencies it finds in your documents until you fix them all. It also includes an option for viewing annotated source code so you can see exactly where it's finding items it doesn't like. This is a great tool, and it is well worth learning and using. This tool is a vital element in building a solid, well-crafted Web site of any kind, and it will help you fix errors and address browser inconsistencies with panache and aplomb.

- ✔ **Built-in validators:** Many tools in this chapter offer HTML validation. These include HTML-Kit, HomeSite, Dreamweaver, and BBEdit. Use 'em if you got 'em; get 'em if you don't!

FTP Clients

After you create your Web site on your computer, you have to share it with the world. So you need a tool to transfer your Web pages to your Web server. One very convenient way to accomplish this task is through FTP (File Transfer Protocol). Many HTML editors include FTP support, but you can also use a separate FTP client to upload and download files to your Web server. FTP has been around since the early days of the Internet (way before the Web came along).

After you select a server host and you know how to access a Web server (your service provider should supply you with this information), you must upload your pages to that server. That means you need FTP, or some reasonable facsimile thereof.

All FTP programs are similar and easy to operate. We recommend these:

- **FileZilla** is a fast, capable, free, open source FTP program with an intuitive drag-and-drop user interface. It's available online at `http://filezilla-project.org`.
- **Cyberduck** (open source for the Macintosh) at `http://cyberduck.ch`.
- **Cute FTP Lite** (shareware, costs $25, but offers great functionality and ease of use) at `www.cuteftp.com`.
- **Fetch** for the Mac is located at `http://fetchsoftworks.com`.

Miscellaneous Helpful Web Tools

Miscellaneous tools can help you manage and control your Web site. Here, we present you with a collection of items that you can try out to see whether they deliver functionality that justifies downloading, learning, and using them (we think they're nifty, but, ultimately, that's up to you to decide):

- **HTML-Kit** supports plugins to add functions, such as link checks and spell checks. Most of these plugins are free or inexpensive. Check out `www.chami.com/html-kit/plugins`.
- **Easy HTML Construction Kit** offers a collection of useful conversion, reformatting, and template management tools for a paltry $25 at `www.hermetic.ch/html.htm`.
- **Firebug** is a Firefox plugin you can use to help you debug programs and Web pages. It lets you click sections of a page and then examine their individual properties and behaviors. Find it at `http://getfirebug.com`.

- **Browser Sandbox** comes from spoon.net; it provides a tool that lets you run multiple versions of IE, Firefox, Safari, Chrome, and Opera inside the following browsers: IE (6, 7, 8), Firefox (2, 3, 3.5), Safari (3, 4), Chrome (all versions), and Opera (9, 10). Browse to `http://spoon.net/browsers`.

- **Dropbox** makes it easy to synchronize files and directories across multiple computers anywhere on the Internet. It supports Windows, Mac, Linux, and various smartphone operating systems. Look it up at `www.dropbox.com`.

- **Google Analytics** provides a plethora of statistics about visitors to your Web site, including user origin, operating system (OS), Web browser, and oodles more. Want to understand your audience? Get Google Analytics free at `www.google.com/analytics`.

- **CrazyEgg** and **ClickDensity** offer heat maps that illustrate exactly how people are using (and moving through) your Web site. No matter what or how you think your users might be using your site, these tools tell you what's really happening. Find them at `www.crazyegg.com` and `www.clickdensity.com`.

- **iPhonetester.com** and **iPadPeek.com** provide helpful tools to see how your Web site looks on an iPhone and iPad without having to buy or otherwise obtain one. Check them out at `www.iphonetester.com` and `www.ipadpeek.com`.

Appendix A

Twitter Supporters

· ·

*T*hank you to the following people that have inspired and influenced the direction of this book: Eric Meyer, Janine Warner, Adam DuVander, *Smashing Magazine,* and the W3C.

Special thanks to the feedback from Twitter reviewers: Matthew Guay @maguay; Brent Wheeldon @BeeEmmDoubleU; Bruno Belotti @abulafio; Ray Mitchell @SixFourWeb; Amber Weinberg @amberweinberg.

Thanks to all our Twitter followers: @tigermain, @robertosolanom, @scotia-systems, @webalyst, @markhughes, @nationalnet, @quantum_dynamic, @condomiami, @apsace, @ivokhin, @anthonyroose, @gusikhwan, @Lorenzo_Vl, @paulcredmond, @KennthPang, @timmetje1990, @CarHeDa, @web_mint, @w3Servcies, @theinklog, @Himmathand, @eleeze, @Jooosieeeee, @Bacterialyrical, @webvana, @Ricksta82, @imaria, @andyhoyland, @hoyland-web, @csswebsiteaward, @shawncampbell, @matt_neary, @Certo, @noufande-sign, @jkatke, @viktor_kkk, @_zehro, @saub09, @karezzy, @mstlaurent, @SMHMAG, @Cleverfidel, @ivy526, @edmossify, @Burton_Boi, @1eme-lyperez1, @damenleeturks, @etemplesmithson, @Nimadera, @jintexas, @dead-meta4, @Fulcan, @sourcecraft, @mordrin, @alexconner, @kyleschem, @Operator1, @shaun_capehart, @cehwitham, @Aanyankah, @Wing_Cheng, @PoorKidOnCrack, @return1_at, @Iamnegative, @newinyork, @mstandage, @favz, @downingbryan, @bobrovnikov, @rrahulprasad, @danieladr, @irSteve, @hidobrado, @Codeclown, @berit_jensen, @Ingenious_mind, @martinbean, @brianarn, @annemckinnell, @Mammas_Crunk, @urbandave, @mauguar, @bebraw, @thedesignloft, @em_two, @mandirice, @steddie1, @doslimones, @wedeacon, @Ade_101, @RedHottopDesign, @marcvangijn, @twahlin, @Xochi_ALC, @tabithakarcher, @DomDanson, @RichardConroy, @diegobetto, @jmanzitti, @Lamc82, @danaeaguilar, @jaslorax, @hellomrtaylor, @design328, @creative_cakery, @hiester, @phlipper, @DejitaruKyonshi, @takingovermiami, @Robert_Cummings, @scott2211, @helvetious, @wesholing, @bklahrke, @swkolupailo, @freundedwerbung, @tweetHOOPLA, @caffeinatedsus, @grey-likeme, @jeclark, @kennydelaney, @POwall, @pyhrus, @cosmive, @sonyaong, @jaimefoxx, @pbz1912, @gorazdmurnik, @adietz, @RorschachDesign, @timfer-rell, @bswatson, @prosurf_pl, @MisaAmiya, @MSoregaroli, @blossomingmind,

@nickludwig, @jaymanpandya, @ReneeShupe, @heitortsergent, @hoshman6000, @kevinpfab, @jaysonlane, @mrkiji, @viacoffee, @sambang, @lawrencetaur, @textusstudios, @Pumpki, @andersandersson, @linglau64, @lookwebdesign, @djbolton, @vtran1, @eddo32, @AmberValDesign, @XploiteDesigns, @khean, @spikeyekim, @ronaldberner, @romymk, @psychopark, @phatchopolis, @GoddamnNoise, @LadyJ389, @hamptonsmedia, @stefan_persson, @lesterho, @evanw, @afreehour, @just_tuts, @pgaboury, @melissapillon, @big_matt_b, @PigOnTheWingDev, @bregtcolpaert, @alistaircalder, @jeffkan, @mmarnall, @_norrsken_, @Brain_Pulse, @KSSpengler, @mrstolt, @tolga_ozdemir, @Xand49, @neur0tica, @thaiszorghi, @theartstadhsmdl, @danfauver, @VGWyvern, @OakesDesign, @thek1w1, @MattVoran, @fcastrovazquez, @Jay_Searra, @rnbjunkiie, @Mcroyle, @andymeek, @klawrenc, @matthewcarleton, @SixFourWeb, @myCodeHeroes, @mannersandpoise, @adorephoto, @brightworks, @mikelitchfield, @jonathanbaltz, @AFFENT0AST, @AliciaLevey, @msteinerweb, @kevinoh, @laraleepalmer, @justbeingarlyn, @darrinmccann, @KimKritzinger, @nixonmedia, @rock2575, @dhulk, @fabsn182, @360construct, @ColorStormGD, @sawayaconsult, @dsellergren, @madhurjain, @ChristinaBruun, @toejklemme, @AndyScherzinger, @donaldpcook, @arghlex, @buraksarica, @2biazdk, @reiot, @tgummerer, @SayHidk, @cabellc, @simplybcreative, @arthurbrownjr, @emilyJbro, @freythman, @JayTillman, @Seich, @wilq_, @kylebellamy, @ElliotLings, @srcarli, @SRotherham, @jaytem, @hollandprdhouse, @MachaSign, @suzannehullah, @krukinternet, @Gargron, @normnode, @erichoffman, @richardkruk, @perfectc_nl, @crumenos, @erwinkerk, @geoffcampbell1, @adamayala, @AndrewChamp, @MatthewCooney, @disseny_web, @Atzimba, @ignacionimo, @KineticKimberly, @ruin11, @MarisBunkovskis, @johannesakesson, @lucky_v, @enkayes, @Revolution1210, @atomrow, @MattTyas, @schofeld, @damsean102, @jchawner, @henasraf, @jmz360, @george_elias, @ddgll, @avgjanecrafter, @Vivid_Ness, @Sophie_will_, @AndyMarkle, @thezenmonkey, @usaps, @robbclarke, @audielle, @woodleader, @dale_moore, @kris860911, @karolinaszczur, @dustyfields, @leevanlog, @gibbon77, @tomhermans, @brotherabstract, @b18269, @sg4380, @JoelCox, @nicolasrauber, @cl_thompson, @nvartolomei, @aklipz, @delphikit, @renaars, @eduardofaria, @SkyZee, @stylishpixel, @vi_rox, @christodhunter, @adhipg, @ar_designs, @nickjvm, @RadDevelopment, @server404, @designpatrol, @HappinessBook, @bbisser, @lizialexander, @iamrewind, @Angelz, @galovesongs, @attawayUCM, @Johnathan1707, @jiminizer, @spacepuddle, @emilyrumbelow, @ShunaP, @iheartrendering, @dren_martin, @NotoriousUSB, @Swrdlw, @aariste, @LeahFreihaut, @CraigTuffs, @eagleseye, @JJ_Web, @ivonakarajlovic, @manion, @mikeheaver, @noiserocker, @hmenon, @andyedinborough, @artrubicon, @MichaelHermus, @dawny_cupcake, @tdwright, @GregHuntoon, @andrewcairns, @Shane_Howell, @virtualizacia, @neilnand, @the18, @urosgruber, @Elisje, @marvos, @Davegood86, @lucraak, @sambell111, @WVMagicDesign, @ValentinoVelez, @datouyL, @Blueys, @Davezilla, @MathRi, @philteague, @ThalAMorgul, @metslifer, @coldwellbnkr, @mantebridts, @douglasradburn, @TutZone, @CynthiaSavard, @marzhal,

@JamesEggers, @BLINDACRE, @thejaycarlson, @meerkw, @zimmiclabs, @haggen, @narelle, @Didifournier, @sonicdivx, @chillman2, @fievelwill, @thomasoffinga, @Fubart, @TimoBakx, @prokka, @phelo, @cssgarden, @aleksandar_k, @SlodiveOnline, @siphilp, @OrionCards, @ZoranJambor, @jalynish, @sethmsparks, @lollyjayne9, @Lil_Tumbelina, @celinemontheard, @oursurveysays, @marklkelly, @aminabbasian, @stephenwalcher, @axing, @ns_museum, @cprowe, @JustinRhodes, @IcarusWingz, @Vinomorph, @TheHundredth, @sillybear, @persocon, @mschatzler, @StevenHook, @hlashbrooke, @spaceghost65, @daninacan, @stakey, @andreaDuquette, @DualDev, @richwilliamsuk, @seanodotcom, @frizzychick, @srikanthpanaman, @ugalem, @vetler, @mattfroese, @foocode, @TWENTY4e, @trickstah, @cl_audio, @rob_norman, @GrayJunior, @ryanriatno, @imrelentless, @forensick, @patricktomas, @whatidraggedin, @Ronsend, @donroyco, @SilverbladeNL, @t_films, @juliegozali, @Zonakusu, @michaelmcguk, @creativeye, @stickyseal, @ren_riz, @Baztoune, @Series3Graphics, @jcboutkan, @randriese, @apinder, @aisy, @Grayski, @fircb0x, @cdg, @drquesh, @amberweinberg, @crashmaster007, @BrokenMichaela, @Tara_Nielsen_, @svendenotter, @webtischler, @magalocr, @brettschumann, @orionweb, @viktoralarsson, @shawnhud, @HannahRampton, @zenom_, @apaatsio, @twit_asim, @piuleony_, @ameershk, @PatrykNr2010, @nerdylamb, @Moodlegirl, @omersilent, @oogyx, @SUEL_Design, @CSSOrg, @usingJquery, @ondoordacht, @kaybrex, @macx, @samswenson, @Jaeesen, @InDieta, @javierland, @RayKayMarketing, @grfxdznr, @mrandmrsBEAR, @dswtpl, @netmoni, @alphahost, @alfonsomm, @nurseito, @BreakinRecClark, @stefstivala, @mmahgoub, @evertonht, @VladanF, @juneja_23ravi, @ayoungh, @Prog5rammer, @gustotech, @AganHoating, @annannaiholu, @xhtmljunction, @infocuswebsolu, @iAndroid_SA, @dtli, @actionmoviefrea, @techGURUtwit, @OgleMedia, @smashingmag, @jnelson74, @brandjane, @BKB_mschroeder, @EvernetUK, @eminaya, @eightfivezero, @Vera2106, @normalnorman, @justinmcgarry, @danielgrieve, @anaura, @snow_burger, @TotalBodyMgmt, @tim_gleeson, @moshner, @ryan_yates, @fittrainerchris, @xteban, @noveltysystems, @almakov, @Vtomatis, @mytwitacct, @1111theatre, @fointypinger, @msux, @Zabisco, @ryanbarr, @kristerkari, @JeroenEijkhof, @mitsubstanz, @theandym, @inxilpro, @bavaga_com, @Dharmangp, @Ed_sin, @twelveofour, @shiftyp, @misteraj, @equinlan, @vivek2562, @prayagn, @nlronald, @marcogallen, @blaneywebdesign, @atatz, @Vrean, @hameedraha, @darkforce_er, @ReinierButot, @SaraKalinoski, @goncaloborrega, @Designerwitter, @chris_gg, @torrentroot, @UserStudio, @vherrin, @AhtiK, @marie_luce, @evaryont, @daniele_360, @eirikhm, @michelgort, @albertlo, @reggielamson, @iambca, @stewartritchie, @jabridesign, @BurkHufnagel, @siderakis, @edmeehan, @soyrosa, @schoot, @naamyo, @TechAsNeeded, @amyberger, @neilthurlwell, @MMudassir, @chimericdream, @metalchic, @chrisajohnso, @the_jchristie, @piksal, @blueeyesben, @josephj60, @riscaa, @anthonypants, @chucken, @BeeEmmDoubleU, @mgjesdal, @Fas75, @spyn, @cameronbaney, @intuitionhq, @10For2, @mike_o_sullivan, @chrislevy, @javaph, @bslavinator,

@Larsenal, @scans007, @Saucerdk, @rockyroadizme, @davidnilsson, @Sorcix, @LoudaMedia, @andrewinebarger, @maguay, @jessamazing, @mixrecords, @iThorning, @AddictToSystems, @anderschdk, @Jeepers1993, @gnoruhs, @mcgrafics, @jayjdk, @ryankaye, @yellowllama, @LeeTurley, @Jaswinder-Virdee, @jbayone, @Velehto, @charlesboyung, @mywayhome, @whitbread-design, @leanderdirkse, @mys7, @mattrogowski, @iconfinder, @coaststudios, @sunilsk, @MJKilgore, @allanberger, @spodalicious, @TheRealKartik, @thisiswilson, @shahrilabdullah, @abulafio, @dalesimpson, @racshot653, @garethspictures, @bretbouchard, @brendadhk, @chucke, @moo_marketing, @megrw, @Brer, @ghostdog23, @mysticode, @crmunro, @davidvivero, @LisaWeik, @juarezpaf, @mloweris, @tudorizer, @FrankS, @georgel, @Kathryn_Wells, @Yuibox, @ronwikso, @_ambrose, @JeffAwesomeribrahimali, @ryanmargheriti, @tumbledesign, @robbygoodwin, @chrisk_de, @japellerano, @d_winter, @paulaceva, @BrianBBrian, @CreativeQA, @fabbrikk, @cmaddi-son, @vgreano, @felipus, @mistercameron, @webtehdas, @NateReid, @hune-falk, @johncloys, @seengee, @amanaplan, @rmanzanet, @cobradave, @marcseyon, @illustrationdan, @UncleBumpy, @Danger_Mouse, @kielabok-kie, @rafaeluzzi, @zitrusfrisch, @sensorsicht, @yummygum, @andrewingram, @mentalartist, @kworry, @ljohndotnet, @IoNPulse, @IvanSF, @rourkery, @kev-inhorek, @AnotherAxe, @davidmcooper, @frankwatervoort, @AlwaysTyred, @ciberch, @cs188, @ekochman, @parisvega, @Gidgidonihah, @yoannjaffre, @Alec_, @ashleyw, @robrubinoff, @purplehayz, @gregrwilkinson, @rumblepup, @SachaGreif, @swinefever, @wwfa, @adambrehm, @RedstageMagento, @AnthonyLatona, @csskarma, @Maximegalon, @edhassinger, @SelAromDotNet, @douglasrogers, @afxjzs, @brianmark, @tb623, @jhontr, @ruudburger, @Flash_Rabbit, @web2000, @3ch0, @krusipo, @userintuitive, @slawekp, @teabass, @bartaz, @yngveh, @middlep, @adomas_s, @maartenmachiels, @doodlemoonch, @iamntz, @micahbrich, @marele, @hendynz, @petechappell, @bmcmann88, @Fatherof1, @janinewarner, @_Atticus, @eckermanj, @hagel, @ImpressiveWebs, @guywithabike, @SonicInteractiv, @Whiskers, @thereal-geddylee, @csonski, @iAquarian, @benrabicoff, @38thirty, @cinderstudios, @autodafe, @poneal, @The_Slade, @TexasMonique, @JustinIsADbag, @ChillyP77, @bloodycheese, @katevanderploeg, @Falcor00, @russwilson, @tombrokeoff, @AndreaKStout, @JimFl, @bgraesser, @jeffersonnoble, @gmcbride.

Index

& (ampersand), 23–24
(#) sign, 100
: (colon), 96
; (semicolon), 137
@ import keyword, 158
@font-face pseudo-class, 331, 340
< (less-than sign), 23–24
> (greater-than sign), 23–24
6 Lightbox Plugins for WordPress
    Web site, 277

• A •

A List Apart Magazine Web site, 374
<a> tag, 156
absolute links, 93
absolute value measurements, 133
Accept attribute, 246
Acceptcharset attribute, 246
acronym (rarely used) attribute, 316
action attribute, 225, 226
:active pseudo class, 174, 207
addresses, 300
AddThis Web site, 258
Adobe Fireworks tool, 367
Adobe Flash program, 308
Adobe Photoshop tool, 366–367
:after pseudo class, 207
Align attribute, 317
Align deprecated attribute, 125
aligning
  images, 114
  text, 182–183
alink attribute, 317
All media type, 158
alt attribute, 117, 125, 240
alternative text, 110–112
American Standard Code for Information
    Interchange (ASCII), 22–23

ampersand (&), 23–24
Analytics tool, 371
anchor elements, 91, 93, 101
animations, 338–339
Apple company, 308
applet attribute, 316
applet element, 123–124
applets, 213
Aptana Studio tool, 364
archive attribute, 125, 317
<area /> element, 116
aria-* attribute, 315
<article> element, 311
ASCII (American Standard Code for
    Information Interchange), 22–23
<aside> element, 311
async (script) attribute, 313
attributes
  element-specific attributes, 312–314
  forms, 225–226
  global HTML5 attributes, 315
  images, 116–117
  overview, 17
  removed from HTML5, 316–318
<audio> element, 311
aural media type, 158
aural styles, 167
autocomplete (input) attribute, 313
autofocus (input, select,
    textarea, button) attribute, 313

• B •

background attribute, 125, 176, 317
background property, 132, 192
background-attachment property, 192
Backgroundcolor property, 159, 176, 192
Backgroundimage property, 159, 192
background-position property, 192

`background-repeat` property, 192
backgrounds
  color, 192
  CSS3, 334
  image, 192–193
  overview, 175–176
bandwidth, 296–297
`basefont` (presentational)
    attribute, 316
`basefont` deprecated element, 123
`:before` pseudo class, 207
`bgcolor` attribute, 125, 317
`blank` value, 98
`blink` value, 187
`<blockquote>` element, 77
blocks of text
  aligning text, 182–183
  block quotes, 77–78
  horizontal rules, 80–82
  indenting text, 183
  preformatted text, 78–80
`<body>` element, 36, 71, 154–155, 286
bold text, 184
`bolder` value, 184
`border` attribute, 125, 317
`Border` property, 132, 163, 194
`border-bottom` property, 194
borders
  CSS3, 332–333
  images, 114
  properties of, 193–195
`border-style` property, 162
`border-width` property, 163
`bottom` property, 161, 202
`box-shadow` attribute, 336
`braille` media type, 158
breadcrumbs, 298
broken links, 95
Browser Sandbox tools, 371
browsers
  dependencies of, 349
  graphical, 76–77
  overview, 13–14

text, 77
windows of, 216–217
bugs
  live links, 355–356
  making site maps, 353–354
  old links, 356
  peer reviews, 358
  revisiting material, 357
  scheduling site reviews, 358–359
  testing tools, 358
  text, 354–355
  user feedback, 359–360
bulleted lists, 85–87
buttons, 271

• C •

`%CAlign` attribute type, 127
Candidate Recommendation (CR), 325
`<canvas>` element, 311
capitalization
  markup for, 186
  syntax for, 186
  of URLs, 95
CAPTCHA, 249
cascading, 145–146
Cascading Style Sheets. *See* CSS
`CDATA` attribute type, 127
`cellpadding` attribute, 317
`cellspacing` attribute, 317
`center` (presentational)
    attribute, 316
`center` deprecated element, 123
centimeters, 133
CGI (Common Gateway Interface), 241
CGI Resource Index, 243
`char` attribute, 317
characters
  (X)HTML, codes, 23
  codes, 378
  HTML5 encoding, 309–310
  non-ASCII, 22–23
  spacing, 180–181
  tag, 23–24

charset (meta) attribute, 313
check boxes, 230–231
Checked attribute, 246
class attribute, 138, 315
classid attribute, 317
Classification properties, 132
clear attribute, 125, 317
clear property, 202, 203–204
ClickDensity tool, 371
clients, 370
client-side scripts
    adding rollovers to pages, 265–271
    working with cookies, 272–274
    working with jQuery and FancyBox
        lightbox, 274–278
clip property, 202
CMS (Content Management System)
    customizing CSS on, 283–289
    Drupal, 281–282
    to HTML sites, 279–280
    Joomla, 282
    WordPress, 281
CMS-based Web sites, 280
Code deprecated attribute, 125
codebase attribute, 125, 317
codetype attribute, 317
colon (:), 96
color
    backgrounds, 175–176
    color names, 170–171
    hexadecimal color codes, 171–172
    links, 173–175
    RGB values, 172
    text, 173
%Color attribute type, 127
Color deprecated attribute, 125
color keyword, 319
color property, 159, 205, 206
cols attribute, 236
<command> element, 311
comma-separated values (CSV), 242
common font families, 177
Common Gateway Interface (CGI), 241
compact attribute, 125, 318

compressed files, 102–103
content attributes, 68
#content element, 284
Content Management System. *See* CMS
contenteditable* attribute, 315
contextmenu* attribute, 315
cookies
    expiration dates of, 274
    working with, 272–274
coords attribute, 117
cords attribute, 317
CR (Candidate Recommendation), 325
CrazyEgg tool, 371
cross-platform file formats, 106
CSS (Cascading Style Sheets)
    background properties, 191–193
    border and outline properties, 193–195
    cascading, 145–146
    changing fonts, 153–157
    custom button rollovers with, 271
    dimension properties, 195–196
    and Drupal, 285–287
    Eric Meyer's reset, 209
    external style sheets, 144–145, 157–158
    Firebug Web site, 209
    fonts and font properties, 197–199
    image rollovers with, 268–271
    internal style sheets, 143–144
    and Joomla, 287–289
    margin and padding properties, 200–201
    markup, 26–27
    positioning, 151–153
    positioning properties, 201–204
    pseudo classes, 207–208
    sizing text fonts with, 179
    Spoon Browser Sandbox Web site, 209
    structure and syntax, 134–142
    style sheets, 130–134
    text properties, 204–206
    text rollovers with, 266–268
    using CSS with multimedia, 158–167
    visual layouts, 149–151
    W3C CSS validation service, 209
    W3Schools Web site, 208

CSS (Cascading Style Sheets) *(continued)*
  Web-developer's handbook, 210
  and WordPress, 283–285
  YSlow add-on, 210
CSS3
  animations, 338–339
  backgrounds, 334
  borders, 332–333
  fonts, 331–332
  limitations of, 340–341
  overview, 325–330
  resources for, 341
  shadows, 334–337
  transforming content, 339–340
  transitions, 337–338
CSS-Tricks Web site, 375
CSV (comma-separated values), 242
cursor property, 164, 202, 204
Cute FTP Lite program, 370
Cyberduck program, 370

• D •

data
  collection forms of, 223–224
  processing, 241–244
data-* attribute, 315
<datalist> element, 311
date keyword, 319
datetime keyword, 319
datetimelocal keyword, 319
declarations
  (X)HTML DOCTYPE, 64–65
  CCS, 136–138
  HTML DOCTYPE, 64
declare attribute, 317
definition lists, 87–89
demos, 300
deprecated (X)HTML markup, 121–128
  attributes, 124–127
  elements, 123–124
  overview, 121–123

designing
  forms, 244–245
  Web pages, 33–34
  Web sites, 45–46
<details> element, 311
DHTML (Dynamic HTML), 265
dimension properties, 195–196
dir attribute, 315, 316
dir deprecated element, 123
direction property, 205
directory paths, 97
disabled (fieldset) attribute, 313
Display property, 161, 202
<div> tag, 268
DOCTYPE declarations, 64–65
document tree, 174
Document Type Definitions (DTDs),
  64, 376–377
documents
  (X)HTML, 63–64, 71–72
  <html> element, 65
  adding (X)HTML DOCTYPE declarations,
    64–65
  adding (X)HTML namespaces, 65–66
  adding headers, 66–71
  adding HTML DOCTYPE declarations, 64
  headings, 26
  heads, 25
  images in, 27
  structuring, 346
domains, 16, 57
draggable* attribute, 315
Dreamweaver tool, 362–363
Dropbox tool, 371
drop-down list fields, 234–236
Drupal CMS, 281–282, 285–287
DTDs (Document Type Definitions), 64,
  376–377
Dynamic HTML (DHTML), 265
dynamic pages, 213

• E •

Easy HTML Construction Kit, 370
editors
 graphics, 365–367
 helper HTML, 363–365
 WYSIWYG HTML, 362–363
elements
 for adding document headers, 68
 attributes specific to, 312–314
 deprecated, 123
 images, 116–117
 nesting, 20
 new in HTML5, 311–312
 removed from HTML5, 315–316
 single tags, 19–20
 tag pairs, 19
<em> element, 74
e-mail
 addresses, 103–104
 sending form data by, 243–244
email keyword, 319
<embed> element, 311
embedding
 creating maps, 256–258
 Flickr, 255–256
 using Twitter widgets, 252–255
embossed media type, 158
empty elements, 19, 108
encoding, 309–310
Enctype attribute, 246
entities
 (X)HTML character codes, 23
 non-ASCII characters, 22–23
 overview, 17
 tag characters, 23–24
Eric Meyer's reset, 209
expiration date of cookies, 274
eXtensible Markup Language (XHTML)
 <html> element, 65
 adding DOCTYPE declarations, 64–65
 adding document headers, 66–71
 adding HTML DOCTYPE declarations, 64
 adding namespaces, 65–66
 character codes, 23
 creating document body, 71–72
 difference from HTML, 16–17
 Document Type Definitions (DTDs),
  376–377
 establishing document structure, 63–64
 markup, deprecated, 121–128
extensions, 96
external style sheets
 importing, 145
 linking, 144–145
 overview, 129
externalizing style sheets, 157–158

• F •

Face deprecated attribute, 125
FancyBox lightbox, 274–278
feedback, 359–360
Fetch program, 370
<figcaption> element, 311
<figure> element, 311
file formats
 .htm and .html, 38
 GIF, 106
 JPEG, 107
 PNG, 107
File Transfer Protocol (FTP)
 clients, 370
 moving files with, 58–59
 overview, 15
file upload fields, 233–234
filenames, 16, 96
files
 choosing location and names for, 37
 downloads, 102–103
 .htm and .html formats, 38
 moving to Web servers, 58–60
FileZilla program, 370
Firebug Firefox plugin, 370

Firebug Web site, 209
Fireworks tool, 367
:first-child pseudo class, 207
:first-letter pseudo class, 207
first-level headings, 76
:first-line pseudo class, 207
Flash tool, 307–308
flat files, 242
Flickr app, 255–256
float property, 202
Float/uO property, 163
flush alignment, 182
:focus pseudo class, 174, 207
font (presentational) attribute, 316
font deprecated element, 123
font property, 197
font-family property, 137, 159, 176, 197
font-family value, 188
fonts
  body text, 154–155
  character spacing, 180–181
  CSS3, 331–332
  family, 176–178, 197–198
  font property, 187–188
  headings, 155
  hyperlinks, 155–157
  line height, 179–180
  size of, 178–179, 198–199
  weight of, 198
font-size property, 159, 197, 198
font-size value, 188
font-style property, 197
font-style value, 188
font-variant property, 197
font-variant value, 188
font-weight property, 160, 197
font-weight value, 188
<footer> element, 311
For attribute, 246
form (input, output, select,
    textarea, button, fieldset)
    attribute, 313
form gateway page, 245
form handlers, 225
<form> element, 217, 225

formaction (input, button)
    attribute, 313
formatting text
  headings, 76–77
  paragraphs, 74–75
formenctype (input, button)
    attribute, 313
formmethod (input, button)
    attribute, 313
formnovalidate (input, button)
    attribute, 313
forms
  CAPTCHA, 249
  check boxes and radio buttons, 230–231
  customizing Submit and Reset buttons,
    239–241
  designing, 244–245
  drop-down list fields, 234–236
  file upload fields, 233–234
  frameworks, 248–249
  hidden fields, 231–232
  input tags, 226–227
  markup, 246–248
  multiline text boxes, 236–237
  password fields, 229–230
  processing data, 241–244
  structure, 225–226
  Submit and Reset buttons, 237–239
  text fields, 227–229
  uses for, 221–224
  validation of, 241
formtarget (input, button)
    attribute, 313
frame (negative usage) attribute, 316
frame attribute, 318
frameborder attribute, 318
frameset (negative usage)
    attribute, 316
frameworks
  forms, 248–249
  mobile, 301–303
FTP (File Transfer Protocol)
  clients, 370
  moving files with, 58–59
  overview, 15

• G •

generic font families, 177
GIF (Graphics Interchange Format), 106
global HTML5 attributes, 315
GNU Image Manipulation Program v(GIMP), 366
Google Analytics tool, 371
Google maps
  and Twitter mashup, 262–263
  and yelp mashup, 259–262
graphical browsers, 76–77
graphics editors
  inexpensive, 365–366
  professional, 366–367
Graphics Interchange Format (GIF), 106
greater-than sign (>), 23–24

• H •

<h1> element, 36, 75
<h4> element, 268
<h6> element, 75
handheld media type, 158
hash mark, 152
<head> element, 36, 268
<header> element, 311
headers
  CSS, 155
  formatting, 76
  giving pages titles, 66–67
  graphical browsers, 76–77
  metadata, 68–69
  redirecting users to other pages, 69–71
  text browsers, 77
height attribute, 112, 125, 318
height property, 164, 196
helper HTML editors, 363–365
hexadecimal color codes, 171–172
<hgroup> element, 311
hidden fields, 231–232
hidden* attribute, 315
horizontal rules, 80–82

hosting Web sites
  moving files to Web servers, 58–60
  obtaining domains, 57
  overview, 55–56
  using hosting providers, 56
hostname, 97
:hover pseudo class, 174, 207
<hr /> element, 80
href attribute, 104, 117, 145
hreflang (area) attribute, 313
hspace attribute, 125, 318
.htm file format, 38
HTML. *See also* CSS
  4.01 Frameset DOCTYPE declaration, 64
  4.01 Strict DOCTYPE declaration, 64
  4.01 Transitional DOCTYPE declaration, 64
  difference with (X)HTML (eXtensible Markup Language), 16–17
  document headings, 26
  document heads, 25
  lists, 26
  paragraphs, 26
  sites, comparing to CMS sites, 279–280
  tables, 26
  validators, 368–369
  Web sites based only in, 280
<html> element, 36, 65
HTML references, online
  character codes, 378
  HTML and (X)HTML Document Type Definitions (DTDs), 376–377
  resource sites, 373–375
  specifications, 375–376
Open Source Notepad++ tool, 365
HTML5
  additional resources, 322
  attributes removed from, 316–318
  elements removed from, 315–316
  and Flash, 307–308
  limits to access and usage of, 320–322
  markup, 308–310
  new attributes, 312–316
  new elements, 311–312
  new input types in, 318–319

HTML5 *(continued)*
  sample Web pages of, 323–324
  Web APIs, 320
HTML-Kit tool, 365, 370
HTTP (Hypertext Transfer Protocol), 15, 95
`http-equiv` attribute, 71
hyperlinks
  absolute, 93
  broken, 95
  building image maps, 116–118
  choosing, 53–54
  color of, 173–175
  e-mail addresses, 103–104
  external style sheets, 144–145
  file downloads, 102–103
  live, 355–356
  locations in Web pages, 99–101
  new windows, 97–99
  old, 356
  overview, 27
  relative, 93–95
  text, 54
  triggering, 115–116
hypertext, 10–13
HyperText Markup Language. *See* HTML
HyperText Transfer Protocol (HTTP), 15, 95

• I •

`<i>` tag, 184
`%IAlign` attribute type, 127
icons used in this book, 6
`id` attribute, 315
`id="name"` attribute, 140
images
  alignment of, 114
  adding alternative and title text, 110–112
  borders of, 114
  editing software for, 172
  in HTML documents, 27
  linking, 115–118
  location of, 108
  maps, 116, 118
  optimizing, 107
  role of in Web pages, 105–106

  rollovers with CSS, 268–271
  specifying image size, 112–114
  using `<img>` element, 108–110
  Web-friendly, 106–108
`<img>` element, 20, 108–110, 112, 116
`<img src>` element, 257
inches, 133
indenting text, 183
inheriting styles, 141–142
inline elements, 74, 93
inline styles, 129, 142, 144
`<input />` element, 227, 229, 232, 240
input fields
  check boxes and radio buttons, 230–231
  customizing Submit and Reset buttons, 239–241
  drop-down list fields, 234–236
  file upload fields, 233–234
  hidden fields, 231–232
  multiline text boxes, 236–237
  password fields, 229–230
  Submit and Reset buttons, 237–239
  text fields, 227–229
input tags, 226–227
input types, 318–319
internal style sheets, 129, 143–144
Internet protocols, 15
intradocument hyperlinks, 99, 100
iPadPeek Web site, 371
iPhonetester Web site, 371
`isindex` attribute, 316
`isindex` element, 123–124
italics, 185

• J •

Java programming language, 213
JavaScript
  arranging content dynamically using, 214–216
  forms, 241
  libraries, 277
  scripting Web pages using, 212–214
Joint Photographic Experts Group (JPEG), 107
Joomla CMS, 282, 287–289

jQTouch framework, 302–303
jQuery library, 274–278
jQuery Validation Plugins Web site, 248
jQuery Web site, 277
justify keyword, 182

• K •

<keygen> element, 311
Komodo Edit software, 364
Kompozer Web page editor, 363

• L •

Label attribute, 246, 313
labeling documents
  <html> element, 65
  adding (X)HTML DOCTYPE declarations,
    64–65
  adding (X)HTML namespaces, 65–66
  adding HTML DOCTYPE declarations, 64
%LAlign attribute type, 127
lang attribute, 315
:lang pseudo class, 207
Language deprecated attribute, 125
Last Call (LC), 325
LCR attribute type, 127
LCRJ attribute type, 127
left keyword, 182
left property, 162, 202
%Length attribute type, 127
less-than sign (<), 23–24
letter-spacing property, 180, 205
<li> element, 82, 84, 228
lightbox plugins, 277
lighter value, 184
line height, 179–180
line-height property, 160, 205, 206
line-height value, 188
line-through value, 187
link attribute, 317
link checkers, 367–368
Link deprecated attribute, 126
link element, 144
:link pseudo class, 174, 207

links
  absolute, 93
  broken, 95
  building image maps, 116–118
  choosing, 53–54
  color of, 173–175
  e-mail addresses, 103–104
  external style sheets, 144–145
  file downloads, 102–103
  live, 355–356
  locations in Web pages, 99–101
  new windows, 97–99
  old, 356
  overview, 27
  relative, 93–95
  text, 54
  triggering, 115–116
LinkScan program, 368
List properties, 132
lists
  bulleted, 85–87
  defined, 87–89
  formatting, 83–84
  nesting, 89–90
  numbering, 84–85
  overview, 26
ListStyle attribute type, 127
list-styleimage property, 160
list-styleposition property, 160
list-styletype property, 160
local pages, 13
longdesc attribute, 317
lowercase value, 186
LRAN attribute type, 127

• M •

manifest (html) attribute, 313
<map> element, 116
maps
  creating, 256–258
  elements and attributes, 116–117
  markup, 117–118
  using as visual user guides, 48–49
  using for site development, 46–48
margin properties, 132, 164, 200

margin-bottom property, 200
marginheight attribute, 318
margin-left property, 200
margin-right property, 200
margin-top property, 200
<mark> element, 312
Matt's Script archive, 243
max (input) attribute, 313
max-height property, 196
maxlength attribute, 228
max-width property, 196
media (a, area) attribute, 313
media types, 158
menu deprecated element, 123
<meta /> element, 68
<meta /> tags, 69
metadata
  custom names, 68–69
  defined, 66
  elements and attributes, 68
<meter> element, 312
method attribute, 225, 246
Microsoft Expression Web 4 package, 363
millimeters, 133
MIMDisabled attribute, 246
min (input) attribute, 313
min-height property, 196
min-width property, 196
mobile Web design
  addresses, 300
  designing for distracted surfers, 299
  designing for small screens, 297
  frameworks, 301–303
  location, 300–301
  mobile devices, 293–296
  navigating on mobile devices, 298
  optimizing for low bandwidth, 297
  surfing the Web on many mobile
    devices, 299
  typing and clicking, 301
  virtual demos or showcases, 300
month keyword, 319
MooTools Web site, 277

multiline text boxes, 236–237
multimedia, 158–167
multiple (input) attribute, 313
Multiple attribute, 246

● N ●

N/A (None), 325
name attribute, 126, 230, 236, 247, 317
named locations, 100–101
namespaces, 65–66
naming
  files, 37
  link locations, 99
<nav> element, 312
navBar id, 150
navigation, 27, 49–52, 298
navigation bar, 150
nesting
  lists, 89–90
  overview, 20
  tags, 141
noframes (negative usage)
    attribute, 316
nohref attribute, 317
non-ASCII (American Standard Code for
    Information Interchange) characters,
    22–23
None (N/A), 325
none value, 186, 187
nonpareil CSS references, 191
normal value, 184, 185
noshade attribute, 318
Noshade deprecated attribute, 126
Noupe Web site, 375
novalidate (input) attribute, 314
nowrap attribute, 318
nowrap deprecated attribute, 126
Number attribute type, 127
number keyword, 319
numbered lists
  formatting, 83–84
  numbering, 84–85

• O •

Object deprecated attribute, 126
oblique text, 185
octothorpe, 152
<ol> attributes, 84–85
<ol> element, 82, 84
online HTML references
  character codes, 378
  HTML and (X)HTML Document Type
    Definitions (DTDs), 376–377
  resource sites, 373–375
  specifications, 375–376
Open Source Notepad++ tool, 365
<option> tag, 234
orphans property, 165
outline properties, 193–195
outline-color property, 194
outline-style property, 194
outline-width property, 194
<output> element, 312
outside links
  choosing, 53–54
  link text, 54
overflow property, 202
overlapping CSS, 152–153
overline value, 187
overlow-clip property, 202

• P •

<p> element, 36, 93
padding property, 132, 164, 200–201
padding-bottom property, 200
padding-left property, 200
padding-right property, 200
padding-top property, 200
pagebreakafter property, 165
pagebreakbefore property, 165
pagebreakinside property, 166
pages
  adding alternative and title text, 110–112
  adding rollovers to, 265–271
  attractiveness of, 347
  browsers, 13–14
  CSS markup, 26–27
  document headings, 26
  document heads, 25
  editing, 40–41
  HTML5, 323–324
  hypertext, 10–13
  image borders and alignment, 114
  image location, 108
  images in HTML documents, 27
  links and navigation tools, 27
  links locations in, 99–101
  lists, 26
  local, 13
  low scroll, 350
  mobile Web design, 293–304
  paragraphs, 26
  planning design, 33–34
  posting online, 41–42
  processing forms on, 242–243
  role of images in, 105–106
  saving, 37–38
  scripting, 211–220
  specifying image size, 112–114
  tables, 26
  titles, 66–67
  using <img /> element, 108–110
  viewing, 38–39
  Web servers, 14–15
  writing HTML, 34–37
Paint Shop Pro Photo X3 graphics editor, 366
paragraphs, 26, 74–75
password fields, 229–230
paths, 16
pattern (input) attribute, 314
PDF files, 102
peer reviews, 358
Photoshop tool, 366–367
picas, 133
Picasa Web site, 258
ping (a, area) attribute, 314
%Pixel attribute type, 127
pixels, 133

placeholder (input, textarea) attribute, 314
plugins, 277
PNG (Portable Network Graphics), 107
points, 133
POP (Post Office Protocol), 15
pop-up windows, 98
Portable Network Graphics (PNG), 107
position property, 162, 202
positioning properties
  clear, 203–204
  CSS, 132
  cursor, 204
  float, 202
  z-index, 202–203
Post Office Protocol (POP), 15
posting Web pages online, 41–42
pound symbol, 152
<pre> element, 79
preformatted text, 78–80
print media type, 158
processing data
  processing forms on pages, 242–243
  sending form data by e-mail, 243–244
profile attribute, 317
<progress> element, 312
projection media type, 158
Prompt deprecated attribute, 126
properties
  background, 191–193
  border and outline, 193–195
  CSS, 134
  dimension, 195–196
  fonts and font, 197–199
  margin and padding, 200–201
  positioning, 201–204
  text, 204–206
protocols, 15, 16
pseudo class selectors, 156
pseudo classes, 173–174, 207–208, 331

● **Q** ●

QuickCheck program, 368
quotation class, 180

● **R** ●

radio buttons, 230–231
ragged alignment, 182
range keyword, 319
Readonly attribute, 247
rel (area) attribute, 314
relative links
  simple links, 94
  site links, 94–95
relative URLs, 94
relative value measurements, 133
required (input, textarea) attribute, 314
Reset buttons
  customizing, 239–241
  overview, 237–239
reset style sheets, 209
rev, charset attribute, 317
reversed (ol) attribute, 314
RGB values, 172
right keyword, 182
right property, 161, 202
role* attribute, 315
rollovers, 265–271
rows attribute, 236
<rp> element, 312
<rt> element, 312
<ruby> element, 312
rules attribute, 318

● **S** ●

s (presentational) attribute, 316
s deprecated element, 123
sandbox (iframe) attribute, 314
saving Web pages
  .htm or .html, 38
  choosing location and names for files, 37
scheme attribute, 317
scoped (style) attribute, 314
screen media type, 158
screens, 296, 297
Scribd Web site, 258

`<script>` element, 217
scripting Web pages
   JavaScript, 212–214
   soliciting and verifying user input, 217–219
   using JavaScript to arrange content
      dynamically, 214–216
   working with browser windows, 216–217
scripts, 211
ScriptSearch Web site, 243
`scrolling` attribute, 318
scrolling pages, 350
`seamless (iframe)` attribute, 314
search forms, 222–223
`search` keyword, 319
`<section>` element, 312
`<select>` tag, 234, 235
selectors, 136–138
`*self` attribute type, 127
semicolons (;), 137
Sencha Touch framework, 302
servers, 58–60
server-side scripting, 220
shadows, 334–337
`shape` attribute, 116, 317
shorthand properties, 151, 195
showcases, 300
simple links, 94
Simple Mail Transfer Protocol (SMTP), 15
single tags, 19–20
singleton tags, 108
site maps, 354
sites. *See also* bugs
   building navigation, 49–52
   comparing HTML to CMS, 279–280
   content embedding, 252–258
   content of, 345–346
   design, 45–46
   hosting, 55–60
   HTML references, 373–375
   links, 94–95
   mapping, 46–49
   maps, 353–354
   mashups, 258–263
   navigate, 349–350

planning outside links, 53–54
scheduling reviews, 358–359
structuring documents, 346
6 Lightbox Plugins for WordPress
   Web site, 277
sixth-level headings, 76
`size` attribute, 126, 228, 247, 318
Size properties, 132
`sizes (link)` attribute, 314
sizing text
   character spacing, 180–181
   font size, 178–179
   line height, 179–180
SlideShare Web site, 258
Smashing Magazine Web site, 374
SMTP (Simple Mail Transfer Protocol), 15
soliciting user input, 217–219
SourceForge LinkChecker program, 368
spacing properties, 200–201
`span` element, 139
specifications, 375–376
`spellcheck*` attribute, 315
Spoon Browser Sandbox Web site, 209
`src` attribute, 110, 240
`srcdoc (iframe)` attribute, 314
`standby` attribute, 317
`start` attribute, 84, 314
`Start` deprecated attribute, 126
`step (input)` attribute, 314
`strike (presentational)` attribute, 316
`strike` deprecated element, 123
`<strong>` element, 74
`style` attribute, 315
style classes, 138–140
style IDs, 140–141
style sheets
   external, 144–145, 157–158
   internal, 143–144
   overview, 130–134
`<style>` element, 143, 150
Submit buttons
   customizing, 239–241
   overview, 237–239
`<summary>` element, 312

syntax
  for applying bold, 184
  for applying italic, 185
  for changing capitalization, 186
  for indenting text, 183
  overview, 17
  for text alignment, 182
  for text decoration, 187

● T ●

Tabindex attribute, 247, 315
Table properties, 132
tables, 26
tab-separated values (TSV), 242
tag characters, 23–24
tag pairs, 19
tags, 347–348
%TAlign attribute type, 127
target (base, a, area) attribute, 314
target attribute, 317
tel keyword, 319
testing tools, 358
text
  aligning, 182–183
  alternative, 110–112
  body element, 154–155
  bold, 184
  browsers, 77
  bugs, 354–355
  changing capitalization, 185–186
  color properties, 206
  controlling text blocks, 77–82
  decoration property, 187
  fields, 227–229
  formatting, 74–77
  indenting, 183–184
  italic, 184–185
  line-height properties, 206
  rollovers with CSS, 266–268
  sizing, 178–181
  title, 110–112
  two-dimensional, 351

text, blocks of
  block quotes, 77–78
  horizontal rules, 80–82
  preformatted text, 78–80
text attribute, 317
%Text attribute type, 127
Text deprecated attribute, 126
text-align property, 160, 182, 205
<textarea> element, 236
text-decoration property, 160, 205
text-indent property, 205
text-shadow property, 205
text-transform property, 185, 205
time keyword, 319
<time> element, 312
title attribute, 111, 315
title text, 110–112
<title> element, 36, 67
tools
  Adobe Fireworks, 367
  Adobe Photoshop, 365–367
  Analytics, 371
  Aptana Studio, 364
  Browser Sandbox, 371
  ClickDensity, 371
  CrazyEgg, 371
  Dreamweaver, 362–363
  Dropbox, 371
  Flash, 307–308
  Google Analytics, 371
  HTML-Kit, 365, 370
  for navigation, 27
  testing, 358
  Web, 370–371
Top property, 161, 202
transitions, 337–338
triggering links, 115–116
TSV (tab-separated values), 242
tt (presentational) attribute, 316
Tty media type, 158
tweets, 252

Twitter Web site
mashup with Google maps, 262–263
supporters, 373–376
widgets, 252–255
type attribute, 85, 229, 232, 314
Type deprecated attribute, 126

• U •

u (presentational) attribute, 316
u deprecated element, 123
UI (user inteface), 43, 58
<ul> element, 228
under construction sections, 48
underline value, 187
uppercase value, 186
%URI attribute type, 127
URL (Uniform Resource Locator)
capitalization of, 95
overview, 15–16
relative, 94
url keyword, 319
user agents, 318
user feedback, 359–360
user inteface (UI), 43, 58

• V •

validation, 241, 368–369
Validatious Web site, 248
valign attribute, 318
value attribute, 230, 247, 314
value deprecated attribute, 126
values, 134
version attribute, 317
Version deprecated attribute, 126
vertical-align property, 205
<video> element, 312
virtual demos, 300
visibility property, 162, 202
:visited pseudo class, 174, 207
visual layouts, 149–151
vlink attribute, 317

vlink deprecated attribute, 126
vspace attribute, 318
vspace deprecated attribute, 126

• W •

W3 Schools Web site, 374
W3C CSS validation service, 209
W3C link checker, 367–368
W3C Recommendation, 375
W3C validator, 369
W3Schools Web site, 208
<wbr> element, 312
WD (Working Draft), 325
Web APIs, 320
Web Design Group Web site, 374
Web design, mobile
addresses, 300
designing for distracted surfers, 299
designing for small screens, 297
frameworks, 301–303
location, 300–301
mobile devices, 293–296
navigating on mobile devices, 298
optimizing for low bandwidth, 297
surfing the Web on many mobile
devices, 299
typing and clicking, 301
virtual demos or showcases, 300
Web Developer's Virtual Library
Web site, 374
Web pages
adding alternative and title text, 110–112
adding rollovers to, 265–271
attractiveness of, 347
browsers, 13–14
CSS markup, 26–27
document headings, 26
editing, 40–41
HTML5, 323–324
hypertext, 10–13
image borders and alignment, 114
image location, 108

Web pages *(continued)*
  images in HTML documents, 27
  links and navigation tools, 27
  links locations in, 99–101
  lists, 26
  mobile Web design, 293–304
  paragraphs, 26
  planning design, 33–34
  posting online, 41–42
  processing forms on, 242–243
  role of images in, 105–106
  saving, 37–38
  scripting, 211–220
  specifying image size, 112–114
  tables, 26
  titles, 66–67
  using `<img />` element, 108–110
  viewing, 38–39
  Web servers, 14–15, 58–60
  writing HTML, 34–37
Web servers, 14–15, 58–60
Web sites. *See also* bugs
  building navigation, 49–52
  comparing HTML to CMS, 279–280
  content embedding, 252–258
  content of, 345–346
  design, 45–46
  hosting, 55–60
  HTML references, 373–375
  links, 94–95
  mapping, 46–49
  maps, 353–354
  mashups, 258–263
  navigate, 349–350
  planning outside links, 53–54
  scheduling reviews, 358–359
  structuring documents, 346
Web tools, 370–371
WebDesignerDepot Web site, 374
Web-developer's handbook, 210
Webmonkey Web site, 374
Web-safe fonts, 331
`week` keyword, 319
`white-space` property, 205
`widows` property, 166

`width` attributes, 112, 318
`Width` deprecated attribute, 126
`width` property, 164, 196
windows
  browser, 216–217
  new, 97–99
WordPress CMS, 281, 283–285
`word-spacing` property, 180, 205
Working Draft (WD), 325
World Wide Web Consortium Web site, 373
Wufoo Web site, 248
WYSIWYG HTML editors, 362–363

● *X* ●

XHTML (eXtensible Markup Language)
  `<html>` element, 65
  adding `DOCTYPE` declarations, 64–65
  adding document headers, 66–71
  adding HTML `DOCTYPE` declarations, 64
  adding namespaces, 65–66
  character codes, 23
  creating document body, 71–72
  difference from HTML, 16–17
  Document Type Definitions (DTDs), 376–377
  establishing document structure, 63–64
  markup, deprecated, 121–128
XHTML 1.0 Frameset `DOCTYPE` declaration, 65
XHTML 1.0 Strict `DOCTYPE` declaration, 65
XHTML 1.0 Transitional `DOCTYPE` declaration, 65

● *Y* ●

Yelp Web site, 259–262
YouTube Web site, 258
YSlow add-on, 210

● *Z* ●

`z-index` property, 162, 202–203
`z-index` value, 153
Zip files, 102–103

Apple & Macs

iPad For Dummies
978-0-470-58027-1

iPhone For Dummies,
4th Edition
978-0-470-87870-5

MacBook For Dummies, 3rd
Edition
978-0-470-76918-8

Mac OS X Snow Leopard For
Dummies
978-0-470-43543-4

Business

Bookkeeping For Dummies
978-0-7645-9848-7

Job Interviews
For Dummies,
3rd Edition
978-0-470-17748-8

Resumes For Dummies,
5th Edition
978-0-470-08037-5

Starting an
Online Business
For Dummies,
6th Edition
978-0-470-60210-2

Stock Investing
For Dummies,
3rd Edition
978-0-470-40114-9

Successful
Time Management
For Dummies
978-0-470-29034-7

Computer Hardware

BlackBerry
For Dummies,
4th Edition
978-0-470-60700-8

Computers For Seniors
For Dummies,
2nd Edition
978-0-470-53483-0

PCs For Dummies, Windows
7 Edition
978-0-470-46542-4

Laptops For Dummies,
4th Edition
978-0-470-57829-2

Cooking & Entertaining

Cooking Basics
For Dummies,
3rd Edition
978-0-7645-7206-7

Wine For Dummies,
4th Edition
978-0-470-04579-4

Diet & Nutrition

Dieting For Dummies,
2nd Edition
978-0-7645-4149-0

Nutrition For Dummies,
4th Edition
978-0-471-79868-2

Weight Training
For Dummies,
3rd Edition
978-0-471-76845-6

Digital Photography

Digital SLR Cameras &
Photography For Dummies,
3rd Edition
978-0-470-46606-3

Photoshop Elements 8
For Dummies
978-0-470-52967-6

Gardening

Gardening Basics
For Dummies
978-0-470-03749-2

Organic Gardening
For Dummies,
2nd Edition
978-0-470-43067-5

Green/Sustainable

Raising Chickens
For Dummies
978-0-470-46544-8

Green Cleaning
For Dummies
978-0-470-39106-8

Health

Diabetes For Dummies,
3rd Edition
978-0-470-27086-8

Food Allergies
For Dummies
978-0-470-09584-3

Living Gluten-Free
For Dummies,
2nd Edition
978-0-470-58589-4

Hobbies/General

Chess For Dummies,
2nd Edition
978-0-7645-8404-6

Drawing
Cartoons & Comics
For Dummies
978-0-470-42683-8

Knitting For Dummies,
2nd Edition
978-0-470-28747-7

Organizing
For Dummies
978-0-7645-5300-4

Su Doku For Dummies
978-0-470-01892-7

Home Improvement

Home Maintenance
For Dummies,
2nd Edition
978-0-470-43063-7

Home Theater
For Dummies,
3rd Edition
978-0-470-41189-6

Living the
Country Lifestyle
All-in-One
For Dummies
978-0-470-43061-3

Solar Power Your Home
For Dummies,
2nd Edition
978-0-470-59678-4

Available wherever books are sold. For more information or to order direct: U.S. customers visit www.dummies.com or call 1-877-762-2974.
U.K. customers visit www.wileyeurope.com or call (0) 1243 843291. Canadian customers visit www.wiley.ca or call 1-800-567-4797.

Internet

Blogging For Dummies,
3rd Edition
978-0-470-61996-4

eBay For Dummies,
6th Edition
978-0-470-49741-8

Facebook For Dummies, 3rd
Edition
978-0-470-87804-0

Web Marketing
For Dummies,
2nd Edition
978-0-470-37181-7

WordPress
For Dummies,
3rd Edition
978-0-470-59274-8

Language & Foreign Language

French For Dummies
978-0-7645-5193-2

Italian Phrases
For Dummies
978-0-7645-7203-6

Spanish For Dummies,
2nd Edition
978-0-470-87855-2

Spanish For Dummies,
Audio Set
978-0-470-09585-0

Math & Science

Algebra I For Dummies,
2nd Edition
978-0-470-55964-2

Biology For Dummies,
2nd Edition
978-0-470-59875-7

Calculus For Dummies
978-0-7645-2498-1

Chemistry For Dummies
978-0-7645-5430-8

Microsoft Office

Excel 2010 For Dummies
978-0-470-48953-6

Office 2010 All-in-One
For Dummies
978-0-470-49748-7

Office 2010 For Dummies,
Book + DVD Bundle
978-0-470-62698-6

Word 2010 For Dummies
978-0-470-48772-3

Music

Guitar For Dummies,
2nd Edition
978-0-7645-9904-0

iPod & iTunes
For Dummies,
8th Edition
978-0-470-87871-2

Piano Exercises
For Dummies
978-0-470-38765-8

Parenting & Education

Parenting For Dummies,
2nd Edition
978-0-7645-5418-6

Type 1 Diabetes
For Dummies
978-0-470-17811-9

Pets

Cats For Dummies,
2nd Edition
978-0-7645-5275-5

Dog Training For Dummies,
3rd Edition
978-0-470-60029-0

Puppies For Dummies,
2nd Edition
978-0-470-03717-1

Religion & Inspiration

The Bible For Dummies
978-0-7645-5296-0

Catholicism For Dummies
978-0-7645-5391-2

Women in the Bible
For Dummies
978-0-7645-8475-6

Self-Help & Relationship

Anger Management
For Dummies
978-0-470-03715-7

Overcoming Anxiety
For Dummies,
2nd Edition
978-0-470-57441-6

Sports

Baseball
For Dummies,
3rd Edition
978-0-7645-7537-2

Basketball
For Dummies,
2nd Edition
978-0-7645-5248-9

Golf For Dummies,
3rd Edition
978-0-471-76871-5

Web Development

Web Design
All-in-One
For Dummies
978-0-470-41796-6

Web Sites
Do-It-Yourself
For Dummies,
2nd Edition
978-0-470-56520-9

Windows 7

Windows 7
For Dummies
978-0-470-49743-2

Windows 7
For Dummies,
Book + DVD Bundle
978-0-470-52398-8

Windows 7 All-in-One
For Dummies
978-0-470-48763-1

Available wherever books are sold. For more information or to order direct: U.S. customers visit www.dummies.com or call 1-877-762-2974.
U.K. customers visit www.wileyeurope.com or call (0) 1243 843291. Canadian customers visit www.wiley.ca or call 1-800-567-4797.

DUMMIES.COM®

Wherever you are in life, Dummies makes it easier.

From fashion to Facebook®, wine to Windows®, and everything in between, Dummies makes it easier.

Visit us at Dummies.com